"A first-rate collection on the history of 'intimate violence' in colonial America and the United States from the second half of the seventeenth century to the eve of the Civil War, convincingly demonstrating both the historical context and the nature and patterns of change in the levels of violence over time. The essays, both extremely readable and uniformly of high quality, tell fascinating, often riveting, stories of love, lust, and general mayhem."

—William G. Shade, co-editor of *Our American Sisters: Women in American Life and Thought*

The essays in *Over the Threshold* use a fascinating array of sources, ranging from legal papers and church records to novels and popular ballads, to investigate violence against spouses, lovers, children, slaves, and servants in the American colonies and early Republic. Many commonly held notions about intimate violence during this period collapse under the weight of historical scrutiny in this incisive collection.

"The articles in this anthology cover a wide range of environments, from not so peace-loving Quaker Philadelphia to brutal slave plantations in Jamaica. The authors investigate both patterns familiar to our own times, such as wife and child abuse and infanticide, as well as ones peculiar to those times, such as routine violence directed at servants and slaves. The articles are fresh, eye-opening, and bring to light the extent of routine violence and the extensive communal and legal means available to end it."

—Elizabeth Pleck, author of *Domestic Tyranny: The Making of Social Policy against Family Violence from Colonial Times to Present*

Christine Daniels is an Associate Professor of History and **Michael V. Kennedy** is an Assistant Professor of History. They both teach at Michigan State University.

Over the Threshold

Intimate Violence in Early America

Edited by

Christine Daniels and Michael V. Kennedy

Routledge   1999   New York   London

To our moms:
Alma Teichmann Daniels (1919–1999)
Regina Fanning Kennedy (1928–1994)

Published in 1999 by

Routledge
29 West 35th Street
New York, NY 10001

Published in Great Britain by

Routledge
11 New Fetter Lane
London EC4P 4EE

Library of Congress Cataloging-in-Publication Data

Over the threshold : intimate violence in early America /
    Christine Daniels and Michael V. Kennedy, editors
        p.   cm.
    Includes bibliographical references and index.
    ISBN 0–415–91804–9 (hc.). —
    ISBN 0–415–91805–7 (pbk.)
        1. Family violence—United States—History   I. Daniels,
    Christine, 1953–   .   II. Kennedy, Michael V., 1954–   .
    HV6626.2.O94   1999
    362.82'92'0973—DC21   98-47351
                                                CIP

Contents

Acknowledgments

Since the inception of this project, several people whose names do not appear among the authors have contributed to its completion. First, we would like to thank the editors at Routledge, both past and present, who made this book possible through their suggestions and encouragement. We are indebted to Claudia Gorelick, who first proposed the volume at an AHA session in 1995. We are even more grateful to Brendan O'Malley (who has lived up to his sainted name), Deirdre Mullane, and Derek Krissoff for their long-suffering patience and fortitude, particularly at the end of the project when it seemed that it would never be done. Elizabeth Sherburn Demers was a virtuoso editorial assistant who kept us organized against all odds. William G. Shade, as usual, has always been there when we needed advice, as have Amy Turner Bushnell and Jack P. Greene. Bill also waded through several versions of the introduction without begging for mercy, a measure of his professional stature and personal courage. We truly appreciate the last-minute efforts of Lisa Fine and Leslie Page Moch, our colleagues at Michigan State University, who stepped into the breach at a frenetic time to help a couple of first-time editors. We would also like to thank the College of Arts and Letters at MSU, which funded part of this project when it was barely a gleam in our collective eye.

All of the contributors deserve praise for their ingenious and creative essays, but we owe a few special thanks. G. S. Rowe and Jack Marietta displayed endless patience with us after meeting all of our none-too-realistic deadlines. Ed

Hatton suggested the snappy title. Jacquelyn Miller and Terri L. Snyder were particularly gracious in accepting our sometimes muscular and rugged editorial suggestions, although each author in the volume clearly has a good sense of humor and a strong ego.

Finally, we would like to thank each other for managing to get through the project together without becoming another meaningful statistic.

C.D.
M.V.K.
Mason, Michigan
June 1999

Overviews

one

INTIMATE VIOLENCE, NOW AND THEN

Christine Daniels

T he specter of intimate violence—physical violence between family members or lovers—terrifies most observers. It juxtaposes two antithetical images; that of a loving and nurturing family with that of repetitive violence, pain, sexual abuse, fear, and even murder. And while intimate physical violence is widespread, psychological and verbal aggression within families is virtually universal. Scholars, too, including sociologists, feminists, and legal theorists, have addressed this issue in academic journals and in courtrooms. Some basic aspects of family violence nonetheless remain elusive. Writers cannot define it; researchers cannot design adequate programs to investigate it; statisticians cannot discover its frequency; sociologists cannot discover its causes. Most families, save those already reduced to the refuges of battered women's shelters or juvenile agencies, are reluctant to discuss it. In part as a result, governmental and legal policies on domestic violence remain inchoate or contradictory.[1]

This stubborn evasiveness has created a cottage industry of sociological studies on intimate violence but no consensus on its frequency, context, or causes. According to these studies, intimate violence exists in 16, 20, 33, 50, 60, 75, or 97 percent of American families;[2] domestic homicides account for 8, 20, 30, or 70 percent of all U.S. murders;[3] and alcohol or drugs are present in 30, 50, 70, or 100 percent of those murders.[4] Few works employ standard statistics, such as the number of domestic assaults or murders per 100,000 population.

The same studies, moreover, often reduce "American" society to a vast homogeneity, without class, ethnic, or historical details, possibly because most Americans continue to view themselves as members of a "classless melting pot."[5] But studies of family violence are permeated with class and ethnic assumptions nonetheless. Most scholars define abuse in middle-class Anglo-American terms; they ignore the fact that people of other social strata or family background—Mediterranean-Americans, for example—are not so hesitant to touch each other.[6] Thus many academics define all incidents of pushing, shoving, or grabbing as "violence." A parent who grabbed a toddler roughly to prevent her entering a city street, or who swatted her little behind lightly for doing so, would thereby have abused her. Such definitions lead to estimates that 97 percent of American families "experience some form of domestic abuse."[7]

While the same scholars try to contextualize their work historically, they rely on simplistic models to do so. For example, many writers who address family violence believe in a clear transition point between the past, when families were public, and the present, when they are private. When that transition occurred, they believe, women lost agency within the family; they had been less subject to abuse when neighbors and friends had fewer inhibitions about interfering in a family's private affairs.[8] Feminists who use this argument have suggested a return to the public family, while conservative writers adopt the same idea with a different political twist; they advocate increased state intervention only into historically "unnatural" families, such as those headed by single women.[9] Both arguments rest on a model that reduces considerable historical complexity to a simple false dichotomy.

Finally, the sociological literature of intimate violence also emphasizes victims' experiences rather than perpetrators' motives. This approach reveals patterns of abuse, but divulges little about the causes of intimate violence.[10] For example, one study entitled "What Changes the Societal Prevalence of Domestic Violence?" concluded that children are often abused between the ages of three and eight. But children's ages alone do not change the rate of violence—an abuser's *response* to their development at certain ages changes the rate of violence.[11] A focus on victims can illustrate an association between two or more social factors in abusive families, but not the reasons for abuse. Investigators may be reluctant to examine abusers' objectives for fear that by explaining the causes of intimate violence, they may seem to justify them; if they understand abusers' actions, they become complicit with them.

Over the past two decades, historians too have turned their attention to intimate violence. The essays in this collection address intimate violence in the British-American colonies and the United States before 1865. "Intimate" violence in this volume (rather than "domestic" violence) refers to violence between two or more people who have an intimate relationship; this catchall term includes lovers as well as husbands and wives. It also incorporates the re-

4

lations of children and parents, although modern sociological literature is beginning to define "domestic violence" to exclude child abuse.[12] Finally, it encompasses relations between masters, slaves, and servants. The dependent position of slaves and servants in families was distinct from those of wives and children, but free men and single women were legally and economically responsible for their slaves and servants. Cultural constructs of such people as "family" members followed social fact; slaves and servants were indeed intimates in many early American families.

The authors in this anthology have examined historical violence through a wide variety of sources, in particular contexts, often with attention to abusers' motives. British colonists drew on imperial culture and laws in re-creating families in the New World and adapted them to American realities of ferocious disease environments, slave systems, and westward migration, as several essays in this volume illustrate. The evolution of perceptible urban class structures in late eighteenth- and early nineteenth-century American cities created different "styles" of abuse and reponses to it, while the experiment of nationhood and accompanying discussion of virtue also affected perceptions of the family. As settlers moved west into new rural areas and tied them into existing commercial nexes, British-American systems of patriarchy and responsibility were elaborated into systems of paternalism and honor, especially in southern states. Several essays in this volume consider the effects of these developments on antebellum families. After the end of the Civil War, the presence of federal and state governments in individual Americans' lives expanded, as did that of reform organizations to redress wife and child abuse. Consideration of the relative lack of such entities unites many of these essays on early America.[13]

Most historians' training is rooted in analysis of change over time; a number of them, including Susan Dwyer Asmussen, Linda Gordon, Margaret Hunt, and Elizabeth Pleck, have discussed such change with subtlety. But "time" can be measured in a variety of ways. Chronological time is one gauge, but other means of marking time also reveal details about domestic violence.

Economic and social immaturity and growth—"developmental time"—for example, have an effect on domestic violence. The Jamaica of 1750 that Trevor Burnard describes here may, at first glance, bear little likeness to Jenifer Banks's portrait of mid-nineteenth-century Michigan. But the world of Jamaican planter Thomas Thistlewood was not unlike that of midwestern settler Mary Clavers. Both were frontier environments with few white immigrants. Scattered legal institutions were established, but their scarcity created a void of authority into which free white men strode. As G. S. Rowe and Jack Marietta note, although frontier areas possessed courts, "[o]lder and more settled regions were more efficient in convicting assailants." The lack of well-established—or at least well-used—legal and social governance gave patriarchy more authority in newly settled regions. And, as Banks states, the social disor-

5

ganization and relative deprivation present during the "boom" period of extractive industrial development further intensified problems which contributed to intimate violence.[14] Banks's essay speaks to the purported effects of frontier lawlessness on intimate violence in the United States and suggests that conditions of frontier social development encouraged, but did not create, domestic abuse. As she notes, these conditions included "undeveloped legal structures and a resultant reliance on patriarchal governance; physical and social isolation from family, friends, or protective institutions; alcohol abuse; declining social and economic status; and the temporary weakening of some aspects of gender identification."

Beyond the first generation of settlement, the essays of Terri L. Snyder and Edward E. Baptist discuss family authority in the context of dwindling resources. Snyder portrays the ways in which slavery became legally embedded in late seventeenth-century Virginia as early colonists consolidated their positions. White servants became harder to control, especially for female masters, who were often seen as suspect by their dependents. More than a century later in Baptist's North Carolina piedmont, as land prices rose and competition for access to markets intensified, middling households were less likely to include any slaves or servants; yeomen's fragile mastery focused on white women. Thus economic and social development, with their own internal clocks, affected family relations in early America.

Any account of family, moreover, must recognize the way in which families' internal "time" intersects with that of the larger world.[15] Many wives, for example, were first abused during pregnancy, according to the essays of Randolph Roth and of G. S. Rowe and Jack Marietta.[16] As Roth notes, moreover, most marriages in which family violence became an issue were of several years' standing, when partners had invested a great deal of time and, usually, affection in marriages, when finances were inextricable and children present. When crisis points in "family time" intersect with crises in social developments, intimate violence can erupt. The works in this volume employ a variety of approaches to change over time.

These essays are also particularly sensitive to geographic and spatial contexts. As Stephanie Cole notes, the "current historiography of domestic violence often belittles or ignores the importance" of "localized approaches to violence" which "defined acceptable violence with a precision most historians have missed." The position of Baltimore, for example, as a border city with a large free black population informs and specifies Cole's essay, as well as that of T. Stephen Whitman. The construction of male mastery in such a setting relied on a grammar of paternal benevolence, in which both African-American and Euro-American people participated. Mississippi, on the other hand, was noted for its conservative constructions of patriarchy and dependence as early as the 1820s.[17] Christopher Morris's Mississippi masters would have been

6

scorned in T. Stephen Whitman's Maryland, where local slave owners had the right "to tie up slaves, but a good and fatherly master would have commanded the situation without such tactics." The position of Fells Point as a maritime suburb is key to James Rice's analysis. And Jacquelyn Miller's, Jeffrey H. Richards's, or Merril D. Smith's essays could only describe eighteenth-century Philadelphia, with that city's middle-class emphasis on business, literature, and society.

In fact, many historians who have previously recognized spatial contexts have focused on a gross distinction between "slave" and "free" regions, which overstates Northern and Southern differences and reifies the position of the South as "other." The essays of Edward E. Baptist and Ed Hatton, for example, demonstrate intriguing similarities in constructions of masculinity and violence in the North and South during the early nineteenth century. G. S. Rowe and Jack Marietta identify assault and homicide rates in free Pennsylvania near those of slave North Carolina. Baltimore's free black population resembled that of Philadelphia more than that of Charleston, South Carolina. The frontier in Michigan resembled the frontier in Jamaica. These essays, therefore, illustrate patterns that cannot be classed simply as demarcating differences between regions that (by the early nineteenth century) countenanced slavery and those that did not.

Distinctions between urban and rural areas, on the other hand, are more meaningful. Class distinctions were more obvious in cities, and the development and spread of middle-class mores regarding violence affected most late eighteenth- and early nineteenth-century urban families. As merchants in cities like Philadelphia and Baltimore extended commercial ties, civil manners and emotional restraint became important.[18] Jacquelyn Miller demonstrates that epidemic diseases that often ravaged urban entrepots, such as yellow fever, could elevate desire for emotional control. Eighteenth-century middle-class Philadelphians, advised by doctors, believed that "monitoring one's passions and actions" was "a medical imperative" as well as a path to domestic harmony. Anger could exacerbate or induce "inflammations, fevers, or mortifications" as disease raged through the streets of seaport cities.

Jeffrey H. Richards locates similar class distinctions in expressions of intimate violence in Philadelphia in Rebecca Rush's novel, *Kelroy*, published nineteen years after the yellow fever epidemic Miller's essay describes. Elite Mrs. Hammond is "one of the most noteworthy villains" in American literature and one of its few female scoundrels; she abuses her daughter Emily verbally and psychologically. While Mrs. Hammond never engages in physical violence, secondary characters, some comic, all "lower-class or rising middle-class," do. Observing the stratified classes of early national Philadelphia, Rush concluded that violence existed "throughout society, but its form [was] determined by the class in which it occur[red]."

INTIMATE VIOLENCE, NOW AND THEN

Working-class women in early American cities certainly complained of physical abuse more often than middle-class women, as Stephanie Cole illustrates.[19] While elite women undoubtedly suffered abuse, they often chose "to suffer without public protest, tacitly supporting the patriarchal system that brought their class such power." Baltimore's working women, on the other hand, bought maneuvering room through judicial elites' desire to restrain the free black community and their resultant tolerance for white working-class demands. In fact, the "class and race of victims of domestic abuse affected the ways in which local officials maintained masculine authority." The combination of class, gender, and racial interests in border cities such as Baltimore created an opportunity for working women to seek domestic peace.

Merril D. Smith's essay here portrays the new realities of class for urban working mothers in republican Philadelphia. Elizabeth Wilson became a symbol of efforts to reform infanticide laws after her lover killed her illegitimate twin infants. "Her seduction by a false lover reflected republican fears, and emphasized that young women should not be alone in the city." As Smith explains, Wilson was convicted "under an old Pennsylvania statute based on the English law 21 James I, c.27 (1624)," which assumed that any bastard infant who died had been killed by its mother, unless she could prove otherwise. This statute (which has the flavor of modern "failure-to-protect" laws) fell disproportionately on the poor.[20]

Essays included here also help create standard statistics for intimate assault and homicide in early America. G. S. Rowe and Jack Marietta's piece indicates that both homicide and assault rates in the "peaceable kingdom" of colonial Pennsylvania were higher than historians have believed. They further suggest that "Quaker aspirations aside, more violence occurred among Pennsylvania's vaunted families and friends than has been previously conceded." Randolph Roth's work focuses on spousal homicide in northern New England between the American Revolution and the Civil War. He suggests that a number of factors, including "northern New England's unique social order, grounded in universal literacy and the household economy," dampened spousal assault and murder rates in Vermont and New Hampshire. Indeed, the few comparable statistics on spousal homicide today confirm that antebellum New England's rates were low. These scholars, moreover, study very long-term trends—in Rowe and Marietta's case, more than a century; in Roth's, about ninety years. They conclude that rates of family violence in the eighteenth and nineteenth centuries do not demonstrate either increasing or decreasing linear progression, but cyclical changes. Roth further determines that the nature of family violence in New England changed during the ninety years before the Civil War. Spousal murder, for example, became more common while infanticide declined. Modern scholars might consider the implications of such long-term changes for their own work.[21]

They might also benefit from a historical appreciation for the concepts of patriarchy and paternalism, and their implications for family governance. Many modern scholars ascribe to the idea that patriarchy was the "total, undifferentiated and predictable tyranny of men and helplessness of women." As one noted recently, "both historically and in the present" the law and other institutions "condoned the use of physical abuse by husbands to control wives. In the early nineteenth century, some state laws specifically approved wife beating." She then referred to a supposed nineteenth-century statute from Mississippi.[22] In fact, as historian Elizabeth Pleck has pointed out, "Wife beating in the nineteenth century was not legal, despite sociologist assertions." The Mississippi example (*Bradley v. State*, 1824) did not refer to a statute, but to a state supreme court case that tested Mississippi's antiquated divorce law. It was "extremely conservative" in the nineteenth-century United States—not the rule but a peculiar exception.[23]

Patriarchal control, of course, was an important political and social concept in England and Anglo-America; it "infused the very marrow of the early modern British American world."[24] In societies without social welfare systems, police forces, or penitentiaries, father figures—patriarchs—filled the roles of all three. They did not own wives and children; dependents were persons at law, but could interact with the state only—with rare exceptions—through the person of the independent male. Patriarchs were to keep order in their households and ensure that household members did not disturb the civil peace. If they had to employ "moderate" chastisement to do so, that was their right. When the rule of the state was weak (as it was in England until the eighteenth century and in early America until the nineteenth), patriarchy assumed a great deal of governance.[25]

But patriachy did not mean that husbands or fathers could beat dependents, especially wives, on a whim. While physical correction for children and servants was rarely questioned, most writers and courts agreed that striking wives showed poor judgment. As one seventeenth-century writer noted, such correction seemed "too impious in him to do it, and too servile in her to suffer it." Even the most conservative notions of patriachal power "never gave a husband more than a limited right to correct his wife's behavior through physical force. Such correction was to be used only for serious issues and was distinguished from beating, administered in anger for trivial faults." The "legitimacy of patriarchal power depended on restraint and wisdom in its use."[26]

Its legitimacy also depended on a man's ability to fulfill reciprocal obligations to dependents, something many sociologists ignore. This concept of patriarchal responsibility retained currency long after ideas concerning patriarchy's role in public politics collapsed.[27] Even after women and formerly dependent white men gained visible legal and social personae during the early nineteenth century, independent men still believed "the patriarchal ethos"

9

could be "uplifting." Masters were to "protect, guard, and care" for dependents, "thereby fulfilling a powerful and ancient image of master as provider. Indeed, offering 'protection' was itself a survival of feudal terminology that recalled the ancient origins of the concept of family."[28]

Four of the authors in this volume—Jenifer Banks, Edward Baptist, Stephanie Cole, and Randolph Roth—discuss the role and limits of patriarchy between free men and their wives in early America. Banks demonstrates that frontier author Caroline Kirkland "exposed the inadequacy of women's networks in frontier isolation and the danger inherent in patriarchal family structures" in such settings. Baptist's creative use of eighteenth-century ballads identifies a period when they became concerned with men who killed wives and lovers. Such men "sinned against patriarchal responsibility"; only violent punishment of these offenders "repair[ed] the legitimacy of white male dominance." Cole's subtle analysis reveals that although theories concerning patriarchy were "articulated in high courts" (*Bradley v. State*) they were "contested on a daily basis in lower ones" as wives used magistrate courts—indeed, sometimes used specific justices—to negotiate a practical standard for patriarchal rule. Roth's detailed discussion of spousal relations in New England produces evidence of a nineteenth-century shift in dependents' attitudes as they came to crave, not patriarchal protection, but an "emotional *pater familias*" and "consolation." These essays discuss changes in, negotiations over, and dependents' stake in patriarchy and portray distinctions between theory and practice, policy and process, statutes and cases, political ideas and social responsibilities.

Patriarchal theory in colonial and antebellum America included the added dimension of indentured servants and slaves. Most of the colonies and many of the states depended on staple crop production for their existence, which in turn spawned a large population of bound laborers. By the early eighteenth century, in most regions, the majority of these bound laborers were slaves. Before about 1750, Euro-Americans thought of "blacks—especially Africans—as subhuman and savage," but by the mid-eighteenth century, a growing number of enslaved people were creole African-Americans who generally followed colonial norms of dress and appearance and spoke English. In part as a result, many slaveholders between 1750 and 1820 discovered that "blacks were fellow humans deserving of humane treatment."[29] While shared humanity did not indicate equality, educated masters came to believe that slaves possessed reason and deserved benevolence. Persuasion (or co-optation) had its place; punishment, in many masters' eyes, was relegated to the status of a last resort. Owners began to demonstrate kindness and express affection for their slaves and to emphasize their obligations to them; in doing so, they implicitly recognized and strengthened their slaves' claims to humanity.

This increasingly intense connection between slaves and masters—defined as "paternalism"—included day-to-day gains and losses for slaves. On one hand, paternalism included white recognition of certain slave rights; on the other, it left slaves with less personal autonomy than they had heretofore possessed. It made slavery "a negotiated sphere between social unequals," as masters cloaked legal patriarchal power with an ideology of paternal beneficence. In return, slaves in paternalist societies were supposed to evince "properly" subservient attitudes toward their white governors. Paternalists expected demonstrations of "gratitude, even love" in return for their kindness; they created "the fiction of the contented and happy slave."[30]

Both slavery and indentured servitude were, like other familial institutions, immensely malleable. Local economic and legal conditions and community standards created a multitude of slaveries and servitudes, all time- and place-specific.[31] Very simply put, paternalism was most evident where the number of slaves—especially African-born slaves—relative to that of Euro-Americans was lowest. Slavery, therefore, shed the physical cruelty of patriarchy and acquired the justification of paternalism over time, from the early eighteenth to the mid-nineteenth century, as more slaves were born in the New World. Conversely, paternalism declined as one traveled from north to south, from New England and New York (during the colonial period) through Maryland and Virginia into South Carolina, Alabama, and Mississippi. Patriarchy remained most obvious and unbridled in the eighteenth-century Caribbean, although there too it softened a bit over time. The ideological balance of patriarchy and paternalism within slavery was rooted, in great part, in the staple crops of various North American regions. As one moved south, crops required more workers per acre and thus a larger ratio of slaves to whites, with less opportunity for close relations. Warmer climates also fostered robust disease environments and high mortality rates. As slaves were imported to replace the dead, fewer were American-born creoles.[32]

The essays in this volume that concern relations between masters, servants, and slaves reveal a kaleidoscope of possibilities for patriarchy and paternalism in plantation America. Terri L. Snyder illuminates the sometimes fragile nature of female authority in a patriarchal world. Under English and Anglo-American law, single women and widows (*femes soles*) could head households.[33] Theoretically, female masters met the same obligations as males; they "were to provide indentured dependents with food, shelter, clothing, and freedom dues." (Servants received freedom dues, usually clothing and tools, when they finished their indentures.) Masters were also entitled to use moderate physical correction if necessary. In Snyder's seventeenth-century York County, "ten lashes with a belt was a permissible punishment for a disrespectful servant." For female masters, however, theory belied practice. As Snyder points out, women masters who tried to correct servants physically were likely to have vengeful dependents seize correcting sticks and thrash them. Effective female masters, therefore, relied on the assistance of the county court, offered servants incentives, and eschewed violence. Their recognition of servants' response to perceptions of illegitimate power shaped a lighter authority than that permitted patriarchs.

In the Caribbean as late as a century later, patriarchal "[d]ominant white men," as Trevor Burnard recounts, still "routinely terrorized their bondspeople." Their approach to household governance, moreover, spilled over into both "gendered white violence and black-on-black violence as a means of regulating" family members. Jamaican masters, Burnard tells us, would have found the elaborated sentimental defenses of paternalism "puzzling and foolhardy." They knew they were "surrounded by huge numbers of slaves who would kill [them] given the opportunity." Nor did they expect otherwise; "patriarchal masters" never "deluded themselves that slaves were content."

Burnard describes the planter Thistlewood's reign as one of terror, and uses the word precisely. Thistlewood maintained household discipline as some scholars argue abusive men do today, with a "deliberate savagery" meant to "defend privileges" and to destabilize the social and psychological realities of other household members. The trauma of such tactics often governs victims' "actions and decisions."[34] Thistlewood had an added advantage with this strategy; his slaves' community was "already fragile" and "inherently volatile."

Thistlewood's white contemporaries in republican Maryland, however, as T. Stephen Whitman informs us, clung fervently to paternalist beliefs. White Marylanders had long lived in considerable intimacy with slaves, whom they outnumbered. Masters thought they knew their bondsmen and bondswomen well, and anticipated in them, as Whitman tells us, the characteristics of "contented" slaves, including devotion, gratitude, servility, and patriotism. Masters could forgive subservient slaves for black-on-white violence if their actions could be construed "as occurring outside the world of public space and public speech," especially if the victim were "an outsider." As Whitman demonstrates, even a black man accused of raping a white woman could be exonerated if he were "an obedient worker who feared his master's authority, a faithful husband, and above all, a guileless man" who did not lie to white people. Blacks who were hostile or "refractory and insolent"—who resisted white demonstrations of benevolence—did not have a prayer.

In contrast to these extremes, as Christopher Morris informs us, Mississippi masters in the late eighteenth century had not yet covered patriarchy with an elaborate cloak of paternalism. While mulatto Marie Glass was assuredly not the norm, her household resembled that of Jamaican Thistlewood, not those of mainland Maryland masters during the 1780s. The cruelty of patriarchy ruled in her home. But as with Snyder's female masters of the previous century, Glass's gender made her authority suspect; her race made her even more dangerous. Although she claimed "the patriarchal privilege to discipline household members when they behaved improperly" and asserted that it "was as a mother

Christine Daniels

that she inflicted such corrections," her cruel punishments (coupled with her race and sex) put her outside the bounds of legitimate patriarchal authority. Spanish Mississippi was not quite Jamaica.

By the mid-nineteenth century, however, as Morris demonstrates, Mississippi masters had built a sturdy—almost unassailable—paternalist structure. They felt justified in interfering in cases of domestic violence to restrain "tyrannical" slave fathers and husbands. As a result, "[d]espite a strong family ideal, slaves' power to shape family life was severely limited by their relationship with a master." They had, moreover, "few means to protect their families from the legal patriarch—the master," even when, ironically, "the master himself and the conditions of slavery" were "the source of domestic strife."

While patriarchy assumed some of the authority that would otherwise have been vested in law, the legal process remained an independent agent in the history of domestic abuse.[35] Even rigid hierarchical institutions such as the law, moreover, included some manipulable space. Although American law was patriarchal (and middle-class), Snyder's female masters and Cole's working wives bent the legal process to their purposes; so did Whitman's free black and James D. Rice's working-class pardon-seekers.

Early American law operated in the public sphere, associated with men and male prerogative, while female dependents and children were confined to the private sphere of the home. This was not an unchanging reality, however. Historians of the family have often described a process of increasing domestic "privatization" between the late seventeenth and mid-nineteenth centuries. Early modern families were characterized by "sociability rather than privacy"; households included many nonnatal members, houses provided a high ratio of public to private space, and so on.[36] But this formulation seems rigid; most families today have both private and public presences.[37] Indeed, even the definitions of the words "public" and "private," when applied to families, mutated over time.[38] The theory of increasing privatization, moreover, clearly did not apply to nearly half of the early United States. Slave-owning households, which always included nonnatal family members, retained a highly visible (in fact, exaggerated) public presence throughout the first two-thirds of the nineteenth century. Slaveholding men and women of the Old South elaborated their desire for a virtuous public family presence into a stylized system of honor and shame. Interpersonal violence was ritualized into theatrical displays of male bravery, while women assumed overstated stances of modesty and chastity.[39]

Some essays in this volume indicate that ritualized displays of violence were part of the fabric of households before the nineteenth century and outside the realm of Southern honor. Intimate violence and responses to it were meant, in part, as theater. Thomas Thistlewood used sexual abuse and violence as public statements of his mastery and dared his slaves to challenge him. Marie Glass did the same with her servants. Her liminal position in society, however, made

INTIMATE VIOLENCE, NOW AND THEN

her performance culturally more threatening than Thistlewood's. Snyder's seventeenth-century female masters, though they rode lightly, understood the need for public displays of control at court, while their male dependents wanted publicly to "assert their authority as men." Servants and slaves lived in families but were not of them; they gave a household a public character in an increasingly private world. They often did not share childhood experiences with the family's natal children. To some extent, therefore, public displays of private violence were undertaken to give *all* household members a common grammar and understanding of the nature of authority within that household.

Nineteenth-century working-class urban households also retained their public natures after middle-class homes had moved toward privacy, as James D. Rice demonstrates. "The boundaries between family and community in a working-class area," Rice tells us, "were thin, porous, and contested, as neighbors, friends, and agents of the state" intervened in family life. Working-class households in early national Baltimore "formed but one of several nodes" in families' lives and were "infiltrated by unrelated members of the community." As Rice illustrates, moreover, the Shields family used public displays of violence within the rough neighborhood of Fells Point to establish themselves as people who were not to be trifled with.

On the other hand, working-class people were aware that the middle-class ideal of the family had shifted from one emphasizing sociability to one focused on privacy. As a result, when William and Kitty Shields petitioned Maryland's governor for mercy after their daughter's death, they reconstructed their family in an image he appreciated, and "obscured the presence of other onlookers" at Betsy's deathbed. In doing so, they negotiated a middle-class system of justice that demanded perfect stories pitched at an elite audience.

Maryland's pardon papers, in fact, suggest another dimension to the seemingly clear dichotomy between public and private spheres. As Rice and Whitman intimate, pardon-seekers reconceived their experiences in terms acceptable to elite legal authorities and to the governor of Maryland. They remolded working-class, free black, or female experiences into displays that confirmed the personalities middle- and upper-class white males demanded of them, and reordered the direction of elite legal and social systems. Written petitions established appropriate social positions for nonelites even as their actions challenged them. These successful, semifictional accounts indicate that working men and women of any race could negotiate elite legal systems to achieve their ends.[40]

Finally, many of the essays in this volume strive to provide not just associated factors, but reasons for intimate violence. Three authors particularly—Randolph Roth, Ed Hatton, and Edward Baptist—confront this issue. Roth argues that murderous husbands became abusive because social expectations of their roles changed dramatically in the nineteenth century. As northern New

14

England became progressively more "prosperous and temperate," consumer appetites escalated. "Having a house was no longer enough—it had to be a nice house. Working hard was no longer enough—one's labor had to confer monetary and social rewards." Changing expectations for male behavior exacerbated this situation. "Being a good provider was no longer enough—a husband had to be unfailingly pleasant, sober, and respectable." By the 1840s even respectability fell short, and "a man had to be a person of sentiment: sympathetic, affectionate, and compassionate, especially toward members of his family." When the pressure of rising social and expectations became too great, thwarted New England husbands exploded in frustration and rage.

While Roth examines husband's roles as providers and helpmeets, Hatton and Baptist focus on antebellum constructions of masculinity itself. Hatton's Joel Clough, a rising young professional-turned-murderer, was a controlling man with a bad temper; as a child, when frustrated, he "would burst out in a most violent passion." He mastered his rage through the discipline of apprenticeship and employment, but when unemployed, his anger always lurked just beneath the surface. When he asked Mary Hamilton to marry him and she refused, he " 'through an uncontrollable impulse,' " stabbed her to death.[41]

Clough's actions placed him at the center of a controversy about the nature of masculinity in the antebellum North. The arguments made by the prosecution and defense at his trial anticipated current discussions of abusive men. Was Clough a "monster" (was he "antisocial") or was he a normal young man who, in one uncontrollable moment of frustration, blighted two lives forever (was he "stressed")?[42]

Edward E. Baptist's discussion of Jonathan Lewis and Omie Wise, set in rural North Carolina, echoes many of the same themes. Lewis, under economic and social pressure, murdered his lover; soon thereafter, a murder ballad arose to describe his deed. Many versions of the song describe him as bestial and monstrous, but the same versions include the artistic device of "narrator-switching"; the narrator, the otherwise objective storyteller, becomes the murderer, and all men identify with the fury that sends a young woman to her grave. Although Hatton does not adduce such a device in Clough's written confession, the confession itself betrayed a similar bifurcation. It emphasized Clough's unexceptional life, punctuated with a few episodes of "vindictive passion" that were, in nineteenth-century terms, "integral to masculinity." As Hatton tells us, Clough "thought himself far more typical than most Northern antebellum Americans would have cared to admit."

These essays, like those in the rest of the collection, confront multilayered issues of causality—social, economic, political, and psychological—in intimate violence. They examine, not just association, but causes, consequences, and often remedies. They place the issue of familial abuse in contexts of time, place, and development—from 1646 to 1865, from New Hampshire to Mississippi and Michigan to Jamaica, from the colonial frontier to antebellum cities. They demonstrate its changing dimensions in each particular setting. They consider the intersection of family and social crises. They discuss the nature of patriarchy, class distinctions, female authority, dependence, and the law. Their willingness to analyze familial abuse implies that, even without being foolish optimists, we may yet hope to understand the causes and nature of intimate violence.

Notes

1. R.L. McNeely and Gloria Robinson-Simpson, "The Truth About Domestic Violence: A Falsely Framed Issue," *Social Work* 32 (1987): 485–490, state that 93 percent of families use verbal aggression to solve conflicts. This estimate seems low.

2. Statistics, in order, from Mary Lystad, "Violence in the Home: A Major Public Problem," *The Urban and Social Change Review* 15 (1982): 21–25; Betsy McAlister Groves, "Children without Refuge: Young Witnesses to Domestic Violence," *Zero to Three* 16 (1996): 29–34; Suzanne Steinmetz and Murray Straus, "The Family as Cradle of Violence," *Society* 10 (1973): 50–56; McNeely and Robinson-Simpson, "The Truth About Domestic Violence"; Jeffrey Fagan and Sandra Wexler, "Crime at Home and in the Streets: The Relationship between Family and Stranger Violence," *Violence and Victims* 2 (1987): 5–24; Ronald L. Simons et al., "A Test of Various Perspectives on the Intergenerational Transmission of Domestic Violence," *Criminology* 33 (1995): 141–171; Jill M. Bystydzienski, "Marriage and Family in the United States and Canada: A Comparison," *American Review of Canadian Studies* 23 (1993): 565–582.

3. Statistics, in order, from Michael A. Buda and Teresa L. Butler, "The Battered Wife Syndrome: A Backdoor Assault on Domestic Violence," *Journal of Family Law* 23 (1984): 359–390; Michael Slade et al., "Application of Forensic Toxicology of the Problem of Domestic Violence," *Journal of Forensic Sciences* 36 (1991): 708–713; Murray Straus, "Domestic Violence and Homicide Antecedents," *Bulletin of the New York Academy of Medicine* 62 (1986): 446–465; Lystad, "Violence in the Home."

4. Statistics, in order, from Holly Johnson and Peter Chisholm, "Violence in the Family: Family Homicide," *Canadian Social Trends* (1989): 16–18; Larry Livingston, "Measuring Domestic Violence in An Alcoholic Population," *Journal of Sociology and Social Welfare* 13 (1986): 934–951; Slade et al., "Application of Forensic Toxicology to the Problem of Domestic Violence." Also Judith A. Seltzer and Debra Kalmuss, "Socialization and Stress Explanations for Spouse Abuse," *Social Forces* 67 (1988): 473–491. The same studies disagree on whether abusers or victims are more likely to be drunk or drugged, and whether men or women are more likely to kill while under the influence of these substances.

5. One of the very few American essays to mention class, Steinmetz and Straus, "The Family as Cradle of Violence," notes that 23 percent of middle-class and 40 percent of working-class women report marital abuse, but discounts the difference. Few U.S. scholars consider the issue; see, for example, Jerome R. Kolbo et al., "Children

Who Witness Domestic Violence: A Review of the Literature," *Journal of Interpersonal Violence* 11 (1996): 281–293; Phil Arkow, "The Relationships Between Animal Abuse and Other Forms of Family Violence," *Family Violence and Sexual Assault Bulletin* 12 (1996): 29–34; John Fantuzzo et al., "Domestic Violence and Children: Prevalence and Risk in Five Major U.S. Cities," *Journal of the American Academy of Child and Adolescent Psychiatry* 36 (1997): 116–122. British and Canadian scholars are less squeamish about class; see Russell P. Dobash and Ruth Emerson Dobash, *A Case Against the Patriarchy* (New York, 1979); Eugen Lupri, "Male Violence in the Home," *Canadian Social Trends* (1989): 19–21.

6. One exception is Marie Ashe and Naomi R. Cahn, "Child Abuse: A Problem for Feminist Theory," in Martha Albertson Fineman and Roxanne Mykitiuk, eds., *The Public Nature of Private Violence* (New York, 1994), 166–194, esp. 182–184. Historical exceptions include Linda Gordon, *Heroes of Their Own Lives: The Politics and History of Family Violence: Boston, 1880-1960* (New York, 1988); Christine Stansell, *City of Women: Sex and Class in New York, 1789-1860* (Urbana, IL, and Chicago, 1982), esp. 193–216.

7. In 1973, Steinmetz and Straus estimated that 97 percent of parents physically punish children at least once during childhood, including grabbing or shoving, in "The Family as Cradle of Violence"; Jill M. Bystydzienski repeated that statistic 20 years later in "Marriage and Family in the United States and Canada," but burdened it with the label of "abuse." Murray A. Straus discusses such misrepresentation of family violence statistics in "Conceptualization and Measurement of Battering: Implications for Public Policy," in Michael Steinman, ed., *Woman Battering: Policy Responses* (Cincinnati, OH, 1991), 19–47.

8. Kathleen J. Ferraro, "Review Essay: Culture, Feminism and Male Violence," *Social Justice* 17 (1990): 70–84; Demie Kurz, "Social Science Perspectives on Wife Abuse: Current Debates and Future Directions," *Gender and Society* 3 (1989): 489–505. Some theorists note that the sociological literature views this transition simplistically, Elizabeth M. Schneider, "The Violence of Privacy," in Fineman and Mykitiuk, *The Public Nature of Private Violence*, 36–58, esp. 38. Historians *do* note a public/private dichotomy, but usually with more nuances. Stansell, *City of Women*, 77–83; Roderick Phillips, "Gender Solidarities in Late Eighteenth Century Urban France: The Example of Rouen," *Histoire Sociale-Social History* 13 (1980): 325–337; Nancy Tomes, "A 'Torrent of Abuse': Crimes of Violence between Working Class Men and Women in London, 1840–1875," *Journal of Social History* 11 (1978): 328–345; Jane M. Pederson, "Gender, Justice and a Wisconsin Lynching, 1889–1890," *Agricultural History* 67 (1993): 65–82.

9. Schneider, "The Violence of Privacy," 43; Ronald Niezen, "Telling a Message: Cree Perceptions of Custom and Administration," *The Canadian Journal of Native Studies* 13 (1993): 221–250; Isabel Marcus, "Reframing 'Domestic Violence': Terrorism in the Home," in Martha Albertson Fineman and Roxanne Mykitiuk, *The Public Nature of Private Violence*, 11–35, esp. 17. James Garbarino, "Child Abuse: Why?" *The World and I* 5 (1990): 543–553, advocates state intervention into "unnatural families"; I do not mean to imply that single mothers are "historically unnnatural." Other writers suggest family, community, or church intervention, as these groups seem today to be more effective in countering intimate violence than lawyers, doctors, or social workers. Martha R. Mahoney, "Victimization or Oppression? Women's Lives, Violence and Agency," in Fineman and Mykitiuk, *The Public Nature of Private Violence*, 59–87. A final ironic point was

voiced by a radical feminist who moved to a classic Lockean liberal construction of privacy and freedom, a move applauded as a "new feminist agenda." Battered women, she stated, could benefit "from the material and social conditions of equality and self-determination that make privacy possible." When John Locke argued that individual liberty was private property, he could not have said it better. Schneider, "The Violence of Privacy," 53; Susan F. Hirsh, "Introduction," in Fineman and Mykitiuk, *The Public Nature of Private Violence*, 3–10, quotation from 5; Chris Nylund, "John Locke and the Social Position of Women," *History of Political Economy* 25 (1993): 39–63.

10. Ashe and Cahn, "Child Abuse," 166–174.

11. Lance C. Egley, "What Changes the Societal Prevalence of Domestic Violence?" *Journal of Marriage and the Family* 53 (1991): 885–897. The literature is full of similar examples.

12. Some scholars make the distinction theoretically; others assume the usage. Kurz, "Social Science Perspectives on Wife Abuse"; Connie Dykstra, "Domestic Violence and Child Abuse: Related Links in the Chain of Violence," *Protecting Children* 11 (1995): 3–5.

13. Historians have written more about family violence and responses to it for the period following the Civil War than for the period proceeding it. See, for example, Gordon, *Heroes of Their Own Lives*. Other excellent surveys concentrate primarily, though not entirely, on the late nineteenth century. Elizabeth Pleck, *Domestic Tyranny: The Making of American Social Policy against Family Violence from Colonial Times to the Present* (New York, 1987); Michael Grossberg, *Governing the Hearth: Law and the Family in Nineteenth-Century America* (Chapel Hill, NC, 1985); Peter W. Bardaglio, *Reconstructing the Household: Families, Sex, & Law in the Nineteenth-Century South* (Chapel Hill, NC, 1995).

14. Ruth Seydlitz et al., "Development and Social Problems: The Impact of the Offshore Oil Industry on Suicide and Homicide Rates," *Rural Sociology* 58 (1993): 93–110.

15. This discussion is indebted to the works of Charles Tilly—for example, "Family History, Social History and Social Change," *Journal of Family History* 12 (1987): 319–330; and Tamara Hareven—for example, *Family Time and Industrial Time* (New York, 1982).

16. Lucile Cantoni, "Clinical Issues in Domestic Violence," *Social Casework: The Journal of Contemporary Social Work* 62 (1981): 3–12; David Peterson, "Wife Beating: An American Tradition," *Journal of Interdisciplinary History* 23 (1992): 97–118.

17. Elizabeth Pleck, "Wife Beating in Nineteenth-Century America," *Victimology* 4 (1979): 60–74, discusses Mississippi's law of patriarchy with great sophistication.

18. Thomas Haskell, "Capitalism and the Origins of the Humanitarian Sensibility," *American Historical Review* 90 (1985); Toby Ditz, "Shipwrecked; or, Masculinity Imperiled: Mercantile Representations of Failure and the Gendered Self in Eighteenth-Century Philadelphia," *Journal of American History* 81 (1994): 51–80.

19. See also Darla Brock, "'Domestic Recreation' and 'Household Amusements': Spousal Abuse in Memphis, 1861–1865," *West Tennessee Historical Society Papers* 48 (1994): 81–90.

20. "Failure-to-protect" laws assume maternal guilt when a child is abused by another person. To be acquitted, a mother must prove she acted to prevent the abuse (of which she may have been ignorant). Fathers are rarely, if ever, charged with failure to

protect. Howard A. Davidson, "Child Abuse and Domestic Violence: Legal Connections and Controversies," *Family Law Quarterly* 29 (1995): 357–373, esp. 364.

21. Straus lists spousal homicide rates of 0.89 per 100,000 population (0.55 husband on wife; 0.34 wife on husband) in the U.S. in 1984 in "Domestic Violence and Homicide Antecedents"; Roth's comparable statistics range from 0.03 to 0.19. Lawrence W. Sherman et al. list a total homicide rate of 13.5 per 100,000 for Milwaukee, WI, in 1988 in "Predicting Domestic Homicide: Prior Police Contact and Gun Threats," in Steinman, ed., *Woman Battering*, 73–93. Johnson and Chisholm, "Violence in the Family," claim a rate of 750 spousal assaults per 100,000 in Canada from 1974 to 1987, although Canada's total (not spousal) homicide rate in 1987 was given as only 2.5 per 100,000 in "Violence in the Family." They are clearly using a low threshold definition of "assault" in the first statistic.

22. First quotation and definition of patriarchy from Gordon, *Heroes of Their Own Lives*, vi; second and third quotations from Kurz, "Social Science Perspectives on Wife Abuse," 495–496. See also Norman K. Denzin, "Toward a Phenomenology of Domestic, Family Violence," *American Journal of Sociology* 90 (1984): 483–513; Marcus, "Reframing 'Domestic Violence'," in Fineman and Mykitiuk, *The Public Nature of Private Violence*, 11–35.

23. Pleck, "Wife Beating in Nineteenth-Century America," 60, 62–63.

24. Philip Morgan, *Slave Counterpoint: Black Culture in the Eighteenth Century Chesapeake and Low Country* (Chapel Hill, NC, 1998), 274.

25. And as Pleck notes in "Wife Beating in Nineteenth-Century America," 67, the reverse is true: "law is necessary only when other forms of social control are weak." Mary Beth Norton subtlely discusses patriarchal governance in *Founding Mothers and Fathers: Gendered Power and the Forming of American Society* (New York, 1996), 3–180, although I do not ascribe to the central position she assigns to Sir Robert Filmer's political thought. For patriarchy in nineteenth-century Canada, see Cecilia Morgan, " 'In Search of the Phantom Misnamed Honour': Duelling in Upper Canada," *The Canadian Historical Review* 76 (1995): 529–562.

26. William Whateley, *A Bride-Bush, or A direction for Married Persons Plainely describing the duties common to both, and peculiar to each of them* (London, 1623), 105–109, quoted in Susan Dwyer Asmussen, " 'Being Stirred to Much Unquietness': Violence and Domestic Violence in Early Modern England," *Journal of Women's History* 6 (1994): 70–89. Additional quotations from 72, 82.

27. Gordon Wood notes that "by 1750, ancient patriarchal absolutism no longer had the same ideological significance it had once possessed," in *The Radicalism of the American Revolution: How a Revolution Transformed a Monarchical Society into a Democratic One Unlike Any Other That Had Ever Existed* (New York, 1992), 147–148, quotation from 147.

28. This discussion oversimplifies legal and social changes, particularly for women, as described in such classic works as Linda K. Kerber's *Women of the Republic: Intellect and Ideology in Revolutionary America* (New York, 1986). Historians of both women and labor, on the other hand, are cognizant of patriarchy's reciprocity. Gerda Lerner, *The Creation of Patriarchy* (New York, 1986); Philip Morgan, "Three Planters and their Slaves: Perspectives on Slavery in Virginia, South Carolina and Jamaica, 1750–1790," in Winthrop Jordan and Sheila Skemp, eds., *Race and Family in the Colonial South* (Jackson, MS, 1987), 37–80, quotation from 50.

29. Joyce Chaplin, "Slavery and the Principle of Humanity: A Modern Idea in the Early Lower South," *Journal of Social History* 24 (1990): 299–316, 304, 299, 310.

30. The classic formulation of paternalism is that of Eugene D. Genovese in *Roll, Jordan, Roll: The World the Slaves Made* (New York, 1972), esp. 3–7. For a recent discussion of patriarchalism and paternalism, see Morgan, *Slave Counterpoint*, 273–300, quotation from 284. For a discussion of patriarchy and paternalism based on gender, see Lerner, *The Creation of Patriarchy*, 238–243.

31. Indentured servitude in colonial America has not been scrutinized as closely as slavery. It, too, was a time- and place-specific institution. Acceptable behavior for masters and servants was determined by changing conditions and varied from place to place. Christine Daniels, " 'Liberty to complaine': Servant Petitions in Maryland, 1656–1799," forthcoming in Bruce Mann and Christopher Tomlins, eds., *The Many Legalities of Early America* (Chapel Hill, NC, 1999).

32. Ira Berlin, "Time, Space and the Evolution of Afro-American Society on British Mainland North America," *American Historical Review* 84 (1980): 44–78; Ira Berlin, "The Slave Trade and the Development of Afro-American Society in English Mainland North America, 1619–1775," *Southern Studies* 20 (1981): 123–136; Sidney W. Mintz and Richard Price, "An Anthropological Approach to the Afro-American Past: A Caribbean Perspective," (Philadelphia, 1976).

33. For a discussion of widows as household heads, see Norton, *Founding Mothers and Fathers*, 149–156.

34. Marcus, "Reframing Domestic Violence," 31–33.

35. Morgan, *Slave Counterpoint*, 275.

36. Tamara Hareven, "The Home and The Family in Historical Perspective," *Social Research* 58 (1991): 253–285, quotation from 256; Barbara Todd, "Out of House and Home: Two New Perspectives on the American Family," *Canadian Review of American Studies* 18 (1987): 161–164.

37. Families' public functions become evident during times of stress, such as divorce, when the manipulation of public gossip becomes important in the private family. Abigail Trafford, *Crazy Time: Surviving Divorce and Building a New Life* (New York, 1982), 167–186. Allegations of criminal and sexual abuse also can create a public character for families as word of the abuse spreads. Also Joanne M. Ferraro, "The Power to Decide: Battered Wives in Early Modern Venice," *Renaissance Quarterly* 48 (1995): 492–512, esp. 505.

38. Norton, *Founding Mothers and Fathers*, 18–24.

39. The literature of Southern honor is voluminous. See, for example, Bertram Wyatt-Brown, *Southern Honor: Ethics and Behavior in the Old South* (New York and Oxford, 1982); Stephanie McCurry, *Masters of Small Worlds: Yeoman Households, Gender Relations, and the Political Culture of the Antebellum South Carolina Low Country* (New York and Oxford, 1995); Edward Ayers, *Vengeance and Justice: Crime and Punishment in the Nineteenth-Century Antebellum South* (New York, 1983); Kenneth Greenberg, *Honor and Slavery: Noses, Lies, Duels . . .* (Princeton, NJ, 1996).

40. Natalie Zemon Davis describes a similar process for other pardon-seekers in *Fiction in the Archives: Pardon Tales and Their Tellers in Sixteenth-Century France* (Stanford, CA, 1987).

41. As Jackson Toby argued more than thirty years ago, "those segments of the population unable to wield symbolic power" were particularly likely to batter as a means of control. Jackson Toby, "Violence and the Masculine Ideal: Some Qualitative Data," *The Annals of the American Academy of Political and Social Science* 364 (1966): 19–27, quotation from 19. More recent formulations of this argument include Demie Kurz, "Social Science Perspectives on Wife Abuse," and Norman K. Denzin, "Toward a Phenomenology of Domestic, Family Violence."

42. Ronald L. Simons and his coauthors, in their extremely intelligent article, "A Test of Various Perspectives," argue that men are more likely to use violence in families if their parents—like Hatton's Joel Clough's and Baptist's Jonathan Lewis's—"displayed an antisocial orientation" measured by attitudes and actions "deemed risky, inappropriate, shortsighted or insensitive by the majority of people in the society." These actions include self-absorption, bragging, crude language, and not accepting responsibility for one's actions. Quotations from 141, 152. Many sociologists have argued that family violence results not from antisocial personalities but from stress with numerous etiologies. See, for example, Livingston, "Measuring Domestic Violence in An Alcoholic Population"; Seydlitz et al., "Development and Social Problems"; Seltzer and Kalmuss, "Socialization and Stress Explanations for Spouse Abuse"; Laura Ann McCloskey et al., "The Effects of Systemic Family Violence on Children's Mental Health," *Child Development* 66 (1995): 1239–1261.

two

PERSONAL VIOLENCE IN A "PEACEABLE KINGDOM"

Pennsylvania, 1682–1801

G. S. Rowe and Jack D. Marietta

Observers of early Pennsylvania rhapsodized over the prosperity, opportunity, orderliness, and stability in the colony called "the Best Poor Man's Country."[1] Lieutenant Governor Robert Hunter Morris insisted that Pennsylvanians were "used to Peaceable principles," while evangelical minister George Whitefield observed that in Pennsylvania there was "a greater equality between the poor and rich than perhaps can be found in any other place of the known world."[2] Foreign commentors were if anything more effusive in their praise than residents. Montesquieu tabbed William Penn the greatest lawgiver since antiquity, "a Veritable Lycurgus." In his *Lettres Philosophiques* (1734), Voltaire remarked that "William Penn could boast of having brought to the World that golden age of which men talk so much and which probably has never existed anywhere except in Pennsylvania," while a German visitor, Gottlieb Mittelberger, maintained that Pennsylvania was "a paradise for women."[3]

Modern historians have echoed these sentiments in calling early Pennsylvania "Penn's Holy Experiment," a "peaceable kingdom," "a worldly success," "an ideal colony" and "a hopeful torch in a world of semidarkness."[4] Even scholars who dwell on early Pennsylvania's violence and acrimony, or on its tumult and unrest during and after the Revolution, conclude that Pennsylvania was an essentially affluent, progressive, enlightened, and democratic society, one indisputably entrenched in the forefront of America's republican experiment.[5] They have recognized Pennsylvania as "America's first self-consciously plural society."[6]

Historians, moreover, have argued that Pennsylvanian society typified the Quaker and German pietist principles of love, charity, and brotherhood. They have described the Quaker family as child-centered and peaceful, a model of humility, benevolence, devotion, tolerance, and equality, where women were treated as equals.[7] These caring, affectionate, even doting Quaker parents presaged what some historians have termed the "modern" family. Quaker domesticity, they argue, produced "a new kind of ruling American middle class" which experienced a "more harmonious economic, communal, [and] familial . . . development" than was present in neighboring states.[8] Insofar as Quakers and pietists outnumbered others in Pennsylvania, or set an example that others imitated, Pennsylvania was exemplary.

An examination of violent crimes in Pennsylvania prior to the nineteenth century, however, challenges conventional wisdom regarding Pennsylvania's stability, peacefulness, and orderliness. For its time, early Pennsylvania possessed remarkable overall institutional stability, responsive and popular leadership, economic opportunity, and an astonishing degree of personal freedom. But it also endured an extremely high crime rate by eighteenth-century standards, particularly for crimes of personal violence. Its homicide and assault numbers fell below those of Virginia but were comparable to those of North Carolina, which has been characterized as particularly violent and disorderly. Pennsylvanian assault rates were higher than those of Massachusetts and Connecticut and may have been higher than those of New York.[9] It is provocative to realize that although current society and justice systems are very different from those of early Pennsylvania, the assault rate in all Pennsylvania for 1991 to 1993 was 205 aggravated assaults per 100,000 population, lower than some figures for colonial Pennsylvania.[10]

This essay examines the prevailing characterization of early Pennsylvania as a peaceful haven for contented, loving families embracing tender, affectionate child-rearing practices, and provides a statistical overview of Pennsylvania's violence.[11] If, as it suggests, historians have misjudged the extent of personal violence in Pennsylvania, they have probably underestimated the amount of domestic violence in early America generally.[12]

One clear index of personal violence in early Pennsylvania was the murder rate. A total of 513 homicide cases came before its courts between 1682 and 1801, more prosecutions than in any other continental British colony except Virginia, which had a longer history and larger population. More suspected murderers appeared before Pennsylvania courts in the single decade of the 1780s than Massachusetts prosecuted between 1750 and 1800. Rural Lancaster County suffered a homicide rate above 5 per 100,000 population throughout the 1750s. Philadelphia's totaled 7.4 in the 1760s, almost twice the highest rate found in

23

Pennsylvania
Rural, 1750s	5.0
All, 1990s	6.8
Philadelphia	
1760s	7.4
1839–1841	3.4
1846-1852	2.7

North Carolina
1755	6.0
1760	6.6

London
1750s	2.0
1760s	2.2
1780s	0.5

the same city at any point during the nineteenth century, and more than four times that of London during the same decade. The colony's homicide rate before the American Revolution was just as high and occasionally higher than that of tumultuous North Carolina. During the second half of the eighteenth century, Pennsylvania's murder rate was twice as high as London's. It was, in fact, only slightly lower than it is today; between 1781 and 1790 Pennsylvania's homicide rate was 5.5; between 1991 and 1993 it was 6.8 (see Table 2–1.)[13]

Complaints of nonfatal violence also bloated criminal dockets in the Quaker colony. Before 1801, Pennsylvanians formally complained of more than 31,000 criminal offenses, nearly one-third of which—in virtually every pre-nineteenth-century county—involved violence against persons. A total of 10,646 assaults appear in Pennsylvania dockets, trial transcripts, or criminal file papers between 1682 and 1801.[14] Another 1000 to 1500 assaults may have been noted in court dockets no longer extant.[15]

In some rural counties, the proportion of assaults exceeded one-third of all offenses. In Huntingdon, Mifflin, Somerset, Wayne, and Luzerne, all of which were created in the 1780s and 1790s as people moved west, assaults constituted more than 40 percent of all allegations coming before grand juries. Still, the commonly held belief that western Pennsylvania was more violent and tumultuous than the eastern half of the colony does not hold. Westmoreland County, for example, in the extreme western part of the state (which had been established earlier and developed more extensively than some areas north and east of it) had fewer of its total prosecutions represented by assaults than older, more urbanized areas of the state. A close reading of the criminal record suggests that development and religious and ethnic composition had a larger influence on assault rates than did geography.[16] Even in older counties, however, assaults represented about one-third of accusations, although by midcentury averaged just above one-quarter of complaints in Philadelphia City assaults.[17] In short, about one out of every three allegations coming before Pennsylvania courts was of a personal assault.

Additional assaults, of course, were never recorded because the victim feared prosecution, combatants accepted such violence as a normal part of life, or because one or both parties preferred not to publicize an attack. Some assaults surfaced only in the discipline records of various churches. Still others—the vast majority, in fact—were not tried in criminal courts but were pursued as civil suits in Courts of Common Pleas. Early Pennsylvanians, moreover, commonly took striking children, servants, slaves, and wives for granted; such violence would be called assaults today. Even Quaker mothers, celebrated for their forbearance and tender ways, used the rod to discipline their children.[18]

Assaults against women by male acquaintances were especially underrepresented in criminal dockets. Many women whose names do not appear in court records were brought to the Philadelphia Alms House complaining of being beaten and abused by fathers, husbands, masters, lovers, and other male acquaintances. The justice system's insensitivity to women doubtless assured that some females never brought their troubles before state tribunals.

Despite these evidentiary obstacles, even in Chester County, with its considerable Quaker and pietist population, women were the targets of assault in 15.2 percent of all the cases in which victims were identified. Doubtless the percentage was higher in counties with fewer Quakers and German pietists, and the number of nonprosecuted assaults against women higher still.

Both within and without the household, men committed most assaults in early Pennsylvania. About one-third of all allegations leveled against men centered on assault, including rape. But eighteenth-century women were more violent than a modern reader might anticipate; more than one-fifth of the criminal allegations leveled at women accused them of assaults. The greatest difference between men and women lay, not in the proportion of assaults attributed to them, but in the extent of the violence they allegedly committed. Men were much more likely to be accused of fatal violence than were women; they allegedly committed three-quarters (75.7 percent) of all Pennsylvania's murders. Rape, of course, was far more frequently attributed to males than females. Although rape was a notoriously difficult crime to prosecute (only one in three accused rapists was convicted), fifty-seven cases appear in the record, with an additional thirty-nine cases of attempted rape.[19]

PERSONAL VIOLENCE IN A "PEACEABLE KINGDOM"

Both the numbers and proportion of crimes of personal violence increased after 1750 and accelerated after the end of the American Revolution. Assaults, for example, constituted 36.2 percent of charges considered by grand juries between 1750 and 1759. Because many assaults during the civil disorder and mob violence of the 1760s and 1770s were never prosecuted, the percentage declined to 30.3 and then to 26.8 in those decades. In the 1780s, however, the number of prosecutions for assault climbed precipitously, nearly doubling the previous decades' totals. By 1800, assaults constituted 36.4 percent of all complaints.[20]

More than a quarter (26.7 percent) of all assault complaints were thrown out by grand juries, while in another 3.7 percent, prosecuting attorneys found reasons not to proceed. Still another 17.9 percent of all complaints remained unresolved in dockets, although some of those represent cases truncated by the Revolution when the courts closed, and others were doubtless arbitrated "out of doors." Prosecutorial patterns against women virtually mirrored those against men.[21]

High levels of personal violence, not zealous law enforcement, produced Pennsylvania's elevated assault numbers, although the province's courts were efficient by eighteenth-century standards. Legal effectiveness is usually measured by the Effective Conviction Rate (ECR), which states the ratio of convictions to accusations. Overall, Pennsylvania secured one conviction for every 2.20 criminal accusations, for an ECR of 1:2.20. Increasing numbers of accusations after the Revolution, however, rendered courts less efficent; the colony-wide ECR declined from 1:2.03 in the 1770s to 1:2.23 in the 1780s and 1:2.49 in the 1790s.

Specific courts' efficiency reflected the age of the venue and the experience and numbers of its personnel. Older and more settled regions were more efficient in convicting assailants than were raw, frontier regions. The city and county of Philadelphia, for example, had ECRs of 1:1.69 and 1:1.81 during the 1790s. Long-settled Bucks, Chester, and Lancaster counties followed at 1:2.04, 1:2.35, and 1:2.10, respectively. Frontier counties suffered from less-efficient courts. During the last decade of the eighteenth century, Bedford County had an ECR of 1:3.03, Somerset County 1:4.17, and Fayette County 1:4.22.

But while Pennsylvania courts prosecuted assailants efficiently, the state's record of punishment was mixed. Nearly 14 percent of assailants charged sought jury trials. The state obtained convictions in 68 percent of such cases. On the other hand, 55.3 percent of all assailants charged were exonerated, while nearly two in five (38.7 percent) pleaded guilty or merely submitted. Those who did so often claimed to be guiltless but agreed to pay their fines. Jane Gill was typical. When brought before a Chester court in February 1770 she "did protest her innocence" but "would not contend with our Lord the King & submit[ed] herself to the mercy of the Court" and pleaded for "a small fine."[22]

The real problem for law enforcement personnel lay in bringing perpetrators before the court. The distance and nature of the terrain that authorities policed made rigorous detection and arrest difficult or impossible. Indeed, contemporaries before 1801 lamented the ease with with suspects escaped the law. After 1750, Philadelphia City had a large constabulary and street lights to deter crime as well as the state's most efficient courts. Yet observers there believed (probably correctly) that more than half of those guilty of crimes never faced the courts, escaping into the city's warren of crowded streets and back alleys.[23] Courts might process indictments efficiently, but finding, arresting, and charging perpetrators was quite another matter.

Pennsylvania certainly experienced every bit as much physical violence as other American jurisdictions—and more than those of certain regions, notably New England. Few direct comparisons are available for other areas because historians have supplied crime rates for very few other contemporary localities or have measured different categories of criminal activity.[24] Trustworthy crime rates for the whole of Pennsylvania are limited, too. We can, however, calculate assault rates in the last thirty years of the eighteenth century for all or almost all of Pennsylvania, thanks to good county court records and the federal censuses.[25] In 1780 the rate was 59.7 per 100,000, in 1790 it grew to 100.8, and in 1800 it peaked at 130.2 per 100,000.[26] In comparison, the assault rate of North Carolina in 1735 was 17.5 per 100,000 population and for 1760, 42.5.[27]

Crime rates for Chester County are more dependable because of its complete records and reliable population figures. Even with a large Quaker population, Chester County experienced an assault rate of 74.9 per 100,000 in the first decade of the 1700s, when its people were mostly homogeneous and before many Ulster Scots, Irish, and nonpietist Germans had arrived. By the 1750s its population had increased by 540 percent and its assault rate had risen to 100.8. By the 1790s, Chester experienced a rate of 123.4 assaults per 100,000, and the century closed ominously with a surge to 160.8 for the half-decade 1796 to 1800.

Chester County, moreover, was by no means the worst precinct for assaults. That distinction belonged to Bedford, Huntingdon, and Somerset counties, in what is now south central Pennsylvania. Their assault rate in the 1790s was 286.9 and rising; by 1796 to 1800, it reached 325.3. Nearby Mifflin County had a rate of 218.0 for 1794 to 1800.[28] All of these counties were spun off from Cumberland between 1771 and 1795, while the parent county was left with the older, more developed southeastern area of its original boundaries. Nonetheless, Cumberland's assault rates also rose, from 51.1 and 69.0 in the 1750s and 1760s to 110.5 in the 1790s. Nearby Dauphin County's rates stood at 185.4 in the 1790s; in the single year 1794 it experienced an astonishing 444.1 assaults per 100,000 people.

Philadelphia was the only urban area of Pennsylvania with discrete courts and records. Most of those records are lost but those from the 1790s survive;

27

they disclose an assault rate of 127.4 per 100,000, a rate that peaked in 1796 at 239.2. Partial dockets before 1791 hint that the 1790s probably represented the height of violent behavior in the city. Earlier data indicate that the assault rate rose consistently near the end of the Seven Years' War (1759 to 1763) from 55.3 to 133.4.

The coincidence with the end of the Great War for Empire is suggestive.[29] The war began in Pennsylvania, devastated its western reaches, and brought the colony its first wartime mobilization. By 1758, however, the war in the province had ended. In the aftermath of other British imperial wars, John Beattie found surges of crime in London that he attributed to demobilized soldiers and sailors. The data suggest that this phenomenon touched Philadelphia as well.[30] By 1767 to 1771, the Philadelphia assault rate had fallen to 62.6 or lower. In 1780 it began a climb that may have continued to the unprecedented heights of 1789 to 1800. Understandably, Philadelphians of the 1790s bemoaned the "quarrelsome" men and women who "boxed" and "brawled" in the city's streets.[31]

Violent behavior in Pennsylvania, therefore, rose after American independence and was mounting still in 1800. Though the disorder and tumult during the war years is well documented, the aftermath of the Revolution, like the years following the Seven Years' War, demands more attention. It produced unparalleled unrest and personal violence. By almost every standard, the 1780s were Pennsylvania's most turbulent decade to that date. Berks County, with its large German pietist population, never experienced a total crime rate of over 150 offenses per 100,000 during its first three decades; that rate moved above 220 in the 1780s.[32]

The 1790s were more violent in some areas than in others. Philadelphians suffered a total crime rate of more than 400 per 100,000 throughout the decade, as did adjacent Berks County; in 1795, Berks's rate exceeded 500. Dauphin County suffered a rate of 1095 in the mid-1790s. This evidence of a surge in crime, especially violent crime, in post-Revolutionary Pennsylvania encompasses eastern and western precincts, frontier areas and settled regions, rural counties and Philadelphia City. Such numbers are not the skewed, misleading product of eccentric law enforcement or incomplete dockets; the increase was real.[33]

Ethnicity and religion also modified personal assault rates, although their effects were not as striking as the aftermath of the Revolution. Pennsylvania's Scots-Irish citizens were much more likely to engage in violent behavior than were their pacifist German neighbors. Dauphin County, for example, home of the violent Paxton Boys of 1763 to 1764, was created from Lancaster in 1785. While Lancaster retained its Mennonite and Amish population, Dauphin included the area's Ulster Scots.[34] Lancaster's assault rate was 57.0 in 1783 and 40.5 in 1786, while Dauphin's was 143.8 in 1785 and 98.2 in 1785 to 1789. Mifflin County's dockets also teem with Scottish surnames, and its assault rates in 1794 and 1795 were 511.0 and 289.7. In 1786, Mifflin's parent county, Cumberland, had a rate of 144.2, which fell to 87.2 after Mifflin was separated.

Lancaster and Berks counties had the highest proportion of Mennonites and Amish people in Pennsylvania. Until the years following the Revolution, the two counties enjoyed assault rates often far below those of adjacent Chester County. Berks had only 19.7 assaults per 100,000 in the 1770s, while Lancaster ranged from 44.0 to 56.4 between 1740 and 1780.

While political turmoil, ethnicity, and religion affected rates of personal violence in the peaceable province, class seems to have had only a small effect, although resident laborers without real property were somewhat more likely to engage in personal violence than were property-holding farmers. About 1000 Chester County assailants' vocations can be traced. Farmers comprised more than half of the assailants, although they were less common among assailants than they were among the population at risk. Laborers, on the other hand, comprised nearly one-quarter of the assailants, but were overrepresented compared to their proportion of the population. No other occupation counted for more than 1.5 percent of the assailants.[35] The mean percentile of assessed wealth of assailants who held property fell between the 54th and 58th percentile of Chester County as a whole. Such men, therefore, were neither the rich nor the poor; rather, they were "middling" men.

The wealth of assault victims only slightly exceeded that of their assailants; their mean percentile lay between the 59th and 63rd percentiles.[36] In general, Pennsylvanians were more apt to assault members of their own class and frequently of their own family. Violence occurred more frequently within the intimate bounds of the household rather than across the public boundaries of class.

Establishing statistics for assaults in Pennsylvania is easier than assessing the nature and extent of intimate violence in the colony. The criminal records of early Pennsylvania, like others in early America, are both incomplete and laconic. Physical abuse of spouses, children, servants, and slaves may have been handled—when handled at all—by a single Justice of the Peace. Because few J.P. records have survived, most minor incidents are thus denied us forever. In addition, early clerks of criminal courts seldom distinguished between "assault" and "battery." Any attempt or threat to inflict injury, combined with an apparent ability to do so, or any intentional display of force that might give a victim reason to fear or expect immediate bodily harm constituted an assault. Battery was the unlawful application of force to another person—the "wrongful" beating of another. Because clerks often characterized both assault and battery as "assault" in their records, it is difficult without supplementary court papers to judge the nature of each assault. Harsh or threatening words appear, in dockets at least, as severe as physical attacks leading to bloodshed and injury.[37] When assaults were particularly brutal, however, assailants were charged with

29

"assault with intent to murder" or "to ravish." Clerks were also casual in recording the victim's name, age, and relationship to his or her assailant. The growing prominence of attorneys-general overseeing criminal prosecutions after 1750, moreover, renders the records even more standardized and laconic; the trail of injured parties becomes dimmer and more difficult to trace. Although some county records are more forthcoming than others, the nature of judicial records in early Pennsylvania makes reconstructing most cases of intimate violence problematic.[38]

The law, moreover, acknowledged that physical force could and should be employed by husbands, masters, and teachers to discipline their charges; local people, as officers of the court, therefore, established local standards of wrongful intimate violence. Handbooks for constables, justices of the peace, and sheriffs reminded judicial personnel that parents might strike children, masters might smite servants, and teachers might cuff students without incurring the wrath of the law. Within reason, such beatings were lawful, so long as they did not become battery. Court officials and the populace as grand and traverse jurors judged the point at which husband, father, master, or schoolmaster crossed the line from properly exercising the prerogative of authority to "wrongfully beating another." The standards of intimate violence were unfailingly local.[39]

Efforts to assess and describe violence in Pennsylvania households—white or black—is complicated both by a lack of consensus on how "household" should be defined and by the paucity of records revealing the rhythm and routine of households. Between 1682 and 1801 possibly as many as 1 in 6 (1660 cases) assault and battery prosecutions involved members or individuals in the same household. As many as 1 in 11 (887 cases) of all cases may have involved married couples.[40] These numbers do not include other forms of familial abuse or violence such as murder, rape, or incest, nor adultery, bigamy, infidelity, or other cases of psychological or mental abuse of family or household members. A consistent definition of a "household" and the types of violence possible within it must be established before comparable data may be produced.

Nor have most historians of intimate violence come to terms with the place of neighbors in the early modern world. Most scholars reflexively consider neighbors "outsiders," but court records suggest this assumption is too simple and too presentist particularly during the seventeenth and early eighteenth centuries. Neighbors seem to have been almost constantly present in households. Some were meddlesome and aggressive, others helpful and caring, but all influenced each other's lives through custom and proximity.[41] More than half of all assaults described in Pennsylvania's court records pitted neighbor against neighbor. Francis Smith of Chester County, for example, entered the home of his absent neighbor James Bayless in 1689 and "did violently force" Bayless's wife, Mary "to ye Bed Side in her sd Husbands House with an intent to have . . . fornication with her." In 1764 Joseph Clark and his wife invited

G. S. Rowe and Jack D. Marietta

Mary Burnside, wife of Alexander, to stay in their home during their absence. During her visit, their son David made sexual advances toward her. When she tried to escape, he struck her. Bucks County's Jane Coverdale, a married women, testified in 1687 that neighbor Philip Conway "came to her bed side & did Say he has sworn he would fuck her either by night or by day & about A Month after that he Came to the house & sd he had Sworn about 4 years he would fuck her." Coverdale was "afraid less hee Shuld lay violent hands on her." Early in 1693, Phillip Yarnell came to the home of Elizabeth Woodyard's father. When he encountered her there, Yarnell asked whether she was a woman, and declared he "would feel" whether it was so. When she tried to stop his groping, he forced her hand "into his Codpise and would have her to feele his members how they went limber or stifer."[42]

Neighbors indulged in violent behavior out of doors as well as in each other's homes. In Lancaster in 1772, for example, William and Mary Dickson struck neighbor Allan Regan with a board and killed him instantly. Regan had stormed over to the Dickson home because Mary had been "abusing" Regan's wife, Anne. Samuel Rowland, neighbor of Woley Rosen and his wife, became so incensed with them in 1688 that he shouted epithets at Mrs. Rosen, then laid "violent hands upon [Rosen] and Tricking him [and] throughing him on ye ground [took] him by the throat near to strangling him."[43] Rowland was only one among many who became unhappy with the intimacy of seventeenth-century neighbors.

Even children were not safe from neighbors and workmen who entered their homes easily and often. In 1734, Jean Smith of Chester County informed the court that her daughter, "scarce six years old," told her that a neighbor had come to their house while Smith was away "and laid upon her and was like to kill her and took a long red thing out of his trousers and hurt her belly with it." In 1754, Jean Gordon insisted that servant John McVey sexually molested her eight-year-old daughter while she was away from home. In 1792, Ann Babb discovered a drunken Thomas Hemphill lying on top of her four-year-old granddaughter "with his breeches down and the child struggling and screaming."[44]

In brief, despite the lack of precise quantification on the nature and rate of domestic violence in early Pennsylvania, it seems clear that—Quaker aspirations aside—more violence occurred among Pennsylvania's vaunted families and friends than has been previously conceded. Like crime generally, violence increased rather than decreased in the last half of the eighteenth century.

The starkest and most obvious form of domestic violence was familicide, although such cases were rare. In 1755, for example, John Myriak of Chester County killed and disfigured his wife "so that no Person could know her." He then killed his two children and a neighbor's infant being suckled by Mrs. Myriak by swinging their bodies so that their skulls were "beat to peaces against a rock that was before his door." John Lewis of the same county, who

PERSONAL VIOLENCE IN A "PEACEABLE KINGDOM"

claimed God directed his actions, strangled his pregnant wife in 1760 as she neared her time.[45]

Wife murder was more common than familicide. In the cases examined by this study, fourteen men were formally accused of murdering their wives; eleven were convicted. In 1786, Josiah Ramage of Chambersburg, Franklin County, beat his wife of thrity-seven years to death with fire tongs. Philadelphian John Bullock's "blackest and most Barbarous" murder of his wife in 1741 led to his conviction. Northampton's John DeLong was found guilty in 1792 of spousal murder but escaped punishment because he suffered "fits of lunacy."[46]

Of course not all men who tried to kill their wives succeeded. In 1772, Hector McNeil of Chester was charged with shooting and wounding his wife Catherine. On two previous occasions he had fired a pistol at her. In 1793, Elizabeth Love maintained that her husband "repeatedly endangered [her] Life." A neighbor of Phillip and Catherine Heger, Mary Norris, testified that Phillip routinely treated his wife so brutally that she often heard her scream, "murder, murder." Philadelphia's Henry Higgert was jailed "frequently" for his "violent ill treatment in beating his Wife Ann [which] greatly endangered her life," while Michael Bowyer of the same city not only "violently assaulted and endangered the life of Deborah, his wife," but also mistreated "his Infant child only four days old." In 1750 Samuel Petit, according to his wife, first beat, then sodomized her.[47]

Although in most instances husbands assaulted wives, wives occasionally assaulted husbands. In 1785, Alexander McArthur accused his wife Sarah of pelting him "with sharp objects, bottles, etc.," while in 1795 John Young charged that his wife Ann assaulted and beat him "& threaten[ed] to take his life." He swore "that he believe[d] himself in danger." Such marital battles often became habitual and cyclical. The testimony of neighbors in homicide, assault, and divorce proceedings reveals evidence of longtime but episodic acrimony like that of the Downs of Philadelphia. Margaret Downs came before the Mayor's court in June 1790 for assaulting her husband Robert. Six months later, Robert stood before the same judges for assaulting her.[48]

The records examined in this study reveal that children also suffered at the hands of their parents; between 1682 and 1801, 92 individuals were prosecuted for slaying youngsters. Dockets contain more than 250 cases stemming either from the neglect or mistreatment of children; nonjudicial records reveal more. Parents' assaults against children ran the gamut of physical abuse. Nicholas Wyriak of Lancaster County, for example, systematically tortured his nine-month-old daughter to death in 1748. In September 1785, Kelly Rogers of Boiling Springs, "with the most unheard of barbarity," murdered her eight- or nine-year-old son "by cutting his throat from ear to ear." After a suicide attempt, Rogers told authorities that after a lifetime of hard labor, the thought that her son "should, during life, pursue the same means for a sustenance" prevented her from "letting him survive her in such servility."[49]

G. S. Rowe and Jack D. Marietta

Instances of murder involving illegitimate children and legitimate but unwanted children were common. Between 1682 and 1801, records indicate that 78 persons were accused of killing infants or of being accessories to infanticide under the British statute 21 James I, c. 27 (1624) or its subsequent revisions.[50] Of those, 73 cases involved unmarried women killing their infants; 57 (78 percent) of those accusations led to trials. Most infanticide prosecutions involved young, poor, and uneducated servant girls, although the courts noted a handful of exceptions.[51]

Scores of infanticide cases, moreover, were never prosecuted. Many young women resorted to "baby dropping" to rid themselves of unwanted offspring; without any positive identification of the infants, prosecution was well-nigh impossible. In 1769, for example, officials of Philadelphia's Christ Church discovered "an unknown infant" buried "about ten inches underground" in their cemetery. Another "unknown infant" was found the same year after it had been "thrown into" the Delaware River. In 1772, officials stumbled upon a female child in the city's "Strangers' burying grounds," while another was found "lying dead by a path," "starved" and "exposed to the weather." A coroner's jury subsequently concluded that the baby had "come to her death by the Cruelty of the Parents unknown." Scores of such incidents appear in nonjudicial records.[52] Illegal abortions, moreover—those of fetuses that had "quickened"—were virtually impossible to prove. Abortifacient herbs and other, more violent remedies were often used successfully and surreptitiously.[53]

Many young women escaped criminal charges because of the influence of their natal families or the families they served.[54] They also escaped because of the inability of coroners and inquest juries to judge malice or willful neglect in cases of infant death, or whether a child had been born alive. After the body of Gertrude Popp's infant was discovered in Berks County in April 1772, she maintained that it had been stillborn. She argued that because she had lifted heavy stones while pregnant, the child had not survived. Another Berks County woman, Ann Mertz, told authorities that she had fallen "off a fence" while pregnant and thereafter "never did perceive any life" in her child.[55]

Infanticide laws did not require authorities to establish that a child had been willfully murdered in order to prosecute a woman, nor for a jury to convict her, but jurors virtually never found women guilty of infanticide unless the prosecution established that a callous mother had planned to kill the child. Prosecutors, moreover, understood this and bowed to popular opinion rather than insisting on statute law.[56] Fewer than half (42 percent) of the women tried for infanticide were convicted; only a third (33 percent) of those convicted were executed.[57]

Most parental abuse, however, stopped short of murder. Certainly by the late eighteenth century, most prosecutions focused on neglect rather than physical abuse. John Yard, for example, "a ragged Deserted Child under eight

PERSONAL VIOLENCE IN A "PEACEABLE KINGDOM"

years old," came to the attention of authorities begging in the streets of Philadelphia as his "Parents neglected to provide for him." Four-year-old James Brickel arrived at the Philadelphia Almshouse in 1792 when his mother was arrested for public drunkenness, as did three-year-old Elizabeth Evans when a J.P. discovered her drunken father neglecting her. Elizabeth Nicholson, another "poor feeble Infant, of between 2 & 3 years old," was "veneral"—infected with a venereal disease—when she was abandoned by her parents in February 1790. Elizabeth Phillips, the wife of Mather Phillips, "a Drunken, Disorderly Fellow," brought her three children with her to the Almshouse when she escaped her abusive alcoholic husband.[58] The Daily Occurrence Dockets, the Vagrancy Dockets, and the Prisoners for Trial Dockets for Philadelphia describe a widespread back-alley culture where children routinely suffered from neglect after the Revolution.[59]

Some child abuse, however, especially before the Revolution, resulted not from neglect but from calculated cruelty and mistreatment. In 1781, John Miller of Bucks County, husband of Appelona, not only beat her so "unmercifully" and so routinely "that she was ashamed, for self preservation" to appeal to county officials, but he seduced Appelona's daughter, Elizabeth, from a previous marriage and impregnated her. He then enticed young Elizabeth, a minor, to join him in deserting Appelona and her other children, although he later abandoned Elizabeth as well. In 1698, Bucks County's George Randol was brought to court "for beating and Intolerably abuseing of his grand Child."[60]

For the most part Quakers and their children kept themselves free of criminal prosecution.[61] But if Quaker families were honest and affectionate they could also be rigid and repressive. The French observer Moreau de St. Mery observed that Quaker girls in Philadelphia could be driven from their families by the discipline their parents imposed. Such subjugation, he argued, made them susceptible to unscrupulous men who seduced them and encouraged them to abandon their families and women who lured them into prostitution. Quaker records do not substantiate St. Mery's observation, but prostitution certainly increased dramatically in Philadelphia after the Revolution. Contributing to this phenomenon were youths, both male and female, who found their families unbearable, as well as the men, unhappy with their marriages, who sought them out.[62]

On occasion, children lashed back physically at their parents, although fewer than thirty such cases can be identified. Catherine Carr was jailed in 1795 for "committing An Assault & Battery on the person of her own Mother." Bucks County's Robert Kennedy was brought to court in 1768 for the same offense. Moreau de St. Mery reported that two young boys, the eldest ten years old, stole goods from a Philadelphia shopkeeper. When the ten-year-old's mother insisted that he stay home as punishment, he set fire to the house with her inside.[63]

34

At other times (in some fifty instances that reached the courts) children's ire was directed toward their siblings rather than their parents. In 1739, for example, in Bucks County, two "deaf and dumb" brothers, ages eighteen and ten, went into the woods, where the elder fatally slit the throat of the younger. In 1773, Samuel Brandt shot his brother Valentine following a quarrel, then torched the family home to hide his crime. More typical of docketed sibling assaults was Ann Collins, who simply beat her sister Phoebe in 1781.[64]

Intimate violence involving free and enslaved African-Americans is treated more fully elsewhere in this volume. In Pennsylvania, however, violence on the part of African-Americans was closely monitored by the white community, especially after 1780 when the Act for the Gradual Abolition of Slavery focused provincial attention on blacks and their alleged criminality.[65] Owners of slaves often punished them without reference to the courts, while authorities largely ignored black-on-black assaults. Because of this extralegal and unrecorded behavior, we will never know with any certainty the degree of intimate violence found within black households or among blacks in white families. Still, nearly four hundred African-Americans came before Pennsylvania courts after 1780, when they were tried in regular courts whose records are more complete than earlier "Negro Courts," which operated from 1700 to 1780 and tried only African-Americans. Nearly nine-tenths (86.2 percent) of those tried for assault were accused of simple batteries.[66]

African-Americans were more often the victims than the perpetrators of physical violence.[67] Pennsylvania's slaves, like those elsewhere, were subjected to daily abuse and indignities, usually within households.[68] Authorities in the Quaker colony, again like those elsewhere, betrayed a widespread inclination to leave the punishment of slave misbehavior to masters. Only truly horrifying cases of physical abuse of slaves by masters came before the courts—and sometimes even those did not. Court records confirm Peter Kalm's 1744 observation that Pennsylvania juries would not convict and execute a white man for killing a black.[69] In 1741, for example, William Bullock of Philadelphia was prosecuted for the death of his eight-year-old black servant boy.[70] The fact that he was convicted suggests that his actions were particularly abhorrent. Yet the Council of Pennsylvania voted not to issue a warrant for his execution, and Bullock escaped the hangman.

Most masters who mistreated their slaves not only escaped conviction, but also avoided prosecution. Lancaster County's William Crawford knifed his female slave Dinah to death in 1767. Witnesses established that he had "often severely beat her" and suspected that she was sexually involved with his neighbor. Despite compelling evidence of his culpability, the Grand Jury refused to indict him. John and Elizabeth Bishop of Berks County abused their "negro wench" Lucy until she died in 1772 but, like Crawford, they escaped prosecution.[71]

PERSONAL VIOLENCE IN A "PEACEABLE KINGDOM"

Rapes of African-American women by white men generally stirred no judicial response. In a rare prosecution, "Fat John" Shaeffer, who purportedly raped young Alice Clifton repeatedly and fathered her baby, was tried in Philadelphia in 1788. Vivid testimony against Shaeffer during Clifton's infanticide trial prompted prosecutors to charge Shaeffer with rape. But court officials found that the jurors would have none of it and exonerated Shaeffer. William Bradford, one-time state attorney-general, insisted that sexual assaults upon black women could not be successfully prosecuted for two reasons. First, black victims could not testify in their own behalf; second, Pennsylvania juries were not prepared to find a white man guilty of the rape of an African-American woman.[72] Black women, therefore, had no incentive to relate such assaults to officials, and most white-on-black rapes doubtless went unreported.

White servants, like black slaves, were also physically abused and even murdered by their masters and mistresses. Again, many such cases undoubtedly escaped the notice of authorities. In 1685 Henry Reynold's Chester County neighbors testified that he had beaten his maidservant so badly that she died the next day. In 1710, mariner Chatmall Pride killed his apprentice Thomas Bleasdall. In 1756, Lancaster apothecary Charles Jagler (or Seigler) drew on his professional lore to poison his maid Rosina Holdersinger while in 1772, John Nicholas beat his apprentice John O'Neil to death when he discovered the lad sleeping on the job.[73]

While servant murders were rare, records suggest that beatings were common. Lancaster County's Christopher Riegert beat his maidservant Ann Charles so badly in 1757 that the court released her from service to him. A year later, the same court discovered that Samuel Scott "greatly abused" and "cruelly treated" Ann Long, "an Infant in service to him." The court also released her from her indenture. Similarly, boarding house proprietor Elizabeth Gather was forced "to give up the Indenture" of eleven-year-old servant Mary Duffy when neighbors protested that Duffy was severely mistreated. Authorities packed Mary off to the almshouse instead.[74] Some masters were more creative in their cruelties to servants, as when John Davenport tied his servant Henry Hawkins behind a horse, which kicked and dragged him until Hawkins nearly died.[75]

Servants did not always submit passively to the physical and psychological treatment meted out to them. In Chester County, where servants comprised fewer than 4 percent of the population included on tax lists, they represented 8.5 percent of that county's assailants. For example, William Davis killed his master William Cloud in 1728, while in 1784 James Burke killed his, Timothy McAuliffe. In Philadelphia, Hans Ulrick Seilor stabbed his mistress to death in 1750.[76] In 1795, Philadelphia's Francis McHenry was accused of "threatening his Master Richard Babe and his Family in a very unjustifiable manner," while Negro Henry threatened his master John Lawrence, in 1790. Negro Peter was guilty of "disorderly and turbulent behavior towards his Mistress," and maidservant Sarah Morton badly beat her mistress while inebriated and was incarcerated for this and "other wise misbehaving."[77] Despite their assaults on masters, however, servants primarily attacked other servants, laborers, and artisans with whom they had daily contact.

Masters' sexual exploitation prompted maidservants to complain only occasionally and often only under outside provocation. Sarah Mooney of Bucks County, for example, was charged with fornication before she told J.P. Gilbert Hicks that her master Charles Edgar had pressed her for sexual favors for four years. She bore him four children between 1750 and 1756, but attracted the attention of court officials only after Edgar assaulted her in 1758. Sexual exploitation of servants by masters was easily and frequently hidden from the court. Minister Henry Muhlenberg, for example, knew of a master who often tried to rape his servant girl in the presence of his wife, although the case was never brought before a court. The papers of Jasper Yeates, attorney and later judge of the Pennsylvania Supreme Court, contain examples of servant women raped by men during the harvest in cases that were never prosecuted.[78]

Pennsylvania, the handiwork of William Penn and the cherished exhibit of Enlightment philosophers, liberated free individuals from the constraints of established religion, hereditary class, exclusive privileges, and a single, prescriptive culture. For some skeptical observers, the problem with this venerated new order was this: What in Pennsylvania would curb the liberated, egotistical impulses of men and women? The German visitor Johan Schoepf discovered that Pennsylvanians "dread everything that preaches contraint. . . . Natural freedom . . . is what pleases them."[79] Who or what would teach men to check their impulses to satisfy personal ambitions and teach them to pursue happiness within limits, to sacrifice, to postpone gratification, and to keep pride and personal honor in check? One response that both eighteenth-century Pennsylvanians and modern historians have given was that families would do the work. In this new society, a modern, affectionate family would ideally supply the services that church, class, and state had done for ages in Europe. Domesticity would take up the burdens of producing public virtue and sustaining republicanism after 1776. Parents would nurture and educate as well as correct and punish. Households would become nurseries of goodness as well as units of production and accumulation.

In the case of some Pennsylvanians, families doubtless worked to these specifications and produced the citizens that philosophers and republicans idealized. Quakers, Mennonites, Amish, Moravians, Dunkards, and others gave little trouble to the state and its courts or to other citizens of the counties, townships, and neighborhoods where they lived. But just as many or more did not heed pietist influences and did not trouble themselves over the consequences of their behavior. The domestic and intimate violence that modern observers associate with twentieth-century families was common in seventeenth- and eighteenth-

PERSONAL VIOLENCE IN A "PEACEABLE KINGDOM"

century Pennsylvania. In this province of expansive settlements and an overextended and understaffed constabulary, government was too remote to deter offenders. Quietistic religions had too few subscribers; religion and cultural pluralism made behavioral standards elective and weak; government was passive; and possessive individualism belittled concern for fellow men and women, including one's own family. In many ways that observers praised, Pennsylvania anticipated the future of America, but it also anticipated its future violence and crime—including that within households.

Notes

1. This chapter is based on research completed for a book to be entitled *Law, Liberty, and License: Criminal Offenses and Their Resolution in Pennsylvania, 1680–1801* by the authors.

2. Alan Tully, *Forming American Politics: Ideals, Interests, and Institutions in Colonial New York and Pennsylvania* (Baltimore, MD, 1994), 262; George Whitefield, *Journals (1737–1741)*, introduction, ed. William V. Davis (Gainesville, FL, 1969), 384, 386–387.

3. Oscar Handlin and John Clive, eds., *Journey to Pennsylvania by Gottlieb Mittelberger* (Cambridge, MA, 1960), 93; Durand Echeverria, *Mirage in the West: A History of the French Image of American Society to 1815* (New York, reprint edition, 1966), 17–18.

4. Thomas A. Bailey and David M. Kennedy, *The American Pageant* 9th ed. (Lexington, MA, 1991); Paul S. Boyer et al., *The Enduring Vision: A History of the American People* (Lexington, MA, 1990); Bernard Bailyn et al., *The Great Republic: A History of the American People* 3rd ed. (Lexington, MA, 1985); John W. Davidson et al., *A Nation of Nations: A Narrative History of the American Republic* (New York, 1990); Jack P. Greene, *Pursuits of Happiness: The Social Development of Early Modern British Colonies and the Formation of American Culture* (Chapel Hill, NC, 1988), chap. 6.

5. Alan Tully, *William Penn's Legacy: Politics and Social Structure in Provincial Pennsylvania, 1726–1755* (Baltimore, MD, 1977); Tully, *Forming American Politics*; William M. Offutt, Jr., *"Of 'Good Laws' & 'Good Men'": Law and Society in the Delaware Valley, 1680–1710* (Urbana, IL, 1995); Gary Nash, *Quakers & Politics: Pennsylvania, 1681–1726* (Princeton, NJ, 1968); Steven Rosswurm, *Arms, Country, and Class: The Philadelphia Militia and the 'Lower Sort' During the American Revolution* (New Brunswick, NJ, 1987); Robert L. Brunhouse, *The Counter-Revolution in Pennsylvania, 1776–1790* (New York, 1942; reprint edition, 1971).

6. Sally Schwartz, *'A Mixed Multitude': The Struggle for Toleration in Colonial Pennsylvania* (New York, 1987), 1.

7. J. William Frost, *The Quaker Family in Colonial America* (New York, 1973); Barry Levy, *Quakers and the American Family: British Settlement in the Delaware Valley* (New York, 1988).

8. Levy, *Quakers and the American Family*, 140, 144, 229.

9. W. Watt Espy and John Ortiz Smykla, *Executions in the United States, 1608–1987: The Espy File* (Ann Arbor, MI, 1987), 101–102; Peter C. Hoffer and William B. Scott,

G. S. Rowe and Jack D. Marietta

eds., *Criminal Proceedings in Colonial Virginia* (Athens, GA, 1984), esp. lx; Robert M. Saunders, "Crime and Punishment in Early National America: Richmond, Virginia, 1784–1820," *Virginia Magazine of History and Biography* 86 (1978): 33–44; Hugh Rankin, *Criminal Trial Proceedings in the General Court of Colonial Virginia* (Charlottesville, VA, 1965); Philip J. Schwarz, *"Twice Condemned": Slaves and the Criminal Laws of Virginia, 1705–1865* (Baton Rouge, LA, 1988); Donna J. Spindel, *Crime and Society in North Carolina, 1663–1776* (Baton Rouge, LA, 1989), 46, 59, 65; Douglas Greenberg, *Crime and Law Enforcement in the Colony of New York, 1691–1776* (Ithaca, NY, 1974). Differences in American jurisdictions are explored more fully in Marietta and Rowe, *Law, Liberty, and License*, chaps. 7 and 8.

10. *Statistical Abstract of the U.S.: 1995* (Washington, D.C., 1995), 200; *Sourcebook of Criminal Justice Statistics, 1993* (Washington, D.C., 1994), 367.

11. In Marietta and Rowe, *Law, Liberty and License*, chap. 7.

12. Eighteenth-century Pennsylvania clearly tolerated a great deal of personal violence, although much of it falls outside the purview of this volume. These themes are developed at length in *ibid.*, chaps. 3 and 7. One measure of Pennsylvania's violence was its treatment of men in office. One half (49.1 percent) of all identifiable victims of assault in Chester County (the single most Quaker county in Pennsylvania) were constables attacked while accomplishing their duties. By the same token, the crime most frequently attributed to constables was assault. Sheriffs, too, often faced hysterical people who endangered them and their families. They suffered proportionately as many assaults as did constables. Judges were also assaulted and threatened—even Supreme Court judges occasionally dodged rocks and bullets, eluded mobs intent on their death, and wrestled and boxed with bitter defendants. One J.P. lamented that "I am Daily threatened of my life and property if I proceed to execute my Office." Several magistrates were killed in the line of duty. Another measure of the violence in early Pennsylvania was its violent judicial response; that is, the number of its executions. Pennsylvania sent 202 individuals to their death between 1700 and 1799, twice the number Massachusetts executed and 17 percent more than New York did in the same period. Before 1801, Pennsylvania executed more felons than any American jurisdiction save Virginia. For a people governed during much of their history by nonviolent Quakers who opposed the death penalty—or embraced it only reluctantly—these are remarkable numbers. Espy and Smykla, *Executions*, 101–102.

13. J. M. Beattie, *Crime and the Courts in England, 1660–1800* (Princeton, NJ, 1986), 108; Roger Lane, *Violent Death in the City: Suicide, Accident and Murder in Nineteenth Century Philadelphia* (Cambridge, MA, 1979), 71, 79; Spindel, *Crime and Society*, 59 n27, 65. Current numbers are found in *Statistical Abstract of the United States: 1995*, 200. The Pennsylvania homicide rate in 1992 was 6.2 per 100,000. Pennsylvania witnessed 154 homicide prosecutions between 1781–1790. For Massachusetts, see Linda Kealey, "Crime and Society in Massachusetts in the Second Half of the Eighteenth Century" (Ph.D. diss., University of Toronto, 1981), 8off.

14. Here "assault" refers to verbal assaults such as slander and libel as well as a range of physical assaults, including kidnapping and rape. A total of 30.7 percent of these proceedings involved physical violence. This figure includes the 513 homicides.

15. Individual county dockets are missing for the years 1682 to 1800; virtually all Philadelphia City and County dockets are missing for the years prior to 1759.

PERSONAL VIOLENCE IN A "PEACEABLE KINGDOM"

16. This observation is based on a survey of all extant dockets prior to 1801. Contemporaries insisted that the Scotch-Irish were "audacious and disorderly." Benjamin Rush maintained that they resisted "the operation of the laws" and "cannot bear to surrender up a single natural right for all the benefits of government." Criminal dockets substantiate that impression. See David Hackett Fischer, *Albion's Seed: Four British Folkways in America* (New York, 1989), 777; Terry G. Jordan and Matti Kaups, *The American Backwoods Frontier: An Ethnic and Ecological Interpretation* (Baltimore, MD, 1989); and Fox Butterfield, *All God's Children: The Bosket Family and the American Tradition of Violence* (New York, 1995), 3, 5, 9–10, 15.

17. Bucks and Philadelphia (excluding the city) counties topped the list of older counties with assault prosecutions at 32.3 percent. After 1759, when Philadelphia records are more complete, 27.7 percent of all cases represented some type of assault. Despite the loss of more than fifty years of dockets, the city processed 12 percent of all assaults recorded in Pennsylvania before 1801. When post-Revolutionary counties are removed from consideration, Philadelphia's percentage of assaults to other crimes still ranged from a low of 25.8 to a high of 35.9 percent.

18. Levy, *Quakers and the American Family*, 227.

19. See also the discussion of rape in Cornelia H. Dayton, *Women Before the Bar: Gender, Law, and Society in Connecticut, 1639–1789* (Chapel Hill, NC, 1995), 232–273.

20. Assault complaints increased from 663 in the 1750s to 4865 in the 1790s.

21. The only disparities between men and women defendants prosecuted in assault cases were the slightly lower (15.4) percentage of cases unresolved for women and the slightly lower (44.9) percentage of convictions.

22. Chester County Quarterly Sessions (hereafter CCQS), 2/1770, Chester County Historical Society.

23. "Petition," *Pennsylvania Packet*, 12/30/1787; "A Native of Philadelphia," *Independent Gazetteer*, 12/17/1785; Marietta and Rowe, *Law, Liberty, and License*, chap. 8.

24. Greenberg's *Crime and Law Enforcement* is typical of many studies of crime in early America in not offering rates of crime per 100,000 which provide the basis for serious comparisons. For additional works, see note 9, above.

25. See John J. McCusker and Russell R. Menard, *The Economy of British North America, 1607–1789* (Chapel Hill, NC, 1985), 203. The populations of Pennsylvania counties before the Federal census of 1790 were derived from tax lists and population multipliers. For a fuller discussion of populations, see *Law, Liberty, and License,* appendix. For Chester and Lancaster Counties, where population data is best, see Lucy Simler, "The Landless Worker: An Index of Economic and Social Change in Chester County, Pennsylvania, 1750–1820," *Pennsylvania Magazine of History and Biography* 114 (1990): 163–199; "Tenancy in Colonial Pennsylvania: The Case of Chester County," *William and Mary Quarterly* 43 (1986): 542–569; Simler and Paul G. E. Clemens, "The 'Best Poor Man's County' in 1783: The Population Structure of Rural Society in Late-Eighteenth-Century Southeastern Pennsylvania," *Proceedings of the American Philosophical Society* 133 (1989): 234–261.

26. In order to avoid the possibility that sample years deviated from the norm, we have used five-year averages of assaults for 1780 and 1790, and three year averages for 1800.

27. Spindel, *Crime and Society*, 59 n27.

28. Mifflin County's dockets are missing for 1791–1793.

29. This rise in assaults coincides with a rise in all crime, a distinct rise in violations of public order, and a less pronounced rise in theft and property crimes. See Marietta and Rowe, *Law, Liberty, and License.*

30. Beattie, *Crime and the Courts in England,* 213–235.

31. Henry D. Biddle, ed., *Extracts from the Journal of Elizabeth Drinker* (Philadelphia, PA, 1889), 267; Kenneth and Anna Roberts, eds., *Moreau de St. Mery's American Journey, 1793–1798* (Garden City, NY, 1947), 328, 333.

32. Michael M. Zuckerman, ed., *Friends and Neighbors: Group Life in America's First Plural Society* (Philadelphia, PA, 1982), 197.

33. Bucks, Fayette, Greene, Washington, Westmoreland, and, possibly, York, are counties that do not show the post-Revolution growth rates.

34. George W. Franz, *Paxton: A Study of Community Structures and Mobility in the Central Pennsylvania Backcountry* (New York, 1989).

35. Data on the male Chester populations at risk were obtained from tax lists. The laborers' numbers are more difficult to obtain than those for yeomen. See Jack D. Marietta, "The Distribution of Wealth in Eighteenth-Century Pennsylvania: Nine Chester County Tax Lists," *Pennsylvania History* 62 (1995): 533, 536.

36. The median wealth for both assailants and victims lay between the 63rd and 70th percentiles. For more data on wealth and occupations see *Law, Liberty, and License,* chap. 7.

37. *Black's Law Dictionary,* 5th ed. (St. Paul, MN, 1979), 105, 139.

38. Violence, of course, can be present without physical force. "Domestic violence" can manifest itself in psychological as well as physical terms. Court records—then or now—seldom offer full views of the magnitude or range of psychological abuse present in households.

39. *Conductor Generalis, or, the Office, Duty and Authority of Justices of the Peace, High Sheriff, Under Sheriff . . .* (Philadelphia, PA, 1749), 18–19. For enforcement of local standards in prosecuting familial violence, see Rowe, "Infanticide, Its Judicial Resolution, and Criminal Code Revision in Early Pennsylvania," *Proceedings of the American Philosophical Society* 135 (1991): 200–232, esp. 211–213.

40. Rowe and Marietta, *Law, Liberty, and License.*

41. For the role of neighbors, see Helena M. Wall, *Fierce Communion: Family and Community in Early America* (Cambridge, MA, 1990), 13–18, 53–57.

42. *Records of the Courts of Chester County* (1910), 163, 289–290; Chester County Quarterly Session Papers (hereafter CCQSP), 8/1764, Chester County Historical Society; *Bucks County Court Records* (1943), 37–38, 75.

43. Lancaster County Oyer and Terminer Court Papers, 1772, Pennsylvania Historical and Museum Commission (hereafter PHMC); *Records of the Courts of Chester County,* 130, 135. The Dicksons escaped being executed only because they had been drunk at the time of the murder.

44. Deposition of Jean Smith, 8/5/1734; Deposition of Jean Gordon, 12/1754; Examination of Ann Babb, 11/23/1792, CCQSP. Pennsylvanians initiated 73 prosecutions for slander in criminal courts and hundreds more in civil courts when they judged comments to have damaged their name, reputation, or status in the community or to have weakened their marriage or undermined their ability to function and flourish in the community.

PERSONAL VIOLENCE IN A "PEACEABLE KINGDOM"

45. *Pennsylvania Gazette*, 8/21/1755; 8/28/1755; *The Life and Confession of John Myriak (Phil., 1755); A Narrative of the Life, together with the Last Speech, Confession, and Solemn Declaration of John Lewis* (Philadelphia, 1760). Although listed in several sources, the Myriak confession has not been found.

46. Charles Biddle, *Autobiography of Charles Biddle, Vice President of the Supreme Executive Council of Pennsylvania, 1745–1821* (Philadelphia, PA, 1883), 209–210; *American Weekly Mercury* (Philadelphia), 11/12/1730, 11/5–12/1741; Philadelphia County Oyer and Terminer Court Papers, RG-33, PMHC; Negley K. Teeters, "Public Executions in Pennsylvania, 1682–1832," in Eric H. Monkkonen, ed., *Crime & Justice in American History: The Colonies and Early Republic* (Westport, CT, 1991) 2:802, 825.

47. CCQSP, 11/1772; Records of the Supreme Court: Divorce Papers (hereafter DP), 1786–1815, RG-33, PMHC; Samuel Petit, 4/1750, CCQSP. McNeil was pardoned. Some men simply abandoned their wives. See Merril D. Smith, " 'Whers Gone to She Knows Not': Desertion and Widowhood in Early Pennsylvania," in Larry D. Eldridge, ed., *Women and Freedom in Early America* (New York, 1997), 211–228.

48. From G. S. Rowe and Billy G. Smith, "Prisoners: The Prisoners for Trial Docket and the Vagrancy Docket," in Billy G. Smith, ed., *Life in Early Philadelphia: Documents from the Revolutionary and Early National Periods* (University Park, PA, 1995), 67, 71, 78, 86; Prisoners for Trial Docket, 1790–1797, 11/1/1796; Merril D. Smith, *Breaking the Bond: Marital Discord in Pennsylvania, 1730–1830* (New York, 1991) offers an overview of spousal abuse.

49. DP; Mayor's Court Dockets, 1781, City Archives, Phil; *Pennsylvania Gazette*, 8/11/1748; *Carlisle Gazette*, 9/21/1785. In 1734 a Philadelphia couple was convicted of manslaughter and sentenced to be branded in the death of their 14-year-old daughter born to the husband's previous wife. *Pennsylvania Gazette*, 10/24/1734.

50. 21 James I, c. 27 (1624) presumed that a woman's child was born alive. If she maintained that the infant was stillborn, it was her responsibility to prove it "by one witness at least." Concealment of a newborn's death, even if the death was natural, was to be punished by execution. This statute was "received" in Pennsylvania through legislation in 1718. An act of 1786 allowed for imprisonment rather than death in such cases.

51. A few exceptions contain lurid details, such as the case of Margaret Rauch of Northumberland County, who killed her child in an attempt to keep her new husband from discovering she had been impregnated by another man. For a fuller description of infanticide in the Quaker Colony, see G. S. Rowe, "Infanticide," 200–232.

52. Records of the Supreme Court (Eastern District): Coroner's Inquisitions, 1751–1796, RG-33, PHMC; *Pennsylvania Gazette*, 3/4/1735, 10/21/1736, 8/11/1737.

53. The common law did not consider abortion illegal until the fetus had "quickened"; that is before it moved perceptibly.

54. Some families had the resources, influence, and inclination to protect servants from scandal. Their success and the willingness of "matron juries" to protect neighbors and relatives confuse the number of infanticides in early Pennsylvania. Well-to-do families preferred to suffer the embarrassment of a pregnant servant (though they sought to hide that fact, too) than to endure a public trial for infanticide. By insisting that the child was born dead or that the young mother exhibited sorrow and remorse, or by conspiring to hide evidence, they short-circuited prosecutions. See the efforts of Philadelphia's Drinker family to hide the pregnancy of their servant, Sally Brant. Sharon V. Salinger, " 'Send No More Women': Female Servants in Eighteenth-Century

G. S. Rowe and Jack D. Marietta

Philadelphia," *Pennsylvania Magazine of History and Biography* 107 (1983): 40–41; Elaine Forman Crane, ed., *The Diary of Elizabeth Drinker* (Boston, 1991), 144, 148, 152.

55. Berks County Oyer and Terminer Court Papers, PHMC.

56. Rowe, "Infanticide," esp. 221–232; William Bradford, *An Enquiry How Far the Punishment of Death is Necessary in Pennsylvania* (Philadelphia, 1793), 40.

57. Resolution patterns are discussed in Rowe, "Infanticide," 207–210.

58. Vagrancy Docket, 1790–1932, 1; Daily Occurrence Dockets, 1787–1790, 1, City Archives, Philadelphia.

59. County Prison, Prisoners for Trial Docket, 1: 1790–1797; 2: 1798–1802, City Archives, Philadelphia; Vagrancy Docket, 1: 1790–1932, City Archives; Guardians of the Poor, Daily Occurrence Docket, 1: 1787–1790, 2: 1790–1792, 3: 1793–1797, City Archives.

60. Petition of Appelona Miller, 3/12/1781, Bucks County Quarter Session Criminal Papers, Bucks County Historical Society; *Records of the Courts of Chester County*, 202; *Records of the Quarter Sessions and Common Pleas of Bucks County* (1943), 362; Theodore G. Tappert and John Duberstein, eds., *The Journals of Henry Melchior Muhlenberg* (2 vols., Philadelphia 1942–1953), I: 26.

61. See Marietta and Rowe, *Law, Liberty, and License*, chaps. 7 and 9; Offutt, *"Of 'Good Laws' & 'Good Men.'"*

62. Roberts, *St. Mery's American Journal*, 290, 302–303, 311, 313.

63. Bucks County Quarter Session Dockets, 12/1768; Roberts, *St. Mery's American Journal*, 311.

64. *Pennsylvania Colonial Records* (hereafter PCR) 10:110; *Pennsylvania Gazette*, 10/18/1739; Philadelphia Mayor's Court, 1/1781, City Archives, Phil. Much violence by Pennsylvania children targeted strangers. Philadelphia officials lamented the fact that there was more juvenile violence in their city than in any other in the United States. As early as 1715, sons of privileged Philadelphians raised tumults in the city. *PCR* 2:171, 598; 5:428–430. Drunkenness, riotous behavior, and assaults involving young men increased after the Revolution. A writer in 1785 claimed that children "join in mobs, beat down the watchmen, break open doors . . . and disturb the quiet of honest people." Moreau de St. Mery was appalled by city youngsters' propensity for striking and throwing snowballs at passersby, especially African-Americans. He found Philadephia's children "Naughty," "willful," and without "affection." By the last decade of the eighteenth century, Mayor Mathew Clarkson conceded that complaints against "the disorderly practices of ungoverned boys which take place in our streets" were rife. Such activities cannot be quantified, but it is significant that Clarkson asserted that the disorder and violence of the city's youngsters "exceed[ed] those . . . known in any other city." Philadelphia had become "remarkable" for its childrens' violence and unsocial behavior. Mathew Clarkson, *An Address to the Citizens of Philadelphia, Respecting the Better Government of Youth* (Philadelphia, PA, 1795), esp. 3–6. Extended family members also exhibited violent behavior toward one another. Some 150 such cases were prosecuted, although laconic records make numbers inexact by failing to specify familial links. In Cumberland County, James Anderson killed William Barnet, his son-in-law, in 1774, while Dauphin County's John Hauser killed Francis Shitz, his brother-in-law in 1798. Teeters, "Public Executions," 802, 808.

65. One sixth (16.9 percent) of all criminal accusations leveled against African-Americans in Pennsylvania involved acts of violence against individuals. Each Negro

court included two J.P.s holding special commissions and "six of the most substantial Freeholders of the Neighborhood." For more of the background of Negro Courts and the forces that led to blacks being tried by the same courts as white offenders after 1780, see G. S. Rowe, "Black Offenders, Criminal Courts, and Philadelphia Society in Late Eighteenth-Century Philadelphia," *Journal of Social History* 22 (1989): 685–692.

66. Rowe, "Black Offenders." Six more were tried for murder and three for rape.

67. Rowe, "Black Offenders," 689.

68. Gary B. Nash and Jean Soderlund, *Freedom by Degrees: Emancipation in Pennsylvania and its Aftermath* (New York, 1991); Nash, *Forging Freedom: The Formation of Philadelphia's Black Community, 1720–1840* (Cambridge, MA, 1988); Billy G. Smith, *The 'Lower Sort': Philadelphia's Laboring People, 1750–1800* (Ithaca, NY, 1990). Slaves perceived cruelty and neglect directed toward them with more resentment than did authorities. The plethora of advertisements for runaway slaves testifies to African-Americans' response to abuse. See Billy G. Smith and Richard Wojtowicz, *Blacks Who Stole Themselves: Advertisements for Runaways in the Pennsylvania Gazette, 1728–1790* (Philadelphia, PA, 1989).

69. Peter Kalm, *Travels into North America* (New York, 1937, reprint edition, 1987), 206–207.

70. *American Weekly Mercury* (Philadelphia), 11/5–12/1741.

71. Lancaster County Oyer and Terminer Court Papers, 1767; Berks County Oyer and Terminer Papers, 1772, 1775, PMHC.

72. Bradford, *An Enquiry*, 29–30, 63; Philadelphia Oyer and Terminer Dockets, 2/1788, PMHC; *Independent Gazetteer*, 2/19/1788.

73. *PCR* 2:513; Lancaster County Oyer and Terminer Court Papers, 4030, PMHC.

74. Dominick Fishbaugh of Cumberland County was also charged with physically mistreating his servant, William Cohan, in 1788. Cumberland County Quarter Session Dockets, 10/1788. Also Lancaster County Quarter Session Dockets, 11/1757; 9/1758; Billy G. Smith, "The Institutional Poor: The Almshouse Daily Occurrence Docket," in Smith, ed., *Life in Early Philadelphia*, 45; Chester County Quarter Session Dockets, 12/1727 and CCQSP, 12/1727, CCHS.

75. Deposition of Ester Burt, CCQSP, 2/1724, CCHS.

76. *PCR* 5:488; *Pennsylvania Journal*, 11/15/1750. After 1760, servants were assessed as property.

77. Smith, *Life in Early Philadelphia*, 66–67, 77, 79, 83.

78. Bucks County Criminal Papers, 1758, Bucks County Historical Society; Muhlenberg, *Journals* 1:265; Jasper Yeates, "Republica v. Michael Hevice, Frederick, Gelvix, and His Wife," in *Yeates Legal Papers* 2, folio 7, 4/1783–5/1783, 114–116; folio 2, 3/1789–4/1789; folio 4, 5/1786–6/1786, HSP; *Carlisle Gazette*, 11/9/1788.

79. Johan David Schoepf, *Travels in the Confederation, 1783–1784* (New York, 1968) 1:238–239; Alexander Graydon, *Memoirs of his Own Time, with Reminiscences of the Men and Events of the Revolution* (Philadelphia, PA, 1846), 404; Muhlenberg, *Journals* 2:759. Charles Brockden Brown's use of this theme is discussed in Robert A. Ferguson, *Law and Letters in American Culture* (Cambridge, MA, 1984), 135.

three

GOVERNING THE PASSIONS

The Eighteenth-Century Quest for Domestic Harmony in Philadelphia's Middle-Class Households

Jacquelyn C. Miller

O n a July day in 1793, Philadelphia resident Joseph Willis reached the end of his rope. Plagued with an acrimonious marriage, his anger and frustration got the best of him. On that fateful morning, he picked up a sharp instrument and attacked his wife Elizabeth so ferociously that, according to one chronicler of the event, her life was thought to be in danger. Elizabeth fortunately survived her husband's assault and very soon after filed for divorce. Many details of this incident remain unknown, particularly the underlying reasons for the couple's marital friction. One of Willis's acquaintances, however, tried to explain the short-term cause of Joseph's bloody attack. Quaker merchant Benjamin Smith blamed the violent outburst on Elizabeth's bad temper and abusive nature. Clearly taking Joseph's side, Smith specifically argued that it was Elizabeth's lack of self-restraint that pushed Joseph over the edge, causing him to assail his wife "either in a fit of desperation, or through the sudden burst of malice that he had been long trying to suppress or conceal."[1] Smith implied that had Elizabeth been able to control her anger and her tongue, harmony would have prevailed in the Willis household. As we shall see, attempts by late eighteenth-century middle-class Philadelphians to cultivate emotional self-control and achieve peace within the household were an important reflection of greater social trends in antebellum America.

Middle-class Philadelphians of the Revolutionary era were tiring of political dissension and social strife and yearned for domestic harmony. Much evidence indicates a growing intolerance of conflict and violence both in private and public realms of Philadelphia society during the last half of the eighteenth century.[2] These sensibilities, and particularly the focused effort to moderate passion in order to maintain physical and mental health, were parameters in an emerging middle-class identity.[3] As part of these efforts to eliminate disorder from daily life, middle-class Philadelphians reassessed physical violence between married couples. By the mid-1750s, they viewed marriage as a partnership that stressed mutual affection, companionship, a single standard of sexual behavior, and complementary gender roles. This trend was strengthened by the republican rhetoric of the post-Revolutionary period. As a consequence of this growing assumption that marriages should be loving, "most people were beginning to believe that any physical attack made by a husband on his wife was unacceptable." This view was codified into law when Pennsylvania passed its divorce law of 1785 and became the first state to consider cruelty a ground for legal separation.[4] These trends had important implications for women, as the case of Elizabeth Willis illustrates. In addition to providing legal protection, the new law altered social expectations regarding proper female conduct. Middle-class Philadelphians consequently expected both women and men to present themselves as rational and nonviolent.

These reform efforts certainly fell short of full success in suppressing the violent tendencies of all Pennsylvanians, even those in Philadelphia's middle class. Despite the persistence of violent actions, by the late eighteenth century, middle-class Philadelphians considered physical outbursts like Joseph Willis's to be unacceptable anomalies. The diaries and letters of many Philadelphians reveal people preoccupied with ensuring that emotional and physical expressions of violence be checked. This essay will explore the mechanisms by which individuals hoped to maintain emotional control, and thus to promote domestic harmony and prevent violence in early American homes.[5]

By the late eighteenth century, middle-class Philadelphians of both genders made great efforts to be rational and unemotional in order to maintain physical health and domestic tranquillity. Their actions in this regard were rooted in their belief that middle-class women and children were capable of rationality and in their conviction that emotional restraint was one of the major conditions of physical and mental well-being. Members of the middle class, however, did not always disapprove of the demonstration of intense feelings. On the contrary, they sometimes admired fervent expressions of love and affection in the domestic context because these emotions promoted familial harmony. They believed that balance was the key and that danger lay in a lack of emotional restraint.[6]

Middle-class Philadelphians rarely assumed that servants or other members of the lower class possessed rationality. During this period, middle-class men did not regard middle-class women as the emotional "other"; rather, both gen-

Jacquelyn C. Miller

ders regarded members of the lower class as emotional "others" with regard to violent emotions and a general lack of self-restraint. Middle-class Philadelphians' writings indicate that they constructed their identities, in part, by defining themselves against lower-class people.[7]

Middle-class individuals who sought to separate their way of life from Philadelphia's violent lower-class culture often justified their cause with references to contemporary medical literature that associated a lack of restraint with disease, madness, and death. During Philadelphia's yellow fever epidemic of 1793, for instance, many residents attributed high mortality rates among the poor to their unrestrained passions—an unruliness that manifested itself in sexual licentiousness, uncleanliness, intemperance, and a lack of emotional self-control. Divergences based on class rather than gender or age were the most important markers of identity in the writings of this self-selected group of Philadelphians. The expectation of female rationality, in contrast, created a space from which middle-class women and men could work together to create a loving and harmonious domestic sphere.

Many Philadelphians desired rationality in their households above all else, and placed great significance on middle-class women as rational beings. Women were often referred to as reasonable, rational, or sensible. The word "sensibility," in particular, signified the psychoperceptual scheme systematized by Isaac Newton and John Locke that came to be known as environmental psychology. This scientific assumption emphasized nurture over nature with regard to human development, and admitted the possibility that women's mental formation might equal that of men.[8] Margaret Morris's story about her response to her son John's death demonstrates just how highly one woman prized the virtue of female rationality. The death of a child, of course, tested anyone's emotional stamina. Margaret Morris's case was no different. When John, a respected Philadelphia physician and Morris's oldest child, died in late September 1793, Morris was at his bedside and remained "sitting by him awhile" after he breathed his last. Morris did not relate her feelings, but she was obviously in control of her emotions; she was soon able to prepare her son's body for the grave, a duty she presumed was hers to perform. Neither was she content to allow others to shoulder the task of overseeing John's burial, but insisted instead on seeing her child laid beside his father, William, who had died in 1766. It meant a great deal to Morris, a Quaker, to be present when her son was buried in the Friends' cemetery next to the man she constantly referred to as "the dear companion of my youth."[9]

Morris soon came to regret taking on so much and thus allowing herself to become exhausted in her grief. "Alas I got off my guard," she revealed later. "I thought that *I* who *had* been thus supported, was equal to every thing." Morris discovered her emotional limits when, during the excursion to the cemetery, she collapsed in delirium. Family members carried her home, where she slept

47

for two days. Morris later castigated herself for being so vain and foolish as to place herself under such intense emotional stress, and she attempted to make the episode a useful lesson. Reminding her surviving children that "resignation is the road to peace," she also instructed them to "let my suffering be a means of preservation to you my tenderly beloved children." In a letter to her sister and brother-in-law, Milcah and Charles Moore, Morris further rebuked her wayward behavior. "Oh that I may be a warning to others," she exclaimed. "For I do believe if I had kept my place, I should have been enabled to do for my dear AM [Abigail Morris, John's wife] all that my good sister W[ells] and her sweet girls did for her."[10] Morris obviously valued female rationality and made no distinctions with regard to emotional standards of behavior on the basis of gender or age. She considered her experience a worthy lesson for male, female, young, and old alike.

The practice of continuously monitoring one's passions and actions, a behavioral ideal that Philadelphia's middle class came to see as virtually a medical imperative, was also advocated as a path to domestic peace. Children in particular were constantly reminded of the necessity of watching their thoughts and behavior. Parents advocated continual self-reflection in the hope that their offspring would develop "internal control constraints." Thus they anticipated that emotional self-control would become second nature to children and would ensure a calm domestic environment. Wishing to instill values and behavior in his son that would assure domestic harmony, J. G. Stedman in 1787 encouraged his son to "fear God," "guard against indolence," "love economy without avarice," "fly from intemperance and debauchery," "beware of passion and cruelty," and love his mother and siblings.[11] Stedman clearly wanted to foster rational, cheerful, and loving children who would make a home pleasant.

Quaker merchant Henry Drinker also had this goal in mind. His wealth and pacifism made him the subject of suspicion by radical patriots during the Revolution; as a result, he was banished to Virginia along with several other members of the Society of Friends. Exile, however, did not deter Drinker from his parental responsibilities. In his letters home, Drinker admonished his children, Sally, Nancy, Billy, and Henry, to cherish "a steady sober and thoughtful frame of mind." Sally, who at sixteen was the eldest, was instructed individually "to watch over thy words and actions every hour in the day, that they be exemplary and tend to promote a kind and loving disposition in thy brothers and sisters towards each other, and especially to incite them to love and respect their affectionate mother and aunt." Thirteen-year-old Nancy was also singled out for advice. Drinker suggested she take "a watchful care and guard over her own temper and natural disposition, so that nothing might escape her that might irritate or promote anger or resentment in her brothers and sisters." He also advised that she be "particularly careful in all her ways, looks and actions, to show herself a dutiful and affectionate child to her dear mother and aunt."

Jacquelyn C. Miller

Implicit in Drinker's letters was the message that if his children failed to adhere to his advice, they might end up like the "lawless and violent men" who ripped him from his loving family and held him captive.[12]

Drinker's admonitions to his children were very much in the tradition of earlier Quaker parents from rural areas of Pennsylvania, who inculcated sentiments of "love and tenderness" while advocating "vigilance and total self-control" to produce loving, moral, industrious, and rational offspring. George Fox, founder of the Society of Friends, advocated the use of noncorporal punishment in disciplining both children and servants to accomplish these goals. Fox also emphasized the need for self-disciplined, rational women in every Quaker household. It is not surprising, then, that Drinker's correspondence with his wife and children resembles a letter that Pennsylvania's Quaker founder, William Penn, wrote to his family in 1682. With domestic harmony in mind, Penn admonished them to "watch against anger; neither speak nor act in it, for like drunkenness, it makes a man a beast."[13] In many ways, these Quaker families were the living ideal upon which nineteenth-century society based its idea of domesticity. By the time of the Revolution, however, both Quakers and non-Quakers in Philadelphia promoted a child-centered family that emphasized self-restraint in a world that seemed filled with violence and disorder.

Advocates of self-control received support from the medical community during the latter half of the eighteenth century, particularly through the powerful influence of physician-authored advice manuals. These popularizers of scientific medicine warned their readers of the connection between physiological disorders and an inability to control their emotions. According to these experts, failing to moderate one's emotions, primarily anger, fear, grief, pride, greed, and even love and joy, could result in physical illness, temporary madness, or possibly death. Physician George Cheyne, for example, informed his readers that in order to maintain a healthy constitution they should "avoid excesses of the passions as they would excesses in high food or spirituous liquors." If passions were not checked, Cheyne asserted, they could "relax, unbend, and dissolve the nervous fibers" or "screw up, stretch, and bend them," depending on whether the passion was "slow and continued" or "sudden and violent." Sudden and violent passions in particular disposed human beings "toward inflammations, fevers, or mortifications." In fact, Cheyne argued, hatred and anger were "but degrees of a frenzy, and a frenzy is one kind of a raging fever." He stressed that "violent and sudden passions are more dangerous to health than the slow and continued, as acute diseases are more destructive than chronical."[14] The quest for rationality, therefore, was often a matter of life and death.

Other writers agreed with Cheyne. According to William Buchan, a widely read eighteenth-century medical writer, "the passion of *anger* ruffles the mind, distorts the countenance, hurries on the circulation of the blood, and disorders the whole vital and animal functions." "The influence of fear," moreover, "in

GOVERNING THE PASSIONS

occasioning [or] aggravating diseases, is very great." In 1775, John Hill reiterated this view, and claimed "the whole frame is disordered by violent passions," and that madness or immediate death was the inevitable consequence "of giving full scope" to one's passions. Controlling one's emotions was of the utmost importance, especially since "nothing in this world" was "worth the trouble and distress men bring upon themselves by giving way to immoderate passions."[15] Clearly these men believed that controlling one's emotions facilitated an orderly and tranquil existence that undoubtedly had important ramifications for the domestic sphere.

Philadelphians' response to the threat of yellow fever in the 1790s demonstrates this connection between emotional control and family harmony. Beginning in August 1793, the same year that Joseph Willis attacked his wife, Philadelphia experienced a major yellow fever epidemic that forced the human body into public consciousness. Diaries, letters, and other records produced during this epidemic reveal a great deal about the emotional and domestic lives of the city's inhabitants. In particular, these documents disclose people's attempts to embrace emotional conventions; they obviously expected severe repercussions for failing to achieve self-control. Many physicians implied that the epidemic rendered the ability to control one's passions a life or death issue. The threat of disease on a grand scale served as a catalyst for Philadelphians to develop skills of self-mastery. Although they themselves did not explicitly connect emotional self-control and the avoidance of disease to their society's growing desire to prevent domestic conflict, the two arenas were linked. At the heart of both concerns was a preoccupation with disorder, whether physical, emotional, or social. Consequently, as Philadelphians struggled to retain their health through a regimen of self-restraint, they also developed behavioral habits with ramifications for domestic relations. An individual who remained consistently calm and sweet was not likely to strike out, either verbally or physically, at other family members. Keeping a check on one's fear, grief, or anger not only ensured one's physical health but also facilitated domestic harmony.[16]

Suppressing negative emotions (especially to maintain one's health) was, of course, only one aspect of this process. Philadelphians did not expect their fellow residents to become unfeeling automatons—domestic harmony demanded more than that. Individuals often praised others for demonstrating feelings of deep love and affection for their families and friends and often regarded tears of grief highly, even when shed by men. Consequently, a key theme Philadelphians articulated with regard to the emotions was that of balance.[17] Navigating between extremes of control and release, individuals attempted to steer a delicate course between repression and expression.

Many Philadelphians viewed popular medical literature as the ultimate authority on emotions. The prevalence of these ideas points to the successful efforts of the medical community to secularize and medicalize passion for many

Jacquelyn C. Miller

eighteenth-century individuals. During the seventeenth century, anger was "one of the evils that Satan could visit on humankind" and wrath "one of the seven deadly sins." Disease, too, was viewed by many people throughout the early modern period as the product of sin and was considered as much a religious as a medical concern, especially in the case of madness. Because of a shortage of university-trained physicians in the colonies during the seventeenth century, medicine usually came under the purview of a variety of laypersons, including clergymen, barbers, herbalists, civil officials, plantation owners, midwives, and folk healers. During the eighteenth century, however, particularly in urban areas, physicians, including Philadelphia's Benjamin Rush, increasingly provided their patients with alternative explanations of physical and mental illness. These explanations were based on scientific and somatic, not theological or spiritual, presuppositions, and offered a new rationale for middle-class reformers' crusade to establish acceptable boundaries for emotional self-expression.[18]

There were, of course, many instances where people fell short of the ideal of calm resignation, castigated themselves for losing control, and determined to keep a check on their emotions in the future. On the morning of September 8, 1793, for instance, physician Benjamin Rush was called to the bedside of a colleague who was suffering from yellow fever, but arrived too late. When he entered the sick room minutes after the patient had expired, the dead man's mother, Rush related, dashed from her son's bed "into my arms, fell upon my neck, and in this position gave vent to the most pathetic and eloquent exclamations of grief that I have ever heard." Disconcerted by her behavior, Rush found himself "sinking into sympathy," but quickly tore himself "from her arms, and ran to other scenes of distress." In relating this story to his wife Julia Rush reported that "through infinite goodness I am preserved not only in health, but in uncommon tranquility of mind, never elevated, and never but twice depressed." He believed, instead, that "the fear of death from the disease has been taken from me, and I possess perfect composure in the room of patients." Rush later explained to the readers of his account of the epidemic that "sympathy when it vents itself in acts of humanity, affords pleasure, and contributes to health, but the reflux of pity, like anger, gives pain, and disorders the body."[19] To remain calm in distressing situations by controlling one's emotions was, in Rush's view, conducive to good health as well as a feat worthy of pride. Throughout the epidemic, individuals continually warned each other of the correlation between emotional excitement and the prospect of infection, a connection that had profound implications for domestic harmony.

One of the emotions people talked about most frequently during the epidemic was fear. Friends and relatives counseled one another about the disastrous consequences that would result if this emotion was not contained. Esther Duché, for instance, advised her aunt to overcome her fears as "they are very prejudicial to health of Body and Mind." Margaret Morris cautioned her servant Peggy "against spreading alarms amongst my children" as "the very apprehension of danger will sometimes occasion" infection. Although many writers did not mention fear specifically, their general warnings clearly encompassed that emotion. For instance, several weeks into the epidemic, Quaker merchant Samuel Fisher reminded his brother, Miers, to keep his "mind firm and unshaken" and "free from all encumbrances—as much as you can, for therein may be your safety."[20]

Others emphasized the relationship between emotional self-control and illness by relating stories about people who died as a result of unbridled fear. In his autobiographical account of the epidemic, Charles Biddle discussed the case of his friend Captain Sharp. Sharp was a veteran of the Revolution and a man "of undoubted courage," who nevertheless was "much terrified at this disorder." As Biddle told the story, when Sharp's wife complained one night of being ill with the fever, the Captain "immediately jumped out of bed; and shut himself up in another room." Although his wife soon recovered, Sharp was so frightened that, according to Biddle, he caught the fever and died. Margaret Morris relayed a similar message when she informed her daughter that the "panic struck" Benedict Dorsey had died of the fever. In another instance, Samuel Massey told his daughter Ann about William Temple, a "very industrious man" who usually made his living by taking people on "pleasurable excursions" in his wagon. During the early days of the epidemic, however, he transported fleeing Philadelphians to the countryside. Temple was found dead in his wagon following one such trip to New Jersey. Massey believed his death resulted from "an apoplectic fit" following a spell of "fatigue and anxiety."[21]

Jacob Ritter recounted a similar tale concerning his uncle during the yellow fever epidemic of 1798. Uncle Ritter's "turn of mind and deportment" differed greatly from those of his brother, Jacob's father. As a result, he was very frightened of the epidemic. His fear was so great that, despite his desire to visit his nephew who was suffering from the fever, he refused to go near the invalid. Instead, he communicated with the boy by standing at the foot of the stairs and yelling up such questions as: "Jacob how are you?" The implicit moral of Jacob's story was that despite all the precautions his uncle took to escape the disorder, his fear weakened his body until he contracted the disease toward the end of the epidemic and died.[22]

Philadelphians also discussed how freedom from fear could preserve one's health. Timothy Pickering wrote to a friend in Boston that "happily my wife and her sister have no fear of the disease; and that fortitude will contribute to preserve them." Others professed similar feelings. John Welsh wrote to his employer that he was certain not to succumb to the disorder since he was not "susceptible of fear." For those easily frightened, however, Welsh believed that the shock of the "almost certain estrangement of relations and friends" was

Jacquelyn C. Miller

"enough to plunge an unfortified mind into a complicated scene of agitation, doubt, and horror" that could eventually lead to death.[23] Philadelphians hoped that a rational demeanor would ensure the continued health and happiness of both individuals and families.

Such fortitude also allowed individuals a praiseworthy selflessness born of firm faith and reason. Because she believed her fate and that of her family was in God's hands, a disposition that innumerable Philadelphians felt to be the ideal state of mind, Margaret Morris was not "afraid to go where duty calls me." Charles Biddle also expressed great admiration for the courage of those "who behaved with great firmness and benevolence." In particular, Biddle praised Peter Helm who, along with Steven Girard, agreed to manage the newly established epidemic hospital at great risk to his own safety. Helm deserved special recognition because, unlike Girard, he was of the opinion that the fever was contagious and therefore had to overcome greater fears of personal danger. Biddle also respected his clerk I. A. Lewis, a former Hessian soldier who, despite being "terrified at staying in town," a fear exacerbated by having "seen twelve corpses going to be buried," had the sense to hire a carriage and to seek the refuge of the countryside. Comparing Lewis's presence of mind to that of a soldier in war, Biddle declared that "no man . . . in battle would behave with more courage than Lewis." According to Biddle's diary account, many others acted with bravery even though they were as much or more terrified than Helm, Girard, or Lewis and were "generally thought to be so timid that they would have fled as soon as there was any danger." Instead, many of them remained in town and distinguished themselves by their courage and goodwill. Biddle, however, deemed Lewis and others courageous not on the basis of whether they left the city or remained behind, but according to whether they controlled their fear and took rational, positive action. "Fear," in the words of Esther Duché, "was the image of death," while "love and confidence were the images of life."[24]

Death was, of course, common during the epidemic, and many survivors discussed another emotion—grief—in detail. Physician William Buchan ranked grief as the most destructive of the passions. "Its effects are permanent," he wrote, "and when it sinks deep into the mind, it generally proves fatal." He added further that "anger and fear being of a more violent nature, seldom last long; but grief often changes into a fixed melancholy, which preys upon the spirits, and wastes the constitution." Because grief weakened the body's resistance to disease, Philadelphians wrote frequently about their efforts to resign themselves to the loss of loved ones. After learning, for example, that there was little hope for their son Jabez's recovery, Miers and Sally Fisher wept together only briefly before controlling their grief. Losing control of one's emotions could lead to terror, panic, and fits—all behaviors that could lead to agitation and a disordered household. Maintaining one's emotional equilibrium was cru-

GOVERNING THE PASSIONS

cial in reaching the state of "tranquility which is founded in resignation" that many Philadelphians wanted to experience in the domestic realm.[25]

Most Philadelphians grieved during the 1793 scourge; between three and five thousand people died out of a population of fifty thousand. Nearly every resident, therefore, lost at least one family member, friend, business associate, or acquaintance to the fever. Many Philadelphians, however, were dismayed by effusive expressions of grief. William Smith, for example, was highly concerned by his wife's behavior after two of her closest friends died. Although Smith did not make an explicit connection between his wife's unstoppable "sympathetic foreboding tears" and her own death from the disease, the two events were discursively linked in the narrative he sent his close friend Benjamin Rush.[26] Expressions of excessive grief like that of Mrs. Smith could not only occasion one's death, but threatened the social fabric of the domestic sphere.

But feelings themselves were not considered wrong or dangerous. Margaret Morris's emotional journey during 1793 illustrates this belief. The widowed mother of four grown children, Morris remained in the city during the epidemic. She continued caring for her sister Hannah, who had been bedridden for years with palsy. A devout Quaker, Morris explained her decision to her daughter Gulielma not to "retreat from the spot where Providence has placed me." Her fate at God's hands would find her. "[W]e cannot fly from the rod if commissioned to strike *us* among the rest" and "the hand that directs it can preserve us amidst the thousands slain." Despite Morris's hope for God's protection and her use of a variety of safeguards against infection, including burning tar and tobacco several times a day, disaster struck her family. Her son John died first. He was soon followed by his wife, Abigail, and his sister Debby's husband, Benjamin Smith.[27] These deaths illustrated the fragile nature of human existence and the necessity of keeping a constant vigil over one's emotional impulses.

Margaret Morris's children were concerned about their mother's reaction to John's death. Her eldest remaining son Richard noted that although he knew his mother's "soul is fortified with patience to endure calamity," he dreaded the outcome of that "deep sensibility for which she is so distinguished" and feared the implications of "the grief with which her gentle bosom must be torn." Having been apprised that his mother was unwell, Richard noted "it would have been more astonishing to me to have heard that she was not ill." Indeed, Richard empathized with his mother; he too was "torn with the most exquisite pain when I reflect upon the mournful situation." He was less concerned with his mother's immediate illness than he was with the long-term effects his brother's death would have "upon her spirits." Richard therefore relayed a message of fidelity to his mother via his brother-in-law. "The added claims upon my care and affection, speak to my heart, in a language too powerful for utterance," Richard wrote, "though I wish once

Jacquelyn C. Miller

more to press upon her lips the proof of my love, yet from the prevalence of this cruel disorder I shall conclude to wait."[28]

Richard Morris's letter, like many others of the period, illustrates that demonstrating intense feelings was not necessarily interpreted as negative. Indeed, it was believed that such proclamations of love and affection created an environment where domestic harmony could flourish; the danger lay in unbridled emotions. Eighteenth-century Philadelphians thought that parents and children should feel and profess their love and affection for one another with effusive language. Once a loved one departed, however, individuals were expected to resign themselves quickly to their loss, keep their grieving minimal, and direct positive emotional energies toward family members who remained. To do otherwise would leave the domestic realm open to disruption and commotion.

Similar capacities for emotional control were observed and assumed in both men and women of the middle class. When Margaret Morris recounted her son's final moments by saying that "sweet composure took possession of his features and he departed without [a] sigh, groan, or struggle," her description resembled those of numerous men and women on their deathbeds. Morris's brother-in-law Richard Wells portrayed Abigail Morris as "calm, sensible and affectionate" when she neared the end of her life. In memorializing the death of his wife Annabella, Caleb Cresson stated that "during her indisposition she was preserved in much calmness and sweet composure of mind." Caleb's sister-in-law Mary Cresson similarly detailed the fevered suffering of her husband, Joshua. Throughout his illness, she noted that upon being asked how he felt, he replied "calm and composed" or "calm and easy."[29] Women like Margaret Morris emphasized the necessity of being sensible and retaining their composure even at the point of death. Rational repression might occasionally lead to violent outbreaks, particularly in men, but nonetheless, reason was a core element of a transgendered middle-class identity.

The boundary between personal attributes archetypically viewed as masculine and adult (rationality) and those considered feminine and childlike (emotionality) did not yet exist for middle-class people in late eighteenth-century Philadelphia. While many men tried to restrain negative passions, they were willing to express socially sanctioned—and obviously genuine—sentiments toward people they loved. Thomas Clifford's father, for example, died during the epidemic (though of gout, not yellow fever). "Few can say they have had so kind, so indulgent, so fond a parent," Clifford wrote his brother in late December. Clifford clearly associated child-rearing and the feminine side of one's nature. He reminded his brother that their father had "watched with maternal care our infant years and carefully instructed us in the best of things setting us a bright example of every Christian virtue."[30] For Clifford, as for many of his contemporaries, virtue was becoming feminized and domesticated.

55

By the same token, middle-class masculinity was becoming more emotional; shedding tears at the death of a loved one did not compromise it. Weeping, in fact, could enhance his image as a sensitive and caring husband and father, and garner the approval of his peers. When Daniel Smith first met with his daughter-in-law, Debby, after the death of his son, Benjamin, he clasped her in his arms and wept on her shoulder. Then, drawing his grandchildren to his breast one at a time, he continued to weep, unable to find the words to express his grief or his love. Smith's behavior was considered appropriate, and Margaret Morris described the meeting as "the most affecting scene I can remember to have been present at." John Welsh agreed in his description of a Doctor Sprout, who buried his youngest daughter in late September. "It was truly an affecting sight," Welsh felt, "to see the old man enfeebled, and tottering after the hearse, deeply affected." Middle-class Philadelphians accepted and valued men's emotional outpourings, even though they also recognized a need to control and circumscribe emotional expression for both genders. In his 1787 deathbed letter, J. G. Stedman reminded his son to "let not your grief for my decease overcome you. Let your tears flow with *moderation*, and trust that I am happy." Focusing on the inner life of the middle class reveals that these households did not dichotomize, but synthesized certain traits that came to be seen as masculine and feminine. This process, though it did not eradicate gender tensions, helped create a style of emotional behavior for the middle-class domestic environment that was shared and esteemed by both women and men.[31]

This capacity for rationality was extended to middle-class children, but it only rarely applied to household servants or to others of lower status. In fact, middle-class Philadelphians focused on class distinctions, not on gender or age divergences within the middle class, as a revealing marker in their efforts to understand the implications of unrestrained passions. While rationality was attributed to middle-class individuals of both sexes and of different ages, servants and other members of the lower class were often characterized as "insensible" and as having "weak minds," which could endanger their health. Margaret Morris, for example, in several letters to her sister Milcah, complained of her maid Sally's silliness in "leaving off a jacket in the heat of the day," which resulted in the girl getting sick. On another occasion, Morris referred to the "weak mind" of her son Richard's apprentice, whose fear, she believed, would prove fatal during the fever. Although yellow fever struck individuals from every social stratum, most of the people who died during the epidemic were poor.[32] This fact lent credence to the social assumptions of those middle-class people who found moral rectitude wanting in those persons viewed as less rational.

In their attempts to explain why some people were more prone to fever than others, many middle-class Philadelphians adopted a moralizing tone toward working-class people by focusing on factors such as intemperance and uncleanliness. For instance, according to physician David Nassy, persons "who have observed a good regimen, and have been regular in their eating, and sober in their drinking" survived the epidemic intact. Nassy thought mechanics who, despite their strength, had not observed any regimen but had consumed "meat, salt provisions, and green fruits" as well as "strong drink, an ill fermented beer, and cyder made of green fruit" were most susceptible to the fever. Like Nassy, Lutheran minister Henry Helmuth contended that people who "had given themselves to drunkenness, or in other respects to a loose and abandoned way of living . . . were most commonly the sure victims of death." Another Philadelphian, Mathew Carey, concluded that the disorder was always fatal "to tipplers and drunkards" as well as to the *filles de joie* whose "wretched and debilitated state of their constitutions . . . very soon terminated their miserable career." And Carey, like many others, thought the disease found fertile ground among "the inhabitants of dirty houses" who had neglected "cleanliness and decency." He spoke for people like Benjamin Rush who felt that uncleanliness had long been proven to be "unfriendly to morals."[33] Immoral or disorderly living, then, was perceived by such moralists as the predominating factor that predisposed one to disease.

These texts make it quite apparent that middle-class efforts to restrain the passions associated sexual activity, drunkenness, and dirtiness with the working class. Members of the lower class embodied the negative qualities that middle-class individuals were trying to banish from their own lives. The fear and disdain that middle-class men and women felt toward their own bodies were directed toward people whose bodies could not be ignored because of their presence in middle-class homes as servants. During the latter part of the eighteenth century, the lower class became the "other" against whom middle-class individuals defined themselves, as well as the targets for Philadelphia's social reformers. In hospitals, prisons, asylums, and schools, reformers attempted to inculcate their lower-class brethren with middle-class values and sensibilities, including emotional self-control, personal hygiene, and hard work.[34] These crusaders anticipated that their endeavors would result in greater peace and tranquility in both the public and the private realms of eighteenth-century life.

The self-appointed middle-class reformers, as the following example suggests, also demanded that strangers conform to this emerging standard of behavior or risk social ostracism. Stopping one evening in October 1794 at an inn near Newark, New Jersey, Mary and John Morton took tea and retired early. They soon encountered a swarm of bedbugs that let them sleep only fitfully. At about midnight, the Mortons were startled into consciousness by the "most dreadful screams and blows" and by a "female voice imploring mercy." After inquiring about the disturbance, they discovered that the cries were those of a young servant girl who had received, in Mary's words, "a merciless and, as we

GOVERNING THE PASSIONS

afterwards understood, a most unmerited punishment" from her master. Mary found the incident greatly distressing. In her own words, she "felt such indignation against the *cruel monster*" and was "so offended with the insult offered us, that if we had had no bugs, I was too much discomposed to have slept." In her view, "the house," beset by unhealthy insects and equally unhealthy emotions, "gave the completest image of the infernal regions" she had ever known. Incensed by the innkeeper's behavior, Mary protested his conduct by refusing to eat her breakfast the following morning, remarking that she would "rather ride twenty miles than eat a morsel there." Continuing their journey between New York and Philadelphia, the couple spent the next night at an inn in Kingston, New Jersey, where, in contrast to their earlier experience, they found a clean bed and "very civil treatment."[35] The depth of feeling with which Mary Morton reacted to the beating overheard in Newark indicates that she considered such violence unacceptable in a civilized society. In her response she revealed a middle-class outlook, demonstrating how she valued the inner skills necessary to hold her passions in check.

Eighteenth-century middle-class Philadelphians saw emotional self-restraint as a means by which to achieve domestic harmony. Learning to govern one's passions lay at the heart of bourgeois domestic life, and it was a habit that middle-class adults attempted to inculcate in their children early on. The desire for personal and domestic tranquility was, however, an ideal toward which many middle-class individuals continued to strive.[36] As the unfortunate episode of Joseph and Elizabeth Willis suggests, maintaining the proper balance between expression and repression was often difficult to achieve; it provided a continuing challenge—even a life-and-death imperative—for those ambitious Philadelphians intent on forging an effective emotional style through gender solidarity and class distinctions.

Notes

1. Benjamin Smith to John Smith, 7/11/1793, Edward Wanton Smith Collection, Quaker Collection, Haverford College (hereafter QCHC). Also Merril D. Smith, *Breaking the Bonds: Marital Discord in Pennsylvania, 1730–1830* (New York, 1991), 2, 5, 116, 129. The Willises experienced a long strained marriage with many problems, including verbal abuse and alcoholism. Benjamin Smith characterized Elizabeth as a "bad tempered railing abusive wife," and Joseph as "a good tempered man" who had not been observed "in liquor of late." Joseph broke up his household by putting "his children out among his friends" and by moving his wife from their home to "a few rooms which he took with a view to cheapness."

Jacquelyn C. Miller

2. Jacquelyn C. Miller, "An 'Uncommon Tranquility of Mind': Emotional Self-Control and the Construction of a Middle-Class Identity in Eighteenth-Century Philadelphia," *Journal of Social History* 30 (1996): 130–149; Jacquelyn C. Miller, "The Body Politic: Passions, Pestilence, and Political Culture in the Age of the American Revolution" (Ph.D. diss., Rutgers University, 1995); C. Dallett Hemphill, "Middle Class Rising in Revolutionary America: The Evidence from Manners," *Journal of Social History* 30 (1996): 317–344.

3. This definition provides a corrective to Stuart Blumin's overly materialist interpretation of the middle class, which he defines along sometimes arbitrary occupational lines. Defining class with modern models, Blumin concluded that a middle-class "way of life" resulted from antebellum urbanization and industrialization. See Stuart M. Blumin, "The Hypothesis of Middle Class Formation in Nineteenth-Century America: A Critique and Some Proposals," *American Historical Review* 90 (1985): 299–338; and Blumin, *The Emergence of the Middle Class: Social Experience in the Antebellum City, 1760–1900* (Cambridge, MA, 1989). My approach has been, instead, to document the ways in which eighteenth-century Philadelphians constructed a middle-class identity. I emphasize the construction of culture from within—on the values that guided people's lives and on the ways in which people defined themselves against those above and below them on the social scale.

4. Smith, *Breaking the Bonds*, 2, 5, 14, 105.

5. Institutions such as jails, asylums, and hospitals restrained both male and female perpetrators of domestic abuse. Thomas Morton and Thomas Woodbury, *The History of the Pennsylvania Hospital: 1751–1895* (New York, 1973), 134–135, 139, 140. Jeffrey Richards has argued that middle-class violence among Philadelphians primarily consisted of psychological and emotional abuse in "Decorous Violence: Manners, Class, and Abuse in Rebecca Rush's *Kelroy*," in this volume.

6. Miller, "The Body Politic," chap. 2. This finding complicates the literature that emphasizes the dichotomy of male rationality and female emotionality among middle-class people. Ruth H. Bloch, "The Gendered Meanings of Virtue in Revolutionary America," *Signs* 13 (1987): 48–53; Lori D. Ginzberg, " 'The Hearts of Your Readers Will Shudder': Fanny Wright, Infidelity, and American Freethought," *American Quarterly* 46 (1994): 195–226; Carroll Smith-Rosenberg, "The Female World of Love and Ritual: Relations Between Women in Nineteenth-Century America," *Signs* 1 (1975): 1–29; Mary Ryan, *Cradle of the Middle Class: The Family in Oneida County, New York, 1790–1865* (Cambridge, 1981), particularly chap. 5. For a sampling of eighteenth-century medical manuals, see William Buchan, *Domestic Medicine, or the Family Physician* (Edinburgh, 1769; reprint, Philadelphia, 1772), 66–71; George Cheyne, *Essay on Health and Long Life* (London, 1724), 158–159; George Cheyne, *The Natural Method of Cureing the Diseases of the Body, and the Disorders of the Mind Depending on the Body*, 3rd ed. (London, 1742), 87–88; John Hill, *The Old Man's Guide to Health and Longer Life: With Rules for Diet, Exercise, and Physic* (Philadelphia, 1775), 24–25; and Benjamin Rush, *An Enquiry into the Effects of Spirituous Liquors upon the Human Body, and Their Influence upon the Happiness of Society* (Philadelphia, n.d.), 4.

7. Michael Zuckerman, "Fabrication of Identity in Early America," *William and Mary Quarterly* 34 (1977): 193; Stephen Greenblatt, *Renaissance Self-Fashioning: From More to Shakespeare* (Chicago, 1980), 9.

8. William Smith to Benjamin Rush, n.d., Rush Manuscripts, 35: 121, 128, and 129, Library Company Manuscript Collection, Historical Society of Pennsylvania (hereafter HSP). For a contrary view, see G. J. Barker-Benfield, *The Culture of Sensibility: Sex and Society in Eighteenth-Century Britain* (Chicago, 1992), xvii.

9. Margaret Morris to Milcah and Charles Moore, 9/25/1793, Edward Wanton Smith Collection, QCHC.

10. Margaret Morris to Milcah and Charles Moore, 9/25/1793, Edward Wanton Smith Collection; Margaret Morris to [Richard Hill Morris], n.d., Margaret Morris Papers, QCHC.

11. Norbert Elias, *The History of Manners (The Civilizing Process)*, trans. Edmund Jephcott (New York, 1978), 1:xiv–xvi. J. G. Stedman, 1/14/1787, printed in Abraham Shoemaker, *Poulson's Town and Country Almanac, for the Year of Our Lord, 1795* (Philadelphia, 1794), [not paginated].

12. Henry Drinker to Elizabeth Drinker, 9/16/1777, 9/20/1777, Henry Drinker Correspondence, QCHC.

13. William Penn to Guliema Penn, 8/4/1682, in Jean R. Soderlund, ed., *William Penn and the Founding of Pennsylvania, 1680–1684: A Documentary History* (Philadelphia, PA, 1983), 165–170, 171–172; Barry Levy, *Quakers and the American Family: British Settlement in the Delaware Valley* (New York, 1988), 105.

14. Cheyne, *Essay on Health*, 158–59. Charles Rosenberg calculates that Buchan's *Domestic Medicine* appeared in 142 editions over a hundred years beginning in 1769, in "Medical Text and Social Context: Explaining William Buchan's *Domestic Medicine*," *Bulletin of the History of Medicine* 57 (1983): 22–23. Rush's writings were so widely reprinted as to preclude a bibliographic count, L. H. Butterfield, ed., *Letters of Benjamin Rush* (Princeton, 1951), 1:272–273, n. 1; and 1:501, n. 2.

15. Buchan, *Domestic Medicine*, 66; Hill, *Old Man's Guide to Health and Longer Life*, 24, 26.

16. Peter N. Stearns and Carol Z. Stearns, *Anger: The Struggle for Emotional Control in America's History* (Chicago, 1986); Peter N. Stearns, *Jealousy: The Evolution of an Emotion in American History* (New York, 1989); Peter N. Stearns and Timothy Haggerty, "The Role of Fear: Transitions in American Emotional Standards for Children, 1850–1950," *American Historical Review* 96 (1991): 63–94; Kenneth Lockridge, *On the Sources of Patriarchal Rage: The Commonplace Books of William Byrd and Thomas Jefferson and the Gendering of Power in the Eighteenth Century* (New York, 1992); Jan E. Lewis, *The Pursuit of Happiness: Family and Values in Jefferson's Virginia* (Cambridge, MA, 1983).

17. For a discussion of the model of manly tears associated with the culture of sensibility and "heart religion," see Barker-Benfield, *Culture of Sensibility*, 71–78. Tears in some situations were not considered manly behavior. As Toby Ditz has pointed out, the tears of a cuckold, for example, were viewed as effeminate because they were "the ineffective effusions of a pitiful victim, not the moral tears of the man of sensibility capable of responding with sympathy *to* such a victim." Ditz, "Shipwrecked; or, Masculinity Imperiled: Mercantile Representations of Failure and the Gendered Self in Eighteenth-Century Philadelphia," *Journal of American History* 81 (1994): 65. For temperance and balance among American Protestants whom Philip Greven has termed "moderates," see *The Protestant Temperament: Patterns of Child-Rearing, Religious Experience and the Self in Early America* (New York, 1977), 151.

Jacquelyn C. Miller

18. Quote from Stearns and Stearns, *Anger*, 19. David D. Hall, "The Mental World of Samuel Sewell," in David D. Hall et al., eds., *Saints and Revolutionaries: Essays in Early American History* (New York, 1984), 90–91; Albert Deutsch, *The Mentally Ill in America: A History of Their Care and Treatment from Colonial Times*, 2nd ed. (New York, 1949), 27–39, 57–65; Franz G. Alexander and Sheldon T. Selesnick, *The History of Psychiatry: An Evaluation of Psychiatric Thought and Practice from Prehistoric Times to the Present* (New York, 1966), 144–164.

19. Benjamin Rush to Julia Rush, 9/8/1793, *Old Family Letters Relating to the Yellow Fever*, Ser. B (Philadelphia, 1892) 20-21; and Rush, *An Account of the Bilious Remitting Yellow Fever, as It Appeared in the City of Philadelphia, in the Year 1793* (Philadelphia, 1794), 346.

20. Esther Duché to Miss Hopkinson, 9/26/1793, Redwood Collection, HSP; Margaret Morris to Milcah Moore, 8/1793, Edward Wanton Smith Collection, QCHC; Samuel R. Fisher to Miers Fisher, 10/20/1793, Fisher Family Papers, HSP.

21. Charles Biddle, Autobiography, 283, HSP; Margaret Morris to Gulielma M. Smith, n.d., Margaret Morris Papers, QCHC; and Samuel Massey to Ann Massey, 9/15/1793, Samuel Massey Letter Collection, College of Physicians of Philadelphia (hereafter CPP).

22. Jacob Ritter, Jr., Autobiography, written in 1836, 13 [typescript version], HSP, published eight years later as Joseph Foulke, ed., *Memoirs of Jacob Ritter, A Faithful Minister in the Society of Friends* (Philadelphia, 1844), 32–35. Peter A. Grotjan's Memoirs at HSP include his account of a friend who succumbed to the fever in 1798 after a discussion with his fiancée "seriously agitated his mind," quote from 95–96.

23. Timothy Pickering to James Lovell, 9/16/1793, Dreer Collection, HSP; John Welsh to Robert Ralston, 9/6/1793, Society Miscellaneous Collection, HSP.

24. Margaret Morris to Gulielma M. Smith, 8/31/1793, Margaret Morris Papers, QCHC; Charles Biddle, Autobiography, 282–284, HSP; and Esther Duché to Miss Hopkinson, 9/26/1793, Redwood Collection, HSP.

25. William Buchan, *Domestic Medicine*, 69; Miers Fisher to William Redwood and Charles Wharton, 9/24/1793, Fisher Family Papers, HSP; and Deborah Logan to Mary Norris, 9/27/1793, Dreer Collection, HSP.

26. Smith to Benjamin Rush, 10/23/1793, in Horace Wemyss Smith, *Life and Correspondence of the Reverend William Smith, D.D.* (Philadelphia, 1880), 2:373. Population figures and mortality rates from an unpublished paper by Susan E. Klepp.

27. Margaret Morris to [Milcah and Charles Moore], 9/23/1793, Edward Wanton Smith Collection; Margaret Morris to Gulielma M. Smith, 8/31/1793, Margaret Morris Papers; Margaret Morris, Memorandum, 5/10/1778, and Margaret Morris to Milcah and Charles Moore, 8/30/1793, Edward Wanton Smith Collection, QCHC.

28. Richard Hill Morris to Benjamin Smith, 9/11/1793, Gulielma M. Howland Collection, QCHC.

29. Joshua Cresson, *Meditations Written During the Prevalence of the Yellow Fever, in the City of Philadelphia, in the Year 1793* (London, 1803), 21; Margaret Morris to Milcah Moore, 9/25/1793, Edward Wanton Smith Collection; Richard Wells to Margaret Morris, n.d., Gulielma M. Howland Collection; and Caleb Cresson, "Memorial Concerning my Dear Wife Annabella Cresson," n.d., Morris-Wistar-Wood Collection, QCHC.

30. Thomas Clifford to John Clifford, 12/2[?]/1793, Clifford-Pemberton Papers, HSP.

31. Margaret Morris to Milcah Moore, 11/15/1793, Edward Wanton Smith Collection, QCHC; John Welsh to Robert Ralston, 9/23/1793, Society Miscellaneous Collection, HSP; and J. G. Stedman to his son, 1/14/1787, in Shoemaker, *Poulson's Town and Country Almanac* [not paginated]. Emphasis in quotation is mine.

32. Margaret Morris to Milcah Moore, 9/3/1793; Margaret Morris to Milcah Moore, 9/30/1793; Margaret Morris to Rachel Hill Wells, 9/3/1793, Edward Wanton Smith Collection, QCHC; Mathew Carey, *A Short Account of the Malignant Fever, Lately Prevalent in Philadelphia*, 4th ed. (Philadelphia, 1/16/1794), 61; Abraham Shoemaker, *Poulson's Town and Country Almanac*; Benjamin Rush to Elias Boudinot, 9/25/1793, *Letters*, 2:681.

33. David de Isaac Nassy, *Observations on the Cause, Nature, and Treatment of the Epidemic Disorder, Prevalent in Philadelphia*, trans. from the French (Philadelphia, 11/26/1793), 10–11; J. Henry C. Helmuth, *A Short Account of the Yellow Fever in Philadelphia, for the Reflecting Christian* (Philadelphia, 1794), 1; and Carey, *Short Account*, 4th ed., 61.

34. Carroll Smith-Rosenberg, "Dis-Covering the Subject of the 'Great Constitutional Discussion,' 1786–1789," *Journal of American History* 79 (1992): 841–873; Miller, "Body Politic," chaps. 1 and 3.

35. Mary Robinson Morton to Thomas and Sarah Robinson, 10/6/1794, Robinson Family Papers, QCHC.

36. Deborah Logan to Mary Norris, 9/27/1793, Dreer Collection, HSP; Elias, *History of Manners*, 184–186.

Jacquelyn C. Miller

Husbands,
Wives, and
Lovers

four

SPOUSAL MURDER IN NORTHERN NEW ENGLAND, 1776–1865

Randolph A. Roth

S tudents of contemporary domestic violence have given us a keen understanding of its dependence on family history, gender inequality, economic frustration, and social isolation.[1] Historical studies of the same topic are more onerous to produce. The surviving records are often poor, and, without field research, historians can only suggest explanations for the domestic violence they uncover. Historical patterns, however, such as that of marital homicides in northern New England, confirm that domestic violence is situationally governed; its intensity and character depend as much on the culture and society of a particular time and place as they do on human nature, family pathology, or the institution of marriage.

In the early nineteenth century, spouses in northern New England argued about almost everything spouses argue about today: money, child rearing, gender roles, and so on, but they almost never killed one another. Lethal marital violence increased from the late 1820s through the Civil War. Even so, compared to other regions, murder was rare. By the mid-nineteenth century, only a few men in Vermont or New Hampshire ever "indulge[d] their passions," beating or slashing to death their wives or those who came to their wives' aid. Those who did reveal a great deal about the institution of marriage in northern New England.

Historical patterns of marital violence are difficult to trace. Many marital assaults were not reported, and authorities did not always prosecute those they encountered. Murders, however, were difficult to conceal and left more traces in historical records than other violent assaults. Once suspected, murders attracted the attention of relatives, neighbors, coroners, reporters, and magis-

Table 4–1. *Gross Homicide Rates in Vermont and New Hampshire, 1776–1865 (per 100,000 Persons per Year)*

Years	Neonates	Infants/ Children	Husbands/ Wives/3rd Parties Intervening	Other Domestic[1] (age 12+)	Non-domestic (age 12+)	Total
1776–1793	0.40	0	0.03	0.03	0.43	0.90
1794–1827	0.15	0.07	0.03	0.06	0.27	0.58
1828–1847	0.13	0.14	0.13	0.09	0.34	0.83
1848–1865	0.19	0.17	0.19	0.15	0.95	1.65

[1] Domestic homicides include all homicides committed by relatives (including those by marriage or adoption) or by unrelated household members.

Table 4–2. *Age-Specific Homicide Rates in Vermont and New Hampshire, 1800–1865 (per 100,000 Persons per Year)*

	1800–1827	1828–1847	1848–1865
Husbands/Wives/3rd Parties Intervening (age 24+)	0.10	0.39	0.47
Adults (age 12+)			
Domestic, w/out Husbands/Wives/3rd Parties Intervening	0.11	0.13	0.21
Nondomestic	0.51	0.50	1.33
Children (age 1–12)			
Domestic	0.16	0.24	0.31
Nondomestic	0.05	0.09	0.07
Infants (age 1 day to 1 year)	0.11	1.28	2.54
Neonates	1.98	3.85	6.67

Randolph A. Roth

trates. They were noted in newspaper articles, coroner's reports, vital records, and court records. The overlap of these records generates enough data to yield a fairly complete count of the homicides and suspected homicides that drew public notice in northern New England.[2]

Even if probable homicides—deaths that magistrates or coroner's juries considered homicides, though they could not prove it beyond a reasonable doubt—are included, the gross marital homicide rate in post-Revolutionary New Hampshire and Vermont was only 0.03 per 100,000 persons per year between 1776 and 1827 (see Table 4–1). If only persons who were at risk of marital homicide in the larger population—adults over the age of 24—are included, the rate from 1800 through 1827 was 0.10 (see Table 4–2), a rate only one-third of that in seventeenth-century Massachusetts Bay Colony and Plymouth Colony, heretofore "the lowest ever reported in American history."[3] That rate rose in northern New England to 0.39 from 1828 to 1847 and 0.47 from 1848 to 1865 (Table 4–2), a change caused by a tenfold increase in wife murder.[4] Marital homicide was still rare, but wives in Vermont and New Hampshire were less safe than before.

Although few marriages ended in murder, many were violent, according to divorce proceedings. Eighteen percent of husbands and 35 percent of wives who sued for divorce in Windsor County, Vermont, between 1793 and 1837 did so on the grounds of "intolerable severity": that is, threatening conduct or physical abuse. If we include suits for adultery that cite intolerable abuse as a factor, the totals rise to 43 percent of husbands and 46 percent of wives (see Table 4–4). The Vermont Supreme Court sustained charges in all but a handful of these cases. In its opinion, the violence reported in divorce petitions was real.

The proportion of divorce suits that cited intolerable severity remained high at midcentury, although husbands used those grounds far less often than they had before (see Tables 4–3 and 4–4). Between 1862 and 1866, 7 percent of

Table 4–3. *Divorces in Windsor County, Vermont, 1793–1861 and all Vermont, 1862–1866 [1] by Gender of Plantiff*

Plantiff	1793–1837 (N=207)[2]	1838–1861 (N=164)[3]	1862–1866 (N=571)
Husbands	24%	40%	45%
Wives	76%	60%	55%

[1] Sources for Tables 4–3 and 4–4, 1793–1861: VSCR, vols. 1–6, Clerk's Office, Windsor County Superior Court, Woodstock, Vermont; and VSCR, Divorces, vols. 1–2, Clerk's Office, Family Court, Vermont District Court, White River Junction, Vermont. Sources for Tables 4–3 and 4–4, 1862–1866: Annual Report of the Registrar of Vital Statistics of Vermont, 1866 (Montpelier, 1867), 86–87.

[2] Two cases not included. One wife pleaded that her husband had been sentenced to the penitentiary and another on grounds the court clerk failed to record.

[3] Five cases not included. Five wives pleaded their husbands had been sentenced to the penitentiary.

SPOUSAL MURDER IN NORTHERN NEW ENGLAND, 1776–1865

Table 4–4. *Divorces in Windsor County, Vermont, 1793–1861:* [1]
Grounds for Divorce by Gender of Plaintiff

Grounds, 1793–1837	Husbands	Wives	Total
Intolerable Severity	18%	35%	31%
Adultery/Intolerable Severity	24	10	14
Adultery	31	15	19
Desertion	27	39	36
Total	100	99	100

Grounds, 1838–1861			
Intolerable Severity	2%	40%	24%
Adultery/Intolerable Severity	0	1	1
Adultery	36	7	19
Desertion	62	52	56
Total	100	100	100

Grounds, 1862–1866			
Intolerable Severity[2]	7%	37%	23%
Adultery[3]	46	17	30
Desertion[4]	46	45	46
Other[5]	0	2	1
Total	99	101	100

[1] See Table 4–3 for sources.
[2] Includes cases of intolerable severity and intolerable severity joined with desertion, willful desertion, and nonsupport.
[3] Includes cases of adultery and adultery joined with desertion, willful desertion, or nonsupport.
[4] Includes cases in which the sole charge was desertion, wilfull desertion, or nonsupport.
[5] Includes cases of fraud, bigamy, nullity, insanity, and imprisonment for felony conviction.

Randolph A. Roth

husbands and 37 percent of wives who received divorces did so for intolerable severity (Table 4–4). These records alone indicate that violence or threats of violence were a serious problem in 1 to 2 percent of all Vermont marriages by the Civil War.[6]

New Hampshire's divorce laws defined domestic violence more narrowly than Vermont's in the late eighteenth and early nineteenth centuries. Plaintiffs had to prove not severity but "extreme cruelty"—violence so severe that the abused spouse risked being maimed or killed. New Hampshire courts, moreover, presumed female marital violence nonlethal; husbands had little chance of winning divorces for physical abuse, and few tried. Wives could and did. In Rockingham County from 1785 through 1815, 40 percent of female plaintiffs complained of extreme cruelty.[7] In time, New Hampshire courts extended "extreme cruelty" to include violence that did not threaten life or limb. According to statewide returns filed by New Hampshire's clerks of court from 1882 to 1886 (the first available), a third of husbands and wives who won divorces did so on the grounds of extreme cruelty. Violence was severe in at least 3 percent of all New Hampshire marriages by the 1880s.[8]

Marital violence intensified the longer couples lived together. Only 14 percent of the plaintiffs who had been married for less than four years and who filed for divorce in Windsor County, Vermont, did so on the grounds of intolerable severity, while 47 percent of the plaintiffs who had been married twelve or more years did so (see Table 4–5). Young marriages usually ended with one or both partners simply walking away, a more difficult resolution for older couples bound together by children, property, and community. When their lives or marriages proved unhappy, they often expressed discontent through violence.

Complaints in Vermont and New Hampshire divorce petitions were varied. Nancy Ashley stated that her husband beat her with a walking cane, while

Table 4–5. *Divorces in Windsor County, Vermont, 1793–1861*[1]: *Grounds for Divorce by Years Together*

	Intolerable Severity	Desertion	Adultery	Total
Years Together[2]				
0–3 (N = 126)	12%	63%	25%	100%
4–11 (N = 134)	30	45	24	99%
12+ (N = 111)	45	24	32	101%

[1] See Table 4–3 for sources.
[2] In cases of desertion or separation, years together is the difference between the year of marriage and the year of desertion or separation. In others, years together is the difference between the year of marriage and the year of divorce.

Naomi Lusk said her husband, an adulterer, assaulted her and threw her out of the house naked. Arminda Hoisington complained of her husband's groundless jealousies and plots against her and claimed she was terrified of him from the beginning of their marriage. Mary Powell's husband, an alcoholic, beat her, broke their furniture, and vowed to poison her or burn their house. One night he choked her and held a knife to her throat; she ran away to save her life. Theophilus Bates felt "unsafe" living with his wife. He believed her capable of deadly violence, and possibly mentally ill.[9]

Elizabeth Tilden's story was more complicated. She was a twenty-year-old widow with two children when she married Stephen, a forty-year-old widower with six children. He subjected her to "tyrannical commands" and beat her during their five-year marriage. Worse still, Stephen broke his promise that her children would be cared for and educated by other families. He finally kicked her out of the house and kept her children, her real estate (worth $200 a year in rent), her clothes, and $170 in cash. She wanted her children and her property back.[10]

Spousal violence could be mutual. On various occasions, for example, Oliver Whipple, an attorney and magistrate, beat his wife Abigail black and blue, threw her to the floor, and threatened her with a whip and iron tongs. When she was seven months pregnant, he threw a chair at her so hard that it "broak the plastering from the leaths on the opposite side of the room," and threatened to "split" her "brains out." He also dallied with the servants, holding hands with Violet and offering Mary "as Good a Gownd as he had in his Shop" if she "would tarry with him a little while." But Abigail had her share of secrets and started her share of fights. She once threatened to throw a teapot of hot water on Oliver at the breakfast table; on another occasion she threw a shoe at her husband and kicked him, whereupon he tossed her against the stove. The Superior Court found Oliver at fault in the divorce but recognized that Abigail had contributed to the couple's troubles.[11]

The McNeils of Londonderry, New Hampshire, were also a violent couple, but by the end of their marriage, Elizabeth had the upper hand. The McNeils had owned a substantial farm, but Josiah's drinking dissipated the property. Elizabeth, an "industrious" woman who had "educated her Children well," suffered his drunken assaults for years; by the time her children were teenagers, however, she had had enough. One winter day, Elizabeth asked a neighbor who called if he had come to see "the prisoner." Josiah lay on the floor, bound hand and foot. A month later, neighbors found him lying wet and muddy in a public road, beaten, bound, and surrounded by his wife and children, who told them they would "smart for it" if they tried to rescue Josiah. The following November, nearby neighbors stepped outdoors after hearing cries at the McNeil place. They saw Josiah run from his house into the woods, his wife, son, and daughters "runing after him with Clubs or Sticks in their hands." An

Randolph A. Roth

hour later, Josiah came to the neighbors' door for protection, with his "head and face" all "bloddy."[12]

Despite this violence, however, the records show that only two husbands and three wives were murdered in Vermont and New Hampshire from the 1790s to the late 1820s and only four more husbands and 27 more wives by 1865. None of them were victims of deliberate murder. Some were murdered by mentally ill persons with homicidal tendencies; the others died after assaults that became unintentionally lethal.

David Wallingford of Milton, New Hampshire, who beat his wife Sarah to death with the brace of a weaver's loom in 1815, was deemed "insane" and not indicted. He had surprised his wife at breakfast and so "fractured and mangled" her head "that much of her blood and some of her brains" were "upon the floor of the house." Contemporaries were not convinced that the wife of Alexander Patterson of Rutland was likewise insane, given her calculated actions, but she too showed signs of mental illness, especially in her anticipatory declarations and her disregard for her children's lives.[13] Mrs. Patterson had threatened her husband so often that "he thought his life was in danger." He disappeared in July 1792. Soon afterward Mrs. Patterson packed her pewter, bedding, and clothing and told her children she would be away at a neighbor's that evening. Late that night, the Pattersons' house burned, and the children barely escaped the flames. A search in the ruins for Mrs. Patterson's valuables uncovered human remains "just where the bed stood." While the coroner's jury gathered, Mrs. Patterson hid the skull and teeth and smashed the rest of the bones to pieces, "in order to render all further enquiries fruitless." The coroner's jury could not identify the deceased as Mr. Patterson and brought in a verdict of death by suspicious means. Mrs. Patterson's valuables were later found hidden in the woods.[14]

In 1800, Mrs. Holgate of Milton, Vermont, killed one of her children and a maid while trying to kill her husband. Holgate quarreled with her husband when he discovered that she had "secreted his books and papers." When he reprimanded her, she "threatened to burn the house and him with it." Mr. Holgate was awakened by flames that night. He managed to save one of his children, but both he and the child were seriously burned and another child and the family maid killed. A man who slept in a store adjacent to the house was trying to escape when he saw "Mrs. Holgate in her usual dress, walking the room." She "had given no alarm, notwithstanding the next room in the house was wrapped in flames." He broke the window, threw her out, and leapt to safety. At the inquest, Mrs. Holgate blamed the maid for the fire, claiming she had "stuck a candle against the ceiling with a fork and left it burning." But a neighbor contradicted her, observing that the maid's room had been filled with smoke, not fire, when he heard her cries before the roof collapsed. The coroner's jury found Mrs. Holgate guilty of murder, but the grand jury believed that her disregard for her own life and the lives of her children indicated mental illness. She never went to trial.[15]

These three cases fit a persistent pattern of spousal murder in that they all involved mental illness, which remained a common cause of domestic murder into the 1840s. In most cases, northern New Englanders realized before the murders occurred that the person who suffered from mental illness posed a threat to his or her family, and tried to take preventive measures. In one case, a neighbor took in threatened family members. In another, a husband won custody of his children, who had been threatened by his wife. In yet another, neighbors looked in on a household every two hours after a family member's mental condition took a turn for the worse. Such measures were often ineffective, however; all the above cases ended in murder.[16]

The state asylums that opened in Vermont in 1836 and New Hampshire in 1840 contributed to the decline in such spouse and family murders during the 1850s and 1860s. The physicians and trustees of these public hospitals—the second and the fourth in the United States—believed their institutions could lessen the "number of cases of violence and murder committed by the insane." They recognized that some mentally ill people were prone to violence, "sometimes from feelings of revenge for some real or fancied injury, and sometimes from kindness to their victims, to save them from the miseries which they fancy are inevitable." Officials touted the asylum "as a place of custody for those endangering the lives and safety of the community and their own persons" and as a means of "removing the immense weight of anxiety and distress and danger of their connections and relations." They reported cases in which the asylums cured violent patients and returned them safely to their families, and urged friends and relatives to send such patients to the asylums, where they were most likely to recover.[17]

Treatment at these public hospitals was not free to families or individuals with property, but public and private subsidies made it reasonably affordable for middle-income families ($2.50 to $3 a week). Public funds paid for the care of indigents.[18] By midcentury, families, townships, and courts sent threatening persons who exhibited signs of mental illness to asylums as a matter of course, especially if they had committed assaults or attempted murder. By 1850, the asylums included 450 patients and by 1865, 700—2 out of every 1000 people aged over eighteen.[19] That rate of commitment was high enough to protect most spouses and families.

Public health officials realized the asylum system was not perfect. Northern New Englanders were far less willing to hospitalize depressed family members than erratic or violent ones, despite the asylum trustees' warning that severe depression was as much a "pathological condition" as any other mental disorder, "often complicated with dangerous delusions and homicidal and suicidal

Randolph A. Roth

tendencies."[20] The persistence of murder-suicides committed by depressed and other nonviolent family members—particularly mothers who killed their children—proved them right. Another persistent problem was recurring violence by former patients who had been released with or without their physicians' blessing.[21] But on the whole, the asylums appear to have saved lives.

Many spousal murders in northern New England between the early 1800s and the Civil War were cases of manslaughter—violent assaults that ended unintentionally in death. Mr. Maxfield of Ryegate, Vermont, died a day after his wife, a Scots immigrant, pummelled him in 1805 during what turned out to be their last drunken fight. In 1812, Elizabeth Duty of Haverhill, New Hampshire, died two days after her husband Moses hit her on the head and side with a hoe and threw her to the ground. Amelia Lamphier of Windsor, Vermont, took seven days to die in 1806 from what an inquest determined were her husband George's kicks to her back, side, and loins, although she, her husband, and her mother-in-law denied that her injuries stemmed from his attack.[22]

Local authorities jailed Mrs. Maxfield and several acquaintances at her house at the time of the assault. Moses Duty was indicted. George Lamphier was tried as a murderer and his mother as an accessory. But Maxfield was released, Duty never tried, and the Lamphiers found not guilty. Court records and newspaper accounts indicate that the community did not sanction their brutal behavior. But they were not, as one jury and two prosecutors realized, willful murderers. They did not intend to kill their spouses, and called physicians once the injuries proved serious.

Nevertheless, people who committed manslaughter were not necessarily less serious abusers than willful murderers. George Lamphier, for instance, who struck his wife only on parts of her body concealed by her clothes, was clearly a cold, calculating, vicious man. Moses Duty and Mrs. Maxfield, who expected their spouses to be up and about after prolonged assaults, were equally brutal. But their behavior helps us understand why domestic violence seldom led to homicide in northern New England. Abusive spouses had strong incentives to hide their cruelty and keep their spouses alive.

Abusers meted out violence carefully in part to avoid prosecution. Bradbury Ferguson, a hatter in Exeter, New Hampshire, beat his wife Eliza Ann repeatedly, but was careful not to leave scars or break bones. In 1840, she told him she was going to swear a complaint against him; he replied "Shew your marks." She rightly feared for her life, but all she could show constables at the time was a household item her husband had hurled at her and "stove . . . all to pieces." Benjamin Smart of Concord lost his temper with his pregnant wife, Nancy, in 1836 with a visitor present. Smart waited until their guest left before he followed her upstairs to the bedroom, kicked her in the back and side, and hurled her to the floor.[23]

Table 4–6. *Prosecution Rates of Spouses[1] in State and County Courts*
for Attempted Murder, Assault, and Threats to Kill, 1800–1865
(per 100,000 Persons Age 24+ per Year)[2]

	1800–1827	1828–1847	1848–1865
Attempted Murder[3]	0.10	0.21	0.49
Assault	0.45	0.81	0.29
Threat to Kill	0.18	0.52	0.07
Total			
All Domestic Violence	0.73	1.54	0.75

[1] Includes crimes against spouses and possible spouses. Only in cases of "threatening to kill" did court clerks record systematically whether the accused and the victim were married.

[2] Approximately 65 percent of spouses accused of attempted murder were convicted, as were 63 percent of those accused of assault and 14 percent of those accused of threats to kill. These percentages do not include suspects in attempted murder who fled prosecution.

[3] None of the 23 cases of threats to kill represented crimes by women against men. Only four of 30 cases of attempted murder did, and one of 62 cases of assault.

But continually abusive spouses risked prosecution if violence became open or obvious (see Table 4–6). Husbands and wives tried for assault or attempted murder faced near-certain conviction; penalties for husbands could be very stiff. Two-thirds of husbands found guilty of attempted murder between 1790 and 1865 were sentenced to five to ten years in prison. Sentences for assault or assault and battery were less severe. Only one-seventh of those convicted in state or county courts spent from one to six months in jail, and fines seldom exceeded $25. When prosecution costs (usually $25 to $50) were added, however, a farm laborer faced the loss of half a year's wages (which averaged $100 to $150 per year, along with room and board).[24] Threats were harder to prosecute; they resulted neither in marks nor witnesses other than the victim, and only one-seventh of these cases ended in conviction. But prosecutors still had an effective sanction, forcing suspects to post bonds of $100 or more for "good behavior." The bonds were forfeited if suspects further threatened or abused their spouses.

Despite high conviction rates, only one adult annually in 100,000 was prosecuted for domestic violence (Table 4–6). Between 1793 and 1861, only four of the spouses in Windsor County, Vermont, who were accused of intolerable severity in divorce petitions were prosecuted for assault.[25] Prosecutions for attempted murder increased in the 1850s and 1860s, but that reflected, as homicide rates did, an actual increase in willful, lethal violence in marriages and in society. Prosecutions for threats and common assaults declined dramatically in these years in state and county courts; state attorneys had their hands full prosecuting lethal and near-lethal cases. New municipal courts took up some nonlethal cases in several cities in Vermont and New Hampshire, but most cases fell to justices of the peace, who had lesser sanctions at their disposal and whose courts were in decline by midcentury.[26]

Few prosecutions for threat, assault, or attempted murder led to divorce; most prosecutions for domestic violence may have been requested by abused wives who hoped state intercession would restrain their husbands and save their marriages. They were *de facto* civil suits. The state intervened decisively only in murders—when spouses could no longer speak.

Violent spouses in northern New England had reason to fear the state, however, in divorce proceedings. Vermont and New Hampshire were the first in the nation to sanction divorce on the grounds of domestic violence and to grant alimony to abused wives. New England's colonial governments had always viewed marriage, in the tradition of radical or Reformed Protestantism, as a civil contract. It could be voided if one party failed to live up to the terms of the contract through adultery, desertion, or impotence. But in their opinion, violence did not violate the marriage contract. Marital violence could be prosecuted only as an assault—a violation of the general civil contract. New England's colonial governments believed physical coercion necessary for correcting the behavior of dependents (children, servants, slaves, and sometimes wives) because they feared marriage and household government would collapse if violence were recognized as grounds for divorce. The same governments certainly realized that such violence could also threaten the institution they wished to protect, and thus allowed testimony about physical and emotional cruelty in divorce petitions brought on other grounds. They were also willing to grant separations in some instances on grounds of physical abuse, but were reluctant to grant divorces solely on those grounds.[27]

The American Revolution led northern New England's governments to a radical new defense of the right of spouses to live free from violence. Marriage, like any civil compact among freeborn citizens, could rest only on consent, not coercion. In 1787, Vermont made "intolerable severity" grounds for divorce. In 1791, New Hampshire followed with a less-sweeping but still-forceful law against "extreme cruelty."[28] These laws were not dead letters—abused spouses used them freely to protect themselves and their families against violence, and courts used them to punish violent spouses. The courts granted victims property, alimony, and child custody, and thus abusive spouses had good reason to hide or moderate their behavior. They stood to lose a good deal in divorce proceedings if they left sufficient evidence of their violence.

Abusers in northern New England had much to fear aside from the state; in-laws, relatives, neighbors, and others in the community reacted strongly to domestic abuse. In some instances, abusers faced vigilante violence. In Kennebunkport, Maine, in the winter of 1824, three women surprised a chronic abuser who had beaten his wife that day. They dragged him by the ears from his house and pushed him facedown in the snow. One woman held his head and another his legs while a third "paid him back with interest, the full amount of flagellations, which he had bestowed on his wife." In Antrim, New Hampshire, in 1837, two men hog-tied a drunken man who had beaten his wife with a chair and then set him against a wall with a noose around his neck while they went for the authorities. The man strangled to death before they returned. In Lincoln, Vermont, in 1863, townspeople mobbed another abuser who had beaten his wife and kicked her out of bed for not rising as early as he had told her to. When she left him and sued for divorce, he seized their six-month-old child. The mob surrounded his house and threatened to tar and feather him unless he returned the child, which he did.[29]

Abusers also faced public ridicule. Newspapers often depicted violent spouses as fools, drunks, and thugs. The account of the Kennebunkport beating in the Concord *New Hampshire Patriot*, for instance, portrayed the abusive husband as a man "who for a long time" had "paid particular honors to Bacchus" and who "in his fits of devotion" had "often assumed the ancient privilege of flogging his wife, turning her out of doors, &c." Of the "Female Retaliation" he suffered "after he had been at this honorable business," "It was a piteous sight to ken—Yet all the people said—AMEN." In 1829, the Montpelier *Watchman and Gazette* scorned wife-beating as a particularly Irish (and hence brutish) way of displaying "patriotism and conjugal affection." It described an assault the editor and a justice of the peace had been asked to quell on Christmas Day. They found the husband seated at the kitchen table, "gnawing the carcass of a baked goose," while his wife lay "groaning upon the bed." The boiling dinner pot "had been arrested in its aim at the head of the wife, and lay upon the floor—the pot here,—the pork there,—the potatoes every where; interspersed with the demolished stove and pipe and soot, and blood and hair, mingled and mingling in one common mass." The husband, "by the help of the constable, was aided to the 'jug,' other than the one from which he had been quaffing copious libations," but was released when his wife refused to press charges. "He who doubts *the love of a woman* must be a dunce—and he who abuses her—a brute." Mrs. Wilson of Middlebury, Vermont, accused in 1859 of trying to murder her husband while both were drunk, claimed that her mutilated husband had "blarneyed about the house and cut himself." The *Rutland Herald* declared that "the love of such a wife lies beyond all comprehension."[30]

Perhaps more important than scorn or vigilantism in preventing domestic abuse was the day-to-day intervention of relatives and neighbors who interceded, often at risk to themselves, to prevent violence against people they knew. A neighboring family gave Eliza Ann Ferguson sanctuary when she fled her husband and refused to surrender her when he arrived and threatened to murder everyone in the house. When her husband persisted in his threats and began to search the house, an elderly gentleman in the household grabbed his cane and chased him away. Matilda Nash of Sullivan, New Hampshire, a widow aged seventy, lost her life in 1829 protecting the wife and children of Daniel Corey, a mentally ill farmer. Corey threatened to kill the members of his family; they took refuge in Nash's house while she went to the Corey house to talk to Daniel. He smashed her head with a gun stock when she refused to leave.[31]

Sheldon Loggins of Williston, Vermont, a fifty-three-year-old farmer, showed similar courage in protecting Mary Allen from her husband in 1850. Allen had grabbed her young child and run across a field to escape a beating, only to be caught by her husband a few yards short of Loggins's door. George Allen threw Mary against a fence and struck her, leaving her bloody. Loggins's daughter raised an alarm and Mary ran for the Loggins house. George took a pistol from his pocket and fired at Mary. Hearing the shots, Loggins came out and, unarmed, confronted Allen before he could fire again. George, "in a violent manner and in a passion," asked Loggins "if he wanted anything of him." Loggins answered that "he wanted he should leave the state." George "said he would have revenge" and fired at Loggins. Missing his mark, George asked Loggins "if He intended to harbor that woman." Loggins, who had known Mary since she was nine years old, vowed that he "would protect her . . . under his roof." George stalked off, telling Loggins: "Remember me, for revenge I will have."[32]

Most interventions ended more peaceably than those described above. Constables and justices of the peace were sometimes called upon to intervene in violent situations, but they often did so more as neighbors than authorities. Even when marital violence was mutual, as it was with the Whipples and McNeils, neighbors or servants stepped in, regardless of which spouse had the upper hand or who had started the fight.[33] Relatives, especially siblings and adult children of the abused, also intervened. Abigail Powers of Bath, New Hampshire, who had been beaten throughout her marriage and who had learned to her horror that her daughter had been a victim of incest, had the support of her brothers and sisters. They offered her and her children shelter and urged her to take her husband to court. Nancy Bean's children, who were grown and settled, invited her to live with them so that she might be free of her husband's drinking and assaults.[34] Relatives, neighbors, and domestic employees also supported abused spouses in court when they decided to prosecute or divorce.

Public scorn for abusers, neighborly support for victims, and the threat of divorce—all of which had roots in seventeenth-century New England—restrained marital violence more effectively than criminal prosecution. But post-Revolutionary northern New England was *less* violent than colonial New England had been. And until the late 1820s, far fewer people belonged to churches in Vermont and New Hampshire than in colonial New England. State-sponsored worship and morals prosecutions, moreover, had disappeared. Alcoholics faced criminal prosecution only if they left families in want, fornicators only if they refused to support illegitimate children, and abusers only if their spouses pressed charges. The inhabitants of post-Revolutionary Vermont and New Hampshire were as well armed as colonial New Englanders, and they drank more.[35] But they killed less.

Clearly, post-Revolutionary northern New Englanders kept measures that had proved effective in colonial New England and added new ones of their own. They augmented hellfire sermons with worldly ridicule, mutual surveillance with compassion, forbearance with physical intervention (a truly "muscular" Christianity), and tolerance of divorce with intolerance toward violent marriages.

More important, however, abusers may have moderated their violence because they recognized their dependence on their spouses. They needed them alive. Marriages in northern New England were partnerships, however unequal the terms. Given the challenges of settling New England's rocky frontier and the difficulty of getting and keeping a farm or shop, husbands and wives needed all the help they could get from each other.[36] Independent proprietorship was a goal northern New Englanders sought and achieved to a greater degree than anyone else in the Western world. The ideal and the reality of independent proprietorship were born from a struggling regional economy. Northern New England was the poorest region in colonial America. It had fewer bound laborers, greater equality of wealth, and higher levels of self-employment than any other region. Survival and success depended on family labor and the continued production of diverse goods for changing local and international markets. In short, the regional economy required that husbands and wives work in complementary ways.[37]

As letters and diaries from happy families reveal, marriages in post-Revolutionary Vermont and New Hampshire sometimes came close to the twentieth-century ideal of unions between friends and equals.[38] More often, spouses lived as unequal partners. Husbands certainly had greater control over finances and investments in land and capital than wives did. Even most unequal partnerships were marked, however, by mutual regard and satisfaction at achieving "self-employment" together. And northern New Englanders began to lessen the inequality in these partnerships after the Revolution by committing themselves to the universal education of both men and women; female literacy rates soared and soon approximated those of men. As a result, Vermont and New Hampshire had the highest literacy rates in the nation, and wives and husbands had a more equal hand in business affairs and in educating their children.[39]

Mutual regard, of course, did not always prevail in these domestic partnerships. Marriages could be torn apart by adultery, jealousy, drinking, or disagreements over work, raising children, or handling property.[40] Yet however angry one or both spouses became in these circumstances, they almost always stopped short of crippling or killing. Mutual dependence might generate violence, but it also set limits, especially once abused spouses had the option of ending marriages that became too violent.

Another reason why most angry spouses in northern New England may have stopped short of killing one another is because they had better ways of getting even. After the Revolution many disgruntled husbands and wives placed ads in local newspapers accusing their partners of indolence, abuse, adultery, theft, and other crimes. Phebe Darling "posted" her husband Enoch in the *Vermont Gazette*, claiming that he squandered their money in taverns and had "at sundry times used me in so improper and cruel a manner, as to destroy my happiness, and endanger my life." Clara Thrall complained in the *Vermont Republican* of her husband's failure to support her and her child and of having "received many a bitter blow from his unfeeling hand."[41]

These postings sometimes rehearsed the entire history of a troubled marriage. Hannah West asked readers of the Windsor *Vermont Journal* to "Hear the Truth" about her husband, who absconded with most of their possessions, leaving her penniless after nine years of marriage. He took "all my cloth that I had to clothe my family with, and all my yarn I had spinned." He also "carried away my flax, wood, and all the provisions which we raised on our farm the last year" and sold them. He left "five children to cry and sob to see the desolation of my family. Since last winter he had been more cruel, and has abused me and his children in a shameful manner, and jamming me till I was black and blue."[42]

Mercy Griffis told *Vermont Gazette* readers of the suffering she endured over sixteen years of marriage to Benjamin Griffis. He and her stepchildren hated her "so much I dare not venture my life with them." Her husband, whom she had nursed "in the tenderest manner during six months sickness, with nobody to help me" had taken "his bed and fatting cow, in August, and swine that never any person took care of or fed but myself, and went away and left me alone," with only "one cow and a little meat and meal enough to last a month." Benjamin told her not to follow him to his son's. Mercy knew it was "dangerous" to do so, but "I knew I had a right to go there for all that," and she had no choice. When she arrived, Benjamin "took part with his children against me." He had "always had been spiteful toward me, and always wanted to revenge on me. Ever since I lived there with him, the common words used by his son to me have been—*God damn you, you damn'd bitch*—or *damn'd curse*." Mercy "lived there till November; I suffered cold and hunger, and had no wood but what I brought myself in storms and tempests." Nor had she "run them in debt"; she had supported herself. She was the worthy partner.[43]

Postings often marked the end of marriages. They were meant to destroy the reputation of spouses who had failed as partners, but they deterred vio-

SPOUSAL MURDER IN NORTHERN NEW ENGLAND, 1776–1865

lence by giving aggrieved spouses a nonviolent means of avenging themselves and defending their honor. They also served as a warning to abusers and potential abusers that they ran the risk of being humiliated publicly.

Another nonviolent means of revenge that was popular in northern New England was the defiant gesture: sometimes a small action meant to demonstrate contempt for a spouse's controlling ways, sometimes a deed so shocking that it became part of local legend. Mary Welch of Two Heroes, Vermont, was unhappy in her marriage, although her in-laws and neighbors laid the blame for that squarely on her own shoulders. She would often ride to town several times in a day; sometimes she would stay with friends in town for several days at a time, leaving her husband Nathaniel alone to care for their three children, run the household, and tend the farm. When Nathaniel asked her to perform her duties, she threatened his life. She told Royal Welch, her brother-in-law, that "she would Burn up & Destroy their own House and every thing they had and that she would kill her husband." When he asked her why she was so angry, she asked "what was that to him?"

Mary's in-laws were certain she would murder Nathaniel if "she could find a favorable opportunity." But she never laid a hand on him; instead, she found other ways to spite him. Nancy Cade, a longtime neighbor, heard Nathaniel ask Mary to make a small cake, at which "Mary got up and fetched about a Bushel of good flower and puts it into a Tub about half full of swills which was put by for the Hogs and after swearing an Oath said to her Husband there's a Cake for you." Another time when he asked her to mend his shirts, she took out one of his "Holland shirts nearly as good as new which she cut to pieces." Yet another time, when asked to clean the house, she broke the furniture into kindling and burned it.[44]

Azuba Brooks of Winhall, Vermont, did on occasion kick her husband or throw things at him, but more regularly preferred to defy him. His complaint (and that of the neighbors) was that Azuba, despite her industriousness, "did not manage her household concerns as well as women in general," and that "her manner of cooking and taking care of her household concerns was such that her family could not be decent." She turned the charges on her husband, telling neighbors he was a "Thumb sucking child" and a "Dirty Mangy Puppy." She answered one of his complaints about her cooking "by taking a cake hot from the Fire and throwing it Spitefully Into his Face," and another about her manners by "blowing her nose and throwing It in his Face." "God Dam You David Brooks I Know how to torment you and I will Do It" was a common refrain for Azuba. An even more bizarre act of defiance was that of a man who married a propertied widow in Cornish, New Hampshire. She complained constantly during the first year of their marriage that "things didn't go so" when her first husband was on the farm. One day her new husband got up and without a word "proceeded to the grave yard, and actually dug up the remains of the first husband,—carried the coffin home, and set it down in the kitchen—declaring that if it would make so much difference he should be on the farm."[45]

Yet another example of defiance was that of a woman living not far from Bangor, Maine, who was "cursed and tormented by a drunken husband." She told him "that if he ever came home again drunk, she would throw herself into the river." The next Saturday evening he staggered home drunk, abused his wife, and fell asleep; when he awoke, she was gone. From the evidence she had left, he and his neighbors could conclude only that she had indeed drowned herself. Stricken with remorse, the husband reformed. Five years later he was appointed to a land agency in Illinois, and one afternoon, overtaken by a storm, he sought shelter at a house by the wayside. "On knocking at the door, judge of his surprise to find the summons answered by his own wife."[46]

Conduct of this sort, though often admired and considered a sign of strong character in New England, was not universally applauded. Respectable society considered it evidence that the defiant partner was at fault. Newspapers declared the grave-robbing husband of Cornish a "monster in human shape." Mary Welch's neighbors, in-laws, and even her own sister were so incensed by her defiant acts that they advised her husband to "whip her severely if ever he thought to live with her."[47] He refused and tried to reconcile with her, but his friends' advocacy of physical chastisement (almost unheard of in early nineteenth-century Vermont and New Hampshire) shows that people who behaved as she did risked putting themselves beyond the protection of society. Still, they had the satisfaction of confounding their adversaries, at least temporarily. And if their humor was sufficiently singular, they stood a chance of being immortalized in local lore as husbands or wives who knew how to put a spouse in her or his place. Mary Welch had her friends and sympathizers in town; the husband from Cornish doubtless had admirers among readers of the *Burlington Free Press*. None of the people who committed these acts, moreover, lifted a hand against their spouses. Like spouses who "posted" their husbands or wives, they vented their anger nonviolently and thereby won some community support.

Beginning in the late 1820s, however, records indicate that more men in northern New England deliberately began to murder their wives. These murders were not numerous, but their cold-bloodedness shocked communities. In Kennebunkport, Maine, in 1828 for example, James Murphy and his wife were both drunk one morning, when he decided to kill her. As she lay unconscious, he heated a Dutch oven lid until it was red hot and laid it on her back. That failed to ignite her, so he went to the pasture, gathered brush, piled it around her and set her on fire. A neighbor arrived and pulled her from the flames, but she died three weeks later.[48]

Twelve years later, in 1840, another infamous incident occurred. Bradbury Ferguson and his wife had quarrelled one day, and that night she refused to come up to bed. Enraged, he grabbed his shotgun and shot her in the stomach. Their children raced downstairs to see what had happened. As his wife lay bleeding to death on the floor, he packed his things for an escape to Canada, but could not find everything he needed. He demanded that she tell him where his best clothes were; her last words were "in the closet." A year later, in 1841, James Sweeney of Norwich, Vermont, beat his wife to death in a neighbor's garden and also fled to escape prosecution. That same year, Richard Bean of Brentwood, New Hampshire, a chronic abuser, gouged out his wife's eye and crushed the bones in her face with repeated blows from a heavy wooden stake. Another incident involved James Powell, a farmer from Georgia, Vermont, who owned one of the most beautiful farms on the Lamoille River; he had not lived on "peaceable terms" with his wife for years. In 1842, he smashed her skull and dumped her body in the river.[49]

The murderous assaults abated for a few years, then resumed in earnest in the 1850s and 1860s. Both deliberate murders and nonfatal assaults by husbands who meant to kill their wives increased in these decades. In 1852, John Dow of Seabrook, New Hampshire, seized his wife by the hair, dragged her into the street, and began sawing at her neck with a pocket knife. It was too dull to sever an artery before a passerby intervened. Jonathan Tebbetts of Kensington vowed to kill his wife Hannah if she tried to leave him. One day in 1853, she grabbed their infant daughter and fled the house. He fired a shotgun at her from an upstairs window. Both she and the baby were hit but survived. Henry Leader of Keene had been jailed for failing to post a bond for good behavior. When his estranged wife visited him at the jail "to perfect some pecuniary arrangements between them," he stabbed her three times. She had left him a short time before "on account of cruel treatment." Only the thickness of her clothing and the quick action of another prisoner, who threw Henry into a cell and locked it, saved her life.[50] If these (and other) willful assailants had had better weapons, more skill, or more time, the marital homicide rate could have doubled.

Neighbors or relatives who came to the aid of battered wives were also clubbed, shot, and stabbed. In 1835, a drunken Theodore Wilson of Kittery, Maine, furious when he came to home to an empty house, went to a neighbor's where his wife and two friends were visiting a sick woman; he demanded that his wife come home with him immediately. Against her friends' advice, she did so. Her friends worried about Wilson's temper, and followed close behind, only to discover that Wilson had already beaten his wife to death in their front yard. When the two women pulled him off, he tried to kill them as well.[51]

In 1848, Titus Foster, Jr., of Hebron, New Hampshire, went to his parents' home to help his mother move out. She had been abused for years by her husband, a wealthy farmer, and had finally asked her son for protection. Titus Sr. flew into a rage as Titus Jr. gathered up his mother's belongings, so his son threw him to the floor and left the house. Titus Sr. followed him down the road and wounded him mortally with a knife. In 1855, Mrs. John Crowley of Portsmouth, New Hampshire, left her abusive husband and took refuge with the family of Hugh Pindar. John Crowley showed up four days later, demanding that his wife and children return, but his wife refused. Crowley tried to strike her, and when Pindar intervened, Crowley hit him in the chest with such force that Pindar's heart stopped. He was dead in minutes. In yet another case in 1859, John Gleason of Middlesex, Vermont, stabbed John Courtney several times in the neck when Courtney tried to stop a drunken quarrel between Gleason and his wife. Courtney died of his wounds.[52]

The most notorious murder of an intercessor in this era occurred in Lisbon, New Hampshire. Ralph Bishop had put a stop to violence several times on the farm of Brewster Young, his neighbor. In June 1862, he heard Young, drunk again, screaming at his family and threatening his wife and daughter, Emerritta, who lay ill. Emerritta recalled that her father was "taking oaths and calling members of the family bad names." He said that he was "the damndest blood thirstiest creature that ever lived" and that he "longed for someone's blood." When his wife asked him to stop for his daughter's sake, he said "he didnt care a God damn" what she or the rest of the family wanted. He complained of the doctor's bills and called Emerritta "vulgar names." He then kicked a kettle off the stove and onto his wife.

When Bishop arrived, Young ordered him out, telling him "he had a right to shoot any one that came that he didn't want should come, & the law would bear him out in it." He seized his gun and raised it to Bishop's head, saying that he "shot a God Damned rooster through the neck this morning" and promising to shoot Bishop "in the same place." Lowering the gun, Young walked into the next room. Mrs. Young told Bishop he should leave, but he refused while the family was in danger, telling her, "Law, I ain't afraid of him. He hain't courage enough to shoot any one." Mrs. Young then heard her husband throwing chairs around the front room. When Bishop went to investigate he was met by a shotgun blast to the face.[53]

The murders and attempted murders of the years examined in this study did not form a single, monolithic pattern, with the exception that the victims were almost invariably wives or people who came to their aid. Each was the consequence of a unique chain of events. But some motifs emerge from the data that suggest reasons for the increased risk of marital homicide in northern New England.

First, poor people who drank tended to be, by the 1830s, more isolated socially than they had been earlier, especially if they lived in the rough neighborhoods that had developed in northern New England's larger towns. Such neighborhoods as "Hayti" in Rutland and "Water Street" in Burlington arose in part because of a decline in independent proprietorship. During this era, it

SPOUSAL MURDER IN NORTHERN NEW ENGLAND, 1776–1865

often took couples longer to accumulate the capital necessary to establish their own shops, farms, or households; more couples in their thirties and early forties lived as renters and laborers. Some couples responded by working harder, saving more, drinking less, having fewer children, and joining churches whose members enjoyed a reputation for reliability, which gave them greater access to credit and good jobs. Others, however, were unwilling or unable to take that course, especially if one or both partners drank heavily.[54]

Before the 1820s, the drinking poor were not highly visible or concentrated. Most northern New Englanders drank heavily on weekends and holidays, and jobs were plentiful in the frontier economy. Forests needed cutting; land had to be cleared. But as these jobs disappeared and drinking in general declined, the drinking poor came to live in run-down neighborhoods in larger towns, where rents were cheap, taverns plentiful, day labor in greater demand, and neighbors less intrusive or judgmental. These neighborhoods gave many of their inhabitants an economic boost; for others, they proved to be, quite literally, dead ends.

Newspaper accounts of murders in these neighborhoods were spare and contemptuous, so we can only guess at the motives, immediate and remote, for husbands in these neighborhoods to kill their wives. In 1838, Henry Damon, a white resident of Rutland's "Hayti," a mixed-race neighborhood, cut his wife Sophia's throat with a razor while she lay in bed. The Damons lived with several unrelated couples in a house of poor reputation and had quarreled that evening about visitors there. Henry may have been jealous; his wife had been indicted five years earlier for adultery. When Sophia Damon cried out for help, however, she received none. A couple that "belonged to the house" lay in another bed in the same room at the time of the assault; the husband hid under the covers, while the wife fled. A woman in an adjacent room jumped out of a window and ran when she heard the "racket."[55] People in "Hayti," where bloody fights and arrests were common, had learned it was safer not to get involved in neighbors' quarrels.

Nor did Catherine Cavanaugh receive help when her "notorious" husband, Sandy, beat her and slashed her to death with a jackknife in her bed in January 1862. They lived in a basement apartment in a tenement on Burlington's Water Street, a place infamous "for its brawls." The Cavanaughs quarreled frequently, and Sandy had once tried to shoot his wife. Tenement residents knew the Cavanaughs were arguing and drunk that night. Mrs. Young heard a scream "together with a blow, as if made by something flat striking against some part of the person protected by clothing." But neither she nor the other lodgers in the house dared intervene.[56]

Most wife-murderers were not abjectly poor, however, and many lived among neighbors who worked to prevent violence, even when they were not asked to intervene. Middle-class husbands could be demoralized, and middle-class marriages could disintegrate. Abusers may have sensed that they had failed in society's eyes, in their spouse's, and in their own.

One source of middle-class frustration was the rising expectations of a northern New England society that by midcentury was, in general, prosperous and temperate. Having a house was no longer enough—it had to be a nice house. Working hard was no longer enough—one's labor had to confer monetary and social rewards. Being a good provider was no longer enough—a husband had to be unfailingly pleasant, sober, and respectable. By the late 1840s and 1850s, even respectability was not enough in many social circles—a man had to be a person of sentiment: sympathetic, affectionate, and compassionate, especially toward members of his family.[57]

These expectations crippled marriages, especially if a sense of failure drove a husband to drink. Drinking made failure more certain: it wasted money, alienated friends and relatives, damaged reputations, and upset households' emotional balance. In these circumstances, husbands' violence against wives and neighbors who came to their aid became more probable. A wife who pointed to her husband's limitations, even with silence, was a thorn in his side; a neighbor who interceded when she was beaten or threatened was a reminder of humiliation. Murderous men were failures.

Wives' tactics for reforming faltering husbands varied. Some tried confrontation, ridicule, and violence, both retaliatory and anticipatory—the same tactics discontented wives favored after the Revolution, when two-fifths of all husbands petitioning for divorce complained of emotional and physical abuse (Table 4–4). But such tactics had fallen out of favor by the 1830s and 1840s. Husbands' complaints of intolerable severity dropped to less than 10 percent of all complaints (Tables 4–3 and 4–4). Overall, discontented wives became less aggressive, verbally and physically, and sought other means of reforming their husbands' behavior. Nancy Bean, who believed it "her duty . . . to toil and suffer" with her husband, "cleaved" to him, hoping the sight of her bruised body would excite feelings of pity and remorse. Mrs. Young kept her children out of her husband's way when he was on one of his "trains," but she also pleaded with him, asking "Brewster, why do you do so?"[58] Abused wives asked their husbands to search their souls and feel compassion for those they hurt, and tried to make their husbands feel guilty or ashamed. And they refused to answer abuse with abuse.

By the 1830s, many abused wives embraced evangelical and sentimental religion and believed it their duty (and best hope) to minister to their husbands. And many embraced the cults of respectability and domesticity, which encouraged women to be aggressive morally and spiritually, but not physically. It is tempting to blame these movements for the deaths of women who stayed too long in abusive marriages and refused to fight, but it can also be argued that these religious and cultural crusades may have reduced domestic violence, especially nonlethal violence, by persuading wives to leave husbands they considered morally or spiritually flawed. The proportion of husbands who complained of desertion in divorce suits rose from less than a third to half (Tables 4–3 and 4–4). In any case, wives' physical and verbal aggression did not always prevent homicide. Women who stood up to their husbands as forcefully as any post-Revolutionary wife were murdered, too.

The shift from violent to nonviolent tactics probably contributed less to the tenfold increase in wife-murders than the sense of failure that gripped many husbands. Violent tactics may have succeeded in some marriages, nonviolent tactics in others. But when either failed, these attempts to reform almost always made matters worse. Failed husbands were dangerous when challenged in any way.

William Barnet, a fifty-seven-year-old Protestant immigrant from England, worked as a cattle farrier and privy cleaner. His wife, Ann, a thirty-five-year-old Irish Catholic from Canada, took in needlework and made cushions. Together they worked their way up from Water Street to a better neighborhood in Burlington, Vermont, where they had a house to themselves. But their industry did not win them respectability. Ann's employer testified at William's hearing that Ann was "not a common woman," indicating that many people might have thought otherwise. William's occupation was a problem, as was the condition of their home, "an old wooden building" on Skinner Street, which was all they could afford. A greater problem, however, was that all their acquaintances knew they drank and quarreled. In 1858, on Water Street, they had had a row that made the newspapers. William had threatened Ann with a knife, which she wrenched from his hand, whereupon he hit her with a flatiron and laid her skull open. He had been prosecuted and publicly humiliated for the assault.

Before the murder, the Barnets' new neighbors on Skinner Street recognized the couple's unhappiness and kept a close watch on them. Ann appeared distracted and disheveled in the weeks before her death in August 1862, but she stayed sober and kept working. On the fatal day, William pressed her employer for her pay and used it to buy whiskey and tobacco for himself. That purchase may have set off the quarrel that G. N. Isaiah heard between nine and ten o'-clock that evening, when he knocked on the door to see if everything was all right. The couple appeared to assure him they were fine. But William's waste of her hard-earned money doubtless infuriated Ann; they fought, and by midnight she lay dead, her throat cut with a rusty butcher knife.[59]

Similar circumstances lay behind Brewster Young's assaults on his family and his aforementioned murder of Ralph Bishop. Young was a hardworking man in his fifties who was affable when sober. He had a respected wife, promising children, and many friends. He was not, however, as prosperous as he thought he deserved to be, and was hard pressed to raise five children on his modest farm. He grew bitter when neighbors testified against him in a civil case about a debt. He vowed he would get even with them and with his wife, who reproached him, albeit gingerly, for his drinking and threats. He promised to grind her "as fine as mince meat." Matters grew worse when his daughter Emerritta took sick and the doctor's bills mounted. Young compounded his family's financial problems by destroying furniture and dishes in fits of frustration and anger. "When he would throw them round he would say, 'there goes them, now make all out of that you can.' He said what things he brake up & destroyed the family would have to go without & suffer for the want of them." Nor could he repair his deteriorating house, with its "rotten shingles." It appears that Young felt that if he suffered, his family should suffer, especially if its members dared criticize him.

Young's eldest son, Woodbury, kept his father's violence in check. But when Woodbury joined the Union Army in 1861, the management of his father and protection of the family fell to Woodbury's best friend, Ralph Bishop. Ralph and Woodbury were so close that they had a system of signals to summon one to the other's house if there was trouble. Ralph was a favorite of Woodbury's mother, brother, and sisters, the youngest of whom was thirteen. Brewster Young, however, hated Bishop, whom he always referred to as the "bobbin Nigger." He had threatened him, as well as his wife and children, throughout the year before the murder; he claimed Bishop had started the feud when he threw Young's axe into the river in 1861.

What really upset Young, however, was the intimacy between Bishop and his family. Woodbury sent long letters about the war to Bishop, who brought them to Mrs. Young to read. The younger children loved Bishop, too. Young claimed Bishop had told him he "had *fucked* every *tuppance* in the house, 'even the thing I live with,'" although no evidence supports his statement that Bishop said anything so crude, nor that he showed more than a brotherly interest in Young's daughters. The family turned to Bishop, not Brewster, for protection or consolation. Bishop had become the emotional *pater familias* of a household that longed for a sentimental father. Young, however, as patriarch, threatened to kill Bishop if he "should come to the house to help the family." He swore to be "damned if I won't rule my shingles while I occupy them." Young alienated his family, and ironically considered himself the victim of disloyalty. He told a friend with whom he shared a drink that he wished Woodbury would get killed in the war so that he would never know the pain of having a family turn against him. "I hope he will get killed instantly. I don't want to have him suffer as I do."

As Emerritta's illness lingered, Young came unstrung. "I don't care a God damn, the quicker she dies, the better," he shouted. Edney, his sixteen-year-old son, told him to stop slamming the door against her bed or "you will kill my sister." Young forbade further visits from the doctor and threatened to shoot Edney if he went for help, but Edney defied him and, encouraged by his mother, ran for the doctor.

It is little wonder that Bishop lost his life when he arrived to support what Young interpreted as a family mutiny. In Young's view, Bishop had tried to supplant him as head of the family. Bishop had not even been summoned; he just walked in as if he owned the place. "You God Damned Bobbin Nigger, you, you came over here on your own account this time," Young shouted when he first saw Bishop. "I have taken pains to see if there was any sign hung out, and there ain't any."[60] Young had lost control of his finances and his family. In his mind, another man was taking over his house, and he was not about to stand for it. Young demonstrates how rising middle-class expectations could feed feelings of failure, and thus contribute to violence.

By midcentury, there was one notable change in spouse murder patterns. Whereas separation or divorce never led to murder in the post-Revolutionary era, in the 1840s and 1850s murders sometimes occurred as abused spouses left troubled marriages, or even after they had left. Each of these murderers or would-be murderers was sober and legally sane at the time of the assault. Each willfully attacked his wife after his marriage was irretrievably broken; none hid or denied his crime. Prosecutors thus had little trouble determining the facts in these cases. In cases for which evidence of the couple's relationship before the murder has survived, the wives had been victims of chronic abuse.

These murders form a pattern that has persisted in northern New England to the present. Legal support for abused spouses who sought separations or divorces saved lives, but threatened the husbands' authority. This support allowed women to walk away from abusive marriages with their children, their property, and some measure of dignity. By the 1840s, violent husbands seem to have recognized these consequences. Henry Leader had already agreed to give his estranged wife Lucinda a share of their property when he tried to kill her. Bradbury Ferguson had also said he would give his wife Eliza Ann a divorce before he murdered her.[61] These men had little hope of gaining anything in court.

Hopelessness may have bred a dangerous fatalism in husbands who had expected their wives' service and obedience but had failed to win either. They may have resigned themselves to their crimes and punishments because they had lost everything that, in their eyes, made them true men. Perhaps their wives were more resolute and defiant on the eve of their emancipation from their troubled marriages. If so, it was a fatal combination.

Marital homicides nonetheless remained rare in northern New England. Murders increased in the 1830s through the Civil War and beyond, but forces that worked against homicide in this region were still powerful. Intervention by neighbors and relatives, the commitment of the mentally ill, public condemnation of marital violence, and the acceptance of separation and divorce did much to dampen and restrain deadly passions. So did northern New England's unique social order, grounded in universal literacy and the household economy, which encouraged economic interdependence and mutual regard among spouses.

Notes

1. I would like to thank Norma Basch, Irene Brown, Joan Cashin, and Tamara Thornton for their comments and helpful suggestions. Murray A. Straus, Richard J. Gelles, and Suzanne K. Steinmetz, *Behind Closed Doors: Violence in the American Family* (Garden City, NY, 1980); Richard J. Gelles, *The Violent Home* (Newbury Park, CA, updated ed., 1987); and Richard J. Gelles and Murray A. Straus, *Intimate Violence: The Causes and Consequences of Abuse in the American Family* (New York, 1988).

2. The best sources for studying homicides in New Hampshire and Vermont are court and coroner records, located in county courthouses [hereafter, County Court: CC; County Court of Common Pleas: CCCP; Superior Court: SC; Superior Court of Judicature: SCJ; Records: R]. The records of Hillsboro, Rockingham, and Strafford counties (NH) are in the New Hampshire State Archives, Concord, NH [NHSA]; those of Addison County, VT, in the Vermont State Archives, Montpelier, VT [VSA]; some records of Chittenden County, VT, are in the Special Collections of the University of Vermont Library [UVL-SC]. Records of the Council of Safety, July 1777 to March 1778 in E. P. Walton, ed., *Records of the Council of Safety and Governor and Council of the State of Vermont, to Which Are Prefixed the Records of the General Conventions from July 1775 to December 1777* (Montpelier, 1873), 1:130–229. Newspapers include: *Burlington Free Press*, 1822–1865; *Farmer's Cabinet* (Amherst, NH), 1803–1820; *Farmer's Museum* (Walpole, NH), 1793–1810; *New Hampshire Gazette* (Portsmouth), 1776–1820; *New Hampshire Patriot* (Concord), 1818–1865; *Rutland Herald*, 1792–1865; *Vermont Gazette* (Bennington) [various titles], 1783–1820. Population estimates used for homicide rates from 1790 to 1865 from the United States Census and from *Historical Statistics of the United States, Colonial Times to 1970* (Washington, D.C., 1975), 1:31, 35. Population estimates from Jay Mack Holbrook, *New Hampshire 1732 Census* (Oxford, MA, 1981), 10; and Holbrook, *Vermont 1771 Census* (Oxford, MA, 1982), xxi.

3. Elizabeth Pleck, *Domestic Tyranny: The Making of Social Policy against Family Violence from Colonial Times to the Present* (New York, 1987), 4, 19–20, reports a gross rate of 0.1 husband-wife murders per 100,000 persons per year in seventeenth-century Massachusetts Bay and Plymouth colonies. Rates may have dropped by the 1690s and early 1700s, possibly approximating northern New England's post-Revolutionary rates. Wife-murder also surged in the late 1820s beyond New England. Martin Wiener of Rice University and Kenneth Wheeler of Ohio State University have found similar patterns in England and in Ohio in the late 1820s (personal correspondence with the author).

4. Marital homicide patterns differed historically from those of other homicides, which did not increase for teens and adults in the 1830s and 1840s; when other homicides soared in the 1850s and 1860s, the marital homicide rate was steady.

89

5. *Parker v. Parker*, Vermont Supreme Court Records (hereafter VSCR) (Windsor), 5:283, Clerk's Office, Windsor County SC, Woodstock, VT; *Salisbury v. Salisbury, David v. David, Jennison v. Jennison, Avery v. Avery*, VSCR (Rutland), 106:244, 262, 270, 272, Rutland County SC, Rutland, VT. Standards for proof were high in divorce cases sought for cruelty or adultery in Vermont and New Hampshire in the eighteenth and early nineteenth centuries, VSCR (Rutland), 106:244, 261–272. While charges in unsuccessful divorce petitions were not necessarily false, those in successful ones were most likely true.

6. By the 1840s, the Vermont Supreme Court supported divorce for desertion if one spouse refused to live with and/or support the other financially. Petitioners did not have to discuss other problems unless they wanted to win property or child custody in a contested divorce. Still, the change in husbands' divorce petitions (which did not occur in wives') may have signalled a drop in nonlethal female domestic violence. By 1862–1867, one in every eighteen Vermont marriages ended in divorce. Intolerable severity was the primary ground for one in every four divorces. *Tenth Annual Report of the Registrar of Vital Statistics of Vermont, 1866* (Montpelier, 1867), 86–87.

7. In Rockingham County, 1785–1815, two husbands accused of violence responded with similar charges; testimony revealed that violence was mutual in both cases. The Superior Court found in favor of the wives, believing that male violence posed a greater threat. New Hampshire SCJR (Rockingham), files 14012, 14064, 14373, 15395, NHSA; 19 of 47 female petitioners cited extreme physical cruelty as a ground for divorce.

8. *Seventh Annual Report of the Registrar of Vitals Statistics of New Hampshire . . . 1886* (Manchester, 1888), 47. Exactly 500 of 1575 divorces during these years were granted for cruelty (486), treatment injurious to health (12), or treatment injurious to reason (2). Returns do not reveal whether violence was cited in other divorce petitions, including the 130 divorces (8 percent) granted for habitual drunkenness. By 1882–1886, there was one divorce for every eleven marriages in New Hampshire and one divorce for cruelty for every thirty-three, *Seventh Annual Report of the Registrar of Vital Statistics*, 47. New Hampshire's returns do not reveal the number of petitions in which violence was a contributing factor.

9. *Ashley v. Ashley*, 9/1799, VSCR (Windsor), 2:109; *Lusk v. Lusk,* 8/1802, VSCR (Windsor), 2:363; *Hoisington v. Hoisington*, 8/1802, VSCR (Windsor), 2:369; *Powell v. Powell*, 8/1803, VSCR (Windsor), 2:421; *Bates v. Bates*, 8/1803, VSCR (Windsor), 2:426.

10. *Tilden v. Tilden*, 8/1803, VSCR (Windsor), 2:429.

11. New Hampshire SCJR (Rockingham), 6:419; file 15395.

12. New Hampshire SCJR (Rockingham), 6:123, 189; files 14012, 14373, 14064.

13. Coroner's inquest on Sarah Wallingford, 5/5/1815, New Hampshire SCJR Case Files (Strafford), NHSA; Janet Colaizzi, "Predicting Dangerousness: Psychiatric Ideas in the United States, 1800–1983" (Ph.D. diss., Ohio State University, 1983), 32, 256–258, 333–334.

14. *Rutland Herald*, 8/20/1792 and 8/27/1792; Old VSCR Files, 1626, Clerk's Office, Rutland County SC.

15. *Farmer's Museum*, 5/5/1800.

16. Gerald N. Grob, *The Mad Among Us: A History of the Care of America's Mentally Ill* (New York, 1994), 5–21; *Woodstock Observer*, 6/30/1829; 10/19/1830; *New Hampshire Patriot*, 6/29/1829; *Farmer's Museum*, 4/19/1803; 4/27/1805; 5/4/1805; *Farmer's Cabinet*, 6/11/1805.

Randolph A. Roth

17. "Seventh Annual Report of the Trustees of the Vermont Asylum for the Insane" (1843), *Journal of the Senate of the State of Vermont, October Session, 1843* (Montpelier, 1844), 65; *Annual Report of the New Hampshire Asylum for the Insane*, 2nd. ed. (1845), 9; "Second Annual Report of the Trustees of the Vermont Asylum for the Insane" (1838), *Journal of the Senate of the State of Vermont, October Session, 1838* (Montpelier, 1839), xi; "Third Annual Report of the Trustees of the Vermont Asylum for the Insane" (1839), *Journal of the Senate of the State of Vermont, October Session, 1839* (Montpelier, 1840), xlii–xliii; *Annual Report of the New Hampshire Asylum for the Insane* (1851), 25–26.

18. Gerald N. Grob, *Mental Institutions in America: Social Policy to 1875* (New York, 1973), 195, 245, 347–351.

19. Grob, *Mental Institutions in America*, 383, 392, 245. New Hampshire and Vermont asylums accepted all patients deemed mentally ill, but did little to protect children against mothers who suffered from depression or "melancholy"; physicians did not appreciate the threat depressed mothers posed to themselves or their children. By the 1870s, 7 percent of men and 2.5 percent of women in northern New England asylums (about ten persons per year) were admitted for "homicidal" tendencies, "Annual Reports of the Trustees of the New Hampshire Asylum for the Insane, 1872–1880" and "Biennial Reports of the Officers of the Vermont Asylum for the Insane, 1872–1880," in Vermont Legislative Documents and Official Reports, 1873/4–1879/80.

20. "Biennial Report of the Commissioners of the Insane for the State of Vermont, 1875–1876," Vermont Legislative Documents and Official Reports, 1876 (Rutland, 1876), 26–27.

21. "Fourth Annual Report of the Trustees of the Vermont Asylum for the Insane" (1840), *Journal of the House of Representatives of the State of Vermont, October Session, 1840* (Montpelier, 1840), xliv; Annual Report of the New Hampshire Asylum for the Insane (1847), 22–23; "Biennial Report of the Commissioners of the Insane for the State of Vermont, 1875–1876," 12–13.

22. *Farmer's Museum*, 9/7/1805; New Hampshire SCJR (Grafton), 9:538, Grafton County Courthouse, Woodsville, New Hampshire; *Post-Boy*, 11/11/1806; VSCR (Windsor), 3:28.

23. Inquest on Eliza Ferguson, Rockingham CCCP Case Files, 10/1840, B19140; C. E. Potter, *Report on the Trial of Bradbury Ferguson, on an Indictment of the Murder of Mrs. Eliza Ann Ferguson* (Concord, NH, 1841); Inquest on Nancy Smart, Merrimack CCCP Case Files, 2/1837 Term, Merrimack County Courthouse, Concord, New Hampshire.

24. T. M. Adams, *Prices Paid by Vermont Farmers for Goods and Services and Received by Them for Farm Products, 1790–1940; Wages of Vermont Farm Labor, 1780–1940*, Bulletin 507, University of Vermont and State Agricultural College, Vermont Agricultural Experiment Station (Burlington, 1944), 87–88.

25. *State v. Hosmer*, 12/1827, Windsor CCR, 14:179; *State v. Curtis*, 12/1827, 14:193; *State v. Pierce*, 5/1839, 16:203; *State v. Johnson*, 12/1860, Second Series, 1:596; *State v. Johnson*, 12/1856, Windsor CCR, Second Series, 1:538; *Hosmer v. Hosmer*, 2/1827, VSCR (Windsor), 5:34; *Curtis v. Curtis*, 2/1829, 5:67; *Pierce v. Pierce*, 2/1840, 7:7; VSCR, Divorces (Windsor), 2:41–43. Also VSCR, Divorces (Windsor), 1:97, 183; Windsor CCR, Second Series, 1:161, 401.

26. Although justices used their positions creatively to mitigate assault in families, see Stephanie Cole, "Keeping the Peace: Domestic Assault and Private Prosecution in Antebellum Baltimore," in this volume.

27. Sheldon S. Cohen, "The Broken Bond: Divorce in Providence County, 1749–1809," *Rhode Island History* 44 (1985): 67–79; Cohen, "'To Parts of the World Unknown': The Circumstances of Divorce in Connecticut, 1750–1797," *Canadian Review of American Studies* 11 (1980): 275–293; Cohen, "What Man Hath Put Asunder: Divorce in New Hampshire, 1681–1784," *Historical New Hampshire* 41 (1986): 118–141; Nancy F. Cott, "Divorce and the Changing Status of Women in Eighteenth-Century Massachusetts," *William and Mary Quarterly* 33 (1976): 586–614; Cornelia Hughes Dayton, *Women Before the Bar: Gender, Law, and Society in Connecticut, 1639–1789* (Chapel Hill, NC, 1995), 105–156; Lyle Koehler, *Search for Power: The "Weaker Sex" in Seventeenth-Century New England* (Urbana, IL, 1980), 49–50, 152–153, 320–321, 362–363, 453–439.

28. Betty Bandel, "What the Good Laws of Man Hath Put Asunder," *Vermont History* 46 (1978): 222–223; Henry Harrison Metcalf, *Laws of New Hampshire: First Constitutional Period, 1784–1792* (Concord, NH, 1916), 5:732–733.

29. *New Hampshire Patriot*, 3/15/1824; 5/29/1837; *Burlington Free Press*, 2/9/1863.

30. *Burlington Free Press*, 2/18/1859; *Vermont Watchman and Gazette*, 1/6/1829; *Rutland Herald*, 3/3/1859.

31. Inquest on Eliza Ann Ferguson, Rockingham CCCP Case Files, 10/1840, B19140; Potter, *Trial of Bradbury Ferguson*, 19–24; *State v. Corey*, New Hampshire SCJR (Cheshire), 10/1830, 14:427–428, Cheshire County Courthouse, Keene, New Hampshire; *New Hampshire Patriot*, 6/29/1829; *Woodstock Observer*, 6/30/1829; Joel Parker, *Report of the Trial of Daniel H. Corey, on an Indictment for the Murder of Mrs. Matilda Nash* (Newport, 1830).

32. Testimony of Sheldon Loggins, Ellen Lockwood, Webster Lockwood, Orpha Lockwood, Julia Loggins, Alma Loggins, *Allen v. Allen*, Chittenden CCR, 12/1852, UVL-SC, Box 39, Divorces.

33. *Vermont Watchman and Gazette*, 6/6/1829; New Hampshire SCJ Case Files (Rockingham), 14064, 15395; testimony of Jesse Coy, William Ellis, Levi Merriman, *Hunt v. Hunt*, VSC files (Windham), 8/1812 Term, Clerk's Office, Windham County SC, Box 20; testimony of Mathew Huston and Abigail Huston, *Kenyon v. Kenyon*, Chittenden CCR, 1/1843, UVL-SC, Box 38, Divorces.

34. Ann Taves, ed., *Religion and Domestic Violence in Early New England: The Memoirs of Abigail Abbot Bailey* (Bloomington, IN, 1989), 20–24; *State v. Bean*, Rockingham CCCP Case Files, 9/1841, 19516 and 19732.

35. William J. Rorabaugh, *The Alcoholic Republic* (New York, 1979), 7–10, 19–20, 149–152; Randolph A. Roth, *The Democratic Dilemma: Religion, Reform, and the Social Order in the Connecticut River Valley of Vermont, 1791–1850* (New York, 1987), 48–49, 350 n54; Michael A. Bellesiles, "The Origins of Gun Culture in the United States, 1760–1865," *Journal of American History* 83 (1996): 427. Only one spouse in this study was murdered with a gun, and none with a handgun. The weapons of choice—clubs, tools, knives, poison, and physical force—were always readily available.

36. Laurel Thatcher Ulrich, "Deputy Husbands," in *Good Wives: Image and Reality in the Lives of Women in Northern New England, 1650–1750* (New York, 1982), 35–50; Ulrich, "Wheels, Looms, and the Gender Division of Labor in Eighteenth-Century New England," *William and Mary Quarterly* 55 (1998): 3–38; Carol Berkin, *First Generations: Women in Colonial America* (New York, 1996), 26–33.

37. John J. McCusker and Russell R. Menard, *The Economy of British North America, 1607–1789* (Chapel Hill, NC, 1985), 91–111, 258–276.

38. Roth, *The Democratic Dilemma*, 286–288.

39. William J. Gilmore, *Reading Becomes a Necessity of Life: Material and Cultural Life in Rural New England, 1780–1835* (Knoxville, TN, 1989), 114–134.

40. Bandel, "What the Good Laws of Man Hath Put Asunder," 221–233.

41. *Vermont Gazette*, 1/2/1796; *Vermont Republican*, 9/4/1815, quoted in Bandel, "What the Good Laws of Man Hath Put Asunder."

42. Bandel, "What the Good Laws of Man Hath Put Asunder."

43. *Vermont Gazette*, 3/6/1809.

44. Old VSC Files, 1921, 2209, 3075.

45. Testimony of Lanson Brooks, Almira Whitney, Patty Durham, *Brooks v. Brooks*, VSC files (Windham), 8/1813 Term, Box 20; *Burlington Free Press*, 6/12/1846.

46. *New Hampshire Patriot*, 1/9/1837.

47. *Burlington Free Press*, 6/12/1846; Old VSC files, 2209.

48. *New Hampshire Patriot*, 12/15/1828; *Woodstock Observer*, 5/19/1829.

49. *New Hampshire Patriot*, 3/5/1841; *Burlington Free Press*, 11/19/1841; Ann Taves, ed., *Religion and Domestic Violence*, 20–24; *State v. Richard Bean*, New Hampshire SCJR (Rockingham), 9/1841, files 19516 and 19732; Inquest on Sylvia Powell, Franklin CCR, Q: 155, Clerk's Office, Franklin County SC, St. Albans, VT.; *Vermont Phoenix* (Brattleboro), 9/19/1842.

50. *State v. Dow*, Rockingham CCCP Case Files, 9/1852, C1831; *New Hampshire Patriot*, 7/21/1852; *State v. Tebbetts*, Rockingham CCCP Case Files, 2/1854, F2567 and F2598; *New Hampshire Patriot*, 11/2/1853; *State v. Leader*, Cheshire CCCPR, 3/1857, 16:70; *New Hampshire Patriot*, 3/18/1857.

51. *Rutland Herald*, 6/30/1835.

52. *Keene Sentinel* (New Hampshire), 4/20/1848; Inquest on Hugh Pindar, Rockingham CCCP Case Files, C3292; *State v. Gleason*, Washington CCR, 3/1859 Term, Clerk's Office, Washington County SC, Montpelier, VT; *Rutland Weekly Herald*, 3/3/1859.

53. Testimony of Emerritta C. Young, *State v. Young*, Grafton CCCP Case Files, 9/1863 Term.

54. Roth, *Democratic Dilemma*, 117–141, 220–246, 265–279.

55. *State v. Damon*, Rutland CCR, Case Files, 4/1833, Clerk's Office, Rutland County SC; *State v. Damon*, Rutland CCR, 9/1839, 27:124; *Rutland Herald*, 10/9/1838.

56. *Burlington Free Press*, 1/9–10/1862; *Rutland Herald*, 1/11/1862; Chittenden CCR, File 71, 9/1862 Term; 27: 435, Clerk's Office, Chittenden County SC, Burlington, VT.

57. Richard L. Bushman, *The Refinement of America: Persons, Houses, Cities* (New York, 1992); Jack Larkin, *The Reshaping of Everyday Life, 1790–1840* (New York, 1988); Roth, *Democratic Dilemma*, 284–290.

58. *State v. Bean*, Rockingham CCCP Case Files, 9/1841, 19516, 19732; Testimony of Emerritta C. Young, *State v. Young*.

59. *Burlington Free Press*, 8/28/1862; Chittenden CCR, 9/1862 Term, File 66; and 27:441.

60. Testimony of Emerritta C. Young, Lauretta A. Young, Georger D. Cushman, Zacariah C. Ash, Darius George, Rebecca B. Young, Sabin Ash, Levi Parker, Orvis L. Brown, Jonathan Corey, *State v. Young*.

61. *State v. Leader*, Cheshire CCCPR, 3/1857, 16:70; *New Hampshire Patriot*, 3/18/1857; Inquest on Eliza Ann Ferguson, Rockingham CCCP Case Files, 10/1840, B19140.

five

"MY MIND IS TO DROWN YOU AND LEAVE YOU BEHIND"

"Omie Wise," Intimate Violence, and Masculinity

Edward E. Baptist

> She got up behind him and away they did go,
> They rode till they came where deep waters did flow.
> "Now Omie, poor Omie, I'll tell you my mind,
> My mind is to drown you and leave you behind."
> "O, pity your infant and spare me my life,
> And let me go rejected and not be your wife."
> But he kicked her and cuffed her, until she could not stand,
> And then he drowned little Omie below the mill dam.[1]

To a modern listener, the ballad "Omie Wise" seems to float suspended in a timeless past. Songs like "Omie Wise," from "The Banks of the Ohio" to "Tom Dula" to "Little Ellen Smith," all murder ballads from the white South, fit into a template that regards intimate violence as an expected behavior.[2] Images of class, gender, race, and region tie Southern "redneck" men to atavistic, violent, even lethal misogyny in our perceptions.

Much of the historiography of antebellum Southern masculinity could support this interpretation. In the pre–Civil War South, law and the culture of honor demanded that white males establish dominance over women. Mastery was essential to manhood and honor. Only dishonorable men failed to regulate members of their households, whether enslaved blacks, white children, or white women.[3] But while culture permitted men to use violence to control women, it also set limits to that violence, enforcing them through communal condemnation or attacks on men who went too far. Men who killed white dependents, especially their wives, could meet a gruesome retribution in the tar, rough music, and humiliation of the charivari, or even death by lynching.[4] Cultural historians, therefore, might understand the murder ballad as a warning (as some have interpreted "Omie Wise") to white men not to go too far in their prescribed violence.

But ideas and attitudes about masculinity and honor have, of course, changed over time. Songs like "Omie Wise" have meant many things to their singers and listeners and were not always understood to say what they now seem to say. The ballad illustrates an ongoing dialogue between common white men about the contradictions between honor's prescriptions for behavior towards women and the economic and social limits yeomen faced in an increasingly commercialized South. Strong pressures pushed them both toward and away from violence against women.[5]

Murder ballads often reflect changing gender mores. Historians of domestic violence, for example, have identified an early eighteenth-century shift in popular English ballads. What began as fearsome portraits of women who killed their husbands become more concerned with husbands who made patriarchy less legitimate by slaughtering wives and lovers. Intimate violence could corrode implicit bargains of household patriarchy from within; increasing disruptions of lower-class life and economic change in eighteenth-century England already exerted tremendous external pressure on the same structures. Because many songs of the white South came from England, many that survived to be collected by folklorists of the late nineteenth and early twentieth centuries reflect this concern with the legitimation of patriarchal family structures.[6] Other songs, however, display a far more ambivalent relationship to family organization. Their depiction of the moral crime of lethal intimate violence contradicts the image of an unrelentingly violent antebellum South.

Certainly violence and violent crime pervaded the region. Duels and brawls were part of the culture of honor, the presence of slavery institutionalized assaults on one-third of the population, and in some areas, murder rates for white men by other whites reached those comparable to the postindustrial United States. Relatively few men, however, murdered their wives or female lovers.[7] But Southern yeomen sang many more songs like "Omie Wise" than those about the murders of poor white men by their peers in drunken brawls. Intimate murders and the ballads that immortalized them had a strong grip on nineteenth-century male imaginations.

The ballad of "Omie Wise" was based in fact. In 1807, the real Jonathan Lewis allegedly killed the real Naomi Wise in Randolph County, North Carolina. Court documents described his trial: the incident was described in an article written by a local clergyman, Braxton Craven, and published in a local newspaper in 1851 together with bits of local legend about the case, lyrics for the ballad, and Craven's own comments. The spare facts of the legal papers and Craven's florid tale together approximate the historical event. More importantly, they describe what nineteenth-century men *believed* had happened, a belief that shaped the various versions of the ballad.[8]

Randolph County, a rural district in the central North Carolina piedmont, resembled other parts of the Southern backcountry in the early nineteenth century (despite an early Quaker influence). Naomi or "Omie" Wise was an eighteen-year-old orphan bound as a servant and field hand to William Adams. Jonathan Lewis lived over the county line in Guilford, but clerked at a store in Asheboro (the Randolph County seat) owned by a prosperous merchant named Elliott. Jonathan had been born into the notoriously wild Lewis clan, which painted Randolph red with blood in a series of late eighteenth-century feuds. Lewis may have hoped to clerk his way into a more respectable world. A match with a penniless orphan would hardly help him rise, but his roving eye fastened upon Omie's beauty. He paid court to her, and soon she was pregnant. Many common whites in Randolph retained older sexual mores long after the nineteenth century, and premarital sex and pregnancy carried little stigma if a marriage eventually took place. But Lewis had no intention of marrying Naomi Wise, and his rumored involvement with her pregnancy soon impeded his courtship of Hattie Elliott, his employer's daughter. The latter match would have boosted him into the ranks of local notables. Legend holds that his mother especially favored such a marriage.[9]

Under competing pressures from his mother, his lover, and the woman he wished to wed, Jonathan Lewis headed down a murderous path. Naomi demanded to know what she would do when the baby was born; if she were still single, the Orphan's Court, which supervised her until the age of twenty-one could extend her term of service. According to Craven, Lewis promised to elope with her, and arranged a rendezvous that evening at a spring near her master's house. At sunset, Omie met him as he rode up, and mounted behind him. The couple rode through the night to the ford of the Deep River. Oral tradition, recorded by Craven and the ballad, claims that Omie soon realized that Jonathan had lied about going to a justice's house for a speedy wedding. When she asked him what he planned to do, he replied: "My mind is to drown you and leave you behind." The song says Omie begged for mercy, but Lewis tied her long skirts together above her head and pushed her into the water below the ford. As her knotted skirt dragged her under, Lewis dashed on horseback through the water to the opposite bank.[10]

Neighbors suspected Lewis as soon as Wise disappeared. When her body was discovered, a mob went to the Lewis settlement where Jonathan lived with his mother and carried him to the ramshackle Asheboro lockup twenty miles away. He languished in jail from April until autumn. During the October term of the circuit court, he faced indictment for "a charge of murder committed on a certain Omi Wise, found dead in the Deep River." The indictment suggested moving his trial to Guilford County, perhaps because of popular feeling against him in Randolph. But before facing trial, Lewis, "being a person of evil mind and wicked disposition," broke jail and escaped.[11]

Lewis was not captured until 1811. Court documents locate his arrest in Orange County, east of Randolph, while Craven's narrative places it in western Virginia or Kentucky. Whatever the truth, the murderer finally faced a jury. Here the records again disagree—Craven claims Lewis was acquitted of murder in Guilford County, while in the Randolph court documents he faced only the charge of breaking jail. Lewis remained in the Randolph county jail until 1813, when he left as a pauper, unable to pay either fees or bail.[12] He supposedly confessed his crime "on his deathbed." Some versions of the song suggest he confessed when a party of men took him from the courthouse and gave him a charivari-type shaming ritual. In one version of the ballad, Lewis says to his tormentors: "Go hang me or kill me/For I am the man/That drowned little Omie/Below the mill dam." The murderer had sinned against patriarchal responsibility, and only violent punishment could repair the legitimacy of white male dominance.

Lewis may have swung from a gallows or slunk into obscurity.[13] Despite the confusion surrounding the "true crime" of Omie Wise's murder, one fact stands out: common white men and women could not forget her death. Her murder was remembered locally in much detail, real and imaginary. But her memory traveled far beyond Randolph County, in large part because the details of the crime spoke to the fears and obsessions of men in the changing nineteenth-century South. The yeomen and women who created the song about Omie's murder carried it with them to frontiers south and west of North Carolina's piedmont. "Omie Wise" is the most widely diffused ballad from North Carolina—collectors have found it from Florida to Missouri.

The ballad of "Omie Wise" evolved in a constant dialogue between singers and listeners, opening a window onto the roles of gender, honor, and intimate violence in a changing world.[14] The precise course of its evolution between 1807 and the earliest known version of the ballad (Craven's 1851 lyrics) remains a mystery. The 1851 text substantially resembles later versions from various locations, however, and despite the song's wide diffusion most versions share several common elements, which were almost certainly present from the beginning.[15] For instance, all but three of the nineteen collected versions include a variant of the couplet "Little Omie, little Omie, I'll tell you my mind/My mind is to drown you and leave you behind." By 1851, singers and listeners had already shaped the main elements of "Omie Wise."[16]

"MY MIND IS TO DROWN YOU AND LEAVE YOU BEHIND"

As migrants and travelers took the song from one end of the South to the other, geographical and chronological diffusion created divergences. Tunes and words changed over time and space in a process of transformation generated by both error and improvisation. English ballad scholar Cecil Sharp, for instance, collected several versions of the ballad in the southern Appalachian mountains around 1900. His version A, from Hindman, Kentucky, calls the villain "James Luther" and inserts two verses about his capture, probably from a different folk ballad. On the other hand, version B, recorded on the other side of the Appalachians in North Carolina, calls the murderer "George Lewis," a commonly found transformation of "Jonathan Lewis." Version A is sung in the pentatonic mode; version B, with more modern musical influences, in the hexatonic. Conversations between musical generations and changes across space are inevitable parts of any folksong tradition.[17]

The ballad of "Omie Wise" also continued to evolve in its birthplace. Three local versions that did not contain the common structures of the sixteen in the main tradition (such as the customary couplet described above), told the same story. But they emphasize the local fame of Naomi Wise's beauty, and two claim her spirit still haunts the site of her murder, a persistent Randolph County legend. Finally, they emphasize Jonathan Lewis's deathbed confession. None of these elements appear as prominently in the main tradition. North Carolina folklore scholar A. P. Hudson concluded that they represent *rifacimento*, the retelling of a well-known story with added details from local tradition.[18]

Singers and listeners also heard "Omie Wise" as a response to an older tradition of murder ballads. The sixteen versions from the main tradition share certain structural similarities with an Anglo-American song called "The Miller's Apprentice," or "The Oxford Tragedy." This ballad migrated from England to the colonial South during the eighteenth century. Sharp collected versions of it in 1917 from Kentucky and Virginia, and it was doubtless well-known in Randolph County. The creator or creators of "Omie Wise" grafted local events onto the body of "The Miller's Apprentice," which conveniently detailed a similar story of a man killing his lover by throwing her into a river to drown.[19]

But the world in which "The Miller's Apprentice" made sense was disappearing when Jonathan Lewis cast Omie Wise into the Deep River. Crucial differences between the ballads show historical changes between the first song's eighteenth-century origins and its later transmutation in the context of the early republican backcountry. In "The Miller's Apprentice," the murderer is a white male bound laborer. By 1800, white male apprenticeship was disappearing in North Carolina. Like most white men, Jonathan Lewis was an independent laborer and struggled with the contradictions and requirements of that state. By the early nineteenth century, concepts of manhood rested on experiences of mastery that separated independent white men from political and economic dependents—women, children, and slaves. The economically independent yeoman could claim masculine authority; landless or propertyless white men struggled to win recognition as members of a patriarchal community. Lewis's contemporary, Brantley York, for example, born the son of a poor tenant in Randolph County in 1805, worked as a day laborer in his youth. To himself and others, this was a source of shame, although one employer's wife reassured him that he would one day be a master: "Brantley, you will not always be in the field working with negroes."[20]

Even poor white men who owned neither slaves nor land but who headed households could claim the authority of mastery over women. In turn, they asserted their right to participate as fellow masters in the community of white male citizens. Wealthy planters did not necessarily recognize such claims, which implied a degree of equality. Such disagreements were in many states the fodder of post-Revolutionary struggles over the meanings of politics and liberty. Yet by the late antebellum era, a variety of pressures from within and without Southern states had extended the vote—the symbol of citizenship—to all adult white men.[21]

Whatever conflicts the new ballad's original version invoked, by the middle of the nineteenth century the singers and listeners of "Omie Wise" discussed class and gender conflicts of a common white society under increasing tension. Men complained about two pressures. The first demanded they exert control over women, by violence if necessary, to demonstrate mastery in a world where men's ability to head an independent household grew more and more doubtful. Second, they were under a simultaneous injunction to restrain themselves from harming or even killing female dependents.

The question of mastery was grounded in changing economic realities. Although yeomen and even unpropertied white men had by 1851 achieved the vote in most states (North Carolina was one of the last to permit universal white male suffrage, eliminating some final restrictions in 1857), political participation was not the only measure of manhood. Even as the political sphere widened to accommodate virtually all white men, that of economic independence shrank. The early nineteenth century saw a nationwide quickening in market activity that transformed different areas of the United States in different ways and at different times.[22] The economy of the central piedmont became increasingly commercialized from the 1830s onward, and the construction of the North Carolina Railroad in the 1850s accelerated this development. In response to the new access to markets, Randolph County farmers increased wheat production several times over in the 1850s alone. At the same time, land prices more than doubled, putting even a tiny farm of a few dozen acres out of the reach of most landless white men. By 1851, when Braxton Craven recorded the lyrics of "Omie Wise," land ownership, a pillar of white male household mastery, was practically impossible for many local men. Women from poor white households often worked as day laborers for other white families in the

"MY MIND IS TO DROWN YOU AND LEAVE YOU BEHIND"

central piedmont, further undermining male claims to mastery. Of course, the ideal of household independence had been as much myth as reality during the colonial and early republican eras. Early Randolph County had contained a number of landless, even indigent, white men. But now even the myth was shattered. By the 1850s a growing group of landless poor whites gave the lie to visions of household independence for Randolph's white men.[23]

The changing economy of the piedmont threatened others besides landless white men. Most newly market-oriented farmers were nonslaveholding yeomen. Economic success would strengthen their claim to honor, which was not as weak as that of the landless poor white man, to be sure, but clearly below that of planters. The market, however, did not yield its benefits to them as easily as it did to wealthy men. Trade hardly provided equal opportunities; prices could fall, taxes could rise, interest rates could siphon profits and create land-stealing debt, and small producers rarely got the same prices or treatment as wealthy planters. Those who chose to seek their independence in migration to the frontier often found increased poverty, rather than independence, waiting for them. Speculators held most frontier land. Unlike migrant planters, yeomen and poor whites rarely possessed the capital—or family ties to men with capital—to participate in the commercial production of cotton. Common white men thus shaped and heard "Omie Wise" between 1807 and 1851 in the midst of economic transformations that intensified pressures upon the always-elusive ideal of household independence.[24]

For the nonslaveholding majority of Randolph County's white men, only white women were left as possible objects of mastery. At first glance, such mastery seemed inevitable. The cultural system of honor defined patriarchs as the unquestioned rulers of their households and all who lived within them. Women, children, and other dependents (including slaves and white servants like Omie Wise) owed such men deference and labor. White women also owed them sexual fidelity and reproductive power. Males who mastered such dependents were men; those who did not had failed at manhood—or so both law and custom contended. In many Southern states, including North Carolina, the law allowed husbands to correct unruly wives by whipping. In this case, legal guidelines reflected folk beliefs on the role of violence in marriage. Jonathan Lewis's uncle, Stephen Lewis, for example, "often whipped [his wife] with hobblerods." He was seen as a truly masculine, if not necessarily good, man. Chroniclers remembered the Lewises as "tall, broad, muscular and powerful men," the "lions of the county."[25]

The role of a patriarch offered and required power, but also imposed limits. While masters had to discipline subordinates, they were to refrain from causing serious injury or death (although in practice the protection of enslaved African-Americans was of little concern to most whites). Men who exercised violence illegitimately faced community retributive justice—or so claimed the

Edward E. Baptist

theory that justified lynching as justice by other means. Men with a modicum of honor could beat their wives, but in doing so they entered a realm of diminishing returns and ultimately risked their reputations; if honor permitted violence against women, it prohibited uxoricide. These inconsistent demands set up a tightrope of self-restraint on which men walked. Not all masters negotiated it well. As the character and actions of Jonathan Lewis suggest, the wider social valorization of violence made deadly force the first resort of some men faced with a challenge to their masculinity.[26]

Southern yeomen had become accustomed to identifying manhood with violence. Common white men fought in brawls, rather than the scripted duels of planters, but both believed in defending their reputations with force. The Lewis men in particular were known for their aggression; they "sought occasion to quarrel as a Yankee [seeks] gold dust in California." Lewis's father, Richard, reputedly killed his own brother Stephen when Stephen abused his own wife. Violent actions were familiar and ready parts of their social language, and those who interpreted "Omie Wise" understood its grammar clearly. The ubiquity of violence made uxoricide possible, despite harsh social condemnation of wife-murder.[27]

Even before commercialization increased threats to economic independence, contradictory demands for violence and restraint proved unbearable for many men. In almost every version of the song, Jonathan Lewis tells Omie "My mind is to drown you/And leave you behind."[28] By leaving his dead lover behind, and in her corpse the dead child he should have acknowledged, Jonathan cast away an embryonic household. Whether he had married Omie or Hattie Elliott, Jonathan would have had to assume the role of master. Though the role of master entailed privileges and status, it was fraught with responsibility and possibilities for humiliating failures. Lewis killed his lover and ran from a frightening role.

The ambivalence and fear men directed at women in the antebellum South grew not only from male self-doubt, but also from the refusal of many women to accede to total subordination. Common white women, like enslaved blacks, were often verbally "unruly" and resisted domination.[29] Some women, for instance, flaunted their adultery. More frequently, female rebellion was verbal. In yeoman communities, a female grammar of contentious invective that traced its origins to early modern England undermined the ideal of female subservience. Nor were wives the only women who subverted the monologue of absolute male authority: Jonathan Lewis's mother supposedly pressured him to marry his wealthy employer's daughter. An unruly or insistent woman could easily give the lie to a man's claim to dominance over his household.[30]

Women could deprive men of control, and thus of honor and manhood, in other ways as well. The code of honor conceived of sex as an act of male domination and performance; the facts of many cases contradicted this image. In

"MY MIND IS TO DROWN YOU AND LEAVE YOU BEHIND"

contrast to Victorian portrayals of nineteenth-century white womanhood, evidence suggests that, particularly among poor whites, female sexuality was more open and demanding than some Northern visitors or some Southern men could tolerate. A New York *Herald* reporter covering the 1868 trial of Tom Dula (the "Tom Dooley" of folk fame) found both the men and the women of the North Carolina piedmont shockingly non-Victorian: "A state of immorality unexampled in the history of any country exists among these people, and free-loveism prevails."[31] Perhaps even more threatening than the visibility of female sexuality was its frankness. Wives and lovers expected sexual satisfaction from their partners, and impotence was a failure of manhood. Thus, during sex itself, a paradigmatic male encounter with women, men could not always control female bodies—or their own.[32]

In the ballad, moreover, Naomi Wise's pregnancy suggests that men's control of reproduction was even more limited than their control of female sexuality. While some women used birth control or resorted to abortion, Omie obviously did not. Jonathan Lewis—or the ballad's listeners—might have seen Omie's pregnancy as the product of a female sexuality beyond male control. Certainly the child in her womb impeded Jonathan's marriage to Hattie Elliott, which in the limited world of Randolph County also blocked his chance for advancement. Omie's sexuality and reproductive power threatened Lewis's attempt to achieve economic independence and honor.[33]

The realm of male–female relationships was thus in practice much more than an institution dominated by uncomplicated male mastery. Marriage and its antecedents became volatile dialogues in which men could feel pushed to extremes. Becoming a man meant claiming a mastery that had to be constantly asserted and defended against unruly dependents. Male claims to dominance met female resistance, and common white men who hoped to find an elusive manhood on this idealized terrain ran into reality. This reality, and honor's contrasting requirements, trapped male listeners of "Omie Wise" in ambilavent positions. For them, as for Jonathan Lewis, leaving Omie behind in the Deep River may have meant an escape from the crushing burden of a mastery too heavy, for a host of reasons, for many men to carry.

Changing economic contexts and female resistance challenged male honor. In response, the multiple layers of meaning in "Omie Wise" undermined and altered the function of the murder ballad from a simple warning against killing women. Yet on the surface, singers attempted to present this sad story as an object lesson intended to shore up the edifice of patriarchy by warning young men and women away from Omie and Jonathan's errors. Clues about the performance and formal structure of the ballad reveal its ostensibly moral function. In the "objective style," often found in Southern white folk song, the

Edward E. Baptist

singer stands rigidly and attempts to maintain an expressionless face and vocal tone. He or she is merely the vessel through which the song and its communal truths flow.[34] The frequent appearance of the conventions of this style in extant versions of "Omie Wise" suggest that many singers tried to present the material as the objective truth of a male-dominated society. Collected versions of the ballad, for example, often began with the lines "Now come all you young people/And listen while I tell," signaling the song's function as a homiletic device for inculcating morals in the young.[35]

If the community spoke in "Omie Wise," however, it did not speak with the voice of certainty. Beneath the homiletic surface of the ballad, common white men voiced a growing and complex dissent. While we will never know everything about the performative context of "Omie Wise," especially between 1807 and 1851, clues to its contextual meanings remain embedded in the song's lyrics.[36] They reveal a dialogue about the strictures of gender and mastery: murmurs buzzing behind a facade of morality ostensibly warning young women against the lies of another Jon Lewis. As in many murder ballads, the appearance of one or more dissident voices undermines the "objective" style and highlights the conflict within "Omie Wise."[37]

Common white men most obviously voiced their dissent within the structure of murder ballads through the device of "narrator-switching." Sometimes the "Omie Wise" narrator is an outraged observer viewing the murder from outside. At other points, the narrator switches identities and becomes the murderer himself. For example, in a version sung by G. B. Grayson in 1927, the narrator begins by declaring his intention to "tell you all a story about Omie Wise/And how she was deluded by Jon Lewis's lies." He then controls the dialogue by markers such as "saying" to indicate when a character—Omie or Jonathan—rather than the narrator is speaking. But in the last two verses of the song, with no warning marker, the narrator speaks with the murderer's voice: "My name is Jon Lewis, my name I'll not deny,/I murdered my own true love, I'll never reach the sky/Go hang me or kill me, for I am the man,/Who murdered little Omie down by the mill dam."[38] The narrator, initially omniscient as the community's voice (with whom the listener identifies) transfers his identity and the listener's sympathy into the person of the murderer. The listener becomes complicit through the shift in voices.

Narrator-switching counteracts the objective style, which had placed the listener outside the tale and against the criminal. In a sudden movement, a narrative shift places both the listener and the singer within the murderer's soul. They cannot cast him out; they are guilty with him. They too have been pushed; if they have not in fact murdered women, they know why a man might do such a thing. "Poor Ellen Smith," another murder ballad originating in the North Carolina piedmont, uses a similar device. The narrator has heard

"MY MIND IS TO DROWN YOU AND LEAVE YOU BEHIND"

of "Poor Ellen Smith, and how she was found/Shot through the heart, lying cold on the ground" and prays that the murderer will be discovered. Then, without warning, the narrator becomes or is revealed as the murderer. He flees ahead of the bloodhounds loosed by a posse who "picked up their Winchesters, hunting me down/But I'd gone away, to that Mount Airy town." Finally captured, he confesses his guilt and awaits death at the hands of the lynch mob: "Now that they've found me, I know I must die." The tension between the objective style and the practice of narrator-switching reveals murder ballads as conversations about the contradictions of gender roles for men.[39]

The internal dialogue of the song "Omie Wise" reveals that male performers and audiences became both the outraged mob that seized Jon Lewis and Lewis himself. The song's interpreters understood Lewis's predicament. Omie had exposed the tenuous nature of his manhood—and theirs. Her body displayed his inability to control reproduction or, one suspects, her sexuality. And if Lewis married Wise, a poor apprentice, rather than wealthy Hattie Elliott, he would himself be poor and economically dependent on other men. The men who heard echoes of their own stories in the narrator-switching (for the murder of a possible wife-to-be offended a powerful belief about protecting dependents) revealed their understanding of the reasons Lewis used violence to control a woman. Omie refused to be the pure object of his sexuality and honor's monologue. When Jonathan threw Omie into the Deep River, he offered a preemptive strike in a male–female battle. He refused to spare her even after she promised to "go rejected and not be your wife."[40]

While violence made a male into a man, it carried great risks if left unbridled. Men who killed their wives faced massive community responses. In a documented contemporary account, the Mississippi wife-murderer Thomas Foster met a horrifying fate. After his acquittal due to insufficient evidence, a mob seized him at the courthouse steps, partially scalped him, whipped him for an afternoon and evening, poured boiling tar on him, and doused him with feathers. The permanently maimed and scarred Foster survived only because friends rescued him before the mob could finally lynch him.[41] In the three North Carolina murder ballads mentioned above, Tom Dula was legally executed for his murder of Laura Foster, "Peter De Graff" was lynched or hanged (depending on the version) for shooting Ellen Smith, and Jonathan Lewis may have been mobbed or lynched for drowning Naomi Wise.[42]

Community retribution for wife-murder could run the gamut from charivari to lynching, as "Omie Wise"'s audience understood. In real life and in the "objective style" of the murder ballad the community degraded and cast out the wife murderer. The song specifically suggests John Lewis's bestial nature. Lewis, for example, utterly lacked the human qualities of pity or compassion: "No pity, no pity/No pity have I" or "He said that he was heartless to the core" or, most clearly, "No pity, No pity/This monster did cry."[43] Though most ver-

Edward E. Baptist

sions end before local men seized Lewis, people who heard or sang "Omie Wise" might assume the murderer met a horrifying death at the hands of an outraged community in 1807, as a mob put away its own demons. Tar and feathers, dripping blood, and whip-torn flesh illustrated corporally the inhuman monster revealed by Lewis's dishonorable actions. The "objective" singing style reinforced this image of Lewis's fate.[44]

As the nineteenth century wore on, however, common white men felt increasing pressure from constricting opportunities for economic independence and the continued resistance of many women to domination. Mastery and honor became more and more difficult to claim. Many men who sang or listened to "Omie Wise" felt pressure to dominate women with unrestrained violence—the same pressure that, unleashed, drove Lewis to his shameful acts. As the narrative voice shifted, they shifted from sympathy with Lewis's punishers to identification with the murderer himself, and listeners admitted that the monster could live within. Trapped by a monologue whose imperatives of male independence and domination pushed them toward uxoricide, one of its greatest sins, some men sought out alternative models of manhood. Activities as disparate as evangelical pacifism and outlawry became candidates for a new paradigm. In this, Southern common white men were hardly alone. Scholars of nineteenth-century American masculinity have detailed crises that beset identities of white men from various classes and regions.[45]

The relationship between murder ballads and the intimate violence they described, therefore, was complex. Instead of continuity, they show change. Instead of fulfilling our preconceptions, they show multiplicity and ambiguity of meaning. Southern white men sang murder ballads for at least two contradictory reasons. On the surface, such ballads condemned men who murdered dependent women. But deeper in the dialogue of songs like "Omie Wise," they vocalized an ambivalence that became a guarded dissent from a patriarchal pattern of honor as a standard of masculinity. Between the demands of a manhood that required an intractable, violent independence, the constrictions of markets, and the reality that women would not be silenced, poor white men and yeomen saw no easy way out. Few saw themselves as murderers but, consciously or unconsciously, they felt the same pressures as did Jonathan Lewis, pressures that pushed against the heart of their identity as white men. They imagined acting both with and against Lewis. Murder ballads thus provide an important window onto intimate violence in the South, not because the deadly abuse they depicted was typical of gender relations, but because they became forums for a growing dialogue in which white males wrestled with the contradictions and impossibilities of honor's prescriptions.

"MY MIND IS TO DROWN YOU AND LEAVE YOU BEHIND"

Notes

1. The author wishes to thank the following individuals for comments, advice and inspiration: Edward W. Baptist, Stephanie Baptist, Charles C. Bolton, Robey Callaghan, Christine Daniels, Konstantin Dierks, Nancy Farriss, Drew Faust, and Michael Kennedy. Alan Lomax, *Folk Songs of North America in the English Language* (Garden City, NY, 1960), 268.

2. I use the term "common whites," suggested by Bill Cecil-Fronsman, *Common Whites: Class and Culture in Antebellum North Carolina* (Lexington, KY, 1992), to describe all nonplanter Southern whites, from landless poor whites to farmers who owned up to ten slaves. In some cases, however, it is useful to distinguish between groups within that classification.

3. Stephanie McCurry, *Masters of Small Worlds: Yeoman Households, Gender Relations, and the Political Culture of the Antebellum South Carolina Low Country* (New York, 1995); Peter Bardaglio, *Reconstructing the Household: Families, Sex, and Law in the Nineteenth-Century South* (Chapel Hill, NC, 1995); Laura F. Edwards, *Gendered Strife and Confusion: The Political Culture of Reconstruction* (Urbana and Chicago, 1997).

4. The literature on the charivari as a means of enforcing social norms is enormous. For the American South, see, for example, Bertram Wyatt-Brown, *Southern Honor: Ethics and Behavior in the Old South* (New York, 1981), 7–13 and *passim*; for a classic European formulation, Natalie Zemon Davis, "The Reasons of Misrule: Youth Groups and Charivaris in Sixteenth-Century France," *Past and Present* 50 (1971): 41–75.

5. Bertram Wyatt-Brown, "Andrew Jackson's Honor," *Journal of the Early Republic* 17 (1997): 1–35; Edward Ayers, *Vengeance and Justice: Crime and Punishment in the Nineteenth-Century Antebellum South* (New York, 1983); Kenneth Greenberg, *Honor and Slavery: Noses, Lies, Duels . . .* (Princeton, NJ, 1996); Charles C. Bolton and Scott P. Culclasure, eds., *The Confessions of Edward Isham: A Poor White Life of the Old South* (Athens, GA, 1998).

6. For a discussion of "Omie Wise" as a warning for both men and women, see Robert Thomas Roote, " 'Naomi Wise': A Study of a North Carolina Murder Ballad," (M.A. thesis, North Carolina State University, 1982); C. Kirk Hutson, " 'Whackety Whack, Don't Talk Back': The Glorification of Violence Against Females and the Subjugation of Women in Nineteenth-Century Southern Folk Music," *Journal of Women's History* 8 (1996): 114–141, includes an ahistorical interpretation of murder ballads. Susan Dwyer Amussen, " 'Being Stirred to Much Unquietness': Violence and Domestic Violence in Early Modern England," *Journal of Women's History* 6 (1994): 70–89; J.A. Sharpe, "Domestic Homicide in Early Modern England," *Historical Journal* 24 (1981): 29–48. Transitions in murder ballads and other popular images of intimate violence suggest that these stories are not timeless but change according to historical situations and the needs of people who re-create the songs.

7. Ayers, *Vengeance and Justice*, 311 n28; Wyatt-Brown, *Southern Honor*, 367–368, 380–382; H. V. Redfield, *Homicide, North and South: Being a Comparative View of Crime Against the Person in Several Parts of the United States* (Philadelphia, 1880); Edward E. Baptist, "Creating an Old South: The Plantation Frontier in Jackson and Leon Counties, Florida, 1821–1861," Ph.D. diss., University of Pennsylvania, 1997.

8. Indictment of Jonathan Lewis, 1807, "Naomi Wise Case," Criminal Action Papers, 1813–1814, Randolph County, North Carolina Division of Archives and History (NCDAH), Raleigh, NC; Braxton Craven, "Naomi Wise, Or, The Victim," Asheboro *Evergreen*, 1/1851, 78–82, 2/1851, 111–116. Craven placed the date of the murder in 1808, an error all subsequent prose accounts have repeated. Bolden G. Hudson, *The Frank C. Brown Collection of North Carolina Folklore* 6 (Chapel Hill, NC, 1952), 690–693.

9. Hudson, *Brown Collection*, 6, 704; Paul Escott, "Yeoman Independence and the Market: Social Status and Economic Development in Antebellum North Carolina," *North Carolina Historical Review* 66 (1989): 275–300; Brantley York, *The Autobiography of Brantley York*, John Lawson Monographs of the Trinity College Historical Society 1 (Durham, NC, 1910), 31–32.

10. Craven, "Naomi Wise," 81–82, 111–116; Guion Griffis Johnson, *Antebellum North Carolina: A Social History* (Chapel Hill, NC, 1937), 256–257.

11. [Second] Indictment of Jonathan Lewis, 10/8/1813; Zabed Wood to Guilford County Sheriff, 10/8/1813; Indictment of Isaac Lane, 10/1808; Seth Wade, C. Arnold and D. Dawson to Isaac Lane, 10/3/1807, in "Naomi Wise Case," Criminal Action Papers, 1813–1814, Randolph County, NCDAH.

12. Craven, "Naomi Wise," 115; Zabed Wood to Guilford County Sheriff, "Naomi Wise Case," Criminal Action Papers, 1813–1814, Randolph County, NCDAH; Roote, "Omie Wise," 23–27. Some versions suggest a more violent conclusion. Lomax, *Folk Songs of North America*, 262, 268–69; Alton G. Morris, *Folksongs of Florida* 2nd ed. (Gainesville, FL, 1981), 87 [version B]; Cecil Sharp, *English Folk Songs From the Southern Appalachians* 1 (London, 1932), 144–148, versions A and D; Hudson, *Brown Collection*, 691–692, versions F and G.

13. Sharp, *English Folk Songs*, 2, 144–45 (version A). *cf.* Hudson, *Brown Collection*, 690–692; Asmussen, "'Being Stirred to Much Unquietness'," 79–80; Elizabeth Pleck, "Wife-Beating in Nineteenth-Century America," *Victimology* 4 (1979), 69–70.

14. I have adopted many methods of Mikhail Bakhtin for "reading" cultural signs. See Michael Gardiner, *The Dialogics of Critique: Mikhail Bakhtin and the Theory of Ideology* (London and New York, 1992), 1–2; V. I. Volosinov, *Marxism and the Philosophy of Language*, trans. Ladislav Matejka and I. R. Titunik (Cambridge, 1973), 9–15, 17–24; Mikhail M. Bakhtin, *The Dialogic Imagination*, trans. Caryl Emerson and Michael Holquist (Austin, TX, 1981), 206–224, 259–422; Caryl Emerson, *The First Hundred Years of Mikhail Bakhtin* (Princeton, NJ, 1997); Caryl Emerson and Gary Saul Morson, *Mikhail Bakhtin: Creation of a Prosaic* (Stanford, CT, 1990).

15. Seven versions were published in Sharp, *English Folk Songs*, 144–148; one in Lomax, *Folk Songs of North America*, 261–262, 268–269; two in Morris, *Folksongs of Florida*, 85–87; seven in Hudson, *Brown Collection*, 690–698 (Hudson also includes a version faked by Braxton Craven, which Craven claimed to have collected but which was probably a poem he composed). Two more are in recorded collections: one by G. B. Grayson, "Ommie Wise," on *G. B. Grayson* (recorded 1927, master # 40306, original issue Victor 21625B); one by Doc Watson, "Omie Wise," on *Doc Watson and Family: Treasures Untold*, recorded live at the Newport Folk Festival, Newport, RI, July 1964 (Vanguard, 1991).

16. Hudson, *Brown Collection*, 690, 692 nA, 696–697; Craven, "Naomi Wise," 116; Morris, *Folksongs of Florida*, 86–87.

"MY MIND IS TO DROWN YOU AND LEAVE YOU BEHIND"

17. Sharp, *English Folk Songs*, 144–146. Pentatonic scales have fewer notes within the scale or sequence of notes called the octave, creating gaps different from those of modern music. Robert Cantwell, *Bluegrass Breakdown: The Making of the Old Southern Sound* (New York, 1992), 116–142. To modern ears accustomed to the even splitting of an octave into twelve equally divided semitones, such modes "appear" "uncertain or ambiguous," but "the folksinger, whose ear has been tuned by God and not by the local piano tuner, has found in that ambiguity an instrument of exceedingly subtle expressive power." Quote from Cantwell, *Bluegrass Breakdown*, 116. He also suggests that pentatonic structures of many Southern folk tunes owe more to Celtic and African roots than English ones, which adds further to the cultural dialogue in "Omie Wise."

18. Hudson, *Brown Collection*, 696–697; Morris, *Folksongs of Florida*, 86–87. The version in Hudson, *Brown Collection*, 696, has traveled to Florida, as has one from the main tradition.

19. Cecil Sharp, *Cecil Sharp's Collection of English Folk Songs*, ed. Maud Karpeles (London, 1974) 294–299; Hudson, *Brown Collection*, 690; Lomax, *Folk Songs of North America*, 261–262.

20. Brantley York, *Autobiography of Brantley York*, 17.

21. Charles C. Bolton, *Poor Whites of the Antebellum South: Tenants and Laborers in Central North Carolina and Northeast Mississippi* (Durham, NC, 1993), 114; Ralph Wooster, *Politicians, Planters and Plain Folk: Courthouse and Statehouse in the Upper South, 1850-1860* (Knoxville, TN, 1975), 1–27; McCurry, *Masters of Small Worlds*, 37–91, 228–276; Bardaglio, *Reconstructing the Household*, 3–36; J. Mills Thornton III, *Politics and Power in a Slave Society: Alabama, 1800-1860* (Baton Rouge, LA, 1978); Fletcher M. Green, *Constitutional Development in the South Atlantic States, 1776–1860* (New York, 1966).

22. Charles Sellers, *The Market Revolution: Jacksonian America, 1815–1846* (New York, 1991); Harry L. Watson, *Liberty and Power: The Politics of Jacksonian America* (New York, 1990); Christopher Clark, *The Roots of Rural Capitalism: Western Massachusetts, 1780–1860* (Ithaca and London, 1990); Melvyn Stokes and Stephen Conway, eds., *The Market Revolution in America: Social, Political, and Religious Expressions, 1800–1880* (Charlottesville, VA, 1996).

23. York, *Autobiography of Brantley York*, 12–21, 29–31; Escott, "Yeoman Independence and the Market," 280–285; Bolton, *Poor Whites of the Antebellum South*, 20–21, 38–39.

24. Escott, "Yeoman Independence and the Market," 291–299; over half of local farmers grew market-sized quantities of wheat by 1860, up from 19 percent in 1850, Bolton, *Poor Whites of the Antebellum South*, 24, 66–112; U. B. Phillips, "The Origin and Growth of the Southern Black Belts," *American Historical Review* 11 (1906): 798–816; Fabian Linden, "Economic Democracy and the Slave South: An Appraisal of Some Recent Views," *Journal of Negro History* 31 (1946): 140–189; Eugene Genovese, "Yeoman Farmers in a Slaveholders' Democracy," *Agricultural History* 49 (1975): 331–342; Baptist, "Creating an Old South."

25. I. J. Brittain, *Tragedy of Naomi Wise* (Winston-Salem, NC, 1910), 4; Pleck, "Wife-Beating in Nineteenth-Century North America," 60–74; Johnson, *Antebellum North Carolina*, 241–242; Laura F. Edwards, "Women, the Law, and Domestic Discord in North Carolina after the Civil War," paper presented to the Organization of American Historians, Chicago, 1996, 12–14; McCurry, *Masters of Small Worlds*, 72–85.

26. Wyatt-Brown, *Southern Honor*, 62–87, 254–291, 380–382, 462–493; Sellers, *The Market Revolution*, 3–33; David Hackett Fischer, *Albion's Seed: Four British Folkways in America* (New York, 1989), 768–771; Victoria E. Bynum, *Unruly Women: The Politics of Social and Sexual Control in the Old South* (Chapel Hill, NC, 1992) 82–83; Victoria E. Bynum, "Mothers, Lovers, and Wives: Images of Poor White Women in Edward Isham's Autobiography," in Bolton and Culclasure, eds., *Confessions of Edward Isham*, 85–100, quotes from 90–91.

27. Elliott Gorn, "'Gouge and Bite, Pull Hair and Scratch': The Social Significance of Fighting in the Antebellum Southern Backcountry," *American Historical Review* 90 (1985), 18–43; Edward E. Baptist, "Accidental Ethnography in an Antebellum Southern Newspaper: Snell's Homecoming Festival," *Journal of American History* 84 (1998), 1355–1383; Wyatt-Brown, *Southern Honor*, 353; Bolton and Culclasure, eds., *Confessions of Edward Isham*; Brittain, *Tragedy of Naomi Wise*, 4.

28. Hudson, *Brown Collection*, 696–697, versions F and G; and Morris, *Folksongs of Florida*, 86–7, version B.

29. Bynum, *Unruly Women*; McCurry, *Masters of Small Worlds*.

30. Molly Stouten, "'Omie Wise': The Ballad as History," *The Old-Time Herald* 5 (1997), 25–30; Wyatt-Brown, *Southern Honor*, 298–306; Bynum, *Unruly Women*, 1–14; Mikhail Bakhtin, *Rabelais and His World* (Cambridge, MA, 1968), trans. Helene Iswolsky, 15–17; James P. Horn, *Adapting to a New World: English Society in the Seventeenth-Century Chesapeake* (Chapel Hill, NC, 1994), 343.

31. Quoted in Hudson, *Brown Collection*, 3, 704; Fischer, *Albion's Seed*, 680–683.

32. Wyatt-Brown, *Southern Honor*, 289, 298–299.

33. Julia Cherry Spruill, *Women's Life and Work in the Southern Colonies* (Chapel Hill, NC, 1938), 325–326; Cornelia Hughes Dayton, "'Taking the Trade': Abortion and Gender Relations in an Eighteenth-Century New England Village," *William and Mary Quarterly* 48 (1991), 19–49; Wyatt-Brown, *Southern Honor*, 317.

34. Alan Lomax, "Folksong Style," *American Anthropologist* 61 (1959), 927–954.

35. Eight of 19 versions do not utilize a variant of these opening verses. Exceptions in Lomax, *Folk Songs of North America*, 268–689; Morris, *Folksongs of Florida*, 85–86, version A; Sharp, *English Folk Songs*, 144–148, versions A, B, D, and F; Hudson, *Brown Collection*, 692–698, version D. Sharp, B, D, E, F, and Lomax use openings derived from the one detailed in the text. Roote, "'Naomi Wise,'" 54–56, believes this homiletic function is the purpose of the ballad.

36. Charles Joyner suggests a female line of communication in murder ballads, linked to all-female work spaces and tasks, which I would suggest runs parallel to male performance of the song in all-male settings and more public spheres (personal communication from Charles Joyner to the author).

37. Bakhtin, *The Dialogic Imagination*, 276–277.

38. Lomax, *Folk Songs of North America*, 268–269. Grayson recorded a virtually identical version on 10/8/1927 in Atlanta and may have recorded the version transcribed by Lomax the same day. Grayson's recording career began in 1927 and ended with his death in 1930. Ray Parker, "G. B. Grayson: A Short Life of Trouble," *Old Time Music* 35 (1980–1981): 10–14.

39. Hudson, *Brown Collection*, 714–717; Vester Jones, "Poor Ellen Smith," on *Traditional Music from Grayson and Carroll Counties* (Folkways album #FS3811).

"MY MIND IS TO DROWN YOU AND LEAVE YOU BEHIND"

40. Lomax, *Folk Songs of North America*, 268.

41. Wyatt-Brown, *Southern Honor*, 462–493.

42. Hudson, *Brown Collection*, 690–717; W. Fitzhugh Brundage, ed., *Under Sentence of Death: Lynching in the South* (Chapel Hill, NC, 1997), points out that white-on-white lynchings were more common than heretofore suspected.

43. Sharp, *English Folk Songs*, 144, version A; Morris, *Folksongs of Florida*, 86–87, version B; Hudson, *Brown Collection*, 692, version A.

44. Wyatt-Brown, *Southern Honor*, 489.

45. William T. Auman, "Neighbor Against Neighbor: The Inner Civil War in the Randolph County Area of North Carolina," *North Carolina Historical Review* 61 (1984): 59–92; Gail Bederman, *Manliness and Civilization: A Cultural History of Gender and Race in the United States, 1880–1917* (Chicago, 1995); Ted Ownby, *Subduing Satan: Religion, Recreation and Manhood in the Rural South, 1865–1920* (Chapel Hill, NC, 1990); Edwards, *Gendered Strife and Confusion*, 107–183; E. Anthony Rotundo, *American Manhood: Transformations in Masculinity from the Revolution to the Modern Era* (New York, 1993); Michael Kimmell, *Manhood in America: A Cultural History* (New York, 1997), 81–190. By the 1840s, some Lewises were swept up in evangelical revivals and abandoned the aggressive manhood of their fathers' generation, York, *Autobiography of Brantley York*, 38.

Edward E. Baptist

six

"HE MURDERED HER BECAUSE HE LOVED HER"

Passion, Masculinity, and Intimate Homicide in Antebellum America

Ed Hatton

Social and cultural historians of nineteenth-century America have shown that antebellum Americans were overwhelmingly concerned with love and its consequences. Middle-class Americans in particular left a wealth of evidence—in prescriptive literature, in fiction, and in private communications—testifying to a deep faith in the romantic ideal. They believed romantic love was a shared and reinforced emotional bond that elevated and solemnized a courtship or marriage, honored women, and ennobled men.[1] The discourse surrounding romantic love invoked not only strict notions of feminine virtue, but also expectations for masculine behavior and identity. Advice manuals and health guidebooks cautioned men to control their passions and yet admonished them to be forceful in their actions and personal relationships. Regarding love in particular, male readers were warned to distinguish the pure, spiritual bond that joined suitable men and women from the baser physical attraction that men could experience. Lust served only to denigrate women and animalize men.[2]

The difference between love and lust played an important role in the larger antebellum discourse on masculinity. Such discussions usually took place between the covers of medical guidebooks and advice books for young men. On occasion, however, an egregious act of "male passion" galvanized a community, bringing the discordance between love and lust to public attention. One such instance was the murder of Mary Hamilton by Joel Clough in Bordentown, New Jersey, in 1833.

Figure 6–1. *Joel Clough at his murder trial.*

Clough, a New England–born construction engineer who worked on canal and railroad projects in the Delaware Valley, fell in love with and courted Mary Hamilton, the widowed daughter of his boardinghouse landlords, the Longstreths, in late 1832. The young widow was less interested in Clough than he was in her, however, and in the spring of 1833, when he asked her to marry him, she refused. Angered by her rejection, Clough disappeared from Bordentown, and returned to the boardinghouse a week later. The next day, Clough summoned Hamilton to his room on the pretext that he was ill, and again asked her marry him. Clough told her that he had a vial of poison and would kill himself if she rejected him a second time. Hamilton declined his offer, but instead of drinking the poison, Clough grabbed a knife and stabbed her in the chest. Hamilton staggered out of the room onto the landing, where Clough stabbed her several more times until she broke free and ran downstairs before succumbing to her wounds.

When the authorities arrived at the boardinghouse, Clough surrendered without a fight. That he was the murderer was never in question; several men had witnessed the assault, and Clough readily admitted that he had committed the crime. He did not admit guilt, however. Clough told his captors that he was not entirely responsible for Hamilton's murder. He asserted instead that the victim should share the blame for her death; by jilting him Mary Hamilton had caused his mind to become unbalanced and precipitated the attack.[3] Clough, as one observer later noted ironically, "murdered her because he loved her."[4]

The sensation following Clough's crime resulted in a heavily attended trial which became a venue for the discussion of the difference between "love" and "passion" and of male self-control in matters of the heart. In an effort to make sense of a senseless crime, participants in the trial, including witnesses, attorneys, and journalists, created explanatory narratives in the form of trial testimony, attorneys' arguments, and newspaper reports.[5] The murderer himself participated in this process by crafting a lengthy, rationalized confession of the crime. The narratives differed according to whether they condemned, ameliorated, or justified Clough's actions, but they all shared one concern—the dangers inherent in male passion.

Although the phrase "crime of passion" became widespread only in the late nineteenth century, readers in 1833 would have understood it. That strong emotions could exceed an individual's command and lead to criminal actions was a widely accepted truism. Penologists and doctors also equated deviance with a lack of emotional control. Penologists, for example, believed that unrestrained passion, especially when it dated from childhood, was the cause of most crime in America.[6] Although they were less sure that deviance was entirely rooted in environment, antebellum doctors interested in psychology agreed that many individuals committed crimes when their intellect fell under the sway of their emotions. The influential Philadelphia physician Benjamin Rush, for example, believed that murder and theft were symptoms of insanity, not of evil. People became criminals, he wrote, when their "will" became the "vehicle of vicious actions," a transformation caused by "passions."[7]

Antebellum Americans inherited a cultural tradition that identified reason with masculinity and male passions with a loss of self-control, along with aggression, rampant sexuality, and violence. For centuries, philosophers lauded reason as man's most valuable virtue; emotionality was the resort of women, children, and weak-minded men. This belief enabled society's masculine elite to assert a natural, even divine, right to govern political entities and families alike. If reason were masculine, only men should rule.

Lurking beneath the association of masculinity with rationality, however, was the disturbing notion that some men lacked reason and, therefore, the ability to be independent. Not all men were able to act rationally all the time. Such men were subject to emotions, sexual desire, and violence. In order to reconcile experience with ideals, therefore, some philosophers asserted that "reason" and "passion" existed side by side within the masculine soul; each tempered the other. These descriptions elevated reason and submerged emotionality.[8]

"HE MURDERED HER BECAUSE HE LOVED HER"

The masculine ideals that middle-class Americans began to embrace in the late eighteenth and early nineteenth centuries reflected their negative opinion of passion. Before 1830, two discrete ideals of masculinity were well established in Northern middle-class American culture: the "masculine achiever" and the "Christian gentleman." The masculine achiever was rooted in the burgeoning commercial revolution and based on the notion that men were essentially rational. It held that males were naturally active and dynamic; they embodied an ideology of self-advancement based on ceaseless effort, independent action, emotional freedom, and rational decisions. The masculine achiever was the breadwinner of the domestic sphere, a man who supported his wife and children. He protected the financial viability of his family in periods of economic uncertainty.[9]

The Christian gentleman, on the other hand, embodied what the masculine achiever did not. Christian gentlemen stressed godliness, purity, kindness, and compassion, qualities many believed were in short supply in, if not antithetical to, an increasingly capitalistic world. Although the masculine achiever embraced religious piety, the Christian gentleman responded to the moral crisis engendered by the spread of amoral commercial enterprise.

Although the two ideals contradicted each other in theory, they intermixed in practice. Many people, including parents who advised their sons, ministers who wrote guidebooks, and men who recorded their thoughts in journals, described proper masculinity as combining economic success with religious piety and moral restraint.

The suppression of passion was essential for both ideals. Successful businessmen and Christian gentlemen controlled the urges that were a vital component of their natures. Even antebellum Americans who accepted the existence of a male "sex instinct" and valued it as a force for good in society argued that only certain circumstances—specifically, marriage—legitimated sexual expression. This powerful force needed to be regulated and controlled by individuals and society to create a civilized community.[10]

Soon after 1820, however, a third ideal of manliness emerged in American popular culture: the "masculine primitive." Most fully elaborated in the antebellum fascination with health and the body, this view recognized physical strength, powerful instincts, and charisma as desirable in men. It manifested itself memorably in accounts of frontier heroes such as Davy Crockett and in the increasing popularity of sports.[11] When properly controlled and directed, the masculine primitive could harness male animal urges (such as the instinct for sex or survival) to fulfill the goals of a capitalist society. This ideal held that the masculine primitive conceived of life as a struggle for existence in which men "battled one another for mastery and success" in the marketplace, the courthouse, and the classroom.[12]

Ed Hatton

In antebellum society, the ideals of the masculine achiever and the Christian gentleman were well established and broadly embraced; the masculine primitive, however, was problematic. The third ideal, in fact, was not widely accepted until the end of the nineteenth century. In antebellum America, to acknowledge men's animal side as positive contradicted the traditional understanding of masculinity. Many writers saw in men an animal whose savage instincts trembled just below the surface. Male desire and its expression were inherently dangerous and antisocial.

One response to the dangers implied by the effort to harness male passions was an outpouring of advice literature that advocated self-control, written by doctors, teachers, and ministers. In his influential and popular guidebook, *A Lecture to Young Men on Chastity*, health reformer Sylvester Graham warned that sensual urges could control a man and lead to his moral decline and self-destruction.[13] Other writers advised that the mastery of male passions was the key to success in business and happiness in life. Young men were to examine minutely every aspect of their characters, including their desires. If they wished to strengthen their emotional and intellectual abilities, they would have to restrain their thirst for the "sensual," including alcohol, gambling, and sexual gratification.[14] One popular author, for example, told young male readers that to uplift their "moral and intellectual nature," they had to "put down the animal."[15] Advice writers did not go so far as to advocate eradicating male sexual instinct (as they did for women), but they urged young men to channel it toward procreation and self-improvement.[16]

Just as middle-class Americans sought to master and regulate sexual desire, they also sought to eradicate anger, especially in intimate relationships. Before the late eighteenth century, anger caused consternation primarily when it interrupted relationships between equals—that is, between independent men of means—although many elite men attempted to control their emotions.

After 1790 or so, a shift in the perception of anger occurred that paralled a rise in the popularity of romantic love as a literary and aesthetic ideal and represented the degree to which placid domestic relationships symbolized social cohesion. Male anger came to be seen as a threat to the harmony of intimate relations between men and women.[17] A new emphasis on the control of anger in personal relations emerged in middle-class advice literature, and writers began to advise men to suppress anger as well as infelicitous sexual urges.[18] Anger, they conceded, was integral to masculinity, but men were to be held accountable for the control of those feelings. A man of good character "did not let himself get swept away by passion of any sort."[19]

Antebellum American society, however, proffered no consensus on the way in which men should handle their "natural" aggression or sexual desires. Although young men were to control passion, no blueprint existed to assist

"HE MURDERED HER BECAUSE HE LOVED HER"

them to their goal. Most men doubtless embraced contemporary masculine ideals according to their own consciences and abilities, with varying degrees of success. When they faltered, however, where was blame to be ascribed—to the man, to the women in his life, to his parents, or to society? This issue formed the heart of the public sensation caused by the murder of Mary Hamilton, when a man of good character—Joel Clough—was "swept away" by passion.

Clough's trial for murder opened less than two months after the death of Mary Hamilton. Before it began, however, it was clear that some people believed that Clough, although a murderer, was not unambiguously at fault. In the days following the murder, newspaper accounts of the events leading to the killing explained Clough's actions as both the result of a failed romance and an act of unparalleled brutality.[20] The virulence of Clough's attack on Hamilton, conveyed in the press by the detail of her wounds and rapid death, marked the young man as a murderer of unusual cruelty. Even so, the accounts wavered on Clough's culpability, describing him both sympathetically as "unfortunate" and disparagingly as a "demon." This ambivalence implied that Hamilton may not have been the only victim of the failed romance.

The public was fascinated by Hamilton's death. On the first day of the trial, held before the Supreme Court of New Jersey, a thousand spectators congregated in and around the courthouse, which was filled "almost to suffocation."[21] Eminent counsels tried the case. The prosecution was led by the state attorney general, John Moore White, and included Samuel L. Southard, a former U.S. senator and former governor of New Jersey. Clough was defended by two lawyers from Philadelphia: David Paul Brown, an attorney noted for his successful defense of accused murderers, and Isaac Hazlehurst, who later became a Pennsylvania state legislator. The trial began on May 31, 1833, and lasted until June 8.

From the start of the trial, reporters and other observers scrutinized Clough for signs of mental imbalance. The young engineer, however, appeared to be the very opposite of a brutal murderer. His manners were impeccable. One reporter, for example, described Clough as "gracefully" acknowledging Mary Hamilton's family as they entered the courtroom, and noted that he rose and bowed to the murdered woman's mother "in the most grave and respectful manner."[22] A portrait of Clough published in several newspapers depicted him in a pensive pose suggestive of intelligence and even sensitivity.[23]

Such sympathetic descriptions contradicted comments about his behavior published in newspapers before the trial. They suggested that Clough's taste in reading tended toward novels—a decidedly suspect genre—and that he wished to be introduced to attractive women he glimpsed through the bars of his cell. Such scraps of gossip supported the impression that Clough was immoral, a depraved "Othello," in the words of one observer. Hints about his private vices suggested a flawed nature that caused his vicious crime.[24]

Ed Hatton

As the trial began, the initial witnesses (more than forty were eventually called) described what they saw and heard on the day of the murder. They included the group of men who saw Clough stab Hamilton, but who apparently were too stunned or too frightened to intervene, as well as the residents of the boardinghouse, members of the murdered woman's family, and friends and neighbors who rushed to the scene of the crime. Together, they provided the details of the relationship between the murdered woman and her killer.

The exact nature of the connection between Clough and Hamilton was the first issue raised. Although Clough did not take the stand, the jury learned something about him through secondhand accounts. One of the men who captured and guarded Clough on the day of the murder testified that Clough claimed he had been "intimate" with Hamilton and that she had acted immorally. Clough suggested to the witness that Hamilton herself was to blame for her killing. Only "strong causes" could have persuaded him "to commit such an act" Clough said; he insinuated that these causes had been Hamilton's physical intimacy with another man. He added that "he hoped he had taken innocent blood," but "feared that he had not."[25]

Clough's alleged comments to his guard about Hamilton, however, were the only ones throughout the trial that suggested that she was sexually active. Her status as a young widow—the fact that she had been married and was, therefore, sexually experienced—did not figure into courtroom or newspaper accounts of their relationship. This elision reinforced the value placed on female purity in antebellum culture. A comment in the first reports of the murder, for example, that Hamilton had rejected Clough for "a rival suitor" was not pursued during the trial. The name of the other man—if he existed—was never revealed. Other aspects of the crime, moreover, that could have reflected on the victim's purity were never raised. No mention was made of the fact that the murder had occurred in a boardinghouse (a morally suspect location), nor that Hamilton had been stabbed while in Clough's room. In fact, the victim's character was uniformly—even excessively—praised for its purity by witnesses, the prosecution, the defense, the judge, and journalists.[26]

Clough's second assertion, that he and Hamilton were on emotionally intimate terms, was supported by a number of witnesses, however. Clough's friends and acquaintances testified that Hamilton had welcomed his attentions. Some also claimed that rumors of an engagement between the two had circulated through the neighborhood before the murder and had included stories that the couple spent long evenings in each other's company, had exchanged love tokens such as jewelry, miniature portraits and locks of hair, and had taken trips together to Princeton, Trenton, and Philadelphia. Henry J. Pyle, who had lived at the Longstreths' boardinghouse, suspected that they were to be married. In his opinion, Clough's attentions "were kindly received" by Hamilton. In fact, a few weeks before her death, Pyle had joked with

"HE MURDERED HER BECAUSE HE LOVED HER"

Hamilton about marrying Clough, and her mirthful response to his teasing seemed to confirm his belief.

The contention that Hamilton was engaged to Clough, or that he courted her, was nontheless refuted by an equally convincing array of witnesses. Several residents of the boardinghouse, including the servants, Hamilton's sisters, and her oldest daughter testified that they knew nothing of an emotionally intimate relationship, although Clough had boarded at the Longstreths' for nearly two years. Elizabeth Longstreth, Hamilton's mother, provided the most detailed and comprehensive account of the relationship between Clough and the murdered woman. Longstreth denied that the rumors of an engagement were true. She stated that Clough had tried to court her daughter but insisted that Hamilton had never accepted any of his gifts, nor had she traveled anywhere with Clough alone.

According to Longstreth, Hamilton rejected Clough's attempts to court her and objected to his persistence. When he asked her to marry him, she had refused him outright. Clough, however, would not accept her rejection. He became increasingly jealous with regard to Hamilton, and on several occasions threatened men who appeared to be potential suitors. Finally Hamilton refused to appear in public with Clough because she suspected he had spread the rumors that they were engaged. Longstreth categorically told the jury that any such intelligence was unfounded; "I have no knowledge of any engagement between them," she stated, "and I know there was none."

Longstreth's insistence that her daughter had unwaveringly objected to Clough's attentions was significant. A marriage promise, even an unstated one, could not be broken casually. If Hamilton had welcomed Clough's attentions or had in any way encouraged him—even by accepting a small token of affection—his violent response to rejection might be comprehensible if not forgivable. Her mother's denial of any matrimonial agreement upheld Hamilton's honor and absolved her of complicity in Clough's actions. This point was revisited repeatedly throughout the trial by the prosecution, the judge, and reporters.

After examining Hamilton's character, the court turned its attention to Clough's. Several of his business associates testified that Clough had been industrious, honest, sober, and "mild."[27] Others, however, testified that although Clough seemed honorable, he was in fact a thief and a liar. One even suggested that Clough had embezzled funds from his employers.[28]

The most damning testimony regarding Clough, however, came from those who had watched him during the days immediately before the murder. In late March 1833, soon after Hamilton's first matrimonial rebuff, Clough left Bordentown. His sudden departure was not out of character, for he often traveled for long periods when engaged on construction projects, but the Longstreths believed that after Hamilton's rejection he would not return. Clough went first to Philadelphia and then to New York City, where he picked up a prostitute at

Ed Hatton

a theater. Later, in the woman's lodgings, Clough argued with her and took some of her jewelry when he left.

From New York he traveled to Troy and then to Albany, where he encountered a friend, James Wallace. A contractor who had worked with Clough on the Morris Canal in New Jersey in 1829, Wallace expected to receive a new construction contract soon and offered Clough the chance to subcontract it. Wallace stated in the courtroom that he knew Clough to be "more than ordinarily mild and forbearing," but when he met him in Albany he found a changed man. Clough had always been sober and responsible, but now he "showed a disposition to drink more than before" and pressured Wallace to do so as well. His behavior was so odd that Wallace thought that Clough had become mentally unbalanced. On the steamboat from Albany to New York City, the two spent an afternoon in the ship's bar, where Clough drank excessively. By the time they arrived in New York City, Wallace had given up on Clough because of his drinking, and had "abandoned the idea [of the subcontract]." Wallace left a sobbing Clough at the dock in New York, where the distraught man was stopped by the police for the theft of the prostitute's jewelry. Clough sent for Wallace, who provided him with an attorney. Clough bought his way out of the charge with most of his ready cash. In the wake of these tumultuous events, Clough returned to the Longstreths' house in Bordentown, where a few days later he murdered Mary Hamilton.

At the conclusion of the testimony, the prosecution and defense attorneys delivered their speeches to the jury. Both sides presented coherent stories of the events preceding the tragedy, but they differed in their interpretations of Clough's character. In the defense's narrative, Clough was an honorable and hardworking young man who fell in love with a respectable young woman. Clough's lawyers ignored the negative testimony provided by some witnesses and emphasized instead his good reputation, his "mild and amiable" disposition, and his hard work and dedication. What was more natural, they argued, than that a rising young professional man would want to marry an "amiable and accomplished female" like Mary Hamilton? They read Clough's letters to her aloud in the courtroom as evidence of the sincerity of his love. In them he asked Hamilton to "abandon her friends and mother, and sacrifice all for him." In return, Clough promised her "an honorable name, a peaceful home, and means of living comfortably."[29] These letters, argued the attorneys, "breathe[d] a fountain" of "affection, amounting almost to adoration" and demonstrated the honor of Clough's intentions and true "character of his heart."[30] In this version of events, Clough did all that a respectable man could do; he worked hard, earned an estimable reputation, and directed his affections toward a worthy woman. The exchange Clough offered Hamilton—his protection and support in return for her sacrifice and devotion—was the accepted formula for domestic happiness. Clough had done what young men in his position were supposed to do.

"HE MURDERED HER BECAUSE HE LOVED HER"

In order to depict Clough's attraction to Hamilton as honorable love, the defense drew upon the romantic motifs and imagery of antebellum culture. One of these was the notion that affection could be communicated only through a sophisticated language of subtle actions and complex emotional revelation. Clough's love, suggested the attorneys, was not expressed as mere desire, but was conveyed through "the tear of the eye" and "the tone of the voice," clear signs that his motives were chaste and intentions honorable. "His passion was of the purest character," they stated.

In fact, it was the intensity of Clough's "sacred" love for Hamilton that made her rejection devastating. The defense argued that Clough was not simply a rejected suitor, but a man whose deep and abiding love had been destroyed. In this regard, Clough deserved to be regarded as Hamilton's victim, for she had "wounded [him] with an inward woe." Clough had loved Hamilton too much; when she rejected him his reason failed and he lost all control of his actions. This, insisted the defense attorneys, explained Clough's uncharacteristic behavior in Philadelphia and New York City as well as the murder itself. On the fatal day, they argued, "the passion of love" had "rendered it impossible" for him "to control or regulate his conduct, and [it] as much destroyed his mind as if he were a maniac."[31]

The prosecution, on the other hand, granted that Clough might have been attracted to Mary Hamilton, but insisted that the measure of his true nature lay in his actions, not in character references and his supposedly pure love for the victim. While they agreed that "love of a virtuous woman" indeed "fits a man for virtuous and noble actions," this did not describe Clough's relationship with Hamilton, which was based on the opposite of virtuous love—lust.

The prosecution delivered this message vividly through a description of Hamilton's stabbing that used imagery suggestive of rape. Prosecutor Anthony Scott, for example, characterized Clough's initial assault as an embrace: "[T]he lover's right hand held a dagger, with his left hand he totally encompassed her." Later in the melee, Scott noted that Clough had covered Hamilton's mouth to stifle her screams, "pierced her bosom" with his dagger and "replunged it with all his strength." They also displayed the murdered woman's lacerated and bloody underclothes. Although a doctor held up the items to demonstrate the viciousness of Clough's attack, the public and the press saw the stained, torn garments as a visible manifestation of his true motive. Unsatisfied lust, not chaste and virtuous love, led to his violence. Hamilton, the prosecution suggested, had been "sacrificed" to satiate Clough's passionate jealousy and desire for revenge.[32]

The prosecution also made light of the defense's claim that Clough's "mild and moderate" temper had been "corroded" by insanity. Insanity had not led him to spend the night "in the filthy pollutions of a brothel, in the mercenary embraces of a harlot," and then to steal her jewels. Clough's behavior, they argued, was not proof of derangement but of depravity, of a diseased appetite for alcohol and illicit passion. Clough was crazy with jealousy and rage, but he was not insane in a medical or legal sense. "[N]ot every outbreaking of anger, rage, and jealousy," the prosecution argued, "dements a man." While the prosecution admitted that alcohol could lead to insanity, Clough's drunkenness was not "the road to madness" but only "the goadings of a spirit" that was "troubled at the contemplation of his crimes."

In struggling to define insanity, attorneys for both sides invoked popular and professional assessments of the causes and consequences of male mental derangement. Early nineteenth-century American jurisprudence generally followed the *mens rea* doctrine, which held that individuals could not be held responsible for actions they could not control or comprehend. Rooted in ancient Hebraic, Roman, and medieval Christian church law, the doctrine manifested itself in seventeenth-century English courts when jurists tried to correlate degrees of insanity with degrees of punishment.[33] This trend, bolstered by changes in the medical understanding of mental derangement in France, England, and America in the late eighteenth century, acknowledged that insanity was a complex phenomenon resulting in a variety of symptoms, one of which could be a disorder in the so-called "moral sense" brought on by "morbid or excessive passions."[34]

This approach was rooted in a new conception of the mind based on a division of its essential functions into three parts: reason, emotions, and the will. Reason or understanding enabled humans to perceive experience and create ideas. Emotions or passions made feelings comprehensible. The will or volition allowed an individual to act on or restrain those ideas and feelings.[35] A dysfunction in any one of these three systems could result in insanity.

Because no clear agreement about the etiology of homicidal insanity existed, lawyers in antebellum murder trials often peppered their arguments with extended quotes from the texts of recognized medical authorities to prove or disprove claims of insanity. They also provided their own interpretations of the proper application of these principles to the case at hand.[36] While legal professionals may have had an increasing appreciation of psychological factors, however, ordinary Americans were reluctant to accept such interpretations. Despite *mens rea* and the advice of medical writers that insanity did not result from moral failure, juries in the antebellum period tended to rely more on popular notions of sanity and insanity than on expert views when deciding such cases.

Early nineteenth-century juries were also quick to assign blame if "insanity" was traced to moral failure on the part of the accused. A few years before Clough's murder of Mary Hamilton, for example, an Ohioan named James Birdsell was tried in Cincinnati for killing his wife while under the delusion that she was plotting to murder him. Although the judge and jury

"HE MURDERED HER BECAUSE HE LOVED HER"

acknowledged his derangement, they still convicted and executed Birdsell because his insanity could be ascribed to a moral fault—intemperance.[37] As one historian of medical jurisprudence has suggested, while "village idiots" might successfully be acquitted of small crimes, the more heinous the crime, the less likely juries were to exonerate the accused. Whether out of a fear of recidivism (a verdict of "not guilty by reason of insanity" did not ensure institutionalization), or out of a sincere disbelief in the merits of the insanity defense, antebellum juries tended to reject claims of innocence by reason of mental incapacity.[38]

Clough's trial occurred during these jurisprudential changes, but before lawyers routinely asked specialists to provide expert testimony. As a result, no alienists—early psychiatrists—or other doctors testified in Clough's defense. His attorneys instead tried to synthesize scientific and popular understandings of insanity themselves to provide an explanation of the way in which "innocent" passions could overwhelm a man's reason and lead him to violence.

According to the defense, the jury had to remember Clough's reputation as a man of reason, not a man of wayward passions. If Clough "had been an outcast and his trade was in blood," or if he had "rioted and wantoned in human life," then the killing of Hamilton would have been consistent with his life and actions. But as "a man of mild and moderate temper, of honesty and probity, [Clough] is surely not to be considered as a beast of prey seeking whom he might devour." His character could not be "made and lost in one day. A man of good character is entitled to the benefit of that character which he has established." Clough loved Hamilton, the defense argued, and no sane man would kill the woman he loved. "In all the crimson colored records of crime, there is nothing to prove that a man destroys the darling object of his heart, while a scintilla of reason remains," one of the attorneys argued. "While a particle of reason flickers in the socket, love always sanctifies its object."

Clough, therefore, had temporarily succumbed to madness. As the defense attorneys told the jury, "[t]he mechanism of the human mind is so delicate that it is easily disordered." Of all the possible causes of insanity, "[t]he mind is [most] easily affected by maladies affecting the heart. Medical science has reduced this to arithmetical certainty." The blame for Hamilton's death therefore lay with the disturbing effects of overpowering love, which unbalanced Clough's mind and character. "From being economical and saving, he became a spendthrift, from being a sober man, he became a drunkard, from being chaste, he sacrificed himself at the infernal shrine of lusts, from being honest, he became a thief." Clough had, "like Satan," fallen "from heaven to bottomless perdition, and all in the narrow compass of 48 hours. All these instances of conduct are striking evidences of a disordered mind."

Clough's attorneys argued that his behavior was not merely an indication of his lust. Lust and love acted on men in different ways. If Clough had simply lusted after Hamilton, his departure from Bordentown would have lessened his desire, for absence "meliorated passion." Love was not lessened by distance—it was intensified. It developed into "a disease and a scourge. It twine[d] its tendrils around the human heart, and dr[ove] it to madness." Clough, therefore, felt not lust, but a sanctifying and devoted love.

Unable to withstand the pain of separation any longer and finding that "the intoxicating bowl" no longer "quench[ed] the fire of his passions," Clough was urged by an "irresistible" impulse to return to Bordentown. By this time, claimed the defense, he displayed unmistakable signs of mental derangement: "He was no longer gay, but dull, gloomy and demented." He sought only "the solitude of his chamber, and avoided society." Struggling with his disease, he dined at the Longstreths' table, where "[h]is former kindnesses were once again exhibited [and] his amiable disposition remained the same." Despondent, Clough decided to take poison, but he was interrupted by Hamilton and killed her instead.

In their rejoinder, the prosecution objected to the defense's conflation of love with mental instability. Insanity, they told the jury, resulted in total irrationality. "It is when reason ceases that insanity begins." Insanity was not "an ungovernable temper, sudden bursts of passion, or hightened resentment." Nor was it "intemperance, the brooding fear of shame, or the gloom of disappointment from affections scorned." Insanity was more innate. It was "the perversion of the intellect, that illusion of the mind which imagines evils that do not exist; and which compels the disordered mind to deduce false reasoning" from facts. Citing legal and medical precedents, the prosecution insisted that insanity must rest on belief in an illusion and that insane acts must fall within the logic of those beliefs. In order to be considered insane, therefore, Clough would have had to believe that it was a duty, not an opportunity, to murder Hamilton. "He must have deemed it a meritorious act and not an ignominious one. This would have shown clearly the illusion which insanity produces, and he would have gloried in the act after it was committed, as laudable and right." Instead, however, he "did the deed, and spoke of it afterwards as his act, for which he expected to atone to the laws of the country."

Clough's claim of insanity was also suspect for at least two other reasons, according to the prosecution. First, none of his forebears had suffered from true derangement. Second, none of his actions before or after the murder, according to prosecutors, indicated insanity. Clough's seclusion in his room and his moody and sullen deportment before the killing were not signs of mental illness. He was simply plagued by the shameful "recollection of his crime [in New York City]," which "he feared would reach the ears of the family of Mrs.

Longstreth." Nor had he in the aftermath of the murder exhibited any of the signs of a madman. He maintained his composure, conversed with people calmly, and acknowledged that he had done wrong.

Finally, the prosecution concluded, no broken heart brought Clough back to Bordentown, but "gangrened jealousy" and a desire for revenge. When Clough observed the women of the Longstreth household involved in what he mistakenly thought were Hamilton's wedding preparations—dressmaking and furniture purchases—"his morbid imagination feared some other rival," and in anger he struck. In this description, prosecutors asked pointedly: "Where is the sudden cutting down of intellect?" Clough's insanity "was the madness of crime," they asserted, "the madness of human depravity."

Both the defense and the prosecution asked the men in the jury box to consider their own notions of manhood, its risks and responsibilities. The defense asked them to take Clough's life before the murder into account. He had acted honorably—had fulfilled all the requirements asked of any man—and had failed only under external and internal pressure. Should he be condemned to death for a single, albeit extreme, failure not entirely of his own making? The prosecution, meanwhile, appealed to the jurymen to see themselves not as men subject to the same strains and stresses Clough experienced, but instead to identify with the ideal of manhood that held among its cardinal virtues the protection of and respect for women. In a telling aside, a prosecution attorney ridiculed the men in the boardinghouse who had not been able to find the courage to attack Clough as he murdered Hamilton. Honorable men would have jumped into the fray to save her, he asserted, admonishing the jurymen not to follow their example. He implored them to defend Hamilton in death as she had been abandoned in life.

The latter interpretation clearly carried more weight. After an absence of about two hours, the jury returned with a verdict of guilty.[39] Clough was sentenced to hang.

Within 24 hours of his conviction, Clough retracted his plea of innocence and confessed to premeditated murder. According to newspaper reports, Clough then admitted that "he had laid a plan for Mrs. Hamilton's death a month before it took place; that he had determined, if she would not have him, no other person should have her."[40] In the weeks preceding his execution, Clough composed a confession and autobiography. With the assistance of several churchmen who visited him in his cell, Clough wrote his life story and gave it to his attorneys for publication after his execution.[41]

Criminal autobiography was one of the most widely read genres in early America and was a popular literary form dating to the sixteenth century in Europe. Rooted in the Christian tradition of penance, such accounts included the details of criminals' lives and crimes, justifications for their actions or admissions of responsibility, and warnings to readers. Religious and eventually legal views of confession emphasized the individual nature of guilt, but also carried the socially symbolic goal of restoring the criminal to the larger community. Confession provided criminals with the chance to accept "full responsibility for untoward behaviour" and to atone publicly for their sins.[42] They thereby fostered the larger social good as examples of the dangers of transgression.

In antebellum America, criminal autobiographies and confessions served the interests of several groups. Printers profited from them, clergymen propagated messages of piety, lawyers publicized the efficacy of the legal system, and the public validated its understanding of evil and the social means to control it. Condemned criminals like Clough and their clergymen amanuenses continued a long tradition with clear financial, social, and cultural incentives.

The true authorship of criminal autobiographies is usually difficult or impossible to determine. First-person accounts were routinely accompanied by testimony signed by clergymen or jurists, vouching that the text had been written by the criminal "author." Some first-person accounts, however, include impassioned theological arguments against homicide purportedly written by condemned men with rudimentary educations. Clergymen, therefore, certainly assisted in constructing these accounts, although many doubtless reflected the views and experiences of the criminal.

In his confession, Clough wrote of his own experiences and the way in which they shaped the character of a murderer. Although brief sections admonish readers to control their passions, the focus of the document is on Clough's struggle with his moral failings and his state of mind regarding his courtship of Mary Hamilton. Unlike the prosecution, which saw lust and revenge as Clough's critical flaws, or the defense, which insisted that Clough's spotless love for Hamilton temporarily caused him to lose control, the condemned man identified another root cause for his crime: childhood indulgence.

Clough begins by describing his own childhood in New Hampshire, where he was born in 1804, the last of five brothers and two sisters. As the youngest child he was favored by his parents. "[M]ore than ordinary pains was taken by my parents to instil into my mind proper principles," he wrote, "and furnish me with a suitable education." As a child, Clough recalled that he was generally good, claiming that "I am not aware of having been guilty of any improper acts, other than those that are generally connected with schoolboys of my age." He did possess one fatal flaw, however, "a most vindictive passion," which was "the besetting sin of my life." Clough recalled that "being the youngest child, I was gratified by my dear parents in all those indulgences that my boyhood could suggest." Yet "when my wishes were foiled, I would burst out in a most violent passion" even to the point of "denouncing my parents in the most violent manner." Instead of schooling him to control his outbursts, however, his parents would "grant me my requests, and even hire me by presents to cease in my passion." He also bullied other boys at school who bested him at games: "I

"HE MURDERED HER BECAUSE HE LOVED HER"

would fly into a rage, and threaten them in the most violent manner." This uncontrollable passionate rage he saw as the source of his later misfortune.

Clough's elder brothers worked on the farm while he went to school and was "indulged in all my foolish whims." Unlike his hardworking brothers, Clough began to develop immoral habits, such as "a fondness of playing cards." By the time he was sixteen, the pastime had become a "fascination" that could only be satisfied by playing for money, although when he lost, his temper erupted. Before long he became addicted to gambling and stole money from his parents to indulge himself. His father, when he discovered Clough's thefts, only scolded him.

Clough's easy and dissipated life ended when his father died, plunging the family into poverty and ending his education. All of the children were bound out as apprentices; the seventeen-year-old Clough was sent to a stonemason. The change brought him to his senses. "I soon made myself useful to my master," he recalled, for "I had seen the error of my ways." He left "off many of my bad habits, playing cards in particular." In contrast to his earlier incarnation as an uncontrolled and spoiled boy, Clough recalled with pride that he never cheated his employer. He embarked on a career in 1825 as "a complete master of my trade."

Clough's first project was to manage the construction of an aqueduct in Connecticut. After the project was completed, however, he could not find work. Without the discipline of employment, he again fell prey to the temptations of young men and indulged "in all kinds of dissipation," including gambling, dishonesty, and passing counterfeit money. He also claimed to have seduced a young woman who died in childbirth after he abandoned her.

Then Clough met Mary Hamilton. At first he "experienced a most violent attachment for [her], and soon after her husband's death, made advances to her, which like a wise and prudent woman, she refused."[43] Her virtue inspired him to improve himself to win her affections. She received more respectful overtures with greater interest, and he "became sincerely attached to and ardently desired to marry her." Hamilton seemed to return his love but avoided any discussion of marriage. She never formally accepted a proposal, but Clough interpreted her conduct as acquiescence. "[S]he repeatedly confirmed [an understanding] by "receiving attentions from me, and valuable presents."[44]

For several months, relations between the two became increasingly intimate, but Hamilton cooled toward Clough when a wealthier suitor came onto the scene. As a result, she ignored Clough, "repulsed my approaches, seemed desirous of the admiration of others, sought their society, and finally, retracted her engagement." This rejection turned his love, "which was pure and fervent," instead to "hatred," and Clough "made a solemn vow" that Hamilton would "never be the wife of another man."[45] He resolved upon her murder and his suicide because he felt that "the wreck of his happiness entitled him to sweep

Ed Hatton

the cause of it from the world."[46] When he was with her, however, his affection for her revived, and he was unable to carry out the plan.

To escape his inner struggle, he fled Bordentown and sank back into dissipation. For a week he returned to his previous life of immorality and threw himself into gambling, drinking, and illicit sex. He left Bordentown to separate himself from Hamilton, but without her spiritually uplifting presence, he wrote, he found himself sinking lower and lower into iniquity. His arrest for the theft of a prostitute's jewelery finally smashed his fragile sense of self-control, and he decided that Hamilton "should retract or suffer the consequences." Clough then returned to Bordentown and "told her that I had lost my money for her sake." Hamilton thereupon "expressed regret, and offered me all the money she had and her watch." Clough refused her offer but "told her that if she would fulfill her engagement, we might yet be happy." She replied, "What, marry you in your reduced circumstances!"[47] Clough had been prepared to drink laudanum in her presence if she rejected him. At her exclamation, however, his "consciousness" deserted him, and "through an uncontrollable impulse," he stabbed her to death.[48]

In his autobiography, therefore, Clough conceived of his crime as the result of his failure to control his antisocial and "passionate" urges for gambling, fighting, and sexual indulgence. His work warned other "passionate" men to watch their step. Significantly, although he described his murderous attack as "an uncontrollable impulse," he did not ascribe his actions to insanity. In fact, the very act of composing a coherent narrative belied that claim.[49] As he summed it up, "[p]ride of character—and uncurbed passion—has been the ruling and besetting sin of my life."[50]

But Clough was not simply a sinner who followed the wrong path. He cast himself both as villain and victim; his act was the result of childhood indulgence. By identifying his own corrupted youth as the cause of the crime, Clough echoed contemporary fears about American family life. Antebellum social critics often commented on parents' dangerous tendency to spoil children. Similar sentiments were expressed by travelers to America, such as Harriet Martineau, who admired "the independence and fearlessness of American children," but who worried about the implications of such behavior.[51] Early nineteenth-century Americans still debated whether children possessed inherent tendencies to wickedness. Horace Bushnell's *Views of Christian Nurture* (1847), for example, did not abandon the notion of innate depravity, although he believed that proper nurture beginning in infancy could "weed out" bad tendencies. Not until the 1850s was infant depravity abandoned by many Americans as a legitimate concern regarding children.

In Clough's tale, Hamilton's murder was not a single act of violence but the legacy of a lifelong struggle for self-control against immoral impulses. Although he shouldered much of the blame, Clough argued in his confession, as

"HE MURDERED HER BECAUSE HE LOVED HER"

he had done from the moment of his arrest, that he alone was not responsible for the crime. Hamilton—by abandoning him for another suitor—and his parents—by their indulgence of his childhood whims—also made him what he was. He thereby rejected the limited dialogue that had characterized courtroom discussions of male deviance in antebellum America. Men were not solely responsible for controlling their urges; others carried part of the burden. Nor was he alone in his claims that parents or women should also be considered accountable for men's behavior.[52] By insisting that his actions resulted from a wide range of conditions and influences—only one of which was self-mastery—Clough countered the notion that men were solitary and independent agents in the control of their passions.

On the night of July 20, 1833, a week before his execution, Clough escaped from jail. His jailers had allowed him a steel pen and a candle to write his confession, but he used them that night to achieve his freedom. He pried open his leg shackles with the pen and burned a hole in the wooden wall of his cell with the candle. He slipped through the hole and lowered himself to the ground from the jail's second story with a rope made of blankets. The next morning the alarm was sounded; Clough was recaptured later that day on his way to Philadelphia.[53]

Some townspeople regretted that Clough had been recaptured. In the wake of his conviction, popular opinion that he was insane had apparently become stronger. While newspapers reported that Clough had admitted his responsibility, they also noted that he suffered from nightmares. In his dreams, he descended an interminable flight of stairs "ending in a black and indistinct abyss."[54] Sleep brought no relief to his "desolate spirit," and he longed "to escape from the ocean of agony upon which he is tossed, and lie down upon the shore of death."[55] While such a state of penitence and terror may have conveyed his remorse to many readers, before the twentieth century nightmares were often thought a sign of madness. Such images evidently convinced many readers of his insanity and reduced responsibility. As one newspaper commented, "many who were loudest in their cries for vengeance have expressed their regret at his re-capture."[56] A number of local residents, including Elizabeth Longstreth, reportedly prepared a petition to mitigate his sentence.

The petition, if it ever circulated, was not successful, for Clough was hanged on July 26, 1833. That morning, accompanied by the sheriff and representatives of the local Protestant churches and escorted by a troop of calvary, Clough was driven in an open carriage to his execution site outside Mount Holly. An estimated five to fifteen thousand spectators accompanied him; people from all over the Delaware Valley had crowded into the town during the three days before the execution.[57] Five volunteer companies of infantry controlled the assembled crowd.

Clough and the ministers climbed the gallows, where they sang hymns and Clough received last rites. The Reverend Wilmer read an extract of his farewell letter to his mother and a short version of his confession.[58] In it, Clough acknowledged that he had received a fair trial but insisted that Hamilton had given him "full encouragement" to court her and had "freely admitted his attentions." Some reporters objected to Clough's "further assaults on his victim," but because he also praised Hamilton's character, the press was satisfied that Clough "did not seek to justify his deed of murder on that account."[59] Finally, with "fortitude seldom, if ever, witnessed on such an occasion," Clough assisted the sheriff in placing the noose around his neck, At approximately two-thirty in the afternoon the "unfortunate" Joel Clough was "ushered into eternity."[60]

The murder of Mary Hamilton by Joel Clough in 1833, and the popular discourse that it evoked, is a case study of antebellum attitudes toward love, lust, and male self-control. The defense attorneys attempted to portray Clough as a "hard-working young man" whose "love" for Hamilton was "sincere" and "honorable." They suggested that the very intensity of that love "rendered it impossible" for the jilted lover to "regulate his conduct" and that it destroyed his mind "as if he were a maniac." The prosecution, in contrast, argued that Clough's actions arose, not out of insanity but out of the innate "madness of human depravity." They tried to demonstrate that Clough was a liar, a thief, an embezzler, a drinker, and a whoremonger, whose act resulted not from sincere love but from unsatisfied lust.

Clough, in his confession, attempted to reconcile these two polar images. He claimed that he loved Hamilton honorably even as he admitted that he had been haunted by dark desires. A battle for self-control had plagued him throughout his life. He interpreted his life and crime in the context of the struggles of other young men to control their urges. Clough, therefore, humanized the legalistic and clinical explanations of his murderous actions. He highlighted, however briefly, the difficulties of self-control Northern antebellum society advocated for young men.

Three terms played key roles in the discourse surrounding the case: "love," "lust," and "passion." At first glance, it seems that Clough's contemporaries associated lust with passion and considered love something fundamentally different. The distinctions were not so clear, however. Although the prosecution linked passion with lust, defense attorneys referred to the "pure character" of Clough's passion or the "passion of love." They may have been trying, opportunistically, to blur the distinctions between love and passion postulated by the prosecution. A broader cultural ambiguity, however, clouded the place of men's romantic emotions in antebellum America.

Clough presented a liminal argument in popular imagination as well as in the courtroom. Americans' fascination with masculine passion reflected widespread concern, not only with love and gender roles, but also with the changing nature of antebellum society. Rising crime rates—especially among working-class and immigrant men—were often ascribed to their "passionate" natures.

"HE MURDERED HER BECAUSE HE LOVED HER"

When a man like Joel Clough fell victim to passion, middle-class Americans took notice. They expected the lives of working-class and immigrant men to be punctuated by violence. But for Clough, who had enjoyed education, status, and respectability, to lose control suggested widespread moral failure. A self-made man who seemed outwardly respectable but who could not control his base impulses, Joel Clough personified what his middle-class neighbors feared.[61]

In his own self-portrait, however, Clough saw himself as not atypical of antebellum men. In his own mind, he embodied aspects of all three antebellum masculine ideals—the masculine achiever, the Christian gentleman, and the masculine primitive—although he did not embrace any ideal wholly. What in the end may be most notable about Clough was not that he murdered Hamilton and was hanged for it, but that despite his heinous action, he still believed himself ordinary. His actions were a predictable product of antebellum concepts of love, lust, and passion and of a failure to school himself or be schooled in self-control. He thought himself far more typical than most Northern antebellum Americans would have cared to admit.

Notes

1. Useful discussions of middle-class notions of love and marriage include Ellen K. Rothman, *Hands and Hearts: A History of Courtship in America* (New York, 1984); Karen Lystra, *Searching the Heart: Women, Men, and Romantic Love in Nineteenth-Century America* (New York, 1989); Steven Seidman, *Romantic Longings: Love in America, 1830–1980* (New York, 1991), esp. chap. 2; Steven Mintz, *A Prison of Expectations: The Family in Victorian Culture* (New York, 1983), chap. 6.

2. Phillip A. Gibbs, "Self-Control and Male Sexuality in the Advice Literature of Nineteenth-Century America, 1830–1860," *Journal of American Culture* 9 (1986): 37–41; Charles E. Rosenberg, "Sexuality, Class and Role in 19th-Century America," in Elizabeth H. and Joseph H. Pleck, eds., *The American Man* (Englewood Cliffs, NJ, 1980), 219–254.

3. The chief source for this account is the trial transcript, published as *Trial of Joel Clough, On Indictment for the Murder of Mary W. Hamilton Before the Burlington Oyer & Terminer Circuit* (hereafter, *Trial*) (New York, 1833), which is very complete and includes the lawyers' addresses to the jury. Other versions of the transcript appeared in newspapers and pamphlets, and I have used them when necessary.

4. *Trial*, 62.

5. For the history of crime literature and the evolution of criminal narratives and reporting, see Daniel A. Cohen, *Pillars of Salt, Monuments of Grace: New England Crime Literature and the Origins of American Popular Culture, 1674–1860* (New York, 1993); David Ray Papke, *Framing the Criminal: Crime, Cultural Work and the Loss of Critical Perspective, 1830–1900* (Hamden, CT, 1987). On the ways in which different representations of reality can be understood as narratives of the real, see Hayden White, "The Value of Narrativity in the Representation of Reality," in *The Content of the Form: Narrative Discourse and Historical Representation* (Baltimore, MD, 1987), 1–25; and Vic-

Ed Hatton

tor Turner, "Social Dramas and Stories About Them," in W.J.T. Mitchell, ed., *On Narrative* (Chicago, 1981), 137–164.

6. David J. Rothman, *The Discovery of the Asylum: Social Order and Disorder in the New Republic* (Boston, 1971), chap. 2.

7. Quoted in Janet Colaizzi, *Homicidal Insanity, 1800–1985* (Tuscaloosa, AL, 1989), 18.

8. As Victor J. Seidler has observed, the historical concealment of male sexuality by Western culture was "a hidden threat of violence that reason was deemed powerless to control." Seidler, "Reason, Desire, and Male Sexuality," in Pat Caplan, ed., *The Cultural Construction of Sexuality* (London, 1987), 85.

9. This discussion is indebted to E. Anthony Rotundo, "Learning about Manhood: Gender Ideals and the Middle-Class Family in 19th-century America," in J. A. Mangan and James Walvin, eds., *Manliness and Morality: Middle-Class Masculinity in Britain and America, 1840–1900* (New York, 1987), 35–51; and Rotundo, *American Manhood: Transformations in Masculinity from the Revolution to the Modern Era* (New York, 1993). Also Peter N. Stearns, *Be a Man! Males in Modern Society* 2nd ed. (New York, 1990), 108–132.

10. Seidman, *Romantic Longings*, 17–19.

11. See Stephen Nissenbaum, *Sex, Diet, and Debility in Jacksonian America: Sylvester Graham and Health Reform* (Westport, CT, 1980); Carroll Smith-Rosenberg, "Davy Crockett as Trickster: Pornography, Liminality, and Symbolic Inversion in Victorian America," in *Disorderly Conduct: Visions of Gender in Victorian America* (New York, 1985), 90–108; Elliott J. Gorn, *The Manly Art: Bare-Knuckle Prize Fighting in America* (Ithaca, NY, 1988), 34–147. Popular decoration, especially the iconography of the middle-class dining room, also celebrated aggressive and predatory masculinity in the mid-nineteenth century. As Kenneth L. Ames has noted, sideboards, paintings, and statuary depicting hunting and death scenes often emphasized "the particular potential for violence that seethes within" men. Ames, *Death in the Dining Room and Other Tales of Victorian Culture* (Philadelphia, 1992), 68–74, quote on 69.

12. Rotundo, "Learning about Manhood," 41.

13. Graham's guide, published in 1834, went through ten editions in fifteen years, Seidman, *Romantic Longings*, 27.

14. Phillip A. Gibbs, "Self-Control and Male Sexuality in the Advice Literature of Nineteenth-Century America, 1830–1860," *Journal of American Culture* 9 (1986): 37–41; Rosenberg, "Sexuality, Class and Role," 219–254.

15. William Ellery Channing, *Self-Culture* (London, 1844), 144, quoted in Gibbs, "Self-Control and Male Sexuality," 39.

16. Reformers based their views on those of contemporary physicians, who considered semen the source of physical and intellectual strength in men. Writing in a language reminiscent of economics, they advised male readers to "conserve" and "invest" their semen in useful activities such as procreation and in creativity, imagination, and logical reasoning. See Ben Barker-Benfield, "The Spermatic Economy: A Nineteenth-Century View of Sexuality," in Michael Gordon, ed., *The American Family in Social-Historical Perspective,* 2nd ed. (New York, 1978), 374–378.

17. Carol Zisowitz Stearns and Peter N. Stearns, *Anger: The Struggle for Emotional Control in America's History* (Chicago, 1986), 28–36; Jacquelyn Miller, "Governing the Passions: The Eighteenth-Century Quest for Domestic Harmony in Philadelphia's Middle-Class Households," in this volume.

"HE MURDERED HER BECAUSE HE LOVED HER"

18. Peter N. Stearns, "Men, Boys, and Anger in American Society, 1860–1940," in Mangan and Walvin, *Manliness and Morality*, 80.

19. Stearns, *Anger*, 42.

20. *Daily Advertiser* (Newark, NJ), 4/9/1833.

21. *Mirror* (Mount Holly, NJ), 6/13/1833.

22. *Daily Advertiser* (Newark, NJ), 6/5/1833.

23. See the portrait published in the *Atkinson's Saturday Evening Post and Bulletin* (Philadelphia), 6/8/1833.

24. *Daily National Intelligencer* (Washington, D.C.), 6/7/1833 and *Daily Advertiser* (Newark, NJ), 6/6/1833.

25. *Trial*, 42.

26. As a reporter for the New York *Courier and Inquirer* noted, "Throughout this protracted trial, during which an immense mass of testimony was received, not a blot or stain was affixed to the character of the lamented Mrs. Hamilton; her reputation, adorned by every virtue that can dignify and beautify her sex, was most triumphantly sustained; and she was proved to have been chaste, beautiful, urbane, and lively, and as pure as the unclouded sky." This comment was reprinted in the *Report of the Trial of Joel Clough, on the indictment for the Murder of Mrs. Mary W. Hamilton* (Boston, 1833), 3; in the *Trial*, 37; and in George N. Thomson, *Confessions, Trials, and Biographical Sketches of the Most Cold Blooded Murderers, Who Have Been Executed in this Country* (Hartford, CT, 1854), 302–303.

27. *Trial*, 30–31.

28. *Trial*, 34, 36.

29. *Trial*, 55–56.

30. *Trial*, 61, 55.

31. *Trial*, 55–57.

32. *Trial*, 50–53.

33. James C. Mohr, *Doctors and the Law: Medical Jurisprudence in Nineteenth-Century America* (New York, 1993), 143; Thomas Maeder, *Crime and Madness: The Origins and Evolution of the Insanity Defense* (New York, 1985), 1–21; Norman J. Finkel, *Insanity on Trial* (New York, 1988), 3–22.

34. Norman Dain, *Concepts of Insanity in the United States, 1789–1865* (New Brunswick, NJ, 1964), 9.

35. Colaizzi, *Homicidal Insanity*, 13.

36. Beginning in the 1820s, attorneys increasingly called upon alienists—expert witnesses who were doctors specializing in mental diseases—to testify on the insanity claims of accused criminals. See Mohr, *Doctors and the Law*. An informative study of insanity and medical jurisprudence in late nineteenth-century America is Charles E. Rosenberg, *The Trial of the Assassin Guiteau: Psychiatry and the Law in the Gilded Age* (Chicago, 1968).

37. Stanley L. Block, "Daniel Drake and the Insanity Plea," *Bulletin of the History of Medicine* 65 (1991): 326–339. On the Birdsell case, see 332–333.

38. Mohr, *Doctors and the Law*, 143–144. One asylum superintendent argued in 1850 that despite the public concern about the ease of the insanity defense, few cases used it successfully, and in those instances, the verdict was justified. Dr. Bell, "Insanity and Crime," *American Journal of Insanity* 6 (1850): 318–321.

Ed Hatton

39. *Mirror* (Mount Holly, NJ), 6/13/1833.

40. *New Jersey State Gazette* (Trenton, NJ), 6/15/1833.

41. *The Only True and Authentic Confession of Joel Clough, containing his Life and Confession from 14 Years of Age, Anecdotes, Letters, Escape, Capture, etc., Written by Himself and Placed in the Hands of One of His Attorneys for Publication* (Philadelphia, 1833). The version cited here is reprinted in John D. Lawson, ed., *American State Trials* (St. Louis, MO, 1914) 1:762–775.

42. Mike Hepworth and Bryan S. Turner, *Confession: Studies in Deviance and Religion* (London, 1982), 131–132. Citation on 140.

43. *Authentic Confession*, 762–765.

44. *Authentic Confession*, 5–6.

45. *Authentic Confession*, 5–6.

46. *Daily Intelligencer* (Philadelphia), reprinted in the *Daily Advertiser* (Newark, NJ), 7/26/1833.

47. *Authentic Confession*, 6.

48. *Daily Intelligencer* (Philadelphia), reprinted in the *Daily Advertiser* (Newark, NJ), 7/26/1833.

49. Clough's confession was a document that both admitted the crime and asserted mitigating factors, echoing those of other antebellum criminal confessions. One such was that of the French parricide Pierre Riviere, whose elaborately composed confession has been shown to contain two "discourses of knowledge," one representing the murderer as a madman and the other representing him as a clear-minded criminal. As Michel Foucault has noted, early nineteenth-century murder narratives were cultural constructions that existed in "the dangerous area" outside the confines of the law. Foucault, "Tales of Murder," in Foucault, ed., *I, Pierre Riviere, Having Slaughtered My Mother, My Sister, and My Brother. . . : A Case of Parricide in the 19th Century*, trans. by Frank Jellinek (New York, 1975), 206.

50. *Authentic Confession*, 775.

51. Martineau, *Society in America* (New York, 1837), 2:271.

52. Rothman, *The Discovery of the Asylum*, 62–68.

53. *Mirror* (Mount Holly, NJ), 7/25/1833; *New Jersey State Gazette* (Trenton, NJ), 7/27/1833; Lawson, *American State Trials*, 1:760–762. Clough's escape is also described in a letter written by the Mount Holly sheriff, Joshua Hollingswood, printed in *Authentic Confession*, 18–22.

54. *New Jersey State Gazette* (Trenton, NJ), 7/15/1833.

55. *Daily National Inquirer* (Washington, D.C.), 7/19/1833.

56. *Daily Intelligencer* (Philadelphia), reprinted in the *Daily Advertiser* (Newark, NJ), 7/26/1833.

57. *Atkinson's Saturday Evening Post and Bulletin* (Philadelphia), 7/27/1833.

58. This version of his confession, probably based on the longer account, was written out by Bishop Doane and corrected by Clough. Even in shortened form, it was much longer than the usual dying words of criminals presented from the scaffold, and took half an hour to read. This version differed from the longer, unpublished version by leaving out Clough's account of his childhood. Instead, it began with religious warnings typical of the last words of condemned criminals, and then moved to his relationship with Hamilton and the minute details of the crime. It described Clough's past

"HE MURDERED HER BECAUSE HE LOVED HER"

conduct as moral but irreligious. In it, Clough confessed to false notions of honor and revenge and to overindulgence in the pleasures of the world. See the letter from Rev. S. Wilmer to the *Daily Chronicle*, 7/13/1833, reprinted in *Authentic Confession*, 24. The scaffold confession, printed in the Philadelphia *Pennsylvanian*, was reprinted in the Washington *Daily National Intelligencer*, 7/29/1833; the Mount Holly *Mirror*, 8/1/1833; the Trenton *New Jersey State Gazette*, 8/3/1833; the *Confession of Joel Clough, Who was Executed at Mount Holly, N.J., July 26, 1833 for the Murder of Mrs. Mary W. Hamilton* (New York, 1833), 5–7; and in Lawson, *American State Trials*, 1:775–776.

59. *New Jersey State Gazette* (Trenton, NJ), 8/3/1833.

60. *Mirror* (Mount Holly, NJ), 8/1/1833.

61. David Paul Brown, *The Forum; or Forty Years Full Practice at the Philadelphia Bar* (Philadelphia, 1856), 450.

seven

"A NEW HOME" FOR WHOM?

Caroline Kirkland Exposes Domestic Abuse
on the Michigan Frontier

Jenifer Banks

T
he frontier has always evoked ambivalent responses in the American psyche—a tension between idealism and materialism. Until recently, westward expansion has been encoded as a male activity. The publication of letters, journals, and diaries kept by women who lived on the frontier, however, has revealed how central and complex were the roles women played in this enterprise. One such complex but problematic version of women's place on the frontier is Caroline Kirkland's *A New Home, Who'll Follow? or, Glimpses of Western Life*.[1] Published under the pseudonym of Mary Clavers, this work is based on letters Kirkland wrote to eastern friends about her three-year experience on the Michigan frontier from 1837 to 1839. In her preface, Clavers notes that, although tempted to present her work as "a veritable history," in fact "there be glosses, and colourings, and lights if not shadows for which the author alone is accountable." These "glosses, and colourings, and lights" will be seen to reveal her ambivalence toward the frontier.[2]

Clavers's stated goal is to counter the romantic image of the frontier fostered by such writers as James Hall in *Legends of the West* (1832) and Charles Fenno Hoffman in *A Winter in the West* (1835). Such texts "were full of important omissions," she complained—important because they obscured the hardships women faced.[3] Clavers exposes these omissions and presents them in the context of national, political, and social issues. She thereby reveals how much women suffered from the lack of sympathetic networks in frontier isolation and the danger inherent in patriarchal family structures and the nineteenth-century cult of domesticity.[4] Through this counterhegemonic perspective, she implies that frontier conditions fostered—even sanctioned—wife abuse by intensifying attitudes that prevailed throughout the Republic. In *A New Home*, therefore, Kirkland often criticizes the values fuelling westward expansion during the first half of the nineteenth century.

Some scholars have suggested that Kirkland associated women with communal interdependence and men with "a wanton and individualistic pursuit of profit."[5] Such absolute distinctions, however, do not adequately describe Clavers's response to the frontier. Certainly she illuminates a gendered frontier "battleground" based on different value systems and presents women as physical and cultural victims of men's pursuit of profit. By including portraits of women from all social classes, moreover, she projects a common bond of sisterhood among all women. In her commentary on these images, however, she deflects attention away from victims to critique abusers less for wife abuse than for failing to contribute to her middle-class vision of "progress" and the economic development of the frontier. It is this juxtaposition of domestic issues with issues of the marketplace that most clearly reflects her "ambiguous positioning between cultural affirmation and cultural critique."[6]

The two conflicting modes of socioeconomic conduct—interdependence and individual pursuit of profit—were present in Kirkland's own family. In 1835 Caroline and her husband William moved from Utica, New York, to Detroit, Michigan, to head the Detroit Female Academy together. Within a year, however, William acquired over thirteen hundred acres of woodland sixty miles northwest of Detroit, and resigned the couple's secure positions at the Academy. Hoping to capitalize on the Michigan land boom, he sent out advertisements seeking settlers for the proposed village of Pinckney ("Montacute" in *A New Home*). He had 200 acres surveyed and a village laid out. In 1837 he moved his family to the fledgling settlement and devoted himself to his business venture.[7]

Much of *A New Home* details the way in which Caroline Kirkland participated in this enterprise as the settlement developed into a community. Through Clavers, she illustrates two developmental stages on the frontier: first, the initial effort required to settle the land; second, subsequent activities necessary for a sense of community. Initially, for example, Clavers threw herself into her central task as wife and mother and created a home for her family. Then, to provide a measure of stability, she planted a garden. Finally, she helped build a sense of community among the settlers by supporting a Female Benevolent Society (a sewing group) and the construction of a church and a school.

Although in some ways *A New Home* is a success story about a middle-class woman from the East who learned to live in the West, it is also a realistic account of the high price many women paid for emigrating to the frontier.

Many women who moved—or were moved—to the frontier felt trapped in a male enterprise. Clavers sympathizes with these women and details the physical and emotional hardships they endured. Brought by their husbands to isolated areas and deprived of domestic comforts, many were not prepared for the extremely difficult conditions under which they had to work and the sacrifices they had to make. "Women are the grumblers in Michigan, and they have some apology," Clavers notes. "The conviction of good accruing on a large scale does not prevent the wearing sense of minor deprivations."[8] Minor deprivations included loss of familial or social support, social alienation, and domestic abuse.

Many of the social factors particularly common to frontier regions have been identified by contemporary sociologists as catalysts for spousal abuse. These factors included relatively undeveloped legal structures and a resultant reliance on patriarchal governance; physical and social isolation from family, friends, or protective institutions; alcohol abuse; declining social and economic status; and the temporary weakening of some aspects of gender identification. The struggle for solvency in the frontier economy may also have contributed to male feelings of low self-esteem, helplessness, inadequacy, and shame.[9]

In exposing domestic abuse, Kirkland took a bold stance as a social critic; she implicitly criticized the ideology of the Family Ideal, "[t]he single most consistent barrier to reform against domestic violence" in the nineteenth century.[10] As the concept of gendered separate spheres gained popularity, the state became ever more reluctant to interfere in family privacy. Thus families became increasingly isolated from community scrutiny and from outside intervention. Clavers intimates that this situation was exacerbated on the frontier, where neighbors lived out of sight, often hours or even days away.

The dominant cultural and legal system vested authority and legal responsibility in married men as household heads. Under nineteenth-century patriarchy, male violence was to a certain extent sanctioned under the definition of moderate chastisement or correction.[11] Definitions of spousal assault and battery in antebellum America differed widely from state to state and region to region, but black eyes and broken noses were often within the bounds of acceptable, if not admirable, chastisement.[12]

Certainly patriarchal governance was firmly embedded in nineteenth-century statutes, and Michigan territorial law upheld it. In cases of "cruel and inhuman treatment," or such conduct on a husband's part toward his wife that "may render it unsafe for her to stay," she could be granted separation of bed and board, although not absolute divorce. In such cases, territorial courts could order the husband to provide suitable support for his wife and children. If, however, a husband could prove his wife's "ill conduct" as justification for his behavior, her case could be dismissed.[13]

137

Overall, early nineteenth-century family law in Michigan, as in many other regions, provided protection for women who were (or could present themselves as) unable to defend themselves, but undermined the efforts of those who stood up for themselves or disobeyed male wishes. And, like many others, Michigan's territorial courts sustained the "Family Ideal" of domestic privacy and of public intervention as a violation of family intimacy.[14] In the Michigan Territory, moreover, certain legal structures or actors that might have helped control spousal abuse, such as surveillance by grand jury members or justices of the peace, were few and far between. In the absence of such institutions, patriarchal control assumed more authority than it could have asserted in more settled areas.

A second factor sociologists have associated with spousal violence is the victim's social and psychological isolation from family, friends, and protective institutions. In secluded cabins, frontier wives had little access to female or kin networks or to the informal protection such connections could afford from an abusive husband.

Isolation is a dominant theme in Clavers's descriptions, as it was in many Western women's diaries and journals. Transported from her Eastern intellectual and cultural milieu, and then from the nascent social and cultural center of Detroit, Clavers is abandoned on the edge of an unformed village in the wake of her husband's economic ambitions. She distances herself from these ambitions by ascribing agency in the enterprise to her husband and satirizing his efforts. "When my husband purchased two hundred acres of wild land on the banks of this soon-to-be-celebrated stream," she recalls, "and drew with a piece of chalk on the barroom table at Danforth's the plan of a village, I little thought that I was destined to make myself famous by handing down to posterity a faithful record of the advancing fortunes of that favored spot."[15]

Clavers certainly feels isolated in Montacute. Her husband brings her there and leaves her alone in a frightening wilderness to set up home in an unfinished log cabin. Many of her neighbors are two or three days' travel away. Because the open cooking fire overheats the house, she has to leave the doors open, and "in this exposed situation passed the first night in my western home, alone, with my children and far from my neighbor." Her fear of "being devoured by wild beasts, or poisoned by rattlesnakes, caused [her] to start up after every nap with sensations of horror and alarm."[16] If an abused woman sought companionship or contemplated escape she would have known how distant any refuge would be and how difficult and dangerous the journey. Michigan roads developed slowly before 1850, and they were often no more than trails through which one had to cut one's way. Much of central Michigan, moreover, was swamp, and completely impassable without log or plank roads. Clavers herself never overcomes her deep-seated fear of being bogged down in these marshes.[17]

In established towns or communities, kinship networks, particularly among females, enabled women to develop a sense of autonomy within marriage and not to be totally dependent on husbands. Such networks could also be sustained by regular correspondence. Letters, however, were a luxury few frontier settlers could afford. Until 1825, the charge of 25 cents for a single letter travelling from the East was difficult, if not impossible, for many families to afford, and most settlers had to travel great distances to reach a post office.[18] Such isolation put great strain on women. Men usually outnumbered women on the midwestern frontier by ratios of five or six to one, so women often did not see other white women for two or more months.[19]

Continuous out-migration from Michigan further mitigated against the development of kin networks. Michigan was located as a midpoint for further westward movement. Many families had left relatives in the East, and included members who moved farther west. Clavers notes that "the habit of selling out so frequently makes that *home*-feeling, which is so large an ingredient in happiness elsewhere, almost a nonentity in Michigan."[20]

A third factor sociologists have identified as contributing to family violence is alcohol abuse. The period between 1790 and 1830 has been described as "a spectacular [drinking] binge" in America in which all social classes indulged.[21] Such national behavior clearly spread to the frontier, and Clavers describes a world in which drinking to excess was a way of life, with her most vivid depictions of alcohol's destructive force centered in the home.

A painful vignette in her opening chapter emphasizes the devastating impact of alcohol. En route to their new home, the Claverses stop at a "wretched inn" where they witness the "horrible drunkenness" and "insane fury" of the innkeeper, whose wife and children live in "constant fear of their lives." Clavers described a "desolate woman, sitting trembling and with white compressed lips in the midst of her children," as her husband searches for "more of the poison already boiling in his veins." The woman states that her husband had brought her "from a well-stored and comfortable home in Connecticut" to a "wretched den in the wilderness," where she and her children are "worn almost to shadows with the ague." The man is ultimately imprisoned for "stabbing a neighbor in a drunken brawl," and dies of delirium tremens, leaving his family destitute.[22] By juxtaposing images of the man and wife, Clavers reveals that the husband's imprisonment is physical and finite while his wife's is physical, emotional, and unending. Clavers is clearly deeply moved by the tale of this woman, who is left imprisoned deep in the woods, living in the shame associated with poverty, a victim of her husband's failed dreams of frontier conquest.

Through this story, Kirkland anticipates the position and rhetoric used by women in the temperance crusade of the 1840s and 1850s, when alcohol abuse became linked to domestic violence in the public consciousness. Women established a central position in this movement in part by claiming a special understanding of alcohol's effects on intimate relationships; they could "draw aside the curtain, and show us the wreck [alcohol] makes of domestic love and home enjoyments."[23] Clavers, therefore, was among the first to give public voice to an issue often deemed off-limits as part of the private sphere.

Kirkland believed that alcohol abuse as a factor in domestic violence, while not peculiar to the frontier, was more prevalent there than in more settled areas of the United States. As she closes her exposure of the plight of the innkeeper's wife, she wryly notes: "so much for turning our fields of golden grain into 'fire water'—a branch of business in which Michigan is fast improving."[24] Clavers's reference highlights the practice of many Western farmers, who, finding it unprofitable to send grain to Eastern markets, distilled it into whiskey. They thereby converted a bulky and perishable product "into non-perishable spirits that could be easily stored, shipped and sold." Even farmers who paid distillers with half their crops could increase their products' value by 150 percent.[25] Many men, however, had their own domestic stills and therefore a ready supply of whiskey in their own homes. Clavers's juxtaposition affords a rich commentary on alcoholism and its resultant violence on the Western frontier. She replaces the poetic vision of "golden grain" with "fire water" and thus elides the nineteenth-century image of "savage" Native Americans into that of the white sot.

Kirkland herself, however, was also a participant in the frontier enterprise and sympathized with its expansionist goals. Her ambivalence only emerges as she concludes the innkeeper's vignette by directing attention away from the problems inherent in his family's suffering and toward the social and economic scope of his failures. She frames her critique in terms of his inadequacy in furthering the expansionist venture. His house is still "deep in the woods"; he neither clears forest nor cultivates land. When she emphasizes his dereliction of duty in leaving his family destitute, she reflects a growing public resentment in the Michigan Territory at the increasing number of inebriates' families who had to be supported with public funds.[26] Her final emphasis is on public and political problems rather than emotional issues. It is this tension between the human and the economic that problematizes her text.

Alcohol was omnipresent in frontier homes. Clavers replicates this ubiquity through references to it in a wide variety of contexts. Frustrated at the ways in which "that ruinous ally, strong drink" delays the building of her home, she has no sympathy for workmen's "frightfully mashed" thumbs and severely injured heads which she attributes to the effects of whiskey. She is dumbfounded that, despite her promises of extra pay to help their destitute families, workers are lured away to an election or town meeting for two days or more, nominally to exercise their democratic rights, but really to take advantage of the pledges of free whiskey. Indeed, some never return to their families. In an apparent domestic aside on the best way to bake bread, Clavers further emphasizes the destructive intrusion of whiskey into the kitchen, the heart of the family sanctum. Dismissing with contempt the frontier substitution of "salt risin'" or "bran 'east" for dry yeast, because they easily become putrid during the fermentation process and foul the house, she concludes that they "ought to be classed with the turning of grain into whiskey, and both made indictable as offenses."[27]

Clavers regularly associated alcoholism with a decline into brutishness. The first innkeeper they encounter lives in "a wretched den in the wilderness," and comes "raving" through their rooms "in search of more of the posion" [liquor] which had enraged him. The second is reduced to a "great moppy head rested in heavy slumber on [his] brawny arms." In a third vignette, a hard-working and otherwise honorable man sacrifices his reputation because he would "make a beast of himself at times." His wife, who had to take in lodgers to support her family, becomes the victim of cruel gossip, while his reputation as a drunk prevents him from defending her. Imagery such as "den," "great moppy head," and "beast" projected the unspeakable horror of living in frontier isolation with such dehumanized men.[28]

Clavers's most vivid portrait of animalistic self-abandon is of the Newland family, her most obvious target of scorn. The Newlands represent the "vicious and degraded" settlers whose behavior she deplores.[29] She is initially bemused by their ever-worsening poverty, but solves the mystery of their decline when she makes an unannounced visit of mercy and interrupts a family party, the centerpiece of which is a tin pail of whiskey. And while Clavers never speaks directly on the sexual exploitation of women, the implicit association of sexuality and beastliness is dramatized in the horrible death of young Amelia Newland. A product of this alcoholic household, she engages in illicit sex and dies the victim of a botched abortion in her own home.

Kirkland, however, like many middle-class reformers, shared the assumption that while alcohol undermined and brutalized the lower classes, its effects on middle-class people were less extreme. Her portrayals of abused women of the middling classes were far more circumspect than those of lower-class women, for whom she used specific details and emotionally charged language. In the case of middle-class women, small details spoke volumes. When young Mrs. Rivers, the newly arrived wife of a lawyer, first visits Clavers, she is "utterly disconsolate." Mr. Rivers's own father describes him as "a wild chap," disinclined to work. Clavers's sympathy for his wife intensifies when she meets Mr. Rivers himself, whose "face shewed but too plainly the marks of early excess." This "appearance of absence, of indifference . . . spoke volumes of domestic history." Similarly, the charming, graceful Mrs. B—— has "one of the most melancholy" faces Clavers has ever seen. She had discovered too late that Mr. B——, having wasted his own fortune, sought in her a wealthy heiress. "[R]eckless self-indulgence" is obvious in Mr. B——'s face. Although the public parts of their home reflect "the hand of refined taste," all else is desolate and the kitchen literally empty. Where alcohol assumed a role in middle-class abuse, Kirkland softened her description, and in fact alcohol plays no part at all in the sad tale of the Cathcarts, a third middle-class family Clavers encoun-

141

ters. Mr. Cathcart is "horribly jealous . . . of everything and everybody which or whom Mrs Cathcart may chance to look at, or speak to, or take an interest in." Although he might try to "grin" before outsiders "in the effort to suppress the overboiling of his wrath," when they are alone, he abuses his charming and beautiful young wife psychologically. For example, he destroys her garden, "ploughing up the neat flower-beds with his knife, tearing down the vines."[30] Thus, he demolishes his wife's attempt to make her mark on the frontier and provide herself with some sense of stability.

Another factor contemporary sociologists have associated with domestic abuse is a decline in male status and a weakening identification with some aspects of traditional gender roles. The belief that women have usurped male prerogatives is implicit in this theory. Many male abusers have low self-esteem and feelings of inadequacy, helplessness, and shame.[31] Conditions on the nineteenth-century Michigan frontier certainly helped engender such feelings, both in terms of declining economic status for many families and of a blurring of differences in gendered work roles.

The frontier mythos called forth images of strong, active men furthering a national expansionist ideal and their own material well-being. This was complemented by the motif of the Western homestead, owned and run by an independent, autonomous farmer and his family. For many people, such a vision proved a chimera. In Kirkland's work, many men watch in frustration as their families sink into poverty worse than any they have suffered before and recognize that they will never own their own land. Many settlers were cheated by speculators even before they arrived. Clavers excoriates the latter: "it must have required some nerve to . . . stand by, while the poor artizan, the journeyman mechanic, the stranger who had brought his little all to buy government land . . . staked their poor means on strips of land which were at that moment a foot under water."[32] Clavers also targets the greed and corruption of bankers, using metaphors of "fungus growth" and "blood suckers." Bankers' speculations created incredible inflation, but equally devastating were banks established under "the General Banking Law," which went broke. Settlers "from the deep woods many miles distant where no grain had yet grown," who travel "two or three days and nights, with a half-starved ox-team, and living on a few crusts by the way" to purchase flour and other necessaries are told their banknotes are valueless. "Can we wonder that the poor . . . learned to hate the rich and to fancy them natural enemies?" Clavers continues. The rough living on a frontier setting exacerbates this poverty. "When everybody is buying land," Clavers notes, "and scarce any body is cultivating it, one must not expect to find living either good or cheap; but, I confess, I was surprised at the dearth of comforts which we observed."[33]

Many studies show that frontier families tried to maintain established customs, family hierarchies, and conventional sex roles both on the Overland

Trail and in Midwest settlements; in adapting to "harshly different environments," settlers continue "to use the values" they know to "make sense of [their] lives."[34] Frontier conditions, however, quickly forced men and women to modify, if not abandon, the "separate spheres" of influence. Clavers advises readers that "the division of labor is almost unknown" in the Michigan Territory. In this "absolutely savage life" each man and woman is obliged to fill many roles, including those usually associated with the other gender.[35]

Settler families fortunate enough to purchase dry land faced the daunting process of clearing Michigan's untouched woodlands. Trees had to be felled, stumps removed, and grubs cleared. "Grubs," Clavers explains, are "the gnarled roots of small trees and shrubs, with which our soil is interlaced in some places to absolute solidity." Clearing land often took two or three years, during which time nothing could be planted.[36] Even the cheerful Mrs. Danforth admits "we had most awful hard times at first." She worked with her husband "from sunrise till dark in the fields gathering brush heaps and burning stumps."[37] Not all couples could achieve this sense of mutual support. For many, such fluid roles triggered a sense of insecurity and loss of identity.

While this blurring of identity undermined male self-esteem, it affected women's self-perceptions as well, as they tried to come to terms with a male-defined venture. Frontier conditions exacerbated emotions sociologists have defined as common to abused women. They often lacked self-worth, felt inadequate and helpless, and blamed themselves for the situation that triggered abuse.[38]

The cult of domesticity has often been cited as the dominant ideology shaping the lives of nineteenth-century Anglo-American women.[39] Theoretically, the valorization of motherhood and an emphasis on women's moral responsibility to their families gave meaning to domestic work, made blurred sex roles intelligible, and confirmed women's self-worth.[40] According to Clavers, however, domestic conditions on the frontier mitigated against creating and maintaining "a domestic paradise." For women who focused on their failures, the cult of domesticity proved dysfunctional.[41] While men valued their agricultural work as integral to the pioneer venture, they saw women's work merely as domestic support. Many women shared this view and did not recognize the significance of their contribution until long afterward.[42] The first annual report on the condition of farm women published by the Department of Agriculture indicted farmers as insensitive to their wives' work load and their need for authority within the domestic sphere.[43]

While women's work was widely undervalued, the journals and diaries of these women demonstrate how their sense of worth was further undermined by primitive living conditions on the frontier. In a one-roomed cabin, the kitchen was no longer a separate domain under female authority or control but a generally used public space. Clavers's sensitivity to this situation is reflected in her careful descriptions of home interiors and the pride with which house-wives point to newly established partitions that distinguish between working, living, and sleeping spaces. Women's sense of self-worth was further under-mined by their exclusion from important decisions. Because husbands usually made the decision to move to the frontier and gave priority to buying agricul-tural rather then domestic equipment, many wives must have felt that they had lost control over their lives.[44]

Domestic brutality along the frontier must be placed in the larger context of all violence. Literary scholars have often argued that Americans have a high tol-erance for violence precisely *because* of the frontier experience, which placed its citizens beyond law and order and "created a condition that fostered a legit-imization" of violent conflict.[45] Caroline Kirkland's narrative, however, pro-vides evidence that such conditions were not *unique* to the frontier, but *exacer-bated* by it. She marshaled her experience in the Michigan forest to demonstrate that while circumstances conducive to domestic abuse were intensified in that setting, many people who emigrated westward brought with them the proclivi-ties leading to such abuse. This was especially true of a dependence upon alco-hol that, though it reached greater heights (or depths) in frontier settings, was a definitive characteristic of the alcoholic republic in its early years.

Throughout *A New Home*, Kirkland's depiction of frontier life reflected her simultaneous consciousness of more than one point of view: the frontier re-sembled developed areas of America, but was more difficult and dangerous to those who ventured to it. Women were particularly endangered; they were vul-nerable not only to the wilderness and their own fears, but also—as she em-phasized in her narrative—to violent or subtle spousal abuse from husbands who were themselves victimized by natural and human predators.

Yet after graphically delineating the suffering she observed among women in Michigan, Kirkland characteristically diverted her attention to its social and economic, rather than personal, effects. Her own commitment to the expan-sion enterprise, pushing Eastern economic and social values farther west, made it impossible for her to gaze too long or too deeply at the cost paid for such progress by women who went along.

Notes

1. Sandra Zagrell, ed., *A New Home, Who'll Follow? or, Glimpses of Western Life, By Mrs. Mary Clavers, an actual settler* (Reprint ed., New Brunswick, NJ, 1990), (hereafter, Kirkland, *A New Home*).

2. Kirkland, *A New Home*, Preface, 1. In *The Frontiers of Women's Writing: Women's Narratives and the Rhetoric of Westward Expansion* (Tucson, AZ, 1996), 26, Brigitte Georgi-Findlay believes this ambivalence results from women's position both as "part

Jenifer Banks

of an expansionist enterprize and members of that group itself most thoroughly colonized by patriarchal 'civilization.' " Annette Kolodney has praised *A New Home* as "the first realistic depiction of frontier life in American letters," in *The Land Before Her: Fantasy and Experience of the American Frontiers, 1630–1860* (Chapel Hill, NC, and London, 1984), 133.

3. Kirkland possibly also refers to Captain Hall's *Travels in North America* (Edinburgh and London, 1829). James Hall, *Legends of the West* (Philadelphia, 1832); Charles Fenno Hoffman, *A Winter in the West* (New York, 1835); Kirkland, *A New Home*, 49.

4. Several scholars have detailed the role of women in the westward movement as families adapted value systems to frontier conditions. John Mack Faragher, *Women and Men on the Overland Trail* (New Haven, CT, and London, 1979); J. M. Faragher, *Sugar Creek: Life on the Illinois Prarie* (New Haven, CT, and London, 1986); Sandra L. Myres, *Westering Women, and the Frontier Experience 1800–1915* (Albuquerque, NM, 1982); Lillian Schlissel, Vicki L. Ruiz, and Janice Monk, eds., *Western Women: Their Land, Their Lives* (Albuquerque, NM, 1988); Lucy Eldersveld Murphy and Wendy Hamand Venet, eds., *Midwestern Women: Work, Community, and Leadership at the Crossroads* (Bloomington, IN, and Indianapolis, IN, 1997).

5. Kirkland, *A New Home*, xxxix–xl.

6. Georgi-Findlay, *Frontiers of Women's Writing*, xii.

7. Franklin Ellis, *A History of Livingston County, Michigan: with Illustrations and Biographical Sketches of Its Prominent Men and Pioneers* (Philadelphia, 1880).

8. Kirkland, *A New Home*, 146–147.

9. Robert T. Sigler, *Domestic Violence in Context: An Assessment of Community Attitudes* (Lexington, MA, 1989), 8–9.

10. Elizabeth Pleck, *Domestic Tyranny: The Making of American Social Policy against Family Violence from Colonial Times to the Present* (New York, 1987), 7–9, defines three elements of the Family Ideal: belief in domestic privacy, conjugal and parental rights, and the preservation of the family.

11. Sigler, *Domestic Violence in Context*, 2, 64. Two studies of the mythology of the American frontier are particularly useful in placing Kirkland's observations within the context of violence: Richard Slotkin, *Regeneration Through Violence: The Mythology of the American Frontier, 1660–1860* (Hanover, NH, 1973); and Annette Kolodney, *The Land Before Her.* Philip Morgan discusses the power of patriarchs in personal societies in *Slave Counterpoint: Black Culture in Eighteenth-Century Chesapeake and Lowcountry* (Chapel Hill, NC, 1998), 275–276; see also Trevor Burnard, "A Theater of Terror: Domestic Violence in Thomas Thistlewood's Jamaica, 1750–1786," in this volume.

12. Sigler, *Domestic Violence in Context*, 2. The English common law doctrine of the rule of thumb specified that a man could beat his wife with a rod or switch no thicker than his thumb, see Elizabeth Pleck, "Wife-Beating in Nineteenth-Century America," *Victimology: An International Journal* 4 (1979): 61–63, 67. Pleck points out that by the early nineteenth century, however, such chastisement, though legal, was socially unacceptable, and that courts in North Carolina and Mississippi were notoriously conservative in supporting it.

13. *Laws of the Territory of Michigan: Laws Adopted by the Governor and Judges by Authority* (Lansing, MI, 1871) 1:494–499.

14. Pleck, *Domestic Tyranny*, 8, 43, 48.

145

15. Kirkland, *A New Home*, 4.

16. Kirkland, *A New Home*, 43.

17. John A. Caruso, *The Great Lakes Frontier: An Epic of the Old North West* (Indianapolis, IN, 1961), 340–41; *Laws of Michigan* 3:1392–1397; Kirkland, *A New Home*, 5, 6, 73.

18. Ralph R. Tingley, "Postal Service in Michigan Territory," *Michigan History* 35 (1951): 447–460.

19. Myres, *Westering Women*, 168.

20. Kirkland, *A New Home*, 22.

21. W. J. Rorabaugh, *The Alcoholic Republic: An American Tradition* (New York, 1979), 8, 21. Rorabaugh estimates the annual per capita consumption of distilled spirits between 1800 and 1830 exceeded five gallons, a rate nearly triple that of 1979 consumption.

22. Kirkland, *A New Home*, 7.

23. Pleck, *Domestic Tyranny*, 50–52.

24. Kirkland, *A New Home*, 7.

25. Rorabaugh, *The Alcoholic Republic*, 74.

26. "An Act Empowering the Judge of Probate to Appoint Guardians to Minors and Others," *Laws of Michigan* 2:483–484.

27. Kirkland, *A New Home*, 41, 33.

28. Kirkland, *A New Home*, 7, 36, 132.

29. Kirkland, *A New Home*, 111.

30. Kirkland, *A New Home*, 57, 63–64, 74–76, 141–142.

31. Sigler, *Domestic Violence in Context*, 20; David Peterson, "Wife Beating: An American Tradition," *Journal of Interdisciplinary History* 23 (1992): 113.

32. Kirkland, *A New Home*, 30–31.

33. Kirkland, *A New Home*, 121, 126, 33.

34. Faragher, *Women and Men on the Overland Trail*, 88–109; Robert L. Griswold, "Anglo Women and Domestic Ideology in the American West in the Nineteenth and early Twentieth Centuries," in Schlissel et al., *Western Women*, 15–26; Julie Roy Jeffrey, *Frontier Women: The Trans-Mississippi West, 1840–1880* (New York, 1979), 22–23. Quotation from Katherine Jensen, "Commentary," in Schlissel et al., *Western Women*, 36.

35. Kirkland, *A New Home*, 72.

36. Kirkland, *A New Home*, 78–79.

37. Kirkland, *A New Home*, 22.

38. Sigler, *Domestic Violence in Context*, 18–19.

39. Carl N. Degler, *At Odds: Women and the Family in America from the Revolution to the Present* (New York, 1980), 49–50; domestic ideology was "less a set of assumptions than a supple perspective about gender ideals, less a well-defined 'cult of womanhood,' than a way common women made sense of every day existence," Griswold, "Anglo Women and Domestic Ideology," 15–17. Although most women on the overland trail were not upper, nor even middle, class, they exhibited the same belief in women's proper sphere.

40. Griswold, "Anglo Women and Domestic Ideology," 18; Lillian Schlissel, "Family on the Western Frontier," in Schlissel et al., *Western Women*, 81, 87.

41. Julie Roy Jeffrey, "Commentary," in Schlissel et al., *Western Women*, 41; Sarah F. McMahon, " 'The Indescribable Care Devolving upon a Housewife': Women's and Men's Perceptions of Pioneer Foodways on the Midwestern Frontier, 1789–1860," in Murphy and Venet, eds., *Midwestern Women*, 189–190; Myres, *Westering Women*, 146–154; Kirkland, *A New Home*, 49–50.

42. "[T]he question of power is not only a question of what people do but also of the recognition they are granted for what they do and the authority that recognition confers," Faragher, *Women and Men*, 63; McMahon, " 'The Indescribable Care'," 190, 195–197. For a positive reading of women's status, see Myres, *Westering Women*, 146–149, 164.

43. Faragher, *Women and Men*, 59–61.

44. "[A]fter years of having their personal dignity and the control over their lives forcibly taken from them, [women] believe they possess no value," Melody Graulich, "Violence Against Women in Literature of the Western Family," *Frontiers* 7 (1984): 15. Johnny Faragher and Christine Stansell, "Women and Their Families on the Overland Trail to California and Oregon, 1842–1867," *Feminist Studies* 2 (1975): 150–166; Lillian Schlissel, "Women's Diaries on the Western Frontier," *American Studies* 18 (1997): 88. "Women and children were part of the journey because . . . there was no way for them not to go once the decision was made," Lillian Schlissel, *Women's Diaries of the Westward Journey* (New York, 1982), 10.

45. Sigler, *Domestic Violence in Context*, 67.

eight

KEEPING THE PEACE

Domestic Assault and Private Prosecution in Antebellum Baltimore

Stephanie Cole

An historian versed in the idea of nineteeth-century patriarchal power and its corollary assumption, the sacrosanct status of the household, might find antebellum jail records for Baltimore city surprising in the amount of domestic violence they reveal. Despite the values that this society supposedly held, almost a fifth of all individuals committed for assault had allegedly attacked a member of their own household.[1] Wives were the most common victims, and their husbands were often repeat offenders. During the summer of 1831, for example, Baltimore justices made over twenty commitments to jail for domestic assault, including David Beard, a white huckster, or peddler, for "violently beating and abusing his wife and children," John Morrison, a black laborer, for "assaulting and beating his wife," and James Crawford, a white tailor, "for want of security to keep the peace with his wife, Mary." John Starr, a white cooper, was jailed for "threatening the life of his brother," though he had been confined just six months earlier for "beating and abusing" his wife. Peter Ryan, a white man who may have run a disorderly house, was charged with assaulting his wife Sally for the third time in four months.[2]

The incarceration of so many men for domestic abuse seems puzzling in light of the extensive authority of household heads in the Old South. Daily rituals, community relations, and regional politics were constructed, maintained, and depended upon that power.[3] American jurisprudence generally followed English common law, which recognized the right of husbands to "correct" their wives as long as the correcting stick was not wider than "a man's thumb." Southern state supreme courts' acquiescence to the violence of husbands and fathers is well documented.[4] Though local courts took notice of race, social class, and degree of offense when judging spousal discipline, married women had limited recourse from patriarchy in the antebellum South.[5] Nevertheless, hundreds of Baltimore men spent days, sometimes weeks, incarcerated for "want of security to keep the peace" with their wives or were charged under the oath of other family members with violent assaults or threats. Their stories suggest that theories concerning paternalistic patriarchy articulated in high courts were contested on a daily basis in lower ones, while the class and race of victims of domestic abuse affected the ways in which local officials maintained masculine authority.

The current historiography of domestic violence often belittles or ignores the importance of, first, localized approaches to violence, and second, the specific role of the legal process in delineating and containing domestic abuse. Local contexts defined acceptable violence with a precision most historians have missed. These definitions, moreover, help describe the societies in which abuse took place. Examining this process in Baltimore, for example, is helpful because it exposes the social machinations that underpinned patriarchal rule; dependents, particularly wives, constantly participated in negotiations over what that rule meant.

One element of elite male power—the law and the justices who administered it—was especially important in negotiating definitions of domestic abuse. "Keeping the peace" necessitated flexibility in the ways in which authorities responded to the lack of peace within households. Along with the specifics of place, however, the legal process has too long been ancillary to the history of domestic violence. Assault was a matter of law. The procedures for prosecuting criminal assault in antebellum Maryland contributed to dependents' abilities to use the legal system to negotiate patriarchy; consequently, understanding judicial procedures is crucial to interpreting records of domestic assault. In early nineteenth-century Maryland, for example, victims generally had to institute and pursue criminal prosecutions.[6] As Baltimore elites tried to strengthen the bonds of patriarchy, therefore, a remarkable number of the city's men remained behind bars because their wives had put them there.

But while Baltimore's case illustrates the limitations of patriarchy under constant negotiation, the process was not limited to that city alone. Elements of Baltimore's social structure—which existed elsewhere to greater or lesser degrees—shaped its treatment of family violence. The most important regional feature of antebellum cities just below the Mason-Dixon line was their peculiar relationships to the "peculiar institution" of slavery. In Baltimore, Richmond, Washington, and similar places, the power of slavery was declining. Although the institution was legal, it did not function along the border as it did

KEEPING THE PEACE

in the Deep South.[7] During the early nineteenth century, moreover, the large free African-American populations in these cities (and in nearby Philadelphia) were augmented continually by newly freed and escaped slaves. At the same time, the proportion of slaves declined in border cities. The easy inference that black equaled slave, therefore, was questioned sharply. African-Americans in these places, moreover, refused to act like chattel; white residents frequently perceived blacks' activities as emblematic of their effort to elude white control. Indeed, some whites troubled by slavery or searching for a way to retain control over recalcitrant slaves contributed to the erosion of the institution by promising their bondsmen and women freedom after a "term of years" of service. Before 1850, as many as one-third of the slaves sold along the urban border were sold not as slaves for life but as term slaves, which further blurred the opposition of black to white and slave to free.[8]

In the same cities, moreover, whites entered the previously black occupation of domestic service in large numbers. With an influx of new immigrants, employers who sought household help and who were uncomfortable with either slavery or free African-American servants could now opt for white help. White servants who performed domestic service found that it restricted personal freedom more than other forms of wage labor; in some ways, they were not quite free. As a result, the legal status of many nonelites in these cities was somewhere between slave and free, and the theoretical extremes applied to fewer and fewer of them. The rhetorical dichotomy that elites maintained between slave and free did not exist in experience. The underlying social notion of black/slave as "naturally" or inherently different from white/free was demonstrably suspect.[9]

Most interpretations of nineteenth-century family conflict have been divided neatly—much too neatly—into two regional stories. The Northern tale centers on the transforming impact of individualism on family relations; that for Southern slave states revolves around the operation of patriarchal privilege, substantiated by the theoretical paternalism of High Court rulings and the brutality of the whipping post.[10] According to these models, Northern urbanization and market expansion led to the acceptance of individualism and a "separate spheres" ideology. As a result, women assumed a more significant legal and social position, although it never approached that of independent white men. Alterations in divorce laws and custody rights reflected these changes. Lawmakers expanded grounds for divorce to include cruelty, and courts increasingly granted divorced mothers custody of children, particularly when the children were young or female. Though divorce reform ultimately relied upon antebellum ideals of women's natural "domesticity, piety, chastity and submissiveness," their interests as individuals slowly gained credence with the courts at the expense of the patriarchal authority of husbands and fathers.[11]

150

In the South, however, lawgivers had an economic and social interest in preserving slavery, and governed household dependents differently.[12] During the early nineteenth century, ideas of contractualism and the interests of the individual entered family law in Southern states, but just so far as to preserve white male control. Extremely cruel or irresponsible men threatened the public image of a paternalist patriarchy. Not surprisingly, men deemed threats to the system were frequently nonslaveholders with little economic or social standing.[13] For Southern jurists, domestic law both reflected and supported the righteousness of the patriarchal social order. Belief in the efficacy of patriarchal power remained dominant even as ideals of individualism undercut that belief in the North.[14]

The limitations of such archetypical paradigms of North and South are most obvious at their peripheries. Reactions to domestic violence in cities on the border between South and North were more complex than either historiographical paradigm can accommodate. Preserving the institution of slavery and the power of whiteness were important to Baltimore elites, but challenges to racial slavery repeatedly presented themselves. The ambiguities of life in a border city created a dynamic in which legal practice permitted greater nonelite participation and individual action than legal theory would imply.

On the basis of policy alone, the urban border region seems firmly within the Southern legal fold. Maryland legislators and jurists protected the prerogatives of household heads by both mandating against rebellion in the home and ignoring much of what went on there. They persistently offered support to slave owners by increasing punishments for recalcitrant slaves who were, by a larger definition, members of the household.[15] At the same time, they worried about masters who might "excessively beat and abuse" their slaves and offered legislation to mitigate that possibility. Such laws indicated that paternalists allowed slaves protection in return for total obedience.[16]

For the rest of the population, the lack of statutory laws and the force of the common law implied that household heads' authority held sway. As part of a systemic legal reform, the state of Maryland in 1809 codified punishments for assaults when they endangered life and limb. When such crimes were committed in a home, the same punishments applied.[17] Most domestic assaults, however, did not entail murder or maiming and were not covered under statutory law until after 1839. The vast majority of the free men and women who found themselves in Baltimore's jail between 1827 and 1832 for domestic abuse, therefore, had been dealt with under common law.[18]

As Francis Wharton's *Treatise on Criminal Law* illustrates, the common law was, like many statutes, a bastion for paternal power. First published in 1846, Wharton's compendium was "a digest of penal statutes of the general government and of Massachusetts, New York, Pennsylvania, and Virginia," and of court decisions from all states. Wharton noted that "no matter how private or secret the assault may be, it does not thereby cease to be an indictable offence," but also depicted the myriad ways in which the law protected patriarchal rights.[19] Assaults within the family were criminal only when they exceeded "the bound of moderation" or were "cruel and merciless." Admissible defenses against the charge of assault and battery included "the correcting of a child by its parent, [and] the correcting of a servant or scholar by his master." In cases of spousal abuse, Wharton observed that according to "ancient common law the husband possessed the power of chastising his wife, though the tendency of criminal courts in the present day is to regard the marital relation as no defense to a battery." Yet he also highlighted a 1824 case in Mississippi, in which the court allowed that husbands still had the right "of moderate chastisement" and "to use salutary restraints in every case of misbehavior."[20]

Perhaps the best indication that Wharton did not believe that the law could easily interfere in antebellum domestic assault is the contrast between his 1846 volume and his 1885 revision. By 1885, the punishment of children by parents could no longer be "unnecessary" as well as cruel or merciless, and included the "forcible exposure of a child" as an assault. A new section, moreover, in a chapter entitled "Misconduct in Office" listed the responsibilities and recently limited rights of parents, masters, and husbands.[21]

By the early antebellum period, lawgivers had reduced the power of the law to aid husbands or fathers who had been the victims of domestic assault, although some jurists were slow to recognize this change. Wharton noted in 1846 that the definition of the murder of a household head as petit treason had been removed by statute across the United States during the early part of the century. Those convicted of petit treason could be drawn and quartered or burned for their crime. Maryland repealed its petit treason law in 1809, possibly reflecting less intense or less bloodthirsty ideas of patriarchal right. The phrasing of the repeal, however, suggests that some Maryland legislators retained conservative notions: "[E]very person liable to be prosecuted for petit treason shall in future be indicted, proceeded against and punished, as is directed in other kinds of murder, according to degree."[22] This wording implies that jurists would still note in the charge the relationship between the alleged murderer and victim. In fact, in a manual for Maryland justices of the peace, published in 1815—six years after the law was repealed—Justice John Hall insisted that if a wife maliciously killed her husband it was "petty treason" though when a husband maliciously killed his wife, "it is but murder."[23] The slow pace of change in legal perceptions and precedents and the allegiance of lower courts to patriarchal values kept household dependents in a vulnerable position.[24]

When victims initiated actions against abusers, conservative ideals and respect for authority were so intrinsic to the law that legal procedures were designed to keep influence in the hands of appointed court judges. This design was not fail-safe, however, and conservative influence often lapsed. Assault and

battery—the attempt and actual "unlawful beating of another," respectively—
were causes for civil action as well as breaches of the peace. Victims of assault
and battery, therefore, could press for a criminal indictment in addition to or
in lieu of recovering damages by action of *trespass vi et armis*.[25] Battery was
justifiable by parents and masters correcting subordinates and by those who
believed they were protecting their property or families. In all other cases, an
offended party capable of taking an oath and competent to be a witness had
the right to prosecute through the county criminal system.[26] He or she began
this process before the local justice of the peace.

Justices often had no formal legal training and depended upon manuals that
described their duties, summarized pertinent laws, and gave examples of the
forms that legal procedures and documents, such as warrants and recognizances, were supposed to take. An outline of the method prescribed in these
manuals, and in particular one written by Baltimore justice John Latrobe, *The
Justices' Practice*, demonstrates that magistrates were supposed to have enough
power to rid the system of wrongful charges but no more.[27] In practice, however, justices stretched their powers with the help of working-class litigants and
the nodding acquiescence of legally trained court judges. The resultant open
legal process meant that patriarchal power was made from the bottom up as
well as from the top down.

Several different courses of action could usher a domestic assault into the
public realm: neighborly, constabulary, or judicial actions. In each case, however, the prerogative of the victim to prosecute and of the justice to incarcerate
alleged criminals remained critical. In truly dire circumstances, the law permitted neighbors to intervene in intimate violence. In Latrobe's words, "any one
may justify breaking and entering a party's house, and imprisoning him, to prevent him from murdering his wife who cries out for assistance."[28] Private citizens had limited rights in involving themselves further, but they could justifiably hand a perpetrator over to the local jail or to a constable to take him there.

Constables could arrest a perpetrator if given information by a witness, although they were on firmer legal ground if they had witnessed the behavior
themselves. When a domestic assault became an affray—"the fighting of two
or more persons in some *public* place, to the terror of the people of the
state"—constables and nightwatchmen had more right to intervene, and could
arrest a perpetrator without a warrant.[29] Though all affrays were supposed to
be public, several manuals advised that constables could "break open the doors
to preserve the peace" if "an affray be in a house."[30] And domestic battles
could indeed be public; in 1832, Shadrick Hart was arrested twice for "breaking
the peace by fighting and abusing his wife in the public streets" and was described as "a notorious disturber of the peace of the city & citizens."[31] Nevertheless, blurring the line between public and private when it came to domestic
disputes was discouraged; "a constable hath no power to arrest a man for an af-

KEEPING THE PEACE

fray out of his own view, without a warrant from a justice, unless a felony were done," John Hall warned in his guide. Their "proper business" was "to preserve the peace, and not to punish the breach of it."[32] Both constables and citizens were advised in cases of domestic violence to consult justices, who would decide whether commitment to jail or recognizance until the next meeting of the county court was merited.[33] Apparently, Baltimoreans and constables followed this advice; all persons accused of assault and battery on a household member were placed in jail by local justices.

Because of limitations on policing and the private nature of most domestic assault, prosecution was usually left in the hands of the victims or their kin. The primary means by which domestic battery came to the attention of public authorities were individual claims made to justices. The justices were then required to evaluate the claims (or "information" in the manuals' terms) by examining the claimant and any companions he or she brought along to corroborate the story. If a justice were satisfied that the action was not groundless or malicious, he was to send a constable with a written warrant to bring the alleged perpetrator for further questioning, usually with himself or, in rare circumstances, with another justice.[34]

After the justice had confronted the alleged abuser, he had to determine whether a crime had taken place. Most criminal business was, theoretically at least, in the hands of the court of record—in this case, the Baltimore City Court. A J.P. could only cause "the apprehension and commitment of those who are charged or suspected of crimes or misdemeanour."[35] His rights in this duty were extensive; he could issue a warrant for and interrogate the supposed abuser, witnesses, and anyone else he thought might have pertinent information. An accused abuser had the same rights before a J.P. that he had during a trial; he could remain silent, confess, or profess innocence by telling his own side of the story. Although a J.P. was supposed to act as soon as "the case permits," he had "reasonable" time to decide on his actions and could hold or recall the defendant until that time. As Baltimore's justices discovered, this capability was an effective tool.[36]

Upon hearing the evidence, the J.P. could dismiss the accused only if the charges were malicious and/or "wholly groundless." Otherwise, he was compelled to remand the accused for trial, and either set bail or jail the alleged perpetrator to ensure his or her presence in court. In serious cases, offenders were sent to trial even in the face of exculpatory evidence. Justices were also responsible for taking recognizances from all who were to appear at the next court, committing those who refused, and writing on the commitments the names and addresses of the prosecution's witnesses. A copy of this list was placed on the docket and issued to the accused if requested.[37] At this point, the justice's duties were completed and the court of record took over.

Stephanie Cole

Other than deciding whether an assault had taken place, therefore, justices had no power to decide guilt or innocence nor to punish or exonerate the accused. Those tasks were officially left to the City Court, which had assumed control from the old Court of Oyer and Terminer and Gaol Delivery in 1816 to handle the "greatly increased" crimes in the city. The original single judge of the Court had given way to three justices of "integrity, experience and sound legal knowledge" who heard all "felonies, and other crimes, offenses and misdemeanors."[38]

Defendants who found themselves in front of the Baltimore City Court as a result of private prosecution again had options. In cases of assault and battery, the defendant could waive the right to the presentment to the Grand Jury and to a jury trial. Judges of the City Court had the power to determine, "in a summary way," these cases and "other small offenses against the peace." This relieved accused persons who could not make bail from a "long imprisonment . . . oppressive to the accused and expensive to the city." Petty juries also involved high costs that devolved upon the accused if convicted or upon his or her accuser if acquitted. Inexpensive bench decisions were obviously a popular route, and in 1835 the assembly expanded the ability of the judges to hear and determine "all complaints of assault and battery" and a slew of other infractions of the law.[39]

J.P.s had another task in "preventive justice," as Latrobe called it—issuing sureties of the peace. Sureties were bonds that insured peaceable relations between two parties. If an assaulter violated a bond, he or she forfeited a considerable amount of money. A justice was "bound to grant" a surety to anyone of "sane memory" who requested one, including a wife or a child. Once a J.P. granted a surety, the person bound promised a set amount, usually $100 and often with the help of friends, to guarantee that he or she would appear at the next court and keep the peace in the interim. Wives and children whose husbands or parents demanded a surety against them were bound exclusively in the name of friends, a reminder of their lack of personality under the law. Dependents who required a surety of the peace against a family member had to swear under oath that they feared future bodily harm from the party.[40]

As this requirement implies, requests for sureties could easily be manipulated. Differing opinions about the issuance of sureties further confused the situation and increased the J.P.s' flexibility in cases of assault and battery.[41] Latrobe, for example, insisted that a retaliatory surety could not be issued for a past battery, or the person who requested the surety risked indictment. John Colvin, however, who published *A Magistrate's Guide and Citizen's Counsellor* in 1805, described terms that accepted the connection between previous batteries and claims for sureties for the peace. The form Colvin provided as a model for the warrant to apprehend a person for assault and battery was attached to a warrant that demanded a surety to keep the peace. In his guide, a description of a recent "cruel beating" accompanied the request for a bond to keep the peace for "the space of one year."[42] While later descriptions circumscribed J.P.s' powers, therefore, earlier practices permitted justices to act on previous assaults.

Whether justices followed Colvin's or Latrobe's interpretation of the law, however, they relied on the victim's word to initiate action. Dependents victimized by domestic assault thereby gained latitude to steer the legal system in unexpected directions. The combination of private prosecution and surety bonds affords a rare glimpse into ordinary border residents' ideas about familial authority. A legal process open to all free people included those generally not consulted about the structure and operation of households, in particular nonelite women.

Social context shaped the opportunities permitted to women and helped determine those who took advantage of it. Access to and response by Baltimore's legal system may have resulted from the uncertainties created by the declining institution of slavery. Elites may have sought to fortify the allegiance of working-class whites by supporting an egalitarian legal process. If so, they probably did not anticipate that so many women would participate in it by charging their husbands with battering them. Nonetheless, hundreds of abused wives made their stories public, despite the fact that authorities ignored or arbitrated crimes with a schematic that respected men's authority over women's protection.

An analysis of the women who approached justices about intimate violence reveals differences in involvement with or access to the legal system by class and race. The same social context which mandated a legal process unrestricted by class probably solidified racial boundaries. Working-class white women, who had access to the law and used it, demonstrated that patriarchal rule was an edifice daily in the making. Their challenges to patriarchal society, and the carefully gauged responses to such challenges, determined the everyday reality of life in that society.

In the worst cases of wifebeating, judicial responses were severe; if left unpunished, such abusers indicated that Baltimore's social order did *not* protect women. Men who crossed the line from an occasional lapse of control to habitual assaults or who used excessive and life-threatening force against their wives and children undermined patriarchal authority.[43] In November of 1828, Michael O'Brien was sentenced to four months in jail for "being a drunken vagabond & ill-treating his wife and family." He had been charged twice earlier in the year for assault, including once in March for "beating his daughter 13 years of age." Peter O'Hara went further and received a stiffer punishment. In 1831 he began twelve years in the penitentiary for murdering his wife Nancy.[44] Testimony from a murder trial in nearby Washington, D.C., intimates that nonelites agreed with the idea that wife-killing was an egregious

Stephanie Cole

crime. John Day received the toughest possible penalty for manslaughter—eight years in the penitentiary. Day claimed that his wife's actions before her death rendered him insane, singling out the fact that she "gave birth to a full grown living child" three months after their marriage. Despite this evidence that Catharine Day had not resembled the quiescent antebellum "true woman," local men felt John Day had acted indefensibly. Among the defense's exceptions and challenges was a request to ban a juror who supposedly said that "a man who would kill or strike a woman ought to be hung" and that "he would act Jack Kitch [the hangman]."[45]

While officials concentrated on extreme cases of violence, Baltimore women called attention to their husbands' less grievous assaults. They initiated complaints of violence with local justices at a point in the legal process when they could control the procedure. In doing so, they questioned the legitimacy of violence as a part of husbands' authority.[46] Over three-quarters of Baltimore domestic assault commitments, or about 15 percent of the total, came when wives charged husbands with assault or demanded a surety for his peace with her. Most of these women were working-class whites.[47] Their husbands were laborers, Chesapeake Bay pilots, hucksters (peddlers), and manufactory workers, among other jobs. But none were attorneys, gentlemen, or men of similar standing.

Without direct evidence, the absence of elite women is difficult to explain. They undoubtedly suffered from domestic violence, but they may have chosen to suffer without public protest, tacitly supporting the patriarchal system that brought their class such power.[48] The wives of working men had no such commitment. Between 1827 and 1832, between fifty and sixty women annually named their husbands as abusive, although they were doubtless aware that conviction rates were low and that they could expect little response.

Wives were not alone in calling attention to contradictions in the social order. Several charges of domestic assault every year involved other family members; most frequent were grown children's attacks on a parent. Sons who struck their mothers were particularly dissonant in a system that lauded seniority and women's vulnerability; in all cases in which punishments can be determined that message is clear. Sons who beat or threatened their mothers served on average 23 days in the Baltimore County jail, nearly five times longer than husbands who beat their wives. Jared Eichelberger, a white man who worked in a tobacco manufactory, spent nearly a month in jail in 1831 for assaulting his mother. He was released only when William Eichelberger paid $5.87 for his fees. Young Eichelberger may have languished in jail because he did not have a family who depended on his income and pressed friends or relatives to raise his bond money. In any case, he had committed a serious crime in the eyes of Baltimore officials.[49]

If charges of assault by white wives and mothers illustrate their persistence in challenging male authority, African-American women's experiences suggest

KEEPING THE PEACE

alienation from the legal system that prevented similar resistance. If Baltimore elites allowed working-class whites to pursue legal claims to encourage their solidarity, they discouraged such sentiments among African-Americans. Free blacks represented almost a third of the commitments for assault in the early 1830s, although they comprised less than a quarter of Baltimore's population. Private prosecutions, moreover, did not produce these incarcerations. Most assaults that involved African-Americans were public disturbances; their incarcerations were instigated by white constables. Ennals Chase, like Shadrick Hart, was accused of publicly "fighting with" his wife and disturbing the neighborhood, not of abusing her.[50]

Not surprisingly, African-American women were reluctant to accuse their husbands in a racist legal system; few African-American women complained to a J.P. Free black husbands were less than half as likely as white husbands to be accused of spousal abuse relative to their proportion of the population.[51] The legal system was not color-blind, as free black people realized. Margaret Halleday, for example, was certainly suspicious. Although the nature of the relationship between Halleday and July Warner is unclear, they were united in their distaste for the City Court. On the same day in November 1827, Halleday and Warner were both committed to jail, Halleday for refusing "to testify for the state against July Warner," who had stabbed her.[52] Black women like Halleday who were not under the protection of a white man could expect little compassion from judicial authorities. That absence of compassion was doubly true for married free African-American women who did not fit under the rules of white patriarchal governance in their homes. Mary Curtis's experience intimates how white elites discouraged married black women's claims for protection. In the first four months of 1828, free black John Curtis was twice committed for injuring his wife. In both cases, the clerk recorded the attacks in sensational, graphic detail, which he never applied to white-on-white assaults. In January Curtis reportedly "stripp[ed] his wife naked t[ied] both hands & feet & abus[ed] her with an iron." In April he stabbed "his wife in the left eye." For the first attack he spent two days in jail, for the second, six. Such aggravated assaults could easily have been interpreted as intents to kill and thus could have been referred to criminal court and punished with mandatory prison sentences. But nothing in the record indicates that the cases went any further than brief commitments to the county jail.[53] Mary Curtis's own role in her husband's light punishment is unknown, but her experience described an uncaring system that sensationalized African-American violence. Black family violence in Baltimore remained outside the interference and arbitration of white justices.

For whites, however, private prosecution opened the door for active involvement in domestic assault. The most proactive players in violent domestic disputes were justices of the peace, who assumed power not given under the law, an impetus that may well have come from clients of the system. Wives, parents, and other victims of domestic assault may have preferred an official less remote than City Court judges to decide the fate of intimate abusers. In any event, the legal procedures carefully outlined by Latrobe or the more liberal Colvin were not followed in many cases. The notes of the jail clerks, rather than illustrating routine officiating, illuminate the latitude and discrimination J.P.s used in treating domestic assault. They reveal a system that played off severe City Court judges against more lenient local justices, apparently with participants' approval. When victims took abusers to a J.P., they began a process that could send the accused to jail for one day or for several months.

If an accused person were jailed because a family member demanded a surety bond—as happened in about a third of the domestic cases in the records—he (or, in a few cases, she) could expect to stay about a week if a justice could keep the case in his jurisdiction.[54] Justices were entitled to handle these disputes entirely; most of the time they did. Only six of fifty cases ended with the City Court discharging the allegedly dangerous person; most were decided by the original justice or, in a few isolated cases, by another justice. Depending on finances, a person committed for "want of security to keep the peace" could be out on the same day or could spend a month or more cooling his heels. Poor men, or men who had rankled friends who might otherwise help raise the necessary sum, stayed the longest. John P. Benson was "committed until he finds security for keeping the peace towards his wife Lydia Benson and all other persons" on June 3, 1831, and was out two days later. Richard Griffin's experience may testify to the strength of the free black community. In August of 1832, Griffin's wife Mary was one of the few African-American women who demanded a surety to keep the peace against her husband. Though Griffin was "colored" and transient enough not to appear in the city directory, he raised the money for the bond quickly. Justice Bailey released him the next day after Griffin paid 67 cents in fees. Hugh Gallagher, a poor white man, was not so lucky. In March 1831, Gallagher, a tallow chandler, was jailed for "want of security to keep the peace towards his mother Elizabeth Gallagher." He was released 58 days later, by which time he owed jail fees of $12.27.[55]

Gallagher's case was unusual. Half of those committed for "want of security" were out within four days. So slight a penalty implies that both family members and authorities used the law to create a "cooling-off" period. The low rate of interference by the City Court suggests that whatever men and women did to attract the attention of J.P.s, the busy and more mighty City Court judges did not perceive such activities as serious enough to warrant participation. The parties concerned may well have shared the sentiment. For abused wives and parents, bringing husbands and sons before justices for peace bonds was an initial, precautionary step. Some clearly chose this path over assault charges. As Colvin's manual indicated, experiencing abuse and demanding a surety could be linked. In fact, ten abuse victims swore out claims for charges as well as demanding sureties for good future behavior. But most people who undoubtedly could have added an assault charge opted to seek only a surety. An abusive husband's income was important; once a man posted bond he was free to leave the jail to return to work. Like Jared Eichelberger, Hugh Gallagher's long jail stay may have hinged on his status as a son without dependents rather than a husband with them. Demanding a surety was one method by which a wife could resist a husband's abuse of power without risking a sentence that could punish them both.

Most people jailed faced more serious charges, but thanks to the intervention of J.P.s, not always with more serious results. Two-thirds allegedly committed one or more misdemeanors or felonies: threatening an assault, beating a victim, using a "dangerous weapon" to frighten a parent or wife, or maiming or killing a family member. Often public charges were added on, so that some of the accused were listed as "being continually drunk," or using "swearing profane language," or "even cursing our blessed Savior."[56] Once criminal charges were involved, justices of the peace were technically no longer competent to release alleged perpetrators after they had committed them. The exceptions occurred when a magistrate placed a possible criminal in jail while he decided whether the charges against him or her were malicious. But Baltimore's justices took liberties and extended their powers, thereby shielding accused abusers (and again, their dependent victims) from serious penalties resulting from involvement with the bench of record.

The proportion of J.P. cases that involved jail time and the length of time accused abusers were incarcerated indicate that justices' actions were not entirely legal. Over 70 percent of those held for criminal indictment were released by a justice's actions, a figure that seems very high for malicious or "wholly groundless" charges. These prisoners had remained in jail for five days on average—probably more time than a justice required to gather witnesses and decide whether malice prompted charges. A significant percentage of these men were certainly incarcerated too long for a simple investigation in the small world of Baltimore. Nearly a third were held for seven to thirty days, clearly more than enough time for routine examinations. In many of these cases, perhaps most, justices settled the dispute between the aggrieved and the accused by instituting informal jail time and demanding accompanying fees.[57] This procedure, though technically outside the law, apparently had the tacit approval of Baltimore's citizens, judging by their participation.

Individual justices approached this process differently, and their deviations enabled battered family members savvy to the system to teach abusers a lesson without paying too high a price. In 1831, for example, justices left committed persons in jail for an average of five to six days, and charged them $1.78 for the pleasure. This was considerably lower than the nearly three weeks averaged by abusers who came before the City Court, but the time accused people spent in jail varied significantly by justice.[58] Domestic victims clearly preferred Thomas Bailey for private prosecutions; he decided 22 cases between 1827 and 1831—twice as many as the next most popular J.P., William Waite. More important, Bailey's average "sentences" and fees were well below the norm, costing just four days and slightly more than one dollar. Waite, in contrast, gave an average sentence of over fourteen days. Justice Charles Kernan's five commitments in 1831 averaged one week in jail and $3.75 in fees. Wives who wished to reprimand their husbands lightly would register their oaths in Bailey's office on High Street first; those who were angrier or more independent economically headed to Kernan's on Hanover Street.[59] The horror of a crime could, on occasion, prompt justices to leave abusers in jail for a long time; Henry Gray remanded Daniel Perkins to custody for almost a month for "abusing his wife and threatening to poyson himself and family," and William Schaeffer did not release Julia Ann Baily for thirteen days after her husband swore that she had "threatened to kill him and his children."[60]

While there were clear distinctions among individual justices, the most significant difference was between cases resolved by J.P.s and the criminal cases that came before the bench of record. Men and women whose fates were determined by the city Criminal Court spent an average of twenty days in jail, four times longer than those who came before J.P.s. Among those eventually acquitted, the average stay was 15 days, still nearly three times longer. When the court was involved, long incarcerations were normal.[61]

Laconic court notations do not always indicate why some individuals remained in jail so long. A few may have had to wait until the court convened, although judges held weekly sessions to settle misdemeanor cases without juries, a procedure popular among "the poorer classes of the community."[62] More likely explanations for longer jail times include the severity of the crime, common knowledge of a defendant's troublesome behavior, or his or her lack of friends. Baltimore officials regarded using weapons as a serious offense. When William Hicks, for example, was committed "for beating his wife and throwing brick bats at her," the J.P. turned his case over to the bench of record. Disrespect for parental authority also merited severe justice. John Jennings was charged by "Patrick Jennings his father with having assaulted and wounded his father and threatening to take his life." The court let him languish in jail for 42 days before discharging him. Judge Brice freed Jacob Etchberger from a charge of "threatening to beat his mother" in July of 1831 after a few days in jail, but recommitted him two weeks later, either with new evidence or for a second offense. This time, Etchberger languished in jail for over two months. Repeat offenders, as aforementioned, caught the full force of the law. Michael O'Brien, the "drunken vagabond" who abused his wife three times in a year, spent four months in jail. Joseph Clinton was held for nine days in July 1828, while he

KEEPING THE PEACE

gathered funds to guarantee his future good behavior toward his wife. When she swore an oath that he broke his promise just three days after his release, the court issued a bench warrant and reincarcerated him. From there he escaped without waiting for his punishment.[63]

Although contemporary sensibilities may find these sentences light, they indicate the impact of private criminal prosecution. Abused women who were willing to take domestic disputes to a local justice used the law to weaken their husbands' claims for unmediated authority. When antebellum Baltimoreans threatened or abused family members, they knew that private criminal prosecution could mean public repercussions for their actions. Though justices afforded intimate assault a wide range of responses, most claims were not ignored. Justices of the peace, the more common judges of this crime, often issued light punishments, although even these were extralegal. In contrast to their response, the city Criminal Court cast a longer shadow.

By 1835, however, the state assembly registered dissatisfaction with this process, particularly the part played by justices of the peace. In that year, legislators created a system in which the governor and council appointed fifteen aldermen who assumed the responsibilities of the justices. These salaried aldermen were to "perform all the duties belonging . . . to justices of the peace," but were required to serve specific wards within Baltimore and to remit formal quarterly reports of their activities. By putting the process into the hands of accountable professionals, lawmakers signaled their discomfort with the informal power of J.P.s—and perhaps with the way the working-class women of Baltimore maneuvered within and around that power.[64]

Lawmakers and judges designed public policy and legal procedures to support male power by giving men tremendous discretion within households. For the most part, what happened in homes was private, and appointed judges were to arbitrate the most serious disputes that escaped their sacrosanct walls. But dependents within households resisted control. The sheer numbers of cases wives brought, as well as the aggressive behavior of justices of the peace and their willing claimants, edged private matters into a public venue. Women may not have been treated as they wished, but they persevered in forcing authorities to listen to their objections to a social order that gave their husbands unchecked power. Although African-American women distrusted and avoided the legal system, white women learned to use it to their benefit. This frequent legal intervention undermined the claim that a paternalistic patriarchy took care of women.

The shifting terrain of urban border society highlighted the tensions within nineteenth-century patriarchal society. In Baltimore, class and race factored heavily into arbitration over domestic assault. With urbanization, the ability of both the oppressed and the elite to negotiate the terms of patriarchal authority altered. Efforts by elites to fortify their power in one way created interstices that eluded their control in others. By supporting the Anglo-American tradition of an individual's right to sue, they opened the door to its use in cases of domestic assault. The result was that those supposedly protected by paternalism on occasion challenged that protection. Because Baltimore elites sought to keep their peace, white women were able to claim peace in their homes.

Notes

1. I am most grateful to the following for their assistance: Peter Bardaglio, Steve Whitman, Bridget Williams-Serle, and members of the Dallas Area Social History Group for their advice on an earlier version of this essay; Tim Huebner, Eric Rise, Jim Rice, and Allan Steinberg for guidance in legal history; New Mexico State University College of Arts and Sciences for funding archival research; and, especially, Chris Daniels and Chris Morris for continuous listening, reading, and prodding, which ultimately allowed me to develop a much better argument than I began with. Data compiled from the Baltimore County Jail and City Criminal Docket [BCCD], 1827–1832, MSA C2077, Maryland Hall of Records. In 1832, 410 cases of assaults and requests for sureties to keep the peace, 72, or 17.5 percent, involved a household member. The other complete years, 1828 and 1831, had about the same total number of assaults; 1832, therefore, seems representative. Although the records contain intriguing evidence concerning violence against all household members, including servants and slaves, analysis of that violence is beyond the scope of this essay. The 215 cases that form the core of this paper came from the following years: 1827 (partial records)—10 domestic assaults (all husband-on-wife); 1828—68 domestic assaults (58 husband-on-wife, 10 others); 1829–1830—records missing; 1831—65 domestic assaults (50 husband-on-wife, 15 others); 1832—72 domestic assaults (60 husband-on-wife, 12 others).

2. Data compiled from BCCD; occupations from Matchett's Baltimore Directory (1833). BCCD, Record 7105, 11/18/1831; 6921, 5/23/1831; 7097, 7/15/1831; 7280, 9/5/1831; 6820, 4/10/1831; 6824, 4/18/1831; 6866, 5/8/1831; and 7148, 7/271831. Peter Ryan had an address but no occupation in the 1833 directory; possibly the same Peter Ryan was arrested for keeping a disorderly house, BCCD, 7021, 6/21/1831.

3. Scholarship on Southern society is voluminous. Notable works on household relations include Elizabeth Fox-Genovese, *Within the Plantation Household: Black and White Women in the Old South* (Chapel Hill, NC, 1988); Stephanie McCurry, *Masters of Small Worlds: Yeoman Households, Gender Relations, and the Political Culture of the Antebellum South Carolina Lowcountry* (New York, 1995); Nancy Dunlap Bercaw, "Politics of Household during the Transition from Slavery to Freedom in the Yazoo-Mississippi Delta, 1861–1876," Ph.D. diss, University of Pennsylvania, 1996; Laura F. Edwards, *Gendered Strife and Confusion: The Political Culture of Reconstruction* (Urbana, IL, 1997).

4. English common law acceptance of "moderate chastisement" is noted in William Blackstone, *Commentaries on the Laws of England,* Facsimile of First Edition of 1765–1769 (Chicago, 1979), 1:432–433. The two most famous legal cases outlining patriarchal power were *State v. Mann,* 13 N.C. 168 (1829), and *Bradley v. State,* 1 Miss. 156

(1824). In the former, the North Carolina Supreme Court acknowledged that masters were not liable for the slave deaths that occurred as a consequence of punishment. In the latter, the Mississippi Supreme Court disallowed a claim of physical cruelty as grounds for divorce. For a discussion of the Mann decision, see Mark V. Tushnet, *The American Law of Slavery, 1810–1860: Considerations of Humanity and Interest* (Princeton, NJ, 1981), 57–79; Thomas D. Morris, *Southern Slavery and the Law, 1619–1860* (Chapel Hill, NC, 1996), 190–193, 278–280.

5. Peter Bardaglio, *Reconstructing the Household: Families, Sex, and the Law in the Nineteenth-Century South* (Chapel Hill, NC, 1995), 92–106; Victoria E. Bynum, *Unruly Women: The Politics of Social & Sexual Control in the Old South* (Chapel Hill, NC, 1992), 59–87.

6. Philadelphia also permitted private prosecutions, but whether other locales did will remain unclear until there are more studies of nineteenth-century legal procedure. See Allen Steinberg, *The Transformation of Criminal Justice: Philadelphia, 1800–1880* (Chapel Hill, NC, 1989); Lawrence M. Friedman, *A History of American Law*, 2nd ed. (New York, 1985), 285–287.

7. Richard C. Wade, *Slavery in the Cities: The South, 1820–1860* (New York, 1964); Barbara J. Fields, *Slavery and Freedom on the Middle Ground: Maryland in the Nineteenth Century* (New York, 1985). For a different view based upon the demand for slaves rather than the power of the institution, see Claudia Goldin, *Urban Slavery in the American South, 1820–1860* (Chicago, 1976).

8. For term slaves, see T. Stephen Whitman, *The Price of Freedom: Slavery and Manumission in Baltimore and Early National Maryland* (Lexington, KY, 1997), 11–14, 75–79. As the sands of slavery shifted, elites in most Southern cities, Baltimore included, sought to capture control by writing stringent "black codes," which proscribed the movements of Africans–Americans based upon race, rather than status. See Leonard Curry, *The Free Black in Urban America: The Shadow of a Dream* (Chicago, 1981); Ira Berlin, *Slaves Without Masters: The Free Negro in the Antebellum South* (New York, 1974).

9. Unfortunately, historians have reified this artificial dichotomy by consistently separating "slave" from "free" regions in their research. I have outlined social life in border cities in "Servants and Slaves: Domestic Service in the Border Cities, 1800–1850," Ph.D. diss., University of Florida, 1994.

10. North-versus-South dichotomies are apparent in Michael Grossberg, *Governing the Hearth: Law and the Family in Nineteenth-Century America* (Chapel Hill, NC, 1985); Bardaglio, *Reconstructing the Household*. David Peterson del Mar, *What Trouble I Have Seen: A History of Violence Against Wives* (Cambridge, MA, 1996), outlines alterations in cultural ideals that affected the frequency of and response to domestic violence in Oregon between the settlement period and the present.

11. Grossberg, *Governing the Hearth*; Eileen Boris and Peter Bardaglio, "Gender, Race, and Class: The Impact of the State on the Family and the Economy, 1790–1945," in Naomi Gerstel and Harriet Engel, eds., *Families and Work* (Philadelphia, PA, 1987), 132–151.

12. Household dependents who received the most attention from antebellum lawmakers and contemporary historians were slaves. At the end of the eighteenth century, Southern lawmakers banned extremely cruel treatment of slaves. See Willie Lee Rose, "On the Domestication of Slavery," in William Freehling, ed., *Slavery and Freedom*

Stephanie Cole

(New York, 1982). Judicial scholars debate the extent to which legal procedures intended to recognize slaves as having rights. See A. E. Keir Nash, "Fairness and Formalism in the Trials of Blacks in the State Supreme Courts of the Old South," *Virginia Law Review* 56 (1970): 64–100; Nash, "A More Equitable Past: Southern Supreme Courts and the Protection of the Antebellum Negro," *North Carolina Law Review* 48 (1970): 197–242; Mark Tushnet, "Approaches to the Study of the Law of Slavery," *Civil War History* 25 (1979): 329–38.

13. Several scholars emphasize the importance of local control within the South. See Bertram Wyatt-Brown, *Southern Honor: Ethics and Behavior in the Old South* (New York, 1982), 391; Christopher Morris, *Becoming Southern: The Evolution of a Way of Life, Warren County and Vicksburg, Mississippi, 1770–1860* (New York, 1995), 63–83; Bynum, *Unruly Women,* 84–87.

14. Bardaglio, *Reconstructing the Household,* 23–36 and 90–97. In questioning the dichotomy between Northern and Southern law, David Bodenhamer and James Ely, Jr. find that Southerners kept traditional rules regarding the poor and indentured, but for reasons not directly connected with slavery. Because urbanization, immigration, and evangelicalism had not yet transformed the South, old rules continued to work there. Though not denying the exigencies of maintaining white power in a biracial society, Bodenhamer and Ely suggest that in dependent law, Southern exceptionalism was linked more to its rural, culturally unified character. James W. Ely and David J. Bodenhamer, "Regionalism and American Legal History: The Southern Experience," *Vanderbilt Law Review* 39 (1986): 539–567; Bodenhamer, "The Efficiency of Criminal Justice in the Antebellum South," *Criminal Justice History* 3 (1982): 81–95.

15. Colonial Maryland passed a series of laws mandating harsh punishment for insubordinate slaves. Most noteworthy was the 1751 "act for the more effectual punishment of negroes and other slaves" which strengthened the 1729 petit treason law. While the first law punished slaves who had murdered a master or willfully burned a dwelling house with hanging and quartering, the 1751 act extended capital punishment to, and withdrew benefit of clergy from, a longer list of violators: those who conspired or attempted to raise an insurrection, to murder or poison any person, or to "commit a rape upon any white woman." Furthermore, anyone who killed a slave refusing to surrender to officers of the law was indemnified for the murder and, until 1753, would not even be tried. *Laws of Maryland,* July session, 1729, chap. 4; *Laws of Maryland,* May session, 1751, chap. 14.

16. In 1715, the General Assembly provided that masters who gave slaves "above ten lashes for any one offence" could be fined although, with permission of a county court, they could give up to 39 lashes. *Laws of Maryland,* April session, 1715, chap. 44, sec. 21. Appellate courts often gave slaves accused of assault or murder against whites some latitude; when slaves were treated unjustly, whites' claims on their submission weakened. A slave who killed an overseer in self-defense, for example, was guilty of manslaughter, not murder, and by extension was not guilty of petit treason. The implication that slaves gave allegiance for protection was not as important in local courts, which tended to convict trouble-making slaves regardless of circumstances. Morris, *Southern Slavery and the Law,* 279–288.

17. Because this codification was part of an impetus to limit judges' prerogatives, it was concerned with defining crimes and regulating prison sentences. Following the

ideas of Enlightenment thinker Caesare Beccaria, lawmakers acted on the principle that the punishment should fit the crime. Draconian capital sentences led to irresolute juries and large numbers of executive and clerical pardons; rational sentences were supposed to bring more certain justice and fewer criminals to test the system. David Bodenhamer, *Fair Trial: Rights of the Accused in American History* (New York, 1992), 51; Kermit Hall, *The Magic Mirror: Law in American History* (New York, 1989), 169–172. Lawmakers were especially concerned to consider circumstances surrounding murders to determine the degree of the crime. Under the new system, only those guilty of premeditated murder could be executed; those convicted of second-degree murder or manslaughter received prison sentences. The law also mandated that if assault involved maiming or an attempt to rob, murder, or rape, it would be punished by confinement in the penitentiary for two to ten years; rape itself would be punished with death by hanging or between one and 21 years in prison. *Laws of Maryland* 1809, chap. 138, sec. 4. For an example of the use of these laws for domestic crime, see BCCD, 7497, 12/9/1831.

18. Assault was codified as a public crime between 1839 and 1860. The 1839 *Laws of Maryland* do not include this law; an 1860 compilation indicated that the City Council decreed assault and battery on city streets or "place of public resort or amusement, between six o'clock in the evening and six in the following morning" was a crime against the city, and required a minimum sentence of $25 and one month in jail. Given the emphasis on the public location of this offense, it is unlikely that the city became involved with domestic violence even then. *Code of Maryland* 2, art. 4, sec. 155, 180.

19. Francis Wharton, *A Treatise on the Criminal Law of the United States; comprising A Digest of the Penal Statues of the General Government, and of Massachusetts, New York, Pennsylvania, and Virginia; with the Decisions on cases arising upon those statutes; together with the English and American authorities upon criminal law in general* (Philadelphia, PA, 1846), 312. Wharton's compendium is arguably the best antebellum resource for understanding common law and domestic violence.

20. Wharton, *A Treatise on the Criminal Law*, 314–15.

21. Francis Wharton, *Treatise on Criminal Law*, 9th ed. (Philadelphia, 1885), 2:572, 403–405.

22. *Laws of Maryland*, 1809, chap. 138, sec. 3. The New York legislature, in contrast, declared: "The killing of a master by his servant, or of a husband by his wife, shall not be deemed any other or higher offence than if committed by any other person." Wharton, *Treatise on Criminal Law* (1846), 220. Other states used phrasing similar to Maryland's.

23. John E. Hall, *The Office and Authority of a Justice of the Peace in the State of Maryland* (Baltimore, MD, 1815), 283. J.P.s were notoriously undertrained; Hall may only have been behind the times. Bodenhamer, *Fair Trial*, 63; James D. Rice, "Crime and Punishment in Frederick County and Maryland, 1748–1837: A Study in Culture, Society, and Law," Ph.D. diss., University of Maryland, 1994, 143–146. Wharton also found that family ties could change the way murder and assault were perceived, despite statute law. He describes a case in which a man accidentally killed a boy he caught stealing from the boy's master. The fact that the victim was not *his* servant—and their ties not "natural or civil"—made the charge murder rather than manslaughter.

24. The history of petit treason law merits more investigation. Generally, historians associate the repeal of these laws with liberal reform, but inconsistencies in dates and

Stephanie Cole

lawmakers' reasoning suggest something more complex. See Morris, *Southern Slavery and the Law*, 277–279; Kathryn Preyer, "Crime, the Criminal Law and Reform in Post-Revolutionary Virginia," *Law and History Review* 1 (1983): 56–59.

25. Blackstone, *Commentaries*, 3:120. Much of Blackstone is paraphrased in John B. Colvin, *Magistrate's Guide; and Citizen's Counsellor* (Frederick Town, MD, 1805), 110–11.

26. John H. B. Latrobe, *The Justices' Practice under the Laws of Maryland, including the Duties of a Constable* (Baltimore, MD, 1826), 261.

27. Colvin, *Magistrate's Guide*; E. H. Cummins, *The Maryland Justice: Containing Approved Forms for the Use of Justice of the Peace of the State of Maryland* (Baltimore, MD, 1825); Hall, *Office and Authority*; Latrobe, *The Justices' Practice*. For more on this procedure, Bodenhamer, *Fair Trial*, 62–65; Rice, "Crime and Punishment," 134–178.

28. Latrobe, *The Justices' Practice*, 266.

29. Colvin, *Magistrate's Guide*, 111.

30. Hall, *Office and Authority*, 7; Latrobe, *The Justices' Practice*, 266.

31. BCCD, 7898, 5/24/1832; 7998, 7/7/1832.

32. Hall, *Office and Authority*, 7.

33. Latrobe, *The Justices' Practice*, 266–268.

34. Latrobe, *The Justices' Practice*, 270.

35. Latrobe, *The Justices' Practice*, 260–261.

36. Latrobe, *The Justices' Practice*, 294–297.

37. *Laws of Maryland*, 1821, chap. 229; Latrobe, *The Justices' Practice*, 297–299.

38. *Laws of Maryland*, 1793, chap. 57; *Laws of Maryland*, 1816, chap. 193.

39. Before 1838, those who insisted on a trial waited for the next session for a hearing presided over by the two associate justices, the Chief Justice, or any combination thereof. *Laws of Maryland*, 1821, chap. 229; *Laws of Maryland*, 1823, chap. 210. Occasionally, the J.P.'s notes of his examinations of informants could be entered into formal proceedings, see Rice, "Crime and Punishment," chap. 3, 5, and 6. The expansion of the court's power was necessary, legislators claimed, because once again there was a "great increase of business in Baltimore city court." *Laws of Maryland*, 1835, chap. 75.

40. A justice could also demand a surety if he witnessed violent action, an unlikely scenario in the case of intimate abuse. Latrobe, *The Justices' Practice*, 308.

41. A justice in Frederick Town, Maryland, used his ability to require peace bonds to keep some litigants out of court, in order to limit the number of people attending court for minor offenses such as assault and battery. Rice, "Crime and Punishment," 157.

42. Colvin, *Magistrate's Guide*, 112.

43. See Wyatt-Brown, *Southern Honor*; Bynum, *Unruly Women*; Bardaglio, *Reconstructing the Household*.

44. BCCD, 7497, 11/28/1831; 7423, 11/4/1831.

45. *U.S. v. John Day*, 156 (Criminal Court District of Columbia December 15, 1852), Case Papers, Appearance, Trials, Judicials, Record Group 21, E-45, Box 22, National Archives. Evidence from the Washington Criminal Court indicates that border region elites worried about extreme wife-beating but not its less serious counterpart. In only three Washington domestic violence cases that went to trial can a conviction be ascertained. All three involved the murder or attempted murder of a wife; all three men received more than a year in jail. These sentences were among the harshest for aggravated

assaults. Yet, of the almost 500 assault cases that reached the court, only about 20 involved household members; 16 of those were husband-on-wife. This number is not entirely certain, as most cases of domestic violence can be determined only by last names, except for a few warrants that clearly mark the victim as wife, servant, or master. The silence in the record underscores the unwillingness of officials to recognize discord within families as the provenance of the court. Data compiled from District of Columbia Criminal Court Papers, Boxes 18–22, and List of Convictions, 1851–1853, Criminal Court, District of Columbia, Record Group 21, E–41.

46. Steinberg makes a similar point, noting that "because [Philadelphia] magistrates were so receptive to assault and battery prosecutions, battered wives had somewhere to go to exert some control over men who exceeded their authority in the home." They were "able to use the law as a tool" to "challenge the legitimacy of violence as an element" of the power dynamic in the family. Steinberg, *Transformation of Criminal Justice*, 47.

47. In 1831, 54 of 65 complaints of wife abuse came from white women. (In 1832, 50 of 60 complainants were white.) Class status is tricky to ascertain, but 21 of the 25 husbands accused of wife-beating in 1831 who can be traced to the 1833 city directory were artisans, laborers, or hucksters or worked in manufactories. Five men shared names with at least one other man in the 1833 directory, making an occupational determination of the one arrested for wife-beating impossible. In two of the five cases, however, all of the men with the same name held working-class occupations. Another 30 men did not appear in the 1833 directory, which may indicate that they were transients; they were almost certainly not among the elite. Data compiled from BCCD, 1827–1832, and Baltimore Directory (1833).

48. For more on the willingness of elite Southern women to place class above gender, see Fox-Genovese, *Within the Plantation Household*, 34–35.

49. BCCD, 7295, 9/12/1831.

50. Data from BCCD, 1827–1832. Citations: BCCD, 7122, 7/22/1881; 7898, 5/24/1832; 7998, 7/7/1832.

51. Even correcting for the uneven sex ratio of black women to black men in the city—and fewer expected marriages—black wives were less likely to take abusive husbands to court than were white wives. Part of this difference may be attributed to fewer marriages in the free African-American community, and thus fewer families "at risk" for arrest. But that explanation is not sufficient. According to Curry, *The Free Black in Urban America*, 253, sex ratios for blacks in 1830s Baltimore were skewed; there were 1.34 black women for each black man, while white ratios were closer to even (1.09:1). But even if all men married, that would yield 74 African-American marriages for every 100 white marriages. If each marriage yielded the same rate of domestic violence, 15.5 percent of all African-American assault arrests should have involved family members. That number is half again as high as the actual percentage (10) of domestic violence arrests. This may mean black families were more congenial, although contemporary and historic statistics illustrate the tendency of all people to lash out at familiars when faced with social inequity. See Linda Gordon, *Heroes of Their Own Lives: The Politics and History of Family Violence in Boston, 1880–1960* (New York, 1988); Robert L. Hampton, ed., *Violence in the Black Family: Correlates and Consequences* (Lexington, MA, 1987); Hampton, *Black Family Violence: Current Research and Theory* (Lexington, MA, 1991).

52. BCCD, 64, 11/13/1827; 65 11/13/1827. Whites also refused to carry through with assault charges, but never for so serious a crime. For example, in September 1832, Elizabeth Nash was briefly incarcerated for failing to give security to appear in court to testify against her husband for assault and battery. Yet a month later she issued new charges, this time for a threat. BCCD, 8144, 9/4/1832; 8145, 9/5/1832; 8263, 10/11/1832.

53. BCCD, 212, 1/12/1828; 452, 3/16/1828.

54. The average number of days for Baltimore City Jail commitments was 7.1; the median was 4. For a smaller database including just those years in which all records were present, the average was 5.6 days. Data compiled from BCCD, 1827–1832.

55. BCCD, 6761, 6/3/1831; 8095, 8/16/1832; 6745, 3/7/1831.

56. BCCD, 85, 11/23/1827; 34, 11/7/1827; 6, 10/26/1827. All aggregate statistics compiled from this docket.

57. Of 66 cases, 18 had long incarcerations. Steinberg, *Transformation of Criminal Justice*, 41–47, describes a similar informal process for Philadelphia.

58. Arbitrary justice accompanied increased power, as antebellum Americans well knew, Bodenhamer, *Fair Trial*, 51–65.

59. Waite's active phase was before 1831 when fees were not recorded. Steinberg's J.P. dockets allow him to point to wives who retracted charges or issued countercharges and used the law to settle private disputes in a pattern similar to those in Baltimore, Steinberg, *Transformation of Criminal Justice*, 46–48.

60. BCCD, 143, 12/13/1827; 750, 8/12/1828.

61. Although jail records fail to distinguish between charges tried by the court and those mediated summarily, the record indicates that appearing before the bench was more painful. The 20-day average reflects the number of days spent in jail by those convicted and acquitted; the 15-day average considers only the latter group. Thus even those found innocent spent considerable time in jail awaiting judgment.

62. See the preambles for *Laws of Maryland*, 1821, chap. 229, and 1835, chap. 75.

63. BCCD, 718, 7/30/1828; 567, 6/10/1828; 7147, 7/27/1831; 7177, 8/10/1831; 723, 11/14/1828; 673, 7/7/1828; 698, 7/19/1828.

64. *Laws of Maryland*, 1835, chap. 366.

Parents and
Children

nine

"UNNATURAL MOTHERS"

Infanticide, Motherhood, and Class in the Mid-Atlantic, 1730–1830

Merril D. Smith

On January 3, 1786, twenty-seven-year-old Elizabeth Wilson was executed in Chester, Pennsylvania, for murdering her twin infants. Wilson protested to the end that she had not killed her babies, although she admitted hiding the bodies. She refused to utter a word in her defense before the trial; after she was sentenced to death, she expressed grief, confessed her fall from virtue, and finally identified her lover as the murderer. Following pleas by her brother, the executive council of Pennsylvania granted a last-minute delay of execution. It arrived shortly after she was hanged. Although her body was cut down, she could not be resuscitated. Her tragic story fascinated the public, and her tale was told by local residents into the next century.[1]

Women were not often executed for infanticide in post-Revolutionary Pennsylvania.[2] Elizabeth Wilson's case stood out because she was indeed hanged, despite unsuccessful attempts to pardon her. She was sentenced under an old Pennsylvania statute based on the English law 21 James I, c.27 (1624). This legislation, standard in early Anglo-American colonies, required that a mother who secretly gave birth to an infant later found dead had to *prove* that the child had been stillborn or face death. Infanticide, although an act of intimate violence, was rarely associated with the domesticity of marriage; most mothers who killed their infants were unmarried women, not wives. Implicit in the law, therefore, was the belief that a single woman who gave birth to an illegitimate child would murder her baby to hide that fact. The Pennsylvania

173

statute based on this law, passed in 1718, noted that "the bare concealment of the death is made almost conclusive evidence of the child's being murdered by the mother or by her procurement."[3]

Elizabeth Wilson, like many other women charged with infanticide, was a single woman living outside her parents' household. Little is known about her brief life. She was born in Chester County to John and Elizabeth Wilson; her father was a poor but "respectable" farmer. In 1777, her parents, loyalist sympathizers, permitted her to visit Philadelphia while it was occupied by the British Army. After the war, Elizabeth returned to the city and worked, undoubtedly as a servant, in a tavern owned by relatives. At the Cross Keys Inn, she met a man who became her lover and the father of the doomed babies.[4]

The accounts of Wilson's life published after her execution suggest that she left home because she enjoyed the freedom of city life or that she had been asked to leave because she and her parents were at odds. At sixteen, she had been strongly influenced by the teachings of Baptist itinerant preachers but later turned away from these beliefs. The records hint that she found rural life boring and argued with her family. In any case, either while she lived in Chester or shortly after her return to Philadelphia, Wilson became sexually active. She bore three illegitimate children before the twins, although the previous births are not mentioned in most accounts and only briefly in her published confession.[5] Delivering a baby before marriage did not necessarily prevent a woman from later marrying, although delivering five, at least some of whom lived, doubtless reduced Wilson's chances in the marriage market. Nonetheless, although she later professed to believe fornication was sinful, Elizabeth hoped her last lover would marry her and consented "to his unlawful embraces."[6] When she became pregnant, he refused matrimony, but promised financial support. Although emmenagogues (to promote menstruation) and abortifacients were commonly known and used by sexually active women in Philadelphia, Wilson evidently did not attempt to induce an abortion. Neither did she try to hide her pregnancy, though some women, despite close living quarters, were successful in an age of seldom-removed clothing and infrequent bathing in disguising their expanding bodies.[7] Wilson believed her lover would be back for her, and may still have hoped for marriage and respectability.

After the twins were born, Elizabeth demanded financial assistance from her lover and threatened to take him to court. Evidently frightened, he agreed to support the babies, but betrayed her again. He met her in the woods and pretended to examine the infants for a resemblance to himself, then pointed a pistol at Elizabeth and trampled the babies, killing them instantly. Still holding her at gunpoint, he demanded her silence.

After the bodies were discovered, Elizabeth was tried. Possibly in shock over the death of her babies, she refused to talk. She may have been afraid and believed she had sinned; given her religious background, she may have wanted to be punished. She might have feared for own her life as well. A man who murdered her infants and forced her silence at gunpoint might have killed her had she accused him.

The evidence presented in the case strongly implied guilt under the existing law, though only her silence convicted her. The council evidently thought she was innocent, but her refusal to defend herself left its members little alternative. She concealed the babies' death, proof enough to convict her of infanticide under 21 James I, c.27. She was sentenced to hang, and her lover was never apprehended.[8]

Only after her sentence was pronounced did she name her lover as the murderer. For most Philadelphians, and even her own brother, the introduction of Wilson's seducer wholly changed their attitudes toward her.[9] She became a victim led astray by an immoral and unscrupulous man, a monster who murdered her babies. As the mother of five illegitimate children, Wilson could hardly emphasize her virtue, but she could underscore her seduction and allude to feminine frailty when her lover betrayed her. She also publicly repented and accepted religion once more, according to the ministers who visited her between her conviction and execution.

Wilson's case caught the public eye, in part because stories of seduction and betrayal were fashionable in the new Republic.[10] The popular press portrayed her as a target of male lust and a grieving mother. After her death, her account was widely published in narratives and discussed in private journals. Her story became the cautionary tale of a woman who had sinned and the remorseful confession of a bereaved mother.

The tragic tale of Elizabeth Wilson proves instructive for scholars as well. Her case illustrates interactions among law, popular opinion, and infanticide during a transitional period that reflected the effects of the Enlightenment on bourgeois thought. Laws were changing; concepts of punishment were changing; beliefs about the family, gender roles, and sexuality were changing as well. Wilson was executed under a law conceived when women were considered inherently sinful and punishment was public. The response to her printed confession and narrative, published just two days after her death, reflected newer gender beliefs popularized in contemporary seduction tales. Despite her conviction for infanticide, moreover, she soon became idealized as a loving mother; her life and death were thus filled with inconsistencies. This essay will explore the ways in which a woman accused of murdering her illegitimate children came to be viewed as an innocent victim, not a murderer or "unnatural" mother. Her sin, crime, silence, confession, repentance, and execution illuminate changing gender roles and evolving class-based expectations about motherhood and punishment in a late eighteenth-century American city.[11]

When Elizabeth Wilson made her fateful move to Philadelphia, rejecting her parents' control and becoming sexually active, she followed the path of

"UNNATURAL MOTHERS"

many young people in the early Republic. By the late eighteenth century, a decline in patriarchal authority, greater social mobility, and changes in the post-war economy lured single young people into cities. Away from their families and communities, many engaged in sexual conduct unacceptable at home.[12]

Elizabeth probably had some guidance from her tavern-owning relatives, because she was supervised by the innkeeper's wife. Inns and taverns, however, were centers for urban lifestyles, and that is where Wilson encountered a culture that experimented with premarital sexuality. Men and women, often transients, gathered at inns to drink, gamble, and socialize. Elizabeth would have come into contact with men seeking sexual partners or prostitutes and working women looking for a "frolic." Images of men who preyed upon and seduced innocent young women became a staple of late eighteenth-century literature, but the characters that awakened social fears were based in reality.

In general, premarital pregnancy rates increased in the late eighteenth century and were higher among working-class women in Philadelphia than in many other regions. Elizabeth Wilson's own case took shape at the precise moment when ideas about women, sexuality, and the extent to which the state should legislate morality were in ferment. Many single mothers, perhaps most, were servants like Elizabeth Wilson who faced the prospect of losing their place or having their indentures extended as a result. Some may have feared accusing masters who abused them. Nonetheless, these women still had many reasons to conceal illegitimate births.[13] Seventeenth-century laws against fornication and bastardy in England and Anglo-America, including 21 James I. c.27, were constructed to punish sin, preserve families, and promote morality through public example. By concealing a dead baby's body, mothers avoided confessing to and being punished for their prior sin of fornication—sexual relations outside marriage.[14] Women's pre- and extramarital sexuality undermined patriarchal family structures, which maintained society's political and legal stability in the early modern era. These transgressions were not simply moral problems for the individuals involved, but threatened society as well. To maintain order, erring individuals were publicly disciplined. Colonial punishments were based on English methods and were "openly corporal." In displays designed as examples to others who undermine order, "the state seized the body of the condemned and directly inscribed its sanctions on that body." The public execution of a woman charged with infanticide was the most severe action the state could impose upon her body, for she had violated both social and legal standards.[15]

Seventeenth-century writers, theologians, and lawmakers regarded women as the weaker sex. They required the protection of fathers or husbands because their weakness rendered them easily aroused and open to temptation. Lusty and seductive yet frail and ineffective, women were snares the devil used to beguile careless men; they were the sinful descendants of Eve.[16] By the mid-eighteenth

176

century, this image of women was changing. Women were more likely to be regarded as naturally virtuous than naturally seductive. Republican theory and evangelical movements stressed that wives should be faithful and pure. Although marriages were to be companionate, wives were expected to submit to husbands when disagreements arose and were urged to use their inherent grace to instill virtue in their husbands and children. Unmarried women were to listen to their parents' advice and avoid men who would deceive, flatter, and seduce them. Having a child outside marriage, therefore, began to seem more an error in judgment in which a woman, neglecting her guardians' advice, fell victim to a seducer. It was no longer the action of a lustful woman entrapping an unwary man with her sinful charm.[17]

Despite this change, fathers were rarely indicted for or convicted of infanticide, particularly of newborns. It was perceived as a woman's crime, an act committed to conceal the birth of an illegitimate child. Even as the law caught up with the sentiment that unwed mothers were not solely responsible, men still escaped arrest.[18]

At the same time, late eighteenth-century political thought began to emphasize individual rights over patriarchs' control, while the idea of public displays of corporal punishment were increasingly abandoned. Changes in Pennsylvania laws at the end of the eighteenth century reflected these new beliefs about women, individuals, and state discipline: concealing the birth of a bastard child became grounds for imprisonment, not execution.[19]

By the 1780s, in part because of Elizabeth Wilson's case, many Pennsylvanians believed old infanticide laws were too harsh. The statute that made the concealment of an infant's death sufficient proof of infanticide was changed in 1786, after Wilson's execution. Under the new legislation, a mother could not be condemned unless it were proven that her baby was born alive. Even those found guilty rarely faced death, as the new act made imprisonment more likely. Charles Biddle, vice president of the Supreme Executive Council of Pennsylvania in 1786, wrote that "the punishment of death is too great for an unmarried woman who destroys her child. They are generally led to it from a fear of being exposed." When Robert Turnbull visited the Philadelphia prison in 1796, he wrote that a seduced woman should not be "censure[d]" by "any generous mind" when "it was the want of her lover's virtue, not her own, that wrested from her a public esteem she had not deservedly forfeited." In court, however, women were still forced to prove they were pure and virtuous and were unlikely to be pardoned unless they showed remorse or proved that they had prepared to care for their babies by preparing infant clothes and bedding.[20]

Single women faced with pregnancy in post-Revolutionary Philadelphia were confronted with several options, virtually all unpalatable. Some considered abortion, which was legal if accomplished before the mother felt fetal movement, or quickening; most successful abortions induced beyond that

"UNNATURAL MOTHERS"

point were not discovered. A late abortion almost certainly would have been regarded as an unfortunate but unremarkable stillbirth.[21]

Although it was legal, many eighteenth-century Pennsylvanians regarded abortion as a sin. In 1739, for example, Margaret Kain stated that when she was "about 3 or 4 Months gon with Child to Martin" Rierdon, he had procured "a Botle of Stuff, from a Doctr. in order to Make me Miscarrie." Kain refused to drink it and informed him "that it was a Sin to get ye child But a greater Sin to put it back." Rierdon, conflating sin and crime, told her "it was no Sin being it had not Quickened." Kain was steadfast and declared she "might as well go in the bed & kill one of My Masters childer that lay with me."[22]

Many eighteenth-century doctors concurred that abortion was immoral or at least repugnant. In 1799, Jacob Keister allegedly attempted to procure an abortion for his pregnant mistress. He approached a young "Practitioner of Physick" at a tavern and asked him if he would "use his medical knowledge in obtaining an abortion." The doctor was "exceedingly offended." Physician William Buchan also condemned abortion in his 1809 *Advice to Mothers*. While he understood the shame that might lead an unmarried woman to this act, he nevertheless denounced women who obtained abortions as murderers and "unnatural mothers." Dr. Alexander Hamilton believed abortion an "unjustifiable crime" committed to "conceal the indulgence of irregular passion" and which often cost women their lives.[23]

Other single women elected to deliver their babies, despite their precarious economic situations. Some who could not afford to raise them then exposed or abandoned them. In 1751, the *Pennsylvania Gazette* reported "a child of about two months old, supposed to be a Molattoe" was found alive in an alley. Authorities offered a £3 reward for information leading to the mother's discovery. A newborn female infant, whom the coroners' inquest decided was purposely concealed, was found dead in the woods west of Brandywine Creek in 1844.[24]

Other mothers abandoned their babies in populated places where they would be discovered and cared for. Mary Rodgers, for example, left her female bastard child at Tobias Handrie's door in 1726, while a newborn male child was left at Mr. James Burnside's door near Bethlehem, Pennsylvania, in 1755. In such cases, the infants were often carefully swaddled, as when a newborn was found in a Philadelphia alley in 1807 "sewed up in a double blanket with a straw pillow under its head and a sugar teat in its mouth." The baby's mother evidently hoped her child would be comfortable and warm until it was discovered.[25]

Mothers who wished to keep their illegitimate children in late eighteenth-century Philadelphia were faced with the prospect of supporting them. The law was less likely to punish them than it had been during the previous century, but also less likely to ensure their support. In the early eighteenth century, both men and women were sometimes tried and punished solely for fornication, regardless of whether a child resulted from the union. If a baby were born, couples might be ordered to marry to guarantee a man's support for the child. After 1750 or so, however, the state seldom prosecuted women only for fornication and prosecuted men only if a living child were born. In such cases, men named as the fathers of bastards were supposedly forced to pay maintenance for the child in order to relieve the county of its support.[26] Some women, however, refused or were unable to name the father, while some men who were named were not convicted. Others fled, as Elizabeth Wilson's lover did, and the state did not have the means to pursue them. Such cases became more common in post-Revolutionary Pennsylvania.

Working-class women who kept their babies were then forced to chose between entering the Philadelphia Almshouse or working to support them. Hundreds of women chose the almshouse in the late eighteenth century. Between 1796 and 1815, 354 deserted women entered the Philadelphia Almshouse; of these, 202 (57 percent) were pregnant or had young children with them. In the almshouse, though, children were often separated from mothers and could be bound out without their permission.[27]

If they wanted to keep their children and not be subject to the supervision of the almshouse directors, single mothers had to find both employment and child care. They did not always succeed, as when Sophia Fitzpatrick returned to work too soon after the birth of her child in 1800. Her health forced her return to the almshouse, where the Directors condemned her foolish attempt to "better" herself. Most live-in servants were forced to part with their children, although some single working mothers obviated the need for child care by finding jobs they could do at home, such as wet nursing or washing clothes.[28] Widows and women deserted by husbands also had to work to support their families. For Philadelphia's growing number of poor, moreover, survival required two incomes—even married women were forced to find work shortly after giving birth.

As the number of working-class women in Philadelphia increased, the ideal of republican motherhood, a corollary of republican womanhood, assumed a middle-class persona.[29] This was marked, in part, by a proliferation of child-rearing manuals obviously aimed at middle-class women. Their publication presupposed that their audience of women would be able to read and would have the time and inclination to do so. A well-to-do woman like Elizabeth Drinker could note in her diary that she "finish'd reading Letters to Married Woman, on Nursing and the Management of Children," while her servants and working women in her neighborhood read neither this work nor anything similar nor kept diaries. Model republican mothers stayed home with their children. They breast-fed them as infants, nurtured them as they grew, and instilled religion and morals—all the while keeping their home running smoothly. Republican mothers were educated, tender, and loving and maintained close ties to their children, even after they became adults.

"UNNATURAL MOTHERS"

Only mothers who could devote all their time to their children could be trusted with this task. As the anonymous Philadelphia author of *The Maternal Physician* wrote, "none but a mother" could "nurse an infant as it ought to be nursed," could provide the "unwearied, uninterrupted attention necessary to detect in season any latent symptoms of disease lurking in its tender frame, and which, if neglected, or injudiciously treated at first, might in a few hours baffle the physician's skill, and consign it to the grave." *The Maternal Physician*'s anonymous author, therefore, believed that working mothers could condemn their babies to death simply by working.

The model of idealized motherhood was obviously unattainable for most laboring women or for farm women, servants, and slaves. Evidently unconscious of any inconsistency, the author of *The Maternal Physician* noted that "even those mothers who are compelled to work for their subsistence" should nonetheless attend "to their infants during the first year" or at least "until they are firmly on their feet."[30] Other middle-class reformers, however, perceived the problems working women had in approaching this ideal. William Buchan believed that poor women could not easily be good mothers, but sympathized with their plight. "They would willingly devote all their time and care to the nursing of their children; but the want of common necessaries force them to be otherwise employed." Poverty's "icy hand" could "congeal" all "streams of maternal comfort." The advice literature, however, was not explicitly tied to class, but to virtue. Lydia Maria Child's *The Mother's Book* was dedicated to American mothers "on whose intelligence & discretion the safety & prosperity of our REPUBLIC SO MUCH DEPEND."[31]

Within the ideal of middle-class motherhood, breast-feeding represented all that was pure and giving in a woman. Dr. Alexander Hamilton noted that mothers' "milk is the most natural and wholesome food for children in early infancy," while Margaret King Moore bluntly announced that "a woman who cannot submit to a little trouble which lasts but a short time, for the benefit of her child, does not deserve to have a child."[32]

In great part, the maternal virtues associated with breast feeding transformed Elizabeth Wilson, even after her death, from an *unnatural* mother to a worthy one. She had nursed her babies for several weeks before beseeching her lover for help. Charles Biddle, for one, believed her innocent specifically on those grounds; "it appeared highly improbable that a mother, after suckling her children for six weeks, could murder them." A poem published shortly after her execution relied on the image of her nursing her children to maintain her innocence and underscore their father's heinous crime: "See smiling Twins and Innocents/ Upon their Mothers' breast!/But in a trice their breath was spent,/By this inhuman Beast!"[33]

Elizabeth Wilson's untimely execution for infanticide reflected her unfortunate position at the moving interstices of several cultural constructions of infanticide, punishment, and motherhood. Condemned by a seventeenth-century view of infanticide, Wilson was reborn as the ultimate eighteenth-century female victim. She was now seen as having been seduced, betrayed, and frightened into concealing her babies' bodies, but as innocent of their murder. Within the male court system, her fear and resultant silence rendered her insufficiently virtuous. In this transitional era, her execution "was a reminder of past times when sinful women were publicly punished for moral transgressions. Subject to middle-class definitions of motherhood, she was a working-class woman. In breast-feeding her babies, she enabled middle-class people to redeem her memory. The narrative published two days after her execution represented her as a woman trying to make a home for her babies. To a world in which motherhood was becoming the idealized and most central image for women, she stressed that she had nursed her infants and tried to save their lives. She also proclaimed her grief. But the same effort to retain and nurse her infants rendered her destitute and reliant on the lover who betrayed her. Women may have been morally superior to men, but most were economically dependent on them, particularly working-class women within the growing cities of the new Republic.

These lessons obviously struck a nerve among Wilson's contemporaries; ten years after Wilson's execution, Elizabeth Drinker, upon reading the *Narrative*, still remembered "having heard the sad tale at the time."[34] It was the very sadness of the tale which transformed Elizabeth Wilson's image, although it did not save her life. As the vulnerable target of a vile seducer, she became an object of pity. Her seduction by a false lover reflected republican fears and emphasized that young women should not be alone in the city. Elizabeth Wilson the murderer became Elizabeth Wilson the bereaved, not an "unnatural" mother but a tragic symbol of maternal sorrow.

Notes

1. A shorter version of this essay was presented at the 1996 Annual Meeting of the Organization of American Historians. I would like to acknowledge the help of Laurie Rofini and Barbara Weir of the Chester County Archives, Larry Eldridge of Widener University and The Manuscript Archives Project, and Margaret McAleer of the Library of Congress. I received financial assistance from a Gest Fellowship at the Quaker Collection, Haverford College, and an Andrew W. Mellon Fellowship at the Library Company of Philadelphia. This work is part of a larger project on mothers and daughters. For the Wilson case, see Henry Graham Ashmead, *History of Delaware and Chester County, Pennsylvania* (Philadelphia, 1884, Facsimile Ed.: Concord Township Historical Society, 1968), 171. For another analysis, see Daniel E. Williams, "Victims of Narrative Seduction: The Literary Translations of Elizabeth (and 'Miss Harriot') Wilson," *Early American Literature* 28 (1993): 148–170.

2. As G. S. Rowe has shown, the highest incidence of executions for infanticide in Pennsylvania occurred before 1768, with most in the 1760s. Between 1768 and 1785, convictions and executions declined. Between 1786 and 1800, convictions rose, but executions declined due to changes in the law. G. S. Rowe, "Infanticide, Its Judicial Resolution, and Criminal Code Revision in Early Pennsylvania," *Proceedings of the American Philosophical Society* 135 (June 1991): 208–209.

3. Sharon Ann Burnston, "Babies in the Well: An Underground Insight into Deviant Behavior in Eighteenth-Century Philadelphia," *Pennsylvania Magazine of History and Biography* 106 (1982): n171.

4. Information on Elizabeth Wilson is conflicting. See Ashmead, *History of Delaware County*, 171–176; and *A Faithful Narrative of Elizabeth Wilson; Who was executed at Chester, January 3, 1786* (New York, 1786). This narrative was also published in Philadelphia and elsewhere and was widely circulated and read. Williams, "Victims of Narrative Seduction," 149; Charles Biddle, *Autobiography of Charles Biddle* (Philadelphia, PA, 1883), 199–202.

5. Asmead's account mentions a stepmother, but gives no details. Although Asmead is probably not infallible, other records scarcely mention her parents, who are curiously absent from most of her narrative. She may have been estranged from them as a result of her earlier pregnancies. Asmead, *History of Delaware County*, 172.

6. Sally Brant, a servant in Elizabeth Drinker's Philadelphia household, gave birth to an illegitimate child and later married a man who was not that infant's father. The baby died after Drinker sent it away from Sally, who remained in the household. Elaine Forman Crane, *The Diary of Elizabeth Drinker* (Boston, 1991), 1:627, 632; 2:1115, 1683, 1941; *Narrative of Elizabeth Wilson*, 5.

7. Burnston, "Babies in the Well," 180.

8. Michael Grossberg, "Battling Over Motherhood in Philadelphia: A Study of Antebellum American Trial Courts as Arenas of Conflict," in Mindie Lazarus-Black and Susan F. Hirsh, eds., *Contested States: Law, Hegemony, and Resistance* (New York, 1994), 153–183, esp. 155. Like the d'Hautevilles, Wilson felt "the shadow of the law" over her, which dictated her subsequent actions and those of her brother. Unlike the d'Hautevilles, much of this action took place outside the courtroom. *Narrative of Elizabeth Wilson*, 5. Biddle believed her lover was the sheriff of Sussex County, New Jersey, *Autobiography*, 199–200.

9. Biddle, *Autobiography*, 200–201; *Narrative of Elizabeth Wilson*, 3.

10. Fliegelman, *Prodigals & Pilgrims: the American Revolution Against Patriarchal Authority, 1750–1800* (Cambridge, MA, 1982), chap. 2, 83–89; Jan Lewis, "The Republican Wife: Virtue and Seduction in the Early Republic," *William and Mary Quarterly* 44 (1987): 716–720; Rodney Hessinger, " 'Insidious Murderers of Female Innocence': Representations of Masculinity in the Seduction Tales of the Late Eighteenth Century," and Karen A. Weyler, "The Fruit of Unlawful Embraces: Sexual Transgression and Madness in Early American Fiction," both forthcoming in Merril D. Smith, ed., *Sex and Sexuality in Early America* (New York, 1998); Ruth Bloch, "The Gendered Meanings of Virtue in Revolutionary America," *Signs* 13 (Autumn 1987): 37–58.

11. *Narrative of Elizabeth Wilson*; Biddle, *Autobiography*, 199–202; Crane, *The Diary of Elizabeth Drinker*, 918; *Elegy, &c., Fair daughters of America, and eke of Britain's isle* (Boston, 1786); *Minutes of the Supreme Executive Council of Pennsylvania, From its Or-*

ganization to the Termination of the Revolution (Harrisburg, PA, 1853), 14:586, 591; Daniel A. Cohen, "Homicidal Compulsion and the Conditions of Freedom: The Social and Psychological Origins of Familicide in America's Early Republic," *Journal of Social History* 28 (1995): 725–726.

12. Billy G. Smith, *The "Lower Sort": Philadelphia's Laboring People, 1750–1800* (Ithaca, NY, 1990), 24–25; 172–173; Joan M. Jensen, *Loosening the Bonds: Mid-Atlantic Farm Women, 1750–1850* (New Haven, CT, 1986), 68; Fliegelman, *Prodigals & Pilgrims,* 83–89.

13. Carole Shammas, "The Female Social Structure of Philadelphia in 1775," *Pennsylvania Magazine of History and Biography* 107 (1983): 80; Smith, *"Lower Sort,"* 22–23, 178, 194; Jensen, *Loosening the Bonds,* 68; G. S. Rowe, "Female Crime and the Courts in Revolutionary Lancaster County," *Lancaster County Historical Society Journal* 87 (1983): 67–68; G. S. Rowe, "Infanticide," 222, includes a thorough compilation of infanticide statistics for Pennsylvania; Peter C. Hoffer and N.E.H. Hull, *Murdering Mothers: Infanticide in England and New England 1558–1803* (New York, 1981), 95; Smith, *"Lower Sort,"* 178–180; Jensen, *Loosening the Bonds,* 68.

14. Hoffer and Hull, *Murdering Mothers,* 56–59, 65–69; Linda Kerber, *Women of the Republic: Intellect and Ideology in Revolutionary America* (Chapel Hill, NC, 1980), *passim*; Mary Beth Norton, *Liberty's Daughters: The Revolutionary Experience of American Women, 1750–1800* (Boston, 1980); Bradley Chapin, "Felony Law Reform in the Early Republic," *Pennsylvania Magazine of History and Biography* 113 (1989): 163–184; Cornelia Hughes Dayton, " 'Taking the Trade': Abortion and Gender Relations in an Eighteenth-Century New England Village," *William and Mary Quarterly* 48 (1991): 40–41.

15. Michael Meranze, *Laboratories of Virtue: Punishment, Revolution, and Authority in Philadelphia, 1760–1835* (Chapel Hill, NC, 1996), 3, 26–27, 37; Hoffer and Hull, *Murdering Mothers,* 56–57.

16. Laurel Thatcher Ulrich, *Good Wives: Image and Reality in the Lives of Women in Northern New England, 1650–1750* (New York, 1982), 96–98; Barry Levy, *Quakers and the American Family: British Settlement in the Delaware Valley* (New York, 1988), chap. 6.

17. Lewis, "The Republican Wife," 697–708.

18. Laurel Thatcher Ulrich, *A Midwife's Tale: The Life of Martha Ballard, Based on her Diary, 1785–1812* (New York, 1990), 147–155; Rowe, "Infanticide," 227.

19. Kerber, *Women of the Republic,* 9–11; Michel Foucault, *Discipline and Punish: The Birth of the Prison,* trans. Alan Sheridan (London, 1977); Michael Meranze, *Laboratories of Virtue,* 2–3, 21; Rowe, "Infanticide," 202–203; 227–228.

20. *Statutes at Large of Pennsylvania,* 12:284; 13:514; Rowe, "Infanticide," 209, 229; Burnston, "Babies in the Well," 171; Hoffer and Hull, *Murdering Mothers,* 20–22, 36–38, 68–69; Biddle, *Autobiography,* 202; Robert J. Turnbull, *A Visit to the Philadelphia Prison* (Philadelphia, 1796), 92–93; Negley K. Teeters, "Public Executions in Pennsylvania," *Lancaster County Historical Society Journal* 64 (1960): 107.

21. "Where a fetus was born without hair or nails, up to the seventh month of gestation, it was assumed to be not viable by the panels of women called to examine the corpse," Susan E. Klepp, "Lost, Obstructed, and Repressed: Contraceptive and Abortive Technology in the Early Delaware Valley," in Judith A. McGaw, ed., *Early American Technology: Making and Doing Things from the Colonial Era to 1850* (Chapel Hill, NC, 1994), 73–92. Klepp notes that the frequency of abortions is impossible to determine, although they were certainly more common than court records indicate. Also James C.

Mohr, *Abortion in America: The Origins and Evolution of National Policy 1800–1900* (New York, 1978).

22. *King v. Martin Rierdon*, Statement of Margaret Kain, Chester County Quarter Session Indictments, 5/1739, Chester County Archives (hereafter CCA). For an abortion with instruments, Dayton, "Taking the Trade," 19–49.

23. *Andreas v. Andreas*, Deposition of James Taylor, 1799, Divorce Papers, 1786–1815, Division of Archives and Manuscripts, Records of the Supreme Court, Eastern District, Pennsylvania Historical and Museum Commission; William Buchan, *Advice to Mothers, on the Subject of Their own Health; And of the Means of Promoting the Health, Strength, and Beauty of their Offspring* (Boston, 1809), 10–11; Dr. Alexander Hamilton, *A Treatise on the Management of Female Complaints and of Children in Early Infancy* (New York, 1792), 162–164.

24. *Pennsylvania Gazette*, 9/26/1751; Chester County Quarter Sessions, 5/1844, CCA.

25. Chester County Quarter Sessions, 11/1726, CCA; *Pennsylvania Gazette*, 2/18/1755. Crane, *The Diary of Elizabeth Drinker*, 2008.

26. *Records of the Courts of Chester County Pennsylvania, 1697–1710*, 2:118; Rowe, "Female Crime," 67–68; Dayton, "Taking the Trade," 22.

27. Merril D. Smith, "'Whers gone to she knows not': Desertion and Widowhood in Early Pennsylvania," in Larry Eldridge, ed., *Women and Freedom in Early America* (New York, 1997), 211–238; Smith, *"Lower Sort,"* 167.

28. 7/23/1800, Daily Occurrence Docket, Guardians of the Poor, Philadelphia City Archives, hereafter PCA; Priscilla Ferguson Clement, *Welfare and the Poor in the Nineteenth-Century City, Philadelphia, 1800–1840* (Rutherford, NJ, 1985); Sharon V. Salinger, "'Send No More Women': Female Servants in Eighteenth-Century Philadelphia," *Pennsylvania Magazine of History and Biography* 107 (1983): 29–48; in the same issue, Jean R. Soderlund, "Black Women in Colonial Pennsylvania," 49–68; Smith, *"Lower Sort,"* 196; Janet Golden, *A Social History of Wet Nursing in America: From Breast to Bottle* (Cambridge, MA, 1996), 27–37.

29. Although certainly mothers were valued and respected in colonial America, Ulrich, *Good Wives*, 153; Levy, *Quakers and the American Family*, 221.

30. Crane, *Diary of Elizabeth Drinker*, 962; *The Maternal Physician; A Treatise on the Nature and Management of Infant, from birth until Two years Old . . . By An American Matron* (New York, 1811), 7, 132; Jacqueline S. Reinier, "Rearing the Republican Child: Attitudes and Practices in Post-Revolutionary Philadelphia," *William and Mary Quarterly* 39 (1982): 150–163.

31. Buchan, *Advice to Mothers*, 97; Lydia Maria Child, *The Mother's Book* (Boston, 1831), Dedication and Preface.

32. Marylynn Salmon, "The Cultural Significance of Breast-Feeding and Infant Care in Early Modern England and America," *Journal of Social History* 28 (1994): 247–269; Hamilton, *A Treatise*, 278; Margaret King Moore, *Advice to Young Mothers on the Physical Education of Children by a Grandmother* (Boston, 1833), 41.

33. Biddle, *Autobiography*, 199–201; Hoffer and Hull, *Murdering Mothers*, 53–55; *Elegy, &C, Fair Daughters of America*, 1786; Williams, "Victims of Narrative Seduction," 150–151.

34. Crane, *Diary of Elizabeth Drinker*, 918.

Merril D. Smith

ten

LAYING CLAIM TO
ELIZABETH SHOEMAKER

Family Violence on Baltimore's
Waterfront, 1808–1812

James D. Rice

I n 1811, Baltimore had just passed the first bloom of youth and was poised on the brink of economic and social maturity. In 1750 the town had been merely a sleepy village, but by 1790 it contained over 13,000 residents. Its population doubled in the next ten years, making it the third most populous city in the United States behind New York and Philadelphia. Baltimore's strategic location on a broad tributary of the northern Chesapeake Bay allowed it to capture much of the trade of America's first "breadbasket," the fertile crescent between Lancaster, Pennsylvania, and Virginia's Shenandoah Valley. Yet the Atlantic grain trade, the very source of Baltimore's explosive growth, also made it highly vulnerable to changes in international markets. Baltimore's export-driven economy suffered terribly when warring France and England took steps to compel American sailing vessels to conform to their strategic goals, and it suffered even more when the Embargo Act of 1807 restricted U.S. shipping to coastal trade. Lacking a mature, diversified economy, the city was hit hard by the embargo and other mercantile disruptions. The value of goods shipped from the port dropped by 75 percent between 1805 and 1808, with the consequences rippling outwards from the wharves and warehouses through the rest of the economy.[1]

Betsy Shoemaker, like her home town of Baltimore, was also just past the first bloom of youth in 1811. She too was reaching for maturity and had been buffeted and hardened by recent events. Her parents, Catharine (Kitty) and

William Shields, adopted her as an orphaned infant. She turned eighteen just as William, a mariner, struggled to support his family during the economic slump that hit their neighborhood of Fells Point, a maritime suburb of Baltimore, with exceptional severity.[2] In that neighborhood, full of underemployed sailors and maritime tradesmen and laborers, Betsy was constantly exposed to the rough culture of a port city. Kitty and William occasionally immersed themselves in that rough culture themselves, but attempted to shield Betsy from it. As soon as Betsy came of age, however, she dove headlong into waterfront society. Her repeated forays into what her mother called "those sinks of Iniquity where licentiousness is order, and Voluptousness is Law" quickly took a toll on Betsy's health. Ironically, however, it was her parents' violent attempt to control her behavior that killed her.[3]

The disturbing story of Betsy Shoemaker's death at the hands of her parents is a powerful tale of domestic violence. It is also a story about a waterfront community in which Betsy's life was not entirely her own, nor did it belong entirely to her parents. Through her rebellious behavior, Betsy tried to lay claim to her own life. Her parents disputed that claim, as one might expect. More surprisingly, Betsy's friends, the community, and even the United States Navy also tried to exert their claims. The boundaries between family and community in a working-class area were thin, porous, and contested, as neighbors, friends, and agents of the state and national governments freely intervened in the Shields's family life. Although only Kitty and William were charged with Betsy's murder, their trials were as much about the family's place in the community and the community's place in the family as they were about the Shields's treatment of their adopted daughter.

Accounts of Betsy Shoemaker's demise were bound to conflict at some points. Yet all parties agreed on one thing: Betsy suffered a horrible death. According to the coroner, Betsy died from "cruel and inhuman" treatment, particulary at the hands of her mother. "Mrs. Shields," he asserted, "on the morning which she [Betsy] died gave and compeld her to drink one pint of Rum after whipping her overnight and very severely that same morning." Betsy drank all but a spoonful of the rum, which was followed by "a spoonful of Wine Drops, then a dose of Jollop then a dose of Castor or sweet oil then a pint of new milk, then a mixture of vinegar water and sugar about half pint, the same quantity of salt and water then three cups of coffee." Finally, Catharine Shields "made water, about one pint and made her drink that." Betsy downed these "several doses" between sunrise and noon, at which time she "Languished and Died."

All who knew about the incident, concluded the coronor, wanted to see Catharine and William Shields brought to justice.[4] A grand jury concurred with his report, indicting William Shields for the severe whipping he was said to have given Betsy on the night before she died and Kitty for administering

James D. Rice

Table 10–1. *Frequency of Reasons Given in Pardon Texts and Successful Pardon Petitions, 1789–1837*

| | Years | | | |
| Reasons | 1789–1810 | | 1811–1837 | |
	N	*%*	*N*	*%*
Equity (innocent/justifiable)	76	35%	302	28%
Character/connections	68	31	227	21
Reformable/youth	22	10	109	10
Sanity/health	19	9	63	6
Penitence/conduct	6	2	275	25
Dependent family/poverty	21	10	101	9
Informant	7	3	12	1
Total	219	100	1089	100

Source: Pardons database; Governor and Council (Pardon Record and Pardon Papers).
Note: *N* excludes persons for whom sex is unknown.

the "several doses" that killed her. When Kitty was tried in January 1812, the jurors convicted her of manslaughter; William had an alibi and was acquitted.

Had the jury been Kitty's last hope, she might have despaired. But as another pardon-seeker wrote in 1803, "Fortunately for the citizens of this Country, there is a tribunal of mercy, sitting superior to the tribunal of *strict* justice," namely the governor.[5] He did not exaggerate the governor's power to pardon even convicted criminals; indeed, the pardoning process amounted to a whole new trial, based on the same considerations as the original—empirical evidence and testimony of good character—but without the procedural and evidentiary restrictions required in formal proceedings. Counsel for the prosecution, jurors, members of the bar, complainants, clergymen, family members, local notables, and, of course, defendants, also joined in petitions for (and against) pardons at their own initiative. The recommendations were collated and discussed by the governor and his council, which reserved special days for such business. Three options were possible: they could issue a full pardon, attach an alternative punishment to the pardon, or allow the sentence to stand.[6]

Maryland governors pardoned guilty convicts more often than they released people they deemed innocent (see Table 10–1). Indeed, over two-thirds of the lucky convicts were still guilty of capital offenses. In part this was because, before 1811, Maryland law imposed the death penalty for some relatively minor offenses. And penitence on the part of the condemned was considered a sign

187

that reformation was possible; professed remorse was especially likely to be taken seriously when the convict seemed conducive to reclamation. The young offender Hanson Barnes, for example, was spared even a trial because "from his youth and inexperience there may be a prospect of reformation."[7] Youth, family responsibilities, and other incentives to reform were among the most frequently cited reasons for pardoning convicts; 10 percent of all pardons and pardon petitions cited the possibility of reformation.[8] In addition, over 20 percent of all successful pardons cited the character of the defendant, his family, or his connections—considerations perfectly consistent with standards applied at every other stage of criminal prosecutions.[9]

Excessively severe punishments, moreover, eroded respect for the law. William Tilghman, member of a prominent planter family, worried that executing a convict would backfire because "his execution might rather tend to excite compassion, than answer the end for which examples of this kind are intended." Executions were not meant to arouse sympathy, but terror of the state and its law. Petitioner George Plater proclaimed that "rogues" should suffer "punishment" as "examples to others." Ideally, wrote another petitioner, executions created examples of "terrible" punishments.[10] Exemplary punishments were particularly designed to impress the poor and the black, who, it was supposed, comprised an identifiable criminal class. "It might seem expedient," wrote one observer, "that there should be some examples of awful warning to check the atrocious wickedness and licentiousness of those poor unhappy black creatures, who appear to be influenced by no restraining tie but the dread of legal punishment."[11] Governors had to choose between prisoners whose executions would make good examples and those who would simply gain sympathy if they were severely punished.

Successful petitions almost invariably portrayed convicts as fitting certain psychological profiles. They emphasized the defendant's good character, social standing, and reformability. Women also stressed their femininity, suggested their virtue, and especially raised the implicit threat that a severe punishment would arouse sympathy for the convict instead of terror of the law.

Kitty Shields's own pardon petition was finely crafted. She masterfully replotted the coroner's story, agreeing with it in most details but placing Betsy's death in the context of a long-term struggle for the girl's soul. The coroner told a simple and compelling tale, drawing on the archetype of the wicked stepmother. Kitty rewrote the same events into a tragedy. In her version, a doting mother attempted to expel the corruption she saw taking root in her daughter's soul, but made a single fatal mistake and brought ruin upon the entire family. As a loving and devoted mother, Kitty implied, she did not need to be reformed, although in conformity with the conventions of pardons, she displayed her penitence. God help the politician who allowed such a woman to suffer an exemplary punishment.

James D. Rice

Shields began by artfully portraying herself as the reformer, not the person in need of reform; as the transmitter of virtue, not its corruptor. When she and William took Betsy in as an orphaned infant, she stated, they hoped Betsy would become "a virtuous member of society and a consolation to them in their declining years." But they were "fatally deceived." Betsy left home shortly after her eighteenth birthday and returned several weeks later "in that deplorable situation which delicacy forbids your petitioners particularly to describe, but which your excellency may readily imagine" when he considered that she had wallowed in one of "those sinks of Iniquity . . . from which few ever return less contaminated in body than in mind." No one would have blamed the Shields if they had barred the door to Betsy, but "being still anxiously solicitous for the welfare of their adopted child" and hoping "by their admonitions to withdraw her from the evil habits she had contracted during her association with those by whom she had been lured from the path of rectitude," they took her in again. On October 19, 1811, however, Betsy once again left and "spent the night in riot and debauchery." She returned the next morning "in a complete state of intoxication."

Kitty "hoped" Betsy's unusual actions were the result of "the wicked arts and contrivances of others," not "the impulse of an appetite naturally vicious and depraved." Betsy's mother then resolved "by one energetic effort to snatch her, if possible, from the career of prodigality into which she had so unfortunately hurried." With that goal in mind, she administered a massive dose of the hair of the dog (rum) to Betsy, "having been taught to believe that the most effectual mode of correcting a destructive habit was by creating, if practicable, a disgust for it." But this did not work as intended, for Betsy was willing to continue her drinking spree. Discovering that the alcohol produced "an effect different from what she contemplated," Kitty tried to undo the first remedy by purging her daughter of the rum. She tried castor oil, salt water, and other remedies calculated to induce vomiting. Unhappily, though, the effect of purgatives and rum on the "debilitated state" of Betsy's health "produced by her overnights debauch" was so deleterious that she soon expired. Her parents, tender and solicitous to the end, gave her a decent burial.[12]

For all the artistry in her version of the story, the allegation that she forced Betsy to drink urine remained a problem for Kitty. Both the coroner and the Grand Jury were convinced she had given Betsy a full pint of the liquid. This accusation impugned Kitty Shields's motives, suggesting a punitive aspect to her behavior completely at variance with her account of the episode. Thus in a second missive to the governor, accompanied by a series of depositions, Shields took pains to refute this particular charge; in doing so, she revealed the presence of ther witnesses at Betsy's deathbed. Several people testified that Anne Spearman and Sally Falkner (two of Betsy's tavern friends and corruptors) had "first suggested the propriety of administering Urine" to Betsy, and did so

LAYING CLAIM TO ELIZABETH SHOEMAKER

while Kitty was out of the room. As she spooned the noxious substance down her friend's throat, Spearman said "if any Thing in the World would make her puke that would."[13]

Catharine Shields, in sum, had not tortured her adopted daughter to death. If anything, she tormented *herself* over Betsy's refusal to stay on the path of virtue. As a betrayed and bereaved mother she was "rather to be pitied than condemned." Her actions on the morning of Betsy's death proceeded from laudable motives; they demanded not exemplary punishment but compassion. Instead, Kitty nominated the "unfortunate" child Betsy as an example to others; "her fate and indiscretion" would serve as "a melancholy example to the young and credulous to teach them to avoid the snares of voluptousness and the fascinations of vice."[14]

The Shields's correspondence with the governor demonstrates their attentiveness to conventions of pardon-seeking—the requisite remorse, while admitting no guilt, and the semblance of familial concern and good moral character. They were no less attuned to the conventions of family life, particularly to the acceptable use of violence within the family. In Kitty Shields's case, three distinct understandings about family life came together to make it possible for her to claim to have loved her daughter to death: traditional notions about the sweeping power of parents over their households, complex republican notions about innately virtuous yet corruptible women, and the increasingly intimate ideal of household relations.

During the mid- to late eighteenth century, middle-class families became increasingly sentimental as parents began to perceive children as "inherently good and pleasurable creatures" who occupied center stage in the family.[15] Accordingly, Kitty cast aside all subtlety as she portrayed herself as a doting mother who lived only for her child and would gladly sacrifice herself in order to attend to Betsy's needs. By the Shields's account, they acted out of the "purest motives of Humanity" from the moment they adopted Betsy until the day they buried her. Her death left them "afflicted with the keenest anguish that ever tortured the human breast." They asserted that parenthood gave them common ground with the governor and appealed to him to "apply their unhappy case to yourself and to mete out to them, the same measure of mercy as you would think they ought to mete out to you were you in their situation and you in theirs." The Shields spoke the language of domesticity with impressive fluency.

The search for a new social and political order in the wake of the Revolution created a uniquely American variant of the intimate family. A post-Revolutionary uncertainty about the ability of ordinary people to play an active political role in society was often expressed in republican language, which in turn shaped ideas about how "republican" citizens ought to behave. The republican experiment raised parental stakes and placed new demands on children; despite their concern for their children, republican parents expected more emotional and behavioral conformity from them than had been expected from the parents themselves. Betsy's failure to live up to parental expectations had serious consequences in the milieu of the new Republic; her parents' violent reaction was partly rooted, at least in their representation, in their sense of failure according to the standards against which republican parents and children measured themselves.[16]

Although the Enlightenment thought of the eighteenth century and the new romanticism of the nineteenth both undermined traditional notions about original sin and the innate depravity of man, republican ideology also emphasized the ease with which corruption fastened itself upon the soul. For the United States to survive, its ordinary citizens would have to be worthy of their expanded powers. They needed to resist the many temptations of corruption and remain on a virtuous path. If citizens became corrupt, the Republic would fail, or even become malevolent. If they lived virtuous lives, however, the United States would serve as a "cynosure of nations" leading the rest of the world by the force of its example. Or so argued the most ideological writers of the early Republic in their most breathless moments.[17]

Republican ideology imposed upon the Shields a more mundane and messier task: shaping Betsy into a woman capable of inculcating virtue in her own (prospective) husband and children. While the Shields did not live up to middle-class standards of republican morality themselves (more of that later), they spoke the language. Their petitions are shot through with the keywords of republican discourse, most notably "virtue" and "corruption." The first sentence of their first petition sets the tone: they had hoped when they adopted her that Betsy would become "a virtuous member of society." But to their infinite sorrow she instead chose a path which led to "iniquity," "licentiousness," "spoil," "voluptuousness," "contamination," "contagion," "degenerance," "indulgence," "excess," "vice," and similar destinations.

Betsy's behavior suggested a propensity for immoderation and vice which would affect her marital prospects. And to the extent to which she passed on these tendencies to her spouse and children, her behavior would have deleterious consequences for society as a whole. Because of the enthusiasm with which she threw herself into the rough culture of Fells Point's waterfront taverns, the Shields—particularly Kitty, who would bear most of the credit or blame for Betsy's development—appear to have felt acutely their impending failure as parents. Their extravagantly violent reaction to Betsy's last "debauch" may have seemed proportionate to the danger she faced from herself.

These two new phenomena of Euro-American family life in Baltimore in 1811—the increasingly child-centered climate of households and the particularly high moral stakes in the new Republic—coincided in the Shields-Shoemaker case with an older aspect of family life: the almost unlimited authority granted to heads of household by both law and custom.

LAYING CLAIM TO ELIZABETH SHOEMAKER

Maryland statutory law provided no special protection for children against their parents, nor was the common law much help. William Blackstone, whose *Commentaries on the Laws of England* had achieved wide circulation in Maryland by 1812 and was often cited in briefs and decisions, included "Wife [or Children], battery of" in his volume not in the section on "Public Wrongs" but under the heading of "Private Wrongs," along with divorce and other domestic concerns. Children merited attention mostly as servants and orphans, though Blackstone highlighted "Children, their duties" in his volume on "The Rights of Persons."[18]

By custom, even these legal barriers against domestic violence were rarely enforced. An examination of over 7000 criminal prosecutions in Maryland's courts between 1748 and 1837 reveals only a handful of cases of violence between family members. (Prosecutions involving violence between unrelated householders were more common, but differing surnames make it difficult to pinpoint the exact number of cases.) The silence speaks more clearly of public attitudes than household behavior.[19] This low prosecution rate certainly did not result from an absence of domestic violence, but from an unwillingness or inability to prosecute or convict most offenders. And although relatively few well-documented cases of domestic violence have survived from Elizabeth Shoemaker's Maryland, those that do reinforce the impression of a widespread and deep-seated reluctance to use legal sanctions against perpetrators of domestic violence. The law limited violence within the household, but also justified its existence—it recognized the right of a household governor to enforce discipline through violence—and Marylanders took the justifications more seriously than the limitations.[20] In the case of the Shields, the sweeping power granted to parents by law and custom, coupled with the raised stakes in the intimate household in the new Republic, made it possible for Kitty Shields to claim plausibly to have loved her daughter to death.

Moreover, the Shields's treatment of their adopted daughter was of a piece with everyday life on the waterfront. The Shields did not have to peek into neighbors' houses to witness violence; they could see it in their neighborhood streets, wharves, and inns.[21] Baltimore itself was in the process of winning the nickname of "mobtown" for its periodic episodes of collective violence over political issues and rivalries between fire companies. And within Baltimore, Fells Point contained a remarkably high concentration of crime-prone single men, sailors, and taverns—a potent combination that created a volatile, exuberantly masculine, and rough society.

The Shields, then, moved in crude circles—particularly William, who as a sailor experienced the brutality of shipboard life. They also encountered the illness and death that stalked large port cities in the early nineteenth century and the aggressive and often fatal practice of medicine of that era. Yellow fever pursued denizens of port cities especially aggressively; when it visited Baltimore it struck first and hardest in Fells Point and surrounding neighbor-hoods.[22] Unless the Shields stood apart from their tough seaport milieu, the correctives they used to reform Betsy—the beatings, rum, and purgatives—were drawn from their everyday experiences of personal violence, illness, and medical practice.

But of course they had never stood aloof from their neighbors. While schol-ars are much more likely to shape questions in terms of the family's place in the community than in terms of the community's place in the family, the corre-spondence generated in Shields's search for a pardon reveals a very thin and in-distinct line between family and community. Their household formed but one of several nodes of its inhabitants' social lives. Kitty's connections with her neighbors unraveled the intimate circle surrounding the Shields family, as did William's business relations and Betsy's socializing with her young friends.

At first glance, the Shields's correspondence comports with the ideal of a highly private family life. Their portrayal of themselves as devoted parents, ever focused on their poor orphan child, systematically obscured the presence of other onlookers. Their first and fullest pardon petition gave the impression that only three family members set foot in the house during Betsy's troubles, and that only Kitty was present on the morning of her death. Kitty's second petition introduced Anna Spearman and Sarah Falkner to the deathbed scene, but only for the limited purpose of demonstrating that "the Urine, that is to say about a Table Spoon full thereof was administered by them to the deceased and not by your petitioner." Spearman and Falkner had initiated the prosecution against Kitty and William Shields, testifying that Kitty had administered the urine; it was, therefore, necessary to place them at the scene in the second petition.

But the room was still more crowded than the Shields let on; a justice of the peace recorded depositions when several other onlookers entered the debate over who gave Betsy urine. Mary Anne Fischer, a neighbor woman aged at least seventy years, swore she was present in Betsy's room when Spearman and Falkner fed Betsy their urine, and implied that Elizabeth Downing, another of Betsy's friends, was at the scene. Frances Wilson, a thirty-six-year-old neigh-bor, also witnessed the scene and corroborated Kitty's story.[23] Thus, at least five people who were not kin surrounded Betsy's deathbed.

Other nonrelatives, moreover, lived under the Shields's roof. Contrary to the impression created by their correspondence, the Shields household num-bered not three but eight. William had apparently taken up shoemaking dur-ing the hard times of the Embargo Act. At least two apprentices lived with him in 1812, and other nonrelatives may have joined the household. The Shields's correspondence mentions no children besides Betsy, but the 1810 census-taker counted one boy aged 10 to 16, one aged 16 to 26, and William (aged at least 45), as well as one girl under 10 years old, one aged 10 to 16, Betsy and one other woman aged 16 to 26, and Kitty (less than 45 years old). Some of those

LAYING CLAIM TO ELIZABETH SHOEMAKER

aged 16 to 26 may have been boarders; others, employees or older apprentices. It seems unlikely that the Shields had any other children. They took such pains to document their doting, child-centered ethic of family life, and understood the pardoning process so well, that they would never have passed up the opportunity to showcase other children as examples of parental fitness.

The Shields household, therefore, was thoroughly infiltrated by unrelated members of the community. Betsy's friends, neighbor women, and as many as five live-in nonrelatives freely penetrated the inner sanctum of the Shields household. The privatization of family life, a staple of historical writing on the middle-class family in this period, had not yet arrived in the Shields's Fells Point, although it doubtless had in the homes of the governor and his councillors.[24] Perhaps this disjuncture between the Shields's well-peopled world and that of the gentlemen to whom they appealed accounts for their reluctance to mention the presence of nonfamily members in their home; they knew their audience.

The Shields family possessed no private "inner sanctum." The family was but one axis of their social existence, thoroughly intersected by other vectors of social life: the network of friends around Betsy (or her favorite haunts), a cluster of neighborhood women who included Kitty, and the mariners' world to which William still belonged. Before Betsy's death, her friends and her parents competed for her allegiance, although all groups generally deferred to the Shields when they disciplined her. The contest continued after her death, but because of the allegation of homicide the controversy spread through the community to include ever more people.

The events leading up to Betsy's death reveal the community's place in the Shields's household, but the events unfolding afterward speak more to the Shields's place in the community. Although the family had apparently moved to Baltimore only four years before Betsy's death, they compiled quite a history in their brief stay. Every year between 1808 and 1812, William, or Kitty, or William and Kitty together, went before the Baltimore City Court of Oyer and Terminer to answer assault charges. In 1808, their first year in Baltimore, William was charged along with two other men with having assaulted one John Karnes. In 1809 William and Kitty were both indicted and convicted for an assault on William McKee. The court fined each $20 plus costs. In 1810 William again paid a $20 fine plus fees, this time for assaulting George Rogers. Later in 1810, both Kitty and William were convicted on still another assault charge. The next time they faced the court, Betsy was dead.

Two of the cases are particularly revealing. When Kitty and William faced assault charges in the summer of 1809, they stood shoulder to shoulder with some familiar figures. Their codefendants included Anne Spearman, the woman later named as one of Betsy's corruptors and charged with giving her urine to drink. Charges against Anne and another defendant were dropped before trial, but she testified *for* Kitty in her trial. So did Betsy Shoemaker herself, along with Fanny Wilson, who would later attend Betsy's deathbed. A year later, when the Shields again made their annual pilgrimage to the criminal court, they called Mary Fischer as a defense witness, another attendant at Betsy's deathbed. Justice of the Peace Henry Fischer—probably Mary's son—took the recognizance (bond) that ensured the Shields's presence at court, then testified at their trial. Prosecution witnesses included George Rogers of Back River, an agricultural and watermen's district east of Fells Point, the victim of the assault. Jacob Mull, a Sailing Master in the U.S. Navy, also testified against Shields; he lived in Fells Point but patrolled the Back River. Captain Alexander Murray of the U.S. Navy, a powerful and well-known officer of national statue, also weighed in.[25]

Several patterns emerged from this series of complaints against the Shields. First, for better or worse, the Shields had made a name for themselves in local society. Given their well-established propensity for violence, the coroner who examined Betsy's corpse could with some justification assert that "no two can be under worse characters than they are, and every body is wishing them to be brought to punishment." The Shields's brief but notable history of encounters with the legal system surely created a presumption of malevolence against them.

Second, an examination of the people involved as complainants, defendants, witnesses, and justices of the peace in the Shields's several trials revealed that the couple was very much enmeshed in the world from which they claimed to be trying to save Betsy. Anne Spearman, a villain in the Shields's pardon petitions, had been an ally in an earlier fight. Similarly, Mary Fisher and Fanny Wilson played some part in the Shields's earlier violent episodes, then gave exculpatory testimony regarding Betsy's death. Had the Shields genuinely wished to protect Betsy from the rough waterfront society of Fells Point, they would have had to disown their own experiences and behaviors: virtually all of the complainants, codefendants, and witnesses in the Shields's prosecutions lived in or near Fells Point (Figure 10–1).

Third, a clear majority of litigants and witnesses whose occupations can be identified depended upon the sea for their livelihood: William Shields, mariner, William Hill, rigger, James Hooper, waterfront innkeeper, and Mull and Murray of the U.S. Navy. Only a tailor and a painter disturb this pattern, consistent with Fells Point's specialized function as a maritime district concerned with shipbuilding and long-distance trade.[26] Mariners, artisans, and laborers dominated this "distinctly plebian" neighborhood, for merchants, capitalists, and professionals preferred to live west of Fells Point at the mouth of Jones Falls, near the inner harbor (Figure 10–1).[27]

The Shields moved into a crude milieu when they settled in Fells Point. Far from avoiding rough characters, they routinely roughed up other people. But eventually they went too far, exceeding even the loose bounds of propriety in live-and-let-live Fells Point. When Betsy died, the Shields discovered neigh-

195

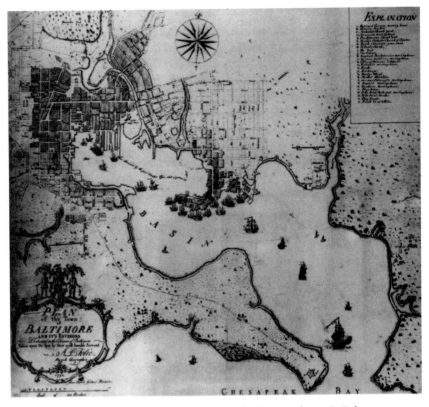

Figure 10–1. *Plan of the town of Baltimore by A. P. Folie.*
Note Fells Point in the center of the map.

borhood limits for tolerance in cases of domestic violence. Taken individually, their previous encounters with the law would not have effected long-term damage to their reputations. Even after Betsy's death, given the widespread reluctance to convict anyone of domestic violence, and given the plausibility of Kitty's claim that Betsy's death was an accident, it seems likely that most cases would have ended with a generous ruling by the coroner or the Grand Jury. But through sheer repetition of violent acts the Shields had established a reputation that predisposed the coroner and others to believe the worst. Thus the coroner, the state's attorney, the Grand Jury, and ultimately the trial jury agreed that Kitty was capable of killing her daughter. On January 11, 1812, a trial jury huddled without leaving the courtroom. Its members accepted William Shields's alibi (the nature of which went unrecorded) and acquitted him of having beaten Betsy the night before she died. Kitty, however, charged

196

with beating Betsy and feeding her a deadly mixture of potions, was convicted of manslaughter.

With the trials, the state encroached upon the domestic affairs of the Shields, but the definition of unacceptable violence remained very local. While participants in the trials acted on behalf of the state, according to rules laid down by central political and legal authorities, the coroner, the jurors, and the witnesses were residents of the same city, often of the same neighborhood, and acted according to local understandings of who the Shields were and how they fit into society.

But with their petitions to the governor, the Shields invited the highest officials in the state into their home. By crafting an effective letter according to conventions that political elites found compelling, they sought connection with still another node of social existence. The state, in the persons of the governor and his councillors, therefore, also had a claim on Betsy Shoemaker. Her posthumous fate and the fate of her mother became entwined with considerations of public policy. This was particularly true in 1812, as concern over criminality and public order in the city of Baltimore mounted. The governor and council's deliberations in Betsy Shoemaker's case followed a watershed decision to combat a percieved crime wave in Baltimore City by transforming the criminal justice system. The number of pardons granted dipped sharply in 1812, as the opening of a new penitentiary raised hopes that prisoners who once might have been hung or perished on a chain gang might instead rehabilitate themselves. This perceived crisis doubtless shaped discussions of Kitty Shields's pardon petition, which received particularly close scrutiny because of its timing, amplifying the intrusion of the state into the Shields household.[28]

One final twist to the story suggests the extent to which Betsy's, Kitty's, and William's social lives intersected with multiple, even competing levels of social existence, of which the household was but one. William, a mariner by trade and resident in one of the early Republic's major ports, enjoyed especially good connections in the U.S. Navy. At least two high-ranking naval officers testified at his earlier trials: Captain Alexander Murray and Sailing Master Jacob Mull. Within weeks of Kitty's manslaughter conviction, Commodore Stephen Decatur, the celebrated hero of Tripoli, offered William a position as a naval recruiter in Virginia, if only the governor of Maryland would make it possible for him to move by pardoning Kitty. The governor acceded to this request, and by March the Shields had packed up and were selling their belongings to prepare for the move. After all the uproar, after numerous court appearance and one terrible tragedy, after all the struggles and negotiations between Betsy, her parents, their neighbors, the legal system, and the state over Betsy's fate, the U.S. Navy authored the end to the story. William knew the waterfront, and the Navy needed sailors in the looming war against the British. The navy got William; Kitty got her pardon.

LAYING CLAIM TO ELIZABETH SHOEMAKER

During their years in Baltimore, the Shields left an unusually wide paper trail through public records. After 1812 they disappear, and we are left to speculate about their fortunes. It is possible that the struggle over Betsy's legacy was definitively won by the navy; when it engineered a pardon for the person convicted of her murder, the navy effectively wrote the posthumous conclusion to the tale of Betsy Shoemaker. The matter was almost certainly not settled so easily, however. The Shields could not have shed all the rough ways that contributed to Betsy's death, especially in another maritime milieu. Betsy's story was ultimately shaped as much by Fells Point as it was by the internal dynamics of the Shields family.

Notes

1. Robert Brugger, *Maryland, A Middle Temperament* (Baltimore, MD, 1988), 141, 152–160; Ronald Hoffman and Carville Earle, "The Urban South: The First Two Centuries," in Blaine A. Brownell and David R. Goldfield, eds., *The City in Southern History* (Port Washington, NY, 1977), 23–51.

2. Lawrence A. Peskin, "Of Ships and Suburbs: Fells Point as Maritime Community and Manufacturing Suburb," paper presented at the Mystic Seaport Museum Conference on Race, Ethnicity and Power in Maritime America, July 1995.

3. Unless otherwise noted, all quotes are from correspondence relating to the Shields's pardon file in Governor and Council (Pardon Papers), folder 106 [MSA S 1061-15], Maryland Hall of Records, (MHR) Annapolis (hereafter Pardons). The file includes a formal pardon petition circulated in late 1811 and presented to the governor before the trials in January 1812 (hereafter "First petition"); a follow-up letter elaborating on certain matters in the first missive (hereafter "Second petition"); a summary of witness depositions given before the trials began (hereafter "Deposition of [deponent's name]"); and a counterpetition written by the coroner who investigated Betsy Shoemaker's death (hereafter "Coroner's letter").

4. Coroner's letter.

5. Emphasis in original, John [illegible] to Governor Robert Bowie, Pardons, 12/10/1803, folder 44; Pardons, 12/17/1803.

6. Governor and Council (Minutes), 1777–1828 [MSA S 1073]; William Browne, ed., *Archives of Maryland*, 28:446–447, 13:119. For more on the pardon process, see T. Stephen Whitman, " 'I have got the Gun and will do as I Please with her': African-Americans and Violence in Maryland, 1782–1830," in this volume.

7. Quote from Pardons, 4/3/1786. Statistics from "Pardons database," a Paradox SE file of all surviving records of *nolle prosequis*, pardons, and executions in Maryland between 1748 and 1837. Sources: Pardons; Browne, *Archives* (volumes of the Governor's office and Council proceedings); Governor and Council (Appointments List), 1792–1837; Governor and Council (Commission Record), 1733–1837.

8. Maryland figures resemble Peter King's findings for a similar study of English cases in 1787 and 1790. When his results are rearranged to match the categories used

James D. Rice

here, previous good character (38 percent) and reformability (28 percent) top the list of favorable petitions and judges' reports, with equity third (15 percent). Differences may be due to the larger number of cases available to King, or different sources available for Maryland and England. King's figures are based on petitions and judge's reports; mine are drawn on pardons themselves. King, "Decision-Makers and Decision-Making in the English Criminal Law, 1750–1800," *The Historical Journal* 27 (1984): 43.

9. James D. Rice, "The Criminal Trial Before and After the Lawyers: Authority, Law, and Culture in Maryland Jury Trials, 1681–1860," *American Journal of Legal History* (Fall 1996): 455–475.

10. Quotes from Tilghman to John Eager Howard, Pardons, 5/19/1789, folder 88; Plater to Horatio Sharpe, 6/22/1766, *Archives*, 32:156–157; Pardons, 1787, folder 81. Dr. Ephraim Howard, Pardons, 9/9/1781, folder 80, urges a dual hanging as an "exemplary punishment." Similarly, petitioners for John Engles, a horse thief sentenced to death by a Frederick County jury, argued his execution would be justified only if it had deterrent value, Pardons, 1782, folder 13. Petitioners for John Selby argued that the execution of his two codefendants "will be sufficient to deter others from similar heinous crimes," Pardons, 10/5/1782, folder 4.

11. John Done to Governor John Stone, Pardons, 11/7/1797, folder 60; George Plater to Governor Sharpe, 6/22/1766, *Archives* 32:156–157; Douglas Hay, "Property, Authority, and the Criminal Law," in Hay et al., eds., *Albion's Fatal Tree: Crime and Society in Eighteenth-Century England* (New York, 1975), 17–63; Joanna Innes and John Styles, "The Crime Wave: Recent Writing on Crime and Criminal Justice in Eighteenth-Century England," *Journal of British Studies* 25 (1986): 380–485; J. A. Sharpe, *Crime in Early Modern England, 1550–1750* (New York, 1984): 68–70, chap. 7.

12. First petition.

13. Depositions of Mary Anne Fischer; Ruth Lawrence; Frances Wilson (quote); Second petition.

14. Second petition.

15. Although the causes, completeness, and timing of this shift have provided ground for debate, a near-consensus has emerged that such a change took place. Quote from Daniel Blake Smith, *Inside the Great House: Planter Family Life in Eighteenth-Century Chesapeake Society* (Ithaca, NY, 1980), 26. Also Phillipe Aries, *Centuries of Childhood*, trans. Robert Baldick (New York, 1962); Lawrence Stone, *The Family, Sex, and Marriage in England, 1500–1800* (New York, 1977); Stephanie Grauman Wolf, *As Various as Their Land: The Everyday Lives of Eighteenth-Century Americans* (New York, 1993), chap. 4; Helena Wall, *Fierce Communion: Family and Community in Early America* (Cambridge, MA, 1990), "Afterward"; Mary Beth Norton, *Liberty's Daughters: The Revolutionary Experience of American Women, 1750–1800* (New York, 1980); Jay Fliegelman, *Prodigals and Pilgrims: The American Revolution Against Patriarchy* (New York, 1982); Barry Levy, *Quakers and the American Family: British Settlement in the Delaware Valley* (New York, 1988); Steven Mintz and Susan Kellogg, *Domestic Revolutions: A Social History of American Family Life* (New York, 1988). For a sharp critique, John Demos, *Past, Present, and Personal: The Family and the Life Course in American History* (New York, 1986), 15–17. On problems of periodization and causation, Peter Burke, *History and Social Theory* (Ithaca, NY, 1992), 53–55; Simon Schama, *The Embarrassment of Riches: An Interpretation of Dutch Culture in the Golden Age* (New York, 1987); David

LAYING CLAIM TO ELIZABETH SHOEMAKER

Cartwright, "New England Families in Historical Perspective," in *Families and Children*, Peter Benes, ed., (Boston, 1987), 21–22.

16. Demos, *Past, Present, and Personal*, 33–34; Daniel T. Rodgers, "Republicanism: The Career of a Concept," *Journal of American History* 79 (1992): 11–38.

17. Catharine Beecher, *A Treatise on Domestic Economy* (1841), in David Hollinger and Charles Capper, eds., *The American Intellectual Tradition: A Source Book* (New York, 1989) 1:233; Kirk Jeffrey, "The Family as Utopian Retreat from the City: The Nineteenth-Century Contribution," *Soundings* 55 (1972): 21–41.

18. It was possible to prosecute parents for assault, homicide, and other offenses against children, but such prosecutions rarely occurred. William Blackstone, *Commentaries on the Laws of England* (Oxford, 1765–1769), 3:140; 1:453.

19. Elizabeth Pleck, *Domestic Tyranny: The Making of American Social Policy against Family Violence from Colonial Times to the Present* (New York, 1987), 30–31, 45; Peter Hoffer and N.E.H. Hull, *Murdering Mothers: Infanticide in England and New England, 1558–1803* (New York, 1981), 46.

20. John Demos has correctly pointed out that evidential and definitional problems prevent historians from measuring the precise extent in the past of child abuse, and by extension other forms of domestic violence, Demos, *Past, Present, and Personal*, chap. 4; Mary Beth Norton, *Founding Mothers and Fathers: Gendered Power and the Forming of American Society* (New York, 1996), 116.

21. Even in Baltimore's rural hinterland, prosecution rates, which can be treated as minimum crime rates, far exceeded what one might expect in the apparently bucolic countryside, see James D. Rice, "Crime and Punishment in Frederick County and Maryland, 1748–1837: A Study in Culture, Society, and Law," Ph.D. diss., University of Maryland, 1994, 86–97; David Hackett Fischer, *Albion's Seed: Four British Folkways in America* (New York, 1989), 768–771, 815.

22. Douglas Stickle, "Death and Class in Baltimore: The Yellow Fever Epidemic of 1800," *Maryland Historical Magazine* 74 (1979): 282–299; Brugger, *Maryland*, 144–147.

23. Depositions of Mary Anne Fischer and Frances Wilson.

24. Aries summarized the link now commonly drawn by historians: when the eighteenth-century family reorganized itself around the child, it "raised the wall of private life between the family and society," Aries, *Centuries of Childhood*, 143. Colonialists adopting this view include Rhys Isaac, *The Transformation of Virginia, 1740–1790* (Chapel Hill, NC, 1982), 72, 76, 302–310; Smith, *Inside the Great House*; and Wall, *Fierce Communion*. Historians of the nineteenth century usually link privatization to some combination of urbanization, commercialization, industrialization, and class formation; Harry L. Watson, *Liberty and Power: The Politics of Jacksonian America* (New York, 1990), 32, 178; Mary P. Ryan, *The Cradle of the Middle Class: The Family in Oneida County, New York, 1790–1865* (Cambridge, MA, 1981); Jeffrey, "The Family as a Utopian Retreat," 38–39; Paul Johnson, *A Shopkeeper's Millennium: Society and Revivals in Rochester, New York, 1815–1837* (New York, 1978), 43–48. Some scholars have commented on the class dimensions of this change. Wolf, *As Various as Their Land*, chap. 4; Tamara Hareven, "Introduction," *Family and Kin in Urban Communities, 1700–1930* (New York, 1977), 4–5; Mintz and Kellogg, *Domestic Revolutions*, 50–51; Demos, *Past, Present, and Personal*, 30; First Petition. The evidence for the Shields's social status is mixed. They kept apprentices, but did not appear in the real property assessments of

the era; few shoemakers rose to the lower ranks of the "middling sort." The Shields's behavior also suggests a non-middle-class ethic.

25. *Baltimore City Directory*, 1807–1813 (Baltimore, annual); David Long, *Gold Braid and Foreign Relations: Diplomatic Activities of U.S. Naval Officers, 1798–1883* (Annapolis, MD, 1988), 19–21.

26. Mariners often stayed in boardinghouses or taverns while ashore; as nonheads of households, they did not appear in the annual city directories from which I derived litigants' occupations. Thus the list probably understates maritime connections.

27. Peskin, "Of Ships and Suburbs"; Brugger, *Maryland*, 14–15.

28. Even the prominent young lawyer Francis Scott Key, author of "The Star-Spangled Banner," was prosecuted for assault in this period. Also James D. Rice, "'This Province, so meanly and Thinly Inhabited': Punishing Maryland's Criminals, 1681–1850," *Journal of the Early Republic* (forthcoming).

eleven

DECOROUS VIOLENCE

Manners, Class, and Abuse in Rebecca Rush's Kelroy

Jeffrey H. Richards

T he nascent American novel is a compelling if peculiar resource for the study of domestic violence in early America. Focused largely on what might be called the comfortable classes, novels in the early Republic follow the reigning English forms, the sentimental and the Gothic, to show threats of violence, sometimes quite sensational, against seemingly virtuous characters. While these works are not literal reflections of life in America, they indicate attitudes about violence and the domestic sphere. In later works, particularly Rebecca Rush's *Kelroy* (1812), increasing realism of method questions assumptions about violence in the first generation of full-length prose fiction in the United States. With *Kelroy*, a novel of manners brings middle-class readers directly in contact with the kind of violence they might observe themselves.[1]

The most noteworthy act of violence in novels of the new republic (1789 to 1800) is seduction, a code word for rape. In works such as William Hill Brown's *The Power of Sympathy* (1789), Susanna Rowson's *Charlotte: A Tale of Truth* (1791), and Hannah Webster Foster's *The Coquette* (1797), women often appear as naïve, even foolish victims of designing rakes. These books are cautionary works, warning young women—that is, unmarried women of the middling and upper classes—to bestow their favors only on suitors who deserve them. Violence in this scenario comes largely from outside to infect the domestic space; the vulnerable young woman may not have sufficient protection within her family to resist seduction because of some familial estrangement such as the death of her father. These novels suggest that violence can be controlled when young women learn to discriminate among suitors as they enter adulthood.[2]

In the novels of Charles Brockden Brown, the most noteworthy writer of the period, the domestic world is internally violent. In *Edgar Huntly* (1799), for instance, guilt for various acts of violence eventually spreads by implication to Huntly himself, a self-declared well-intentioned man whose sleepwalking becomes a metaphor for the possibility that even "good" people are capable of madness and murder. In *Wieland* (1798), a contented group of young adults living in a rural retreat outside Philadelphia begins to disintegrate when various members of the circle interpret voices they hear as malevolent. Clara Wieland, the narrator, records how her married brother goes on a murderous rampage, killing his wife and children, blaming all on the voice of a cruel god. For Clara, the agency of these deaths is complicated by the presence in their midst of a "biloquist," a kind of ventriloquist, who professes no direct guilt. In these and other novels, Brown leaves the origin of the violence obscure. By adding sensational details to a domestic plot—a ventriloquist, for example—he gives the illusion that violence is exceptional and extraordinary, although always threateningly possible. Violence is thrilling to read about, but connected more to literary types and Gothic expectations than to life among the comfortable.[3]

One of the first American novels to use a nearly realistic mode is *Kelroy* by Rebecca Rush.[4] Likened by the few critics of the book to the novels of Jane Austen, whose *Sense and Sensibility* and *Pride and Prejudice* appeared in the years surrounding *Kelroy*'s publication, Rush's novel examines life largely among the wealthy—those who have been and those who want to be.[5] In large measure, the author avoids sensational scenes like those in the aforementioned American novels. No one is tomahawked or strangled or raped, no small child is switched nor maidservant ravished. Nevertheless, *Kelroy* provides evidence that the very composition of American society, classbound in the ostensibly classless republic, creates conditions under which a variety of abuses can occur.[6]

Kelroy is set in Rush's native Philadelphia and environs and centers on the Hammond family. At the beginning of the story, the prosperous Mr. Hammond has died, leaving his wife and two daughters in straitened but by no means impoverished circumstances. Mrs. Hammond, embarrassed by the debts from her husband's estate that her inheritance must cover, decides to conceal her diminished capital. She therefore leaves her fashionable Philadelphia home and moves to the country, where she can pinch pennies and hide from urban high society. After a time, she embarks upon her grand scheme: to return to the city and spend the rest of her money to secure advantageous marriages for her daughters. Once her daughters are sold, Mrs. Hammond can live with one of them or by other means provided by the young women's husbands.

DECOROUS VIOLENCE

Mrs. Hammond's plan succeeds with her first daughter, Lucy. Her beauty captivates a visiting English peer, Lord Walsingham, and the match is settled quickly. But sensitive, artistic Emily, younger and incapable of calculation, follows her heart and fixes on a young poet, Edward Kelroy, whose father, like hers, has lost the family fortune. The plot of the novel then focuses on Mrs. Hammond's increasingly Machiavellian attempts to prevent Emily from marrying Kelroy and to force her into a partnership with a man of property. Rush chooses not to write the kind of comedy of manners that Austen created during the same decade but rather to depict a ruthless woman whose occupation is pretending to be wealthy. The consequences of Mrs. Hammond's success—her actions cause the deaths of the young lovers—show the lengths to which she will go to achieve her ends.

Compared to literature that describes domestic violence, *Kelroy* may not seem at first to be worth consideration. None of the main characters is beaten; no one in the Hammonds' circle comes home drunk or is thrown into debtor's prison. Men for the most part treat women with deference and respect; women rarely utter a discordant word about gender relations. Nevertheless, the book presents two levels of violence more believable than the exotic violence in seduction stories or Brockden Brown's novels. Both levels are tied to Rush's understanding of class divisions in Philadelphia society. The primary level is psychological, as Mrs. Hammond tries to break down Emily's resolve to marry Kelroy. The other is physical, experienced by lower and rising middle-class characters like the Gurnets—more of them later. For Rush, violence exists throughout society, but its form is determined by the class in which it occurs.

The central complication for today's readers is determining the extent to which *Kelroy* has a gendered outlook as well. The introduction to the only modern reprint of the novel offers a standard feminist reading of novels by women of the early republic: "*Kelroy* exposes a social system that limits the physical, educational, professional, and economic aspirations of women."[7] Feminist historiography often identifies patriarchy as the root cause of domestic violence because it fosters unequal power relations between the sexes. Rush, however, complicates the question of gender and patriarchy by portraying Mrs. Hammond as her daughter's abuser. Mrs. Hammond is one of the most noteworthy villains—very few of whom are women—in early American literature.[8]

This essay, therefore, will investigate Rush's treatment of Mrs. Hammond and the depiction of the psychological warfare she wages on her daughter Emily. It will then contrast Rush's delineation of elite life with her portrayal of nonelite characters who perpetrate or suffer physical indignities. Finally, it will offer some concluding remarks about the novel as a resource concerning violence in the early republic.

Contemporary discussions of family abuse often focus on the persistence of violent behaviors across generations. Thus, the son of an abusive alcoholic is

Jeffrey H. Richards

likely to abuse his own spouse and children;[9] a woman who passively accepts violence done to her in a marriage probably learned that strategy from her mother. With this in mind, we would do well to examine Rush's novel for recurring factors. The novel begins when the heroine, Emily Hammond, is twelve. Her father, an emigrant merchant who settled in Philadelphia, has died, and his extravagance has burdened Emily's mother with debts she must satisfy.[10] If Mrs. Hammond felt victimized by a debt accumulated without her knowledge or consent, she might victimize a family member in turn.

Rush, however, reveals that Mrs. Hammond may not have been an unwitting victim and had some degree of complicity in her circumstances. The narrator remarks that upon her husband's death, "the regret of his widow was greatly augmented by a prospect of comparative indigence, which suited neither her habits nor her temper." Nonetheless, unlike many an unprepared widow, Mrs. Hammond "was a woman of fascinating manners, strong prejudices, and boundless ambition, which extended itself to every circumstance of her life." Although she may not have been directly responsible for the "extravagancies" laid to her husband's charge, Rush tells us that economic restriction does not suit her "temper"; thus she may have contributed to her husband's debts, knowingly or unknowingly, to suit her own tastes. Furthermore, in the past she had demonstrated her unwillingness to be a passive player in her own affairs by successfully orchestrating her first marriage. Physically beautiful and socially adept as a young woman, she waited until the age of thirty to marry; now, the narrator tells us, she is a widow "too much on the wane to hope for a second advantageous connexion of that nature."[11]

Despite her age and lack of economic security, "she retained an unabated relish for show and dissipation," the narrator comments, "which her knowledge of the world, on which she prided herself much, taught her could only be obtained in future by concealing as much as possible the alteration of her circumstances." The decision to marry off her daughters to raise capital is, Rush insists, the result of her calculation and decision. Mrs. Hammond discharges her debts, knowing she will still have one-third of her estate left. She says nothing about her financial strain, knowing that "appearances are every thing, whilst they can be continued; and Mrs. Hammond conducted herself with a mixture of cunning and probity, which effectually lulled suspicion, and answered her purposes."[12] She may be seen as an independent person, used to getting her way and determined now, as a *feme sole*, to have her way again.

Nearly every action Mrs. Hammond takes is described by the narrator as being from design. By removing to the country, Mrs. Hammond not only can avoid the gossip of other elites but can cultivate an image of a grieving widow that no one would have the bad taste to question. More importantly, however, being away from Philadelphia gives her maximum control over her daughters' lives. Republican mothers were told in advice literature to guide the young toward their rightful place in society; for Mrs. Hammond, all that is required is the image of devoted guidance. Women in Philadelphia during the first decades of the new republic would have seen countless periodical articles urging them to adopt what is now often described as a "women's-sphere" ideology, based on an appeal to their virtue and their republicanism. Mrs. Hammond may not have absorbed the appeal to virtue, but she understands that fostering its appearance would carry her far.[13]

In private, she acquaints her daughters with the rules of matrimony: "involuntary love" is unacceptable; instead, they must marry sensibly, to someone who can satisfy their material needs. In essence, Mrs. Hammond creates, or attempts to create, an authoritarian setting wherein her word is law and the words of others are carefully filtered, monitored, and contradicted where necessary. Her creed is hardly a "cult of true womanhood" with an emphasis on woman's moral center in the domestic sphere; rather, it is the "cult of personality" maintained by a dictator.[14] This form of thought control over twelve- and thirteen-year-old girls reveals Mrs. Hammond's linking republican motherhood with the prerogatives of the patriarchy as she demands obedience to the laws of the domicile.

In short, she keeps enough power to be frightening; without a husband or enough capital to satisfy her desires for luxury, there are no brakes to her ambition. Given the ferocity and the complex machinations she pursues to ready the girls for marriage, one wonders if she would have been happier applying her energies to entreprenurial endeavors. Certainly, a number of merchant-class widows in Philadelphia did, in fact, maintain businesses after the deaths of their husbands.[15] Thus, Mrs. Hammond might have tried her hand at trade or pursued her husband's business. Of course, she may have shared the fate of many potentially competent women: she may have had no training in the family business nor earned her husband's confidence. The text, however, does not indicate that, with the opportunity to engage in business, Mrs. Hammond would have chosen to do so. Few heads of small businesses could have rivaled her in her control over the production and distribution of the product she had to sell—her daughters. Such power, it turns out, gives her the opportunity to abuse it.

After four years in the country, Mrs. Hammond returns to Philadelphia and works tirelessly to engage Lucy and Emily and to further her reputation as a wealthy woman. Her success with Lucy, whom the narrator describes as a copy of her mother, does not prepare Mrs. Hammond for Emily's resistance to her will. Emily is disgusted by Lucy's behavior, especially in light of Walsingham's honorable, if benighted character. With Lucy settled, Mrs. Hammond focuses on Emily and soon discovers surreptitiously that Emily has her eye on Kelroy and struggles mightily with desires to be direct: "The immediate impulse of her mind was, to assert her own authority, and forcibly prevent her daughter from ever again seeing Kelroy; but," the narrator adds, "a little reflection con-

Jeffrey H. Richards

vinced her of the folly of such a step; and controuling with strong effort, every tempestuous emotion, she listened to the suggestions of her native caution, which pointed out a more difficult, but less perilous course." Calling Emily to her to sew a cap, Mrs. Hammond exploits the oppurtunity. Watching the discomfort that Emily feels under her gaze, Mrs. Hammond "enjoyed her agitation with malicious pleasure; but although she wished to refrain from severity, could not deny herself the satisfaction of tormenting her a little before she proceeded to business." Chiding her on shaking hands and elongated stitches, Mrs. Hammond works the situation to advantageous effect. Emily's attempts to sew even stitches fail as she becomes "discomposed" by Mrs. Hammond's "sarcastic tone."[16] The mother then goes in for the kill, ridiculing her failure to control her sewing or her speech.

But Rush refuses to give to Mrs. Hammond an easy victim. Emily is wounded, but not defeated: "unused to language like this, every particle of pride and spirit in Emily's composition flew to her aid." Discovering heretofore unknown reserves of resistance, "and losing all apprehension in her disgust at so rude an attack, she instantaneously recovered herself, and rising, replied with calm dignity."[17] As in all abuse situations, the victim's response is important to the progress of the situation. For Rush, the attitude maintained by the daughters to their mother's manipulations determines their future. Whereas Lucy adopts her mother's creed of material comfort out of a propensity in that direction, Emily resists her mother's attempts to beat down her pride.

Emily's resources startle her mother. At the time of this episode, she is seventeen, an age Rush presents as old enough to marry, but too young to have that knowledge of the world on which Mrs. Hammond prides herself. Nevertheless, Emily literally stands up to her mother and tells her there is no question she cannot answer truthfully. Her mother is, for the moment, nonplussed: "[Emily's] lofty but respectful air, astonished Mrs. Hammond, who now first became sensible that her daughter inherited a portion of her own haughtiness."[18] Abandoning the sarcastic affront, realizing, in fact, that Emily's character resembles her own, Mrs. Hammond changes tactics and adopts a tone first of softness, then, when Emily confesses that Kelroy has visited her, of "generosity." Despite all of her different strategies, her efforts to persuade, cajole, and plead with Emily to abandon her impecunious lover fail. As with many literary daughters in the early Republic, Emily seeks a path of self-affirmation without rebelling outright against her parent, which for a time works: the abuse stops, and Mrs. Hammond gives Emily permission to see Kelroy. Rush seems to affirm that a little pride, even haughtiness, in a woman has some social utility and ought not be suppressed entirely.

Even so, Emily's challenge to her mother's authority can go only so far. Her filial loyalty will not allow Kelroy to propose any change in their relationship; indeed, she effectively tells him that she fears "some very positive, if not violent

207

conduct in her mother" should she decide to marry him at this juncture. The message is not lost on Kelroy. To Walsingham, who has learned the measure of his mother-in-law only after his marriage to Lucy, Kelroy announces that she has neither honor nor principle: "'I have long been convinced that she . . . could, without compunction, sacrifice her child to the veriest wretch in nature—aye, by heaven! sell her child to a Jew, or a Turk to grace his seraglio, provided she herself were to be exalted by the bargain!'" To Kelroy, Mrs. Hammond is "'like my evil genius, scattering doubt, and frowning darkness wherever she moves.'"[19] Emily, as a dutiful daughter, can only stand up to the most egregious forms of psychological abuse. Despite Mrs. Hammond's severity, readers might still expect the usual neoclassical literary outcome from the situation.

At this point, Mrs. Hammond differs little from parent-villains of Roman comedies who try to prevent young people from marrying, eventually fail, and are reconciled in the happy ending to the successful plot laid by youth against old age. Three crucial events, all of a pecuniary nature, prevent this traditional dénouement. First, Walsingham forces Mrs. Hammond to reveal her relative poverty and the fact that there will be no dower for Lucy. Mrs. Hammond then hardens herself against her son-in-law and becomes determined to retain the money she has borrowed from him. Second, Kelroy sails for India to try to make his fortune before returning to claim Emily's hand; in his absence Mrs. Hammond seizes every opportunity to break Emily's love and spirit. The third and most dramatic event is a fire that destroys Mrs. Hammond's Philadelphia home and expensive furnishings—items which she might have bartered to maintain a modest living. On the heels of this loss, however, comes good fortune: she wins a $50,000 lottery, enough to restore her comfort and security. Money, then, drives Mrs. Hammond's responses to change or crisis. Money, or the carefully maintained illusion of wealth, allows her enormous latitude of behavior and freedom of action.[20]

Both money and illusion underly one of Mrs. Hammond's chief pleasures, the theater.[21] Her sitting in the right box would have signified her elite status. Most of the plays she would have seen on Philadelphia stages would have portrayed elite manners and situations, and thus held a mirror up to her own sense of *politesse* and display. It is not surprising, therefore, that she is skilled at maintaining illusion. She is a consummate actress whose ability gives her a tremendous advantage over those who, like Emily and Kelroy, believe in fidelity to their hearts and truth in the presentation of self. Although the two lovers know what game she plays, "Mrs. Hammond appeared to indifferent spectators to be one of the most amiable, and affectionate of mothers."[22] Thus the sentimental victims, the romantically consistent poet Kelroy and artistic Emily, must contend with a being who can transform herself at will.

Rush's character, Mrs. Hammond, expands the literary possibilities for women to control their world, albeit here for dark purposes. She is a tyrant,

208

and she engenders the fear in her subjects that she may suddenly turn violent and mark out some victim arbitrarily. This power is often motivated by a deep insecurity, a fear that similar violence could at any moment be visited upon the leader. While Mrs. Hammond is careful about her public image among others of her class, she sometimes reveals to her family a propensity to abuse that Emily fears. In one episode, Mrs. Hammond must sit and seethe while Walsingham makes pointed remarks to Emily about sharpers in the world, knowing that she is the target of his insinuations. When a servant suddenly breaks a glass dish, Mrs. Hammond snaps; after her enforced silence, she "fiercely poured on him such a torrent of vindictive reproof, as neither of her auditors had ever heard issue from her lips before." And while the episode allows her to vent enough to regain her composure, her son-in-law finds his bait has brought something to the surface he had never observed: "Walsingham, who had hitherto remarked her moderation on similar occasions, well knew that the accident alone was not the cause of this violence."[23] He discovers that the root of her violence is money—or its lack.

When the fire further reduces her circumstances, Mrs. Hammond gives way to even more arbitrary behavior. She moves in with the gossipy Mrs. Cathcart and her adult twins Charles and Helen, and bears her misfortunes without the grace of a truly stoic republican mother: "Tortured by the consciousness of the degrading exposure of her past deeds which approaching want and dependence must soon effect, Mrs. Hammond had become so horribly perverse and irascible, that her own daughter could with the greatest difficulty accommodate herself to the intolerable caprices of her humour."[24] When left alone, she demands company; when in company, she ridicules or abuses those with her. This imperious irascibility comes to a head when Mrs. Cathcart reads the news in the paper of the winning lottery ticket. For reasons unbeknownst to all save Kelroy, Mrs. Hammond faints, and in her collapse, is hit accidentally in the face by Mrs. Cathcart as the latter tries to prevent her from falling. Blood flows; Mrs. Cathcart inquires openly why she fainted; and Mrs. Hammond, restored, delivers upon her friend a "rough attack" that brings Mrs. Cathcart to tears.[25] Although feeling herself to be the victim of physical abuse, Mrs. Hammond confines her abuse in return to a verbal attack on a member of her own class; as we shall see later, class is an important factor in how Rush depicts violence in her novel.[26]

Curiously, the sudden change in fortune that ought to have ended Mrs. Hammond's manipulative behavior only redirects it. The news that she has indeed won $50,000 causes Kelroy to feel relief; he believes that he can now leave Emily with her mother without fear of the measures she might take in her desperate attempt to get Emily settled with a richer man. True to appearance, with the capital necessary to retrieve her place in elite society, Mrs. Hammond affects a calm and easy demeanor toward Emily that implies that she has no further need to manipulate her daughter's life.

DECOROUS VIOLENCE

However, Mrs. Hammond, the woman who has remarked, "'I have reflected on everything!'"[27] conspires with another suitor, the *nouveau riche* Marney, to forge letters from Kelroy to Emily and back. Each thinks, wrongly, that the other has abandoned the relationship. Emily eventually marries an earnest, monied man named Dunlevy; Kelroy wanders the world and squanders his talent in sorrow and dissipation. Emily's death follows her discovery of the forgery; Kelroy's follows his learning of Emily's and the reason for it. Mrs. Hammond herself dies suddenly in a transport of joy over her enormous success. But her psychological violence toward Emily convinces Rush's readers that her motivation is a belief that "involuntary love" is insupportable in a culture where ambition and money carry the day.

Rush signals to elite young women that belief in romance could make them potential victims of abuse, not from an imagined seducer but from a real parent.[28] She demonstrates that among elites, abuse arises within domestic settings, not outside them. Emily Hammond never faces a physical threat; her "virtue" is never challenged. Yet her innocence is just as surely robbed by the unrelenting, if changeable psychological tactics her mother practices on her.

If elites, or aspiring elites, suffer from nothing worse than a bloody nose occasioned by a faint, members of the lower classes face harsher abuses. For Rush, violence appears among all classes, but whether it is physical or psychological depends on social expectation and decorum. She portrays almost exclusively domestic or semidomestic venues throughout the book; we never see factories or run-down neighborhoods. Yet the author's own attitude toward psychological violence obscures the meaning of physical abuse in *Kelroy*. Because beatings occur among nonelite secondary characters, she feels at liberty to make light of them.[29] Mrs. Hammond's psychological villainy remains Rush's major interest; more overt forms of abuse come across as comic relief.

A pair of episodes involving the comic doctor, Blake, suggest that, for Rush, fisticuffs or their threat are expressions of substandard manners and taste and have no place among the elite. At a party, Blake spills coffee on a stranger; she in turn calls him a "Hottentot."[30] Later, he and Marney argue about a painting. Insulted, Blake leaps up and shakes his fist in Marney's face, while the women fear "an immediate boxing match." Although the elite women at the party might flee the scene to avoid the spectacle of Blake and Marney fighting, whether the men actually hit each other or not has little consequence in the greater scheme of Rush's novel. The elites may leave or laugh, but they assume that physical violence is below their station.

Other situations involve Mrs. Hammond directly. In one, a milliner comes to call for the debt of $500 that Mrs. Hammond owes her. Although the narrator describes the milliner as "a vulgar, passionate woman," we see quite quickly that her complaints are just. Yet Mrs. Hammond, trying to impress the world with money she does not have, resists paying her. As they trade insults, the words of the "vulgar" woman so enrage their target that Mrs. Hammond "with difficulty refrained from striking her." As Emily seeks to stop this dispute—its character being so unexpected among elites that she perceives the conflict as a "violent altercation"—Kelroy's entrance restores Mrs. Hammond's countenance of feigned rationality.[31] With a show of effrontery, she pays the bill.

This conflict and one mentioned earlier, in which Mrs. Hammond verbally assaults a servant for breaking a dish, reflect the harshness of behavior toward servants maintained even by elite women. The treatment of servants in this era, including females, was often violent; even the Quaker Elizabeth Drinker records in her diary the necessity of having to whip servants.[32] The fact that Mrs. Hammond berates her servant or abuses the milliner reflects social expectations in late eighteenth- and early nineteenth-century Philadelphia. For Rush, however, the displays of Mrs. Hammond's passions indicate that she cannot maintain her sense of decorum easily—and that, by 1812, such displays are recognized as unseemly in elite women.

Other characters, including black servants, suffer physical violence, but generally these episodes are unremarked-upon by elites. The most violent scene in the novel, however, occurs when Emily, Helen, Dunlevy, and Charles visit Jeb Gurnet, a poor peddler turned wealthy wholesaler and salt merchant, and his family. Like Marney, the Gurnets are people who have risen economically but have not yet acquired the social graces of the true elite. At this point in the novel—Kelroy has gone to India, but Mrs. Hammond has not yet played her final card—the visit provides, apparently, a comic interlude before the gloomy conclusion; the scenes with the Gurnets have the quality of slapstick. Juxtaposed to the Machiavellian workings of Mrs. Hammond and the Kelroy-Emily plot, however, the Gurnet episode provides an unsettling subtext to the psychological violence of the elite.

Rush takes pains to show that the Gurnets' quick financial rise has not elevated them culturally. Gurnet can now associate with people who would not have admitted him to their homes before; he sends his three daughters to boarding school to give them the finishing that often represented female education in the early nineteenth century. While Gurnet may be able to get in the door, however, his daughters find it difficult to meet suitors in their new socioeconomic class. Eleanor, Mary, and Catharine "were obliged in some measure to conform to the rules of the [boarding school], but they did it mechanically, and went through their lessons without either understanding, or remembering them." Their public personae, however, suffer from more than their lackluster studies. "Old Gurnet was very proud of them," the narrator interjects, "and desirous that they should appear well drest; but his habits were too inveterately low, and sordid, for him to be prevailed on to trust his wife and daughters with money; and when they asked him for new clothes, he would teize them for several days by saying he was sure they did not want

DECOROUS VIOLENCE

them." Gurnet displays what he thinks is his patriarchal right to control all aspects of family life, but Rush insists that he has not adjusted his habits to meet his rising status: "and after worrying them into fits of crying, and sullenness, [he] would march abroad, and without making known his intentions, purchase quantities of ill-chosen, gaudy finery . . . as it often happened that they all fixed their fancy on the same thing, the most violent quarrels ensued, which usually terminated in the entire destruction of the article in question."[33]

Rush portrays the Gurnets' domestic discontent as directly related to their father's ambition; since the daughters have little in the way of personal capital—no especially good looks, talent in music, language skills, or poetic ability—they cannot help but err in front of the elite visitors who have come to observe them. Their "blunders" in society "subjected them to unavoidable ridicule"; but the family situation is strained further by Gurnet's desire to move them to the country, which he accomplishes "with his usual obstinacy . . . much against their inclination."[34] Thus social climbing is a psychologically violent act, exposing those content in one stratum of society to the mockery of those in another, and forcing people—in this case, a family of women under a patriarch—"against their inclination." Although Mrs. Hammond thinks her new neighbors ridiculous, she resembles Jeb Gurnet in her ambition and willingness to bend her family to her will.

The Gurnet daughters, lacking any social graces, immediately descend upon members of the visiting party. Mary clings to Dunlevy, Catharine to Charles, and Eleanor to Helen. Dunlevy reacts as if he were being attacked; Helen, meanwhile, despite trying to change the subject, is forced to listen to Eleanor's gossip about violence between a servant and a maid. All three feel nearly abused by the young Gurnets, yet bear their treatment with predictable decorum. At last, Mary and Catharine are prevailed upon to play the piano. While the latter performs, Eleanor sneaks off, brings in a dog, and pinches "both its ears until it sent forth such a horrible outcry as entirely overcame the little remaining self-command of the company." A row ensues, creating a "hurricane" at the center of which is Catharine, "crying with all the violence of an affronted child."[35] Rush indicates that the infusion of money does not bring manners nor domestic gentility.

Not long after the incident described above, violence springs anew. Following tea, as the company stroll in the garden, Eleanor hears voices and observes that the black servant, Ben, has dropped a punch bowl. Gurnet grabs Dunlevy's cane and pursues him, threatens to " 'pummel' " him, then proceeds to do so. Ben, however, escapes, and flees to the cow pasture, where Gurnet, in pursuit, slips and falls, "his face in the mire." In his pique, Gurnet threatens his laughing daughters with a "box" on their ears and promises to "thrash" Eleanor if she does not quickly clean up Dunlevy's manure-spotted cane.[36] After one more exchange between the senior Gurnets, Emily, Dunlevy, Charles, and Helen leave,

Jeffrey H. Richards

their merriment short-lived when Emily learns on her return that Kelroy's kind and stoic mother has died.

Interestingly, Rush's narrator does not directly criticize the physical violence at the Gurnet home. Rather, the satire, written with careful attention to speech, finds its mark in the Gurnets' lack of decorum. Although Mr. Gurnet comes across as a good-natured fellow, Rush implies that his style of home governance errs by his being too involved with domestic affairs. One token of a civilized society is the trust of a husband in his wife's ability to create and maintain domestic order. Gurnet, by not allowing his wife and daughters greater freedom to spend family money in their own way, forces them into an infantile and crude dependence on him. Rush implies that a more sensible ordering of the domestic sphere, with less violence to the "inclination" of family members by a single, powerful individual, would reduce the amount and degree of abuse the daughters and their father visit on each other. Once again, Gurnet functions as an analogue to Mrs. Hammond, highlighting her own lack of trust of Emily's desires.

These episodes of violence have as their root cause some disparity in class structure. The black servant, Ben, who is nearly beaten senseless for dropping a bowl, suffers the most, as befits those on the bottom of the social scale. The tongue-lashing Mrs. Hammond gives her servant for dropping a glass dish—a parallel to the scene with Gurnet and Ben—and the blistering she gives to the milliner, while not as physical as the violence done to Ben, again indicate that class differences give elites a license to visit harshness on those beneath their station. Finally, the argument between Marney and Blake and the Gurnet episodes are all inspired by their attempts to show themsleves equal to their "betters." In ill-directed attempts to belong to elite society, they display the reasons why membership eludes them. By the same token, with both the Gurnets and the Hammonds, violence in the home comes from discontent with station.

Rush remains equivocal about class, but not about violence. Her novel depicts ambition and will combining to abuse feelings of love and contentment; sincerity is no match for appearance unless it is buttressed by a large and independently controlled fortune. Rather than being a critique of institutional, social, and legal limitations on women, *Kelroy* locates society's ills in a system that rewards social climbing at the expense of other human values. In doing so, Rush may have been castigating her fellow Philadelphian, Benjamin Franklin, whose story of his own rise in society was, by 1812, being presented as a model of American behavior. Rush shows domestic violence at the juncture of a hypocritical doctrine of republican democracy in a society bound by class distinctions. The novel demonstrates that social mobility—the economic promise of republican politics—carries with it an intrinsic propensity to violence because the class structure of British America had remained intact. Within this framework, one can fall as well as rise. Mrs. Hammond fears the former and uses

213

perverse, psychologically violent means to prevent it. Jeb Gurnet desires the second and employs the cane to ensure it. Thus class thinking, as portrayed in Rush's novel, maintains an iron grip on Americans of the early Republic, so that even the most well-mannered elites punish everyone within reach to preserve class status.

As a reflection of Pennsylvania society, *Kelroy* suggests that hidden within the recesses of ordered, decorous, elite domestic worlds, and less hidden in the homes of quickly rising entrepreneurial families, both physical and mental abuse lurks. It is a necessary component of a desperate attempt to maintain or elevate social status. Rush's novel documents the price one pays for participation in elite culture; by forgoing the depiction of sensational violence for the Gurnets' petty thrashings and Mrs. Hammond's sinister manipulations, the author shows that the novel as a form can have more to do with the textures of contemporary society than stories of seduction or murder that dominated American literature previously. For all its humor and witty characterizations, Rebecca Rush's *Kelroy* offers a darker, yet more realistic, vision of the presence of domestic violence than other novels of the time.

Notes

1. Rebecca Rush (1779–?) was the daughter of Jacob and Mary Rench Rush and the niece of the famous physician Benjamin Rush.

2. William Hill Brown, *The Power of Sympathy* (Boston, 1789); Susanna Rowson, *Charlotte: A Tale of Truth* (London, 1791); Hannah Webster Foster, *The Coquette* (Boston, 1797). These and other novels discussed below are available in modern reprints.

3. Charles Brockden Brown, *Edgar Huntly* (Philadelphia, 1799) and *Wieland* (New York, 1798).

4. Rebecca Rush, *Kelroy. A Novel* (Philadelphia, 1812). All references are to the modern edition, Rebecca Rush, *Kelroy. A Novel*, ed. Dana D. Nelson (New York, 1992).

5. *Kelroy* is mentioned in many standard histories of the early novel: Lillie Deming Loshe, *The Early American Novel, 1789–1830* (New York, 1907); Herbert Ross Brown, *The Sentimental Novel in America* (Durham, NC, 1940); and more extensively in Henri Petter, *The Early American Novel* (Columbus, OH, 1971); also Harrison T. Meserole, "Some Notes on Early American Fiction: Kelroy Was There," *Studies in American Fiction* 5 (1977): 1–12. Kathryn Zabelle Derounian-Stodola, "Lost in the Crowd: Rebecca Rush's *Kelroy*," *American Transcendental Quarterly* 47–48 (1980): 117–26 discusses the book as a novel of manners and makes the Austen connection, as does Cathy N. Davidson in a different context, *Revolution and the Word: The Rise of the Novel in America* (New York, 1986), 232–235. Davidson's study, especially attentive to the role of women in early novels, sees *Kelroy* as a mixture of manners and Gothic. Unfortunately,

Jeffrey H. Richards

her discussion includes several misrepresentations of plot details (for instance, Davidson says Mrs. Hammond is widowed at 30, when she is married at 30) and should be read with caution. See also Davidson's foreword to *Kelroy*, Nelson, ed., v–vii. Steve Hamelman, "Aphasia in Rebecca Rush's *Kelroy*," *South Atlantic Review* 62 (1997): 88–110, considers the novel a poststructuralist parable of language and the deficiency of communication, 108.

6. Davidson, *Revolution*, 232.

7. Dana D. Nelson, Introduction, *Kelroy*, xxi; Karen A. Weyler, "'A Speculating Spirit': Trade, Speculation, and Gambling in Early American Fiction," *Early American Literature* 31 (1996): 223–225.

8. "Mrs. Hammond stands supreme as the prototype of the Great American Bitch," quoted from Derounian-Stodola, "Lost in the Crowd," 120.

9. My remarks on abuse are drawn from assumptions underlying Sara Munson Deats and Lagretta Tallent Lenker, eds., *The Aching Hearth: Family Violence in Life and Literature* (New York, 1991).

10. As Marylynn Salmon points out, Pennsylvania probate law, unlike that of many other states, required widows to satisfy all claims against their husbands' estates; they could not retain any of it ("dower") unencumbered. Salmon, "Equality or Submersion? Feme Covert Status in Early Pennsylvania," in Carol Ruth Berkin and Mary Beth Norton, eds., *Women of America: A History* (Boston, 1979), 106–108. On other vulnerabilities of married and divorced women, see Merril D. Smith, *Breaking the Bonds: Marital Discord in Pennsylvania, 1730–1830* (New York, 1991), 10–43, 156–178.

11. Rush, *Kelroy*, 3–4.

12. Rush, *Kelroy*, 4.

13. Karen K. List, "The Post-Revolutionary Woman Idealized: Philadelphia Media's 'Republican Mother,'" *Journalism Quarterly* 66 (1989): 65–75; Linda K. Kerber, *Women of the Republic: Intellect and Ideology in Revolutionary America* (Chapel Hill, NC, 1980).

14. Barbara Welter, "The Cult of True Womanhood, 1820–1860," *American Quarterly* 18 (1966): 151–174.

15. Lisa Wilson-Waciega, "A 'Man of Business': The Widow of Means in Southeastern Pennsylvania, 1750–1850," *William and Mary Quarterly* 44 (1987): 40–64; and *Life after Death: Widows in Pennsylvania, 1750–1850* (Philadelphia, 1992).

16. Rush, *Kelroy*, 55.

17. Rush, *Kelroy*, 56.

18. Rush, *Kelroy*, 56.

19. Rush, *Kelroy*, 67, 83.

20. Davidson, *Revolution*, 232, argues that, as a woman, Mrs. Hammond would not be versed in economic details and would be a victim of merchants. Not only is she not as vulnerable as this view suggests, but recent historical studies of Philadelphia women make clear they possessed cleverness, resourcefulness, and economic savvy. In addition, single women householders often received lower property tax rates compared to men. See Karin Wulf, "Assessing Gender: Taxation and the Evaluation of Economic Viability in Late Colonial Philadelphia," *Pennsylvania Magazine of History and Biography* 121 (1997): 201–237.

21. Mrs. Hammond also likes card parties, another elite diversion. On the development of "polite" manners and the attachment of elites to particular amusements in the

period just before that of Rush's novel, see David S. Shields, *Civil Tongues and Polite Letters in British America* (Chapel Hill, NC, 1997).

22. Rush, *Kelroy*, 47.

23. Rush, *Kelroy*, 86.

24. Rush, *Kelroy*, 125–126.

25. On lotteries in Pennsylvania, see Trina Vaux, "An Evil and a Remedy," *Pennsylvania Heritage* 15 (1989): 32–37. Vaux shows that the sum of $50,000 won by Mrs. Hammond, while high, was not unusual. Also Alan D. Watson, "The Lottery in North Carolina," *North Carolina Historical Review* 69 (1992): 365–387. Both indicate the popularity of lotteries in the period just before the War of 1812. The place of lotteries amidst other speculative economic enterprises that appear in early American fiction is discussed in Weyler, "'A Speculating Spirit,'" 207–242.

26. As Jacquelyn C. Miller demonstrates in "Governing the Passions: The Quest for Domestic Harmony in Eighteenth-Century Philadelphia's Middle-Class Households," in this volume, middle-class Philadelphians felt compelled to restrain any propensity to physical violence. If taken as a reflection of its time, *Kelroy* in many ways validates Miller's documentary research.

27. Rush, *Kelroy*, 88.

28. Rush takes a more realistic approach to this theme than another American novelist, Tabitha Gilman Tenney, whose heroine, Dorcasina Sheldon, suffers beatings and near-rape experiences from acting as if her life were like a romance novel. The moral for both writers, however, is the same: abusers prey on female romantics. See Tenney, *Female Quixotism* (Boston, 1801).

29. Derounian-Stodola, "Lost in the Crowd," 120–124, suggests that the nonelite characters represent various degrees of caricature and typing.

30. Rush, *Kelroy*, 61.

31. Rush, *Kelroy*, 118.

32. Sharon V. Salinger, "'Send No More Women': Female Servants in Eighteenth-Century Philadelphia," *Pennsylvania Magazine of History and Biography* 107 (1983): 29–48.

33. Rush, *Kelroy*, 154.

34. Rush, *Kelroy*, 155.

35. Rush, *Kelroy*, 159–160.

36. Rush, *Kelroy*, 161–162.

Jeffrey H. Richards

Masters,
Servants,
and Slaves

twelve

"AS IF THERE WAS NOT MASTER OR WOMAN IN THE LAND"

Gender, Dependency, and Household Violence in Virginia, 1646–1720

Terri L. Snyder

Elisheba Vaulx had her share of servant trouble. In 1676 William Baker, her indentured servant, ran off to join Nathaniel Bacon, Jr. and his rebel troops. By 1681 Elizabeth Mullins, the recently freed maidservant who continued to work for Vaulx, had become stubborn, willful, and pregnant, while William Stroud, another former servant, had stolen one of Vaulx's hogs. Later that year, her slave Frank and a neighbor's indentured servant brawled with a couple of freemen in her parlor and her yard. Because she was a widow, responsibility for dealing with these unruly family members rested with Vaulx.[1]

Vaulx felt the weight of this responsibility by January 1681, when she sent a note to her attorney, Mr. Smyth, explaining that "my maide Betty will be at Court therefore [I] desire you to speake for me and to say she hath [to serve] according to the act of Assembly, for though she was free before I had her to Court, yet the childe was borne in her servitude, besides she is growne soe high and soe [peremptory], that I can scarce speake to her, pray Assist me in what lyes in your power."[2] Perhaps, Vaulx reasoned, since her own authority failed to awe Mullins, the lawyer and justices could inspire in her the proper respect for her superiors.

Evidently, Vaulx's strained relations with Mullins did not erupt into physical violence although, under legal understandings prevalent in early modern England and Anglo-America, Vaulx was entitled to correct her servant's obstinacy within reason. Masters and mistresses possessed extensive powers—and obligations—in regard to servants. Household heads were to provide indentured dependents with food, shelter, clothing, and freedom dues and were allowed to correct servants moderately. Legal standards permitted physical coercion but prohibited maiming or lasting injury; ten lashes with a belt was a permissible punishment for a disrespectful servant in early modern England or Virginia.[3] In this climate, Mullins's affronts justified physical correction because she violated social hierarchy and disturbed the peace of the household, although clearly she was not the first or last of Vaulx's servants to do so.

Vaulx, however, chose an alternate route. In framing an appeal to the York County court in Virginia, she cited her own ineffectual authority ("I can scarce speake to her") and the servant's sense of entitlement ("she is growne soe high") and relied on the justices to discipline the maid. Mullins may have had little regard for her mistress's opinion, but she did abide by the ruling of the York justices who sentenced her to six months extra service, substantially less than the two years required by statute.[4] The tension between the two women and Vaulx's appeal to the court to buttress her household sovereignty illustrate the complexities of women's authority, household dependency, and the adjudication of such disputes by the local courts in early Virginia.

Contrary to Vaulx's petition for aid, household disputes usually came to the attention of the York justices when punctuated by violence. This essay explores episodes of household violence in York County, Virginia, from 1646 to 1720, their social meanings with regard to authority and dependency, and the legal management of these outbursts by the local court.[5] In York, household brutality had two specific sources. Free white women who crossed gender boundaries by heading households, even temporarily, or by exercising overreaching authority within them, risked a violent response. This retaliatory violence was gendered and aimed to contain white women who were perceived to have overstepped their proper sphere of influence. Other household violence, however, such as marital cruelty, brawls, and excessive violence by masters toward servants, was less clearly gendered. It resulted instead from strains in authority relations and uncertainties over social categories of dependency. In these cases, violence was used to discipline or punish dependents, to claim or contest the authority of superiors, and to demonstrate equality or supremacy.

While authority and violence had gendered dimensions in York County, for the justices who punished excessive and illegitimate brutality, dependency rather than gender was paramount. Regardless of the sex or status of the perpetrator or victim, the court's interest was confined to establishing standards of evidence and righting the transgressions of social hierarchies that household violence represented. The justices were by turns paternalistic and patriarchal. They offered protection to white injured parties, whether they were male or female, free or unfree. But for those who overstepped legitimate authority through excessive household violence, the court demanded compensation and the promise of future good behavior.

Three specific forces brought pressure to bear on the constitution of household authority in the Chesapeake during the last half of the seventeenth century. First, the transformation of the Chesapeake's labor force during this period "revolutionized the social relations of production." The transition to slavery diminished political conflict between whites, who, despite class differences and, for the poor, extremely limited opportunities for mobility, considered blacks inferior. For most of the seventeenth century, planters relied primarily on white male indentured servants, but around 1680 they turned increasingly to African and African-American slaves to meet their labor needs. In York County, for example, one-third of unfree workers were black slaves in the 1670s, four-fifths by 1680, and 95 percent by the 1690s. This shift was accompanied by a decline in freedmen's status and prospects as the amount of inexpensive, available land dwindled.[6]

Second, beginning in the 1660s, slavery became embedded in legal institutions.[7] In 1662, a statute provided that children born to slave mothers became slaves for life; by 1667, baptism as a Christian no longer exempted a slave from bondage. By 1669, Virginia's burgesses deemed it legal for a master to physically injure or kill a slave in the process of correction; it was illegal to do the same to indentured servants.[8] By 1680, more racial distinctions had been legislated: slaves could receive thirty lashes for offering violence to a white, neither free nor enslaved African-Americans were allowed to carry guns, and free blacks were prohibited from owning white servants.[9] The comprehensive 1705 "Act concerning servants and slaves" also protected white servants from immoderate correction, specified that they could not be whipped naked, and outlined procedures for them to file complaints with magistrates. The act simultaneously denied slaves those protections and blocked nearly all avenues to freedom. Clearly servants had rights that slaves did not, for servants were entitled to seek legal protection and ultimately to be made free.[10] The changing labor force and the law of slavery increased the social distance between slave and servant, unfree and free, black and white.[11]

In addition to the changing labor force and the legal creation of slavery, seventeenth-century Anglo family patterns were thrown into disarray. Virginia had a high mortality rate and a surplus of men. Both sexes, moreover, often delayed marriage to serve out their indentures. Women were few, but because they were often younger than their husbands at marriage, they frequently outlived them. White women in the Chesapeake were more independent than their counterparts in England and New England, but they were also less protected.[12] Many women who began their lives in Virginia as indentured servants experienced young widowhood and subsequent remarriages, often more than once. Likewise, family structures themselves were affected, as parental death

"AS IF THERE WAS NOT MASTER OR WOMAN IN THE LAND"

and remarriage created mixed and complex households.[13] These circumstances weakened patriarchal relations within the Virginia households.

Together, the changing labor force, the evolution of the law of slavery, and the constitution of gender and familial connections complicated social attachments within Chesapeake households. In this context, household violence reflected weak spots in the fabric of social relations—power struggles between those with socially legitimated authority and those who wielded power illicitly but not necessarily unsuccessfully. Moderate levels of violence in early modern households were considered legitimate and regular, and, surely, then as today, outbursts of household violence were underreported. The violent episodes discussed here should be understood as excessive ones that required the intervention of the local court. Moreover, household violence and the legal response to it were intimately connected to the larger social changes underway in Virginia.

Tensions between unfree laborers and their masters in York households often found release in the insubordinate behaviors Elisheba Vaulx's servants exhibited—absence, insolence, theft, and violence. One study of servant discipline in all colonial North American courts to 1660 found that 40 percent of criminal charges against indentured servants were for running away and theft, while 44 percent cited violence.[14]

For women who headed households, like Elisheba Vaulx, the use of disciplinary violence was risky. Vaulx herself petitioned the court to buttress her authority, pleading feminine weakness and submission to the justices over an attempt to discipline her maid physically. In dealing with her servants' infractions, Vaulx compromised and settled disputes in ways that lessened the severity of consequences they suffered. In doing so, she surrendered some of the benefits male planters, more certain of their authority, might have reaped. When ex-servant William Stroud stole her hog, for example, he could have been sentenced to pay a thousand pounds of tobacco to Vaulx and to anyone who informed on him or to enter service for two additional years. But because Vaulx intervened before anyone could inform—indeed, she intervened *knowing* that her "neighbors threaten to inform"—Stroud owed damages only to her, and she may not have required the full amount. Her note to the justices indicated only that Stroud had "made satisfaction" to her; they took no further action.[15]

She was equally generous to runaway William Baker. She conferred with the governor's council about his sentence and allowed him to confess his absence in anticipation of a pardon for servants who participated in Bacon's Rebellion. Her actions permitted him to serve a single day, rather than two, for each day he was gone from her service.[16] She also compromised with the recalcitrant Elizabeth Mullins. Her actions suggest that successful women masters of necessity rode their authority lightly to reap the benefits of compromise. Negotiation and settlements served Elisheba Vaulx better than the correcting stick. While they might have questioned the legitimacy of her use of such heavy-

222

handed authority, physical punishment would have only pushed her servants to greater recalcitrance.

Other women in York chose a more authoritarian attitude toward their household dependents, however, and in doing so they risked violent retaliation. In York County, ten cases of servant-on-master violence were brought before the court between 1646 and 1720. Six involved attacks on women—five wives whose husbands were absent and a female bystander. All episodes clearly violated the law: servants were to obey their masters, be they men or women. Servants who violated household hierarchy by striking masters received an extra year of service. Some episodes also violated gender conventions. Generally speaking, men were not to strike women, although such violence was more acceptable in the seventeenth century than it became in the eighteenth. For the most part, however, household violence was homosocial; four female and two male servants struck female masters, while no court records note female servants who struck male masters.

Servant violence in York County was typically retaliatory: in the midst of a beating, servants often grabbed the stick from their masters and struck back. Verbal correction could also result in a violent response from servants, who found tobacco sticks (the rods on which tobacco leaves were hung to dry in the Chesapeake) ubiquitous tools for their vengeance.

Episodes in which servants assaulted female household heads reflect ambivalence on the part of the former toward female dominion. Women transgressed boundaries of gender and authority when they disciplined servants; in response, servants overstepped bounds when they counterstruck. Cases of servant violence toward female masters often explicitly state that the retaliatory violence occurred "in correction." When Ashaell Batten went to England in 1665, he left his wife Anne in charge of the household. When she attempted to discipline indentured servant Andrew Hill, he took "the sticke out of her hand correcting him" and "use[d] other violence toward her." Another servant, Hannah Langley, aided him by laying "violent hands on" Batten.[17] In 1679, as Mrs. Hyde struck her servant Mary Barrow, Barrow laid "hold on her mistriss['s] stick" and returned the blows.[18]

Female bystanders were sometimes drawn into a fray as well. Jane Shurlin deposed in 1682 that Joseph Brookley, servant to Robert Prichard, assaulted herself and his master with a tobacco stick. Shurlin held Prichard in her arms to defend him from the "wide assaults" of Brookley, who continued to "lay about him as if there was not master or woman in the land."[19] Shurlin's words suggest that Brookley breached two conventions: he violated both a culturally defined sphere of gender relations and a legally defined sphere of authority relations.

When servants struck male masters, however, court records do not indicate that their actions were retaliatory. Shurlin, for example, did not state that

"AS IF THERE WAS NOT MASTER OR WOMAN IN THE LAND"

Prichard was correcting Brookley, merely that the servant complained about his diet (which she did not find justified). In other instances of violence toward masters, only one servant seized a correcting stick, which typified violence toward female masters. Even in that case, however, the servant displaced his anger and resentment from his master and struck the master's son instead.[20]

In most servant violence against male masters, the roots of disorder are not recorded. The actions of offending servants are described in general terms: "resisted and struck" or "did assault, beat and wound." Clerks, of course, may have compressed details in general, but that they did so consistently in these particular cases is not meaningless. The use of sticks by women was notable, a visible symbol of their claim to authority, both to their servants and to the court clerks who recorded the cases.[21]

Although servants paid materially in extended service for attacking masters, they may have experienced psychological compensation. Besting one's master was a temporary reversal of social hierarchy that made a short-lived claim to power. By resisting the more brutal conditions of servitude, servants protested their correction and asserted their standing as equals. Retaliation momentarily measured power not through legally legitimated avenues but through the use of force. This psychological compensation became even more critical when female masters struck servants.

The use of correcting sticks by female masters seems to have inflamed servants; disciplinary violence had social meanings related to gender. When women hit servants, they asserted superiority. Female authority, however, was often constituted as unruly and disorderly by early modern people. Ballads, broadside verse, and all manner of early modern English print culture presented parables of physically and verbally ungoverned women and recited their comeuppance with relish—usually in the form of a violent reprisal.[22] Such cultural refrains doubtless stirred in the minds of Virginia servants. They are certainly evident in *The Vain Prodigal Life and Tragical Penitent Death of Thomas Hellier* (1680), a pamphlet that describes the way in which an indentured servant in Charles City County, Virginia, murdered his master and mistress.[23] Hellier bound himself as a tutor, but when he arrived at his master's plantation, he found no children. He was put to work in the tobacco fields, where he resigned himself to hoeing, weeding, and chopping. He could have borne this labor had it not been for his master's wife. He was driven to murder because of the "unworthy ill-usage" which he "received daily and hourly" from his "ill-tongued mistress," who would "not only rail, swear, and curse" him in the house, but also "like a live ghost would impertinently haunt" him when he was "quiet in the ground at work." And although he "silently wrought as fast as she railed," working "without so much as muttering at her, or answering anything good or bad," all his silence "would not harm her vile tongue."[24]

Terri L. Snyder

Hellier's portrait of his carping mistress was echoed by the minister who heard his confession, wrote it down, and contributed his own "Reflections" to the narrative. Both viewpoints frame Mrs. Williamson as a scold, an unruly woman with an ungoverned tongue who deserved her fate. Like Hellier, the clergyman blamed Mrs. Williamson for "exercising her perniciously inventive fancy in heaping on him ironical invectives." Hellier, the clergyman argued, was driven to murder by the "implacable tongue of that shrew his mistress," whose continual "taunts and jears, oathes and curses," and "tyrannical passion" were insufferable.[25]

Female or male household heads could restore order to their homes legitimately by taking unruly servants to court. Husbands like Ashaell Batten and Robert Hyde, prosecuting for their wives under the unity of coverture, sought to protect their authority and their spouses. All injured masters could establish a right to additional time from their laborers, but the 1661/1662 Act "Against Unruly Servants" required a confession or evidence from a witness for conviction.[26] The York justices upheld this standard of evidence, and all episodes of servant–master violence that came to their attention had to be supported with confessions or witnesses' depositions. For example, when Mary Barrow grabbed Mrs. Hyde's stick and returned her blows, Hyde called to a nearby servant, "Looke heare Flower she strikes me," to get help, establish a witness, or both. Defendants found guilty were ordered to serve their masters an extra year plus a few weeks to repay their master's expenses in prosecuting them.

To the York court, on the other hand, gender distinctions were unimportant. In sentencing unruly servants, the justices did not differentiate between men and women—violence from women was neither worse nor better than violence from men. Sentencing unruly servants reinforced their dependency, but this was based on their status, not their sex. Neither did the sex of the victim matter to the justices: servants received the same punishment regardless of whether they had struck male or female masters. In a colony with a large and growing unfree labor force, meting out punishment for violation of dependency relations was paramount.

Physically violent responses to women in authority were not only the province of servants. If women like Anne Batten, Mrs. Hyde, and Mrs. Williamson were vulnerable to counterattacks for correcting servants, other women risked violence by asserting authority over free white men. Widow Mary Butts, for example, disputed with her tenant, James Holloway, in 1690. Witnesses reported two violent episodes between the pair. In the first, Holloway went to look for one of Butts's lost cows, returned to the house empty-handed, and said he would search again if Butts would go with him. She replied that she would rather go alone, grabbed a corn stake and "went to strike him, but he went to take it out of her hand, then shee took fast hold of

"AS IF THERE WAS NOT MASTER OR WOMAN IN THE LAND"

his hare and withall both fell down." On another occasion Holloway came into Butts's house demanding breakfast. When she snapped, "gett you out of my house, I know noe businesse you have here," Holloway replied, "I have as much business here as you have." When Butts followed him out of doors, "biding him to be gone" and tried to strike him with a loblolly stick, Holloway hefted his hoe in defense, saying, "Landlady if you will not be quiett, by God I will knocke you downe." Holloway sued Butts for personal injury; a jury awarded him a modest 150 pounds of tobacco.[27]

As Holloway's landlady, Mary Butts had some authority over her tenant, and requesting some tasks from him was reasonable enough. When she tried to reinforce her position through the threat of violence, however, he not only repelled her blows, he took her to court, where a jury found her threats unreasonable, although their judgment suggests that they did so without enthusiasm. Her resistance to his offer to search for the cow together and her insistence that he should not come unexpectedly into her house suggest that she may have felt threatened in some way, perhaps sexually, by him. Nevertheless, the jury's decision indicated that, landlady or not, Butts had no cause or right to use violence against a free white man.

Similarly, in 1688, William Wade visited the house of John Williams, who was absent. A history of antagonism may have existed between Wade and Mrs. Williams, for, having found that he had quartered his horses in the tobacco house, she said that "shee should turne them out." Wade exploded, beating her with a tobacco stick until it broke and then dragging her by her neckerchief "like to [choke] her." He called her a "spotted bitch," and concluded that "hee had done her kindnesse in washing her ass." By threatening Wade's property, Mrs. Williams assumed an authority usually reserved for free men. Wade resorted to violence as a means of shaming her, but he overstepped his bounds. Her husband successfully prosecuted Wade for assault, and a jury awarded Williams damages of a thousand pounds of tobacco.[28]

Household violence between intimate family members was also formalized into complaints for York justices. Such reports often came from community members such as churchwardens or grand jury members, credible men responsible for scrutinizing social relations. Seven complaints of spouse abuse, for example, came before the justices between 1646 and 1720, five of which centered on the physical abuse of wives by their husbands.[29] Spousal abuse was surely underreported, but the neighborly scrutiny typical of villages in early modern England and New England was also at work in Virginia.[30]

In York County, violence between husbands and wives is revealed in pleas for marital separations. Unlike Massachusetts and Connecticut, colonial Virginia did not permit absolute divorce. When violence between husbands and wives was excessive, however, justices granted separations with maintenance or divorce *a mensa et thoro* to couples.[31] In 1691, for example, Mary Savory peti-

Terri L. Snyder

tioned the court for relief from her marriage, pleading that her husband's "inhumane useage" endangered "her life as well as her bodily health . . . dayly." The court ordered Henry Savory into custody until he gave a bond for his future good behavior, allowed his wife some personal property, and paid the costs of the suit.³² In 1697, a churchwarden complained that Robert Hide starved his wife and that she was "lying in a very weak and despicable condition from her husband's habitation." He noted that Hide "rejected and refuse[d] to allow her sustenance." The justices ordered Hide to allow her to come home, where the children could look after her, and to live with her peaceably.³³

A plea of cruelty, however, did not always result in separation—the court demanded adequate proof. In 1658 Joan Aduston complained that her husband misused her, but she could not prove it. The justices would not grant a separation because no one other than Aduston could testify to the cruelty.³⁴ In all cases where standards of proof were met, however, the York justices acted paternalistically, separating couples and offering protection to wives. Where proof was unclear, the court ordered a reconciliation.

Complaints of mutual cruelty and wives' violence toward husbands also reached the justices. In 1658 "severall complaints" alleged that Richard and Ann Owle "dayly goe in danger of there lives each to other" and the court granted a separation agreement.³⁵ In *Hill v. Slate*, 1692, domestic violence was not the focus of the case but had affected its outcome. James Hill brought an action of defamation against Robert Slate because Slate was spreading rumors about him; Slate claimed he had caught his wife in bed with Hill and that she was pregnant with Hill's child. Slate denied none of the charges and repeated his stories in court, asserting their truth and summoning witnesses who confirmed his statements. They reported that Mrs. Slate had choked her husband, who feared further violence from her and, possibly, Hill.

The choking was verified by three witnesses who reported that Slate had shown them a torn neck cloth and a bloody coat. More damning testimony came from a witness to whom Mrs. Slate had asserted that she "never [had] any reall love [for] her husband," adding that her marriage was a "forced match by my father and mother, but lett me goe and come when I will my husband will not controle me, I might have married forty and not have mett with the like."³⁶ Mrs. Slate may have been deriding her husband, bragging, or both. Her words reveal that although she obeyed her parents, she would act independently of him. As her strategy coincided with adultery and assault, it was not defensible.

The jury found for the defendant and ordered Hill to pay one thousand pounds of tobacco, stipulating that he not come to Slate's home nor "harbor, entertaine or associate himself in company" with Mrs. Slate.³⁷ Mrs. Slate used violence to claim power over her sexual choices, but from the jury's viewpoint, brutality directed at an innocent husband from an adulterous wife was not legitimate. The jury's decision simultaneously reinforced Mr. Slate's authority

"AS IF THERE WAS NOT MASTER OR WOMAN IN THE LAND"

and corrected Mrs. Slate's misbehavior. Mr. Slate used the legal system to re-assert his authority over his wife: he complained to a grand juryman and he successfully pleaded the defamation suit. Like Elisheba Vaulx, he used the legal system to counteract mistreatment. His wife was once again his dependent.

In addition to servants who attacked their masters and spouses who attacked each other, masters who corrected servants excessively also came to the attention of legal authorities. Virginia law protected indentured servants from immoderate correction by masters and mistresses. In practice, the legal response to brutality varied: some county officials followed up on reports of extreme violence, others did not.[38]

Overall, the York County justices acted. Between 1646 and 1720, sixteen complaints of ill-usage reached the court: seven from women and nine from men. As with violence of servants against their masters, excessive abuse was largely a homosocial phenomenon: the nine men complained against eight male masters and one against the wife as well, while the seven maids complained against four male masters, two widows, and one married couple.[39]

But the court demanded evidence and expected respectful behavior from servants before responding to their complaints. In 1661, for example, Governor Berkeley sent a note to the York justices about Mary Rawlins, a servant who had been "most unchristianly and cruelly used by her master," John Russell, and ordered him to give security for good behavior. Rawlins had made two previous complaints of cruelty to the York justices, and Berkeley chided them for failure to provide relief. As a result, York justices required a hefty forty-pound sterling bond from Russell for the "unchristianly usage and unlawfull correction."[40]

Still, the justices had Rawlins examined by a physician and gathered ten depositions to judge her complaint. While the governor accepted her word, York justices demanded extensive confirmation of her injuries. They also questioned her credibility. One justice asked another if Rawlins "disembled," and a witness deposed, with some prompting, that Rawlins's injuries were "reall and not feigned." Other witnesses reported that they had heard Rawlins complain of back and hip pain and had observed bruises and swellings on her arms and back, but were uncertain as to the injuries' cause. One was so appalled by the wounds inflicted that she told John Russell that "shee should think shee would not live if shee was his servant."

The need for an unusual amount of evidence was based in part on Rawlins' behavior. According to a fellow servant, Rawlins loudly complained after a beating that she "wished the plague rott her mistress and said shee would be revenged of hir." To another, she asserted that if her master ever beat her again she would complain and "further worke hir witt but shee would have hir freedome before whitsonday." Rawlins wanted her freedom "for shee was kept from Andrew Lather hir Lover by hir said Master but shee would have him at last come what would of it."[41] Despite visible bruises and the assessment that Rawlins was indeed hurt, her unruly words weakened her credibility; she was expected to accept her punishment without question. Her remarks suggest disorderliness and a lack of respect for her master and mistress that inspired more serious beatings.

After the governor's note, an examination from a physician and two women, and the testimony of seven other witnesses, the justices censured and controlled her master through a substantial recognizance bond. Mary Rawlins returned to his household, but the bond kept him in line. Likewise, in 1693, John Wright was made to give security to not "beat strike whipp or any other waies evilly intreate any Christian servant," nor command any overseer to do the same. If any of his servants needed correction, Wright was to take the servant to a justice before whipping him or her. Wright was also ordered to leave his servant Mary Avery alone, post a bond worth two hundred pounds sterling to guarantee his good behavior, and pay a thousand pounds of tobacco as costs.[42] In such cases, the court interposed its authority between brutal masters and their unlucky servants.

In cases of excessive abuse, the York court protected servants of both sexes. By the early eighteenth century, the justices took even more care to do so. When Anne Carter complained of abuse but did not show up in court, the justices suspected that her master had detained her and ordered her into protective custody.[43] In 1706, Henry Powers, apprentice to Use Gibson, complained of immoderate beatings and lack of instruction in a trade. The court, also citing Gibson's "evil example of life and manners," granted Powers his freedom.[44] Similarly, when Anne Duvall complained of her apprenticed daughter's "ill useage" in 1707, the court allowed Duvall to gain her daughter's release with a payment of six hundred pounds of tobacco. Masters who ignored the ill health of their servants were ordered to seek cures for their afflictions.[45]

In cases of master–servant violence, to be sure, the responsibility for finding a justice rested with the servant, and complainants whose charges were deemed frivolous or could not be proven could be whipped.[46] Once a complaint was lodged, however, York justices took charges seriously and investigated them thoroughly unless a servant had a reputation for unruliness, like Mary Rawlins. The York justices protected servants and punished masters through hefty recognizance bonds.

The court also censured unruly masters, bringing them under the justices' dominion. Officials recognized that excessive household violence itself violated higher judicial authority. If courts supported an unjustified and illicit use of masters' authority, it might undermine the legitimacy of household relations on which political authority was based. To allow masters politically unauthorized and illicit power, therefore, threatened the authority of the law.

Violent episodes in York were driven by tensions in both gender relations and dependency relations; one case from the York records suggests how these

"AS IF THERE WAS NOT MASTER OR WOMAN IN THE LAND"

twin catalysts entwined in Elisheba Vaulx's female-headed household. Here, the absence of a male head of household arguably spurred dependents to defer to Vaulx privately, but publicly to assert their authority as men. In 1680 Vaulx's servant Margaret Stapleforth gave a comprehensive account of a brawl involving Frank, Vaulx's slave, a neighbor's indentured servant, Peter Wells, and freeholders John Macartey and George Burley. According to Stapleforth, the dispute began when Vaulx sent Frank to speak with Macartey and Edward Thomas about some business. Macartey and Thomas, however, told Frank that "they were not company for Negroes" and sent him home without a discussion. Angered, Frank declared that "if John Macartey came downe the next day hee would fight with him."

The next day Macartey arrived at Vaulx's home on Queen's Creek, probably to discuss business. Apparently finding that Vaulx was not at home, he, George Burley, and four other men sat in her parlor to drink. In the meantime, Frank and Peter Wells, neighbor Humphrey Browning's bound tailor, tried to goad Macartey to a fight. Wells, sympathetic to Frank but surely with motives of his own, challenged Macartey to cudgels, but the drinkers walked away. An angry Wells returned to Frank, who asked, "what was the business?" Wells' answer frothed with his frustration; "God Damne them hee was as good a man as the best of them all."

Eventually, Macartey and the others returned to the parlor, and Frank swore "by God hee would goe to them and make one amongst them." Meanwhile, Wells pursued a mystified and increasingly exasperated Macartey, who eventually fired back a contemptuous question: "[W]hat was the matter with this Taylor?" Macartey's slur on Wells's status succeeded, as Wells replied that he was not christened Taylor. The exchanges heated up—Macartey continued to call Wells "Taylor" until Wells exclaimed, "God Damne Humphrey Browning and you," and added for good measure that "hee was as good a man as Humphrey Browning." He struck Macartey, who returned his blows. Eventually Frank joined in as well.[47]

This episode seethes with many layers of social tension. Both Wells and Frank asserted their manhood through conflicting images of gender and dependency relations. In declaring that he was as good a man as Macartey and his chums, for instance, Wells claimed the status of a freeman. He went even farther in insisting that his manhood was equal to that of Mr. Humphrey Browning, his master. Frank's threat to fight sprang from similar sources. That he felt the need to claim authority may have been related to his status in Vaulx's household: he was a slave, but he conducted men's business for his mistress. The responsibility he assumed from Vaulx, combined with his treatment at the hands of Macartey and Thomas, left him in an ambiguous position. He sought to establish his standing, despite the fact that he risked severe punishment for raising his hand against a white man.[48]

Terri L. Snyder

Not all the bystanders appreciated this social dramaturgy; as one of the witnesses hazily recalled, he had helped Macartey dispose of the rum until "one Peter servant to Mr. Humphrey Browning after the drincking of the Bottle had some words with the said John Macartey concerning Planters and Taylors." Most of the depositions recall Wells alone fighting with Macartey; only two of eight witnesses even mentioned Frank.[49]

Clearly, both Frank and Wells felt Macartey's insults and disrespect for their status keenly. Each felt dishonored: violence allowed Frank to prove that he was fit "company" for freemen and Wells to show that he was "as good a man" as the others. Together, the servant and the slave tried to shift the balance of power by punishing Macartey for his disdain; their blows were meant to compromise the legitimacy of Macartey's masculine authority. By fighting, Frank and Peter Wells claimed the status of freemen and the power associated with that rank typically denied to them.[50]

The legal resolution of the dispute was as simple as the social roots of it were complex. It was also fraught with irony: Humphrey Browning served Wells by bringing suit against Macartey for the costs of treating Wells's considerable injuries. The jury found for Macartey, however, and Browning paid both the cost of doctoring his tailor and the cost of his lawsuit.[51]

Although the brawl took place in Vaulx's household, neither she nor her dependents faced charges. Frank was not held legally accountable for striking a white man, nor was Vaulx held responsible for his actions. Her former reliance on the York justices to regulate her household dependents had demonstrated a demeanor of submission; she was not charged with Frank's outburst. Frank, moreover, had done her bidding, a task consonant with his position. It was not his fault that this entailed conducting business with free white men who rebuffed him. Both Vaulx, in requesting that he conduct business, and Frank, in attempting to carry out her order, acted in ways acceptable for their status. The resulting violence in her house by her slave did not concern the court.

Violence directed by free African-Virginians against whites, however, was rarely so privatized. On the contrary, the justices treated it as a public concern. Joseph and Mary Walters were a free black couple living in York County in 1693 when they were charged with assault; Mary was the alleged perpetrator. She was convicted of assaulting Elizabeth Sampson, a white woman, and Thomas Pinckett, a white man, given 29 lashes, jailed, and ordered to provide security for her future good behavior. The justices or the clerk also found it necessary to record a full statement. When they concluded that Walters's "wicked and dangerous life and conversation," expressed "both by her actions and expressions and threats," was likely to "prove of dangerous consequence," she either had to prove her free status or face transportation out of the colony.[52]

The York justices' immediate response to disorderliness from Walters reflected other racial issues facing them. She, as they said, "pretends herself a free

"AS IF THERE WAS NOT MASTER OR WOMAN IN THE LAND"

woman" at a time when legislators and justices were closing avenues of freedom for slaves in the colony. Moreover, she was "ungoverned," using violence to prove her status. In so doing, she claimed authority over, or at least equality with, York County's white residents. The court's message indicated that such claims to authority were not tolerated from black women in 1693.

In early Virginia, therefore, household violence had many sources. Fighting could doubtless simply be an immediate response to a variety of situations—too much beating, too little food, or too much liquor. But beyond these reactions, domestic violence carried social meanings. Women who wielded sticks against servants or physical or verbal threats against freemen risked retaliation for their perceived illicit use of authority. Elisheba Vaulx was no stranger to struggles over power that a household of servants and slaves could engender. Her route—the safest for female masters—was to appeal to the York justices to reinforce her authority and eschew correction in favor of compromise. Buttressed by the court, she and doubtless other successful female masters used a combination of negotiation and reward, not physical discipline, to manage dependents. Violence against women masters, however, had declined by 1700, as sex ratios evened and cultural notions of gentility competed with older visions of the female scold.

Throughout the period, abused spouses and servants enjoyed the court's protection if they could prove their complaints. In fact, the court grew increasingly attentive to servants' problems as distinctions between servants and slaves were legislated. Overreaching authority in the form of excessive violence from *any* free white toward other whites—free or bound, male or female—proved unacceptable in seventeenth-century Virginia and became even more so as the eighteenth century approached. By 1700, excepting the treatment of slaves, masters did not reign unfettered in their households. The court held significant authority. Legitimate complaints from white household dependents brought legal censure; justices worked to bring abusive York householders into compliance with the court's legal power to censure illegitimate authority and to enforce obedience. When masters sought to elude the law's watchful eye and use excessive or illegitimate violence, the court wielded its considerable authority to bring them into the legal realm of patriarchal obligation.

Notes

1. I thank Christine Daniels for her astute criticisms of several drafts of this essay, as well as Elizabeth Young, Roxann A. Wheeler, and the members of the Early Americanists Seminar of Southern California for their helpful comments on an earlier version of the piece. Research was made possible by the generous assistance of a Barbara Thom Postdoctoral Fellowship from the Huntington Library and a Junior Faculty Research

Terri L. Snyder

Grant from the California State University, Fullerton Foundation. Elisheba Vaulx was married to James Vaulx, a York County justice and merchant, who was dead by February 1680. York County Deeds, Orders, Wills [hereafter YCDOW] 6, folios 241, 287; "Kenner Family," *William and Mary Quarterly*, 1st ser., 14 (1905): 178; "History of York County in the Seventeenth Century," *Tyler's Quarterly Historical and Genealogical Magazine* 1 (1920): 255. Servants cases are found in YCDOW No. 6: William Baker, 88; Elizabeth (Betty) Mullins, 279, 288; William Stroud, 288; Frank, 360, 362–364.

2. YCDOW 6, 288. Smyth was probably Lawrence Smith, who practiced law in Gloucester and York counties. "Notes and Queries," *Virginia Magazine of History and Biography* 23 (1915): 87–89; and Lyon G. Tyler, "Temple Farm," *William and Mary Quarterly*, 1st ser. 2 (1893): 5–6.

3. Servants could refuse to work if their masters or their masters' wives beat them, but "the master by law is allowed, with moderation to chastise his servant or apprentice," Michael Dalton, *The Countrey Justice* (London, 1635), 85–86. See also Bradley Chapin, *Criminal Justice in Colonial America, 1606–1660* (Athens, GA, 1983), 136–137; Arthur P. Scott, *Criminal Law in Colonial Virginia* (Chicago, 1930), 293; Elizabeth Haight, "Heirs of Tradition/Creators of Change: Law and Stability on Virginia's Eastern Shore, 1633–1663," Ph.D. diss., University of Virginia, 1987, 10–13, 278–280.

4. The court clerk noted that Mullins was "willing" to serve "halfe a [year]," and Vaulx paid a fine of 500 pounds of tobacco. YCDOW, 6, 279. On the law governing servants' pregnancies, see William Waller Hening, *The Statutes at Large* (New York, 1823), 2:114–115.

5. The data for this study come from an analysis of the caseload of the York County, Virginia court, 1646–1720. A total of 52 cases addressed household violence directly or indirectly. I used established legal categories such as assault, but also included cases in which violence was revealed but was not the legal issue in the case. For discussions of gender and household violence in early modern England and Anglo-America, see Susan Dwyer Amussen, "Punishment, Discipline, and Power: The Social Meanings of Violence in Early Modern England," *Journal of British Studies* 34 (1995): 12–18; Susan Dwyer Amussen, " 'Being Stirred to Much Unquietness': Violence and Domestic Violence in Early Modern England," *Journal of Women's History* 6 (1994): 70–89; Mary Beth Norton, *Founding Mothers & Fathers: Gendered Power and the Forming of American Society* (New York, 1996), 114–137; Cornelia Hughes Dayton, *Women Before the Bar: Gender, Law and Society in Connecticut, 1639–1789* (Chapel Hill, NC, 1995), 105–108; Elizabeth Pleck, *Domestic Tyranny: The Making of American Social Policy Against Family Violence from Colonial Times to the Present* (New York, 1987), 17–33.

6. Allan Kulikoff, *Tobacco and Slaves: The Development of Southern Cultures in the Chesapeake, 1680–1800* (Chapel Hill, NC, 1986), 6, 38–44; David W. Galenson, *White Servitude in Colonial America: An Economic Analysis* (New York, 1981), 149–176; Peter Kolchin, *American Slavery, 1619–1877* (New York, 1993), 8–12; Edmund Morgan, *American Slavery, American Freedom: The Ordeal of Colonial Virginia* (New York, 1975), 218–228, 308–315; Russell Menard, "From Servants to Slaves: The Transformation of the Chesapeake Labor System," *Southern Studies* 16 (1977): 355–390; Menard, "From Servant to Freeholder: Status Mobility and Property Accumulation in Seventeenth-Century Maryland," *William and Mary Quarterly* 30 (1973): 37–64; James Horn, *Adapting to a New World: English Society in the Seventeenth-Century Chesapeake* (Chapel Hill, NC, 1995), 249–250.

"AS IF THERE WAS NOT MASTER OR WOMAN IN THE LAND"

7. For an analysis of this process, see Warren M. Billings, "The Law of Servants and Slaves in Seventeenth-Century Virginia," *Virginia Magazine of History and Biography* 99 (1991): 45–62; and Morgan, *American Slavery, American Freedom*, 311–313, 328–337.

8. Hening, *The Statutes at Large*, 2:170, 260, 270. Morgan has outlined this process as well in *American Slavery, American Freedom*, 311–313, 328–337.

9. Hening, *Statutes at Large*, 2:481, 280–281, 116–117, 195. After servant revolts, lawmakers, evidently fearing joint action between servants and slaves, enacted laws to prevent them from gathering together, penalizing indentured servants who ran away with slaves.

10. Hening, *Statutes at Large*, 2:117–118; 3:447–462. See also Christine Daniels, " 'Liberty to complaine' ": Servant Petitions in Colonial Maryland," in Christopher Tomlins and Bruce Mann, eds., *The Many Legalities of Early America* (Chapel Hill, NC, forthcoming).

11. Lois Green Carr and Russell R. Menard, "Immigration and Opportunity: The Freedman in Early Colonial Maryland," in Thad Tate and David Ammerman, eds., *The Chesapeake in the Seventeenth Century: Essays on Anglo-American Society* (Chapel Hill, NC, 1979), 220–227; Morgan, *American Slavery, American Freedom*, 295–315.

12. Lois Green Carr and Lorena S. Walsh, "The Planter's Wife: The Experience of White Women in Seventeenth-Century Maryland," *William and Mary Quarterly* 34 (1977): 542–571; Lorena S. Walsh, " 'Till Death Us Do Part' ": Marriage and Family in Seventeenth-Century Maryland," in Tate and Ammerman, *The Chesapeake in the Seventeenth Century*, 126–152; Kulikoff, *Tobacco and Slaves*, 167–174; Horn, *Adapting to a New World*, 216–222; Norton, *Founding Mothers & Fathers*, 48–51; Kathleen M. Brown, *Good Wives, Nasty Wenches and Anxious Patriarchs: Gender, Race, and Power in Colonial Virginia* (Chapel Hill, NC, 1996); Terri L. Snyder, " 'Rich Widows are the Best Commodity This Country Affords': Gender Relations and the Rehabilitation of Patriarchy in Virginia, 1660–1700," Ph.D. diss., University of Iowa, 1992.

13. About one-quarter of children in seventeenth-century Virginia had lost one or both parents by the age of five; half had done so by 10, Darrett B. and Anita H. Rutman " 'Now-Wives and sons-in-law' ": Parental Death in a Seventeenth-Century Virginia County," in Tate and Ammerman, *The Chesapeake in the Seventeenth Century*, 158–159.

14. On the whole, however, cases involving servant discipline comprised only 5 percent of 89 cases. Chapin, *Criminal Justice in Colonial America*, 137.

15. Hening, *The Statutes at Large*, 2:129; YCDOW 6, 288.

16. YCDOW 6, 88. Prior to the 1680 pardon, servants who joined Bacon were punished as runaways, doubling the time of their absence. The 1680 act required that they serve only the time of their absence. See Hening, *The Statutes at Large*, 2:395, 462.

17. YCDOW 4, 52.

18. YCDOW 6, 77, 82.

19. YCDOW 6, 455.

20. In 1662, Thomas Morley's servant, John Shelton, "tooke the sticke out of his master's hand (correcting him)" and "strooke his master's son," see YCDOW 3, 176.

21. See for example YCDOW 16, 80; YCDOW 14, 446.

22. Joy Wiltenberg, *Disorderly Women and Female Power in the Street Literature of Early Modern England and Germany* (Chapel Hill, NC, 1992), 106–109; Laura Gowing, *Domestic Dangers: Women, Words, and Sex in Early Modern London* (Oxford, 1996), esp.

111–128; Frances E. Dolan, *Dangerous Familiars: Representations of Domestic Crime in England, 1550–1700* (Ithaca, NY, 1994); Elizabeth Foyster, "A Laughing Matter? Marital Discord and Gender Control in Seventeenth-Century England," *Rural History* 4 (1993): 5–21.

23. Thomas Hellier, "The Vain Prodigal Life, and Tragical Penitent Death of Thomas Hellier," (London, 1680). T. H. Breen, James H. Lewis, and Keith Schlesinger have authenticated the biographical aspects of Hellier's narrative, see "Motive for Murder: A Servant's Life in Virginia, 1678," *William and Mary Quarterly* 40 (1983): 106–110, 111–118.

24. Hellier, "The Vain Prodigal Life," 11.

25. Hellier, "The Vain Prodigal Life," 25, 32.

26. As married women (femes coverts) neither Anne Batten nor Mrs. Hyde could present suits in their own names. On the act of governing unruly servants, see Hening, *The Statutes at Large*, 2:118.

27. YCDOW 8, 467 (order), 474, 478 (depositions). The writ for the case, and therefore Holloway's specific complaint, does not survive. Depositions focus on the two violent episodes, so it is safe to assume that assault was at issue.

28. YCDOW 8, 104 (order), 113–114 (depositions).

29. Six of the seven complaints focused on spousal abuse. YCDOW 2, 168–169; YCDOW 3, 38; YCDOW 5, 117; *Savory v. Savory*, YCDOW 9, 91; YCDOW 10, 365, 371; YCDOW 14, 166. The seventh was presented as a a defamation case, see *Hill v. Slate*, below. For marital relations and separate maintenance in colonial Virginia, see Brown, *Good Wives, Nasty Wenches, and Anxious Patriarchs*, 334–342.

30. This differs from the findings of Norton; see *Founding Mothers & Fathers*, 80–83. Also Amussen, " 'Being Stirred to Much Unquietness,' " 82–83; Pleck, *Domestic Tyranny*, 21–23, 29–33.

31. Walsh, "Marriage and Family," 137–138; Norton, *Founding Mothers & Fathers*, 89–90. For New England, see Dayton, *Women Before the Bar*, 105–156.

32. *Savory v. Savory*, YCDOW 9, 91.

33. YCDOW 10, 370–371; Brown, *Good Wives, Nasty Wenches, and Anxious Patriarchs*, 336.

34. YCDOW 3, 38.

35. YCDOW 2, 168–169.

36. YCDOW 9, 101.

37. YCDOW 9, 99, (suit and trial results), 100–101 (depositions).

38. Christine Daniels finds clear evidence that Maryland's colonial courts attended to servant complaints in " 'Liberty to complaine.' " James Horn finds examples of mortal violence in Lower Norfolk and Lancaster Counties, *Adapting to a New World*, 270. Mary Beth Norton reports that witnesses to the abuse of Chesapeake servants rarely attempted to intercede, which often meant that abuse was mortal, *Founding Mothers & Fathers*, 123–125. For all North American colonies prior to 1660, Chapin finds that complaints of servant abuse comprised only 15 percent of all criminal cases involving servants, *Criminal Justice in Colonial America*, 137. See also Douglas Greenberg, "Crime, Law Enforcement, and Social Control in Colonial America," *American Journal of Legal History* 26 (1982): 293–325; Kathryn Preyer, "Penal Measures in the American Colonies: An Overview," *American Journal of Legal History* 26 (1982): 326–353.

"AS IF THERE WAS NOT MASTER OR WOMAN IN THE LAND"

39. Daniels, "'Liberty to complaine,'" finds that in Maryland, mistresses were more likely to assault their maids than their men, and servant women more likely to be injured by masters or mistresses, while male servants were generally subject only to the violence of their masters.

40. The bond was a written obligation of a sum that Russell would forfeit if he further abused Rawlins. YCDOW, 3, 121 (order), 123–124 (depositions). For statutes protecting servants, Hening, *The Statutes at Large*, 1:440.

41. YCDOW 3, 123–124.

42. YCDOW 6, 493–494.

43. YCDOW 14, 187.

44. YCDOW 12, 408.

45. YCDOW 13, 72.

46. For example, in 1658 Abraham Harman and Samuel Harrison complained against their master, Thomas Beale, but could not provide evidence; they were sentenced to twenty lashes, although Beale remitted the punishment. YCDOW 3, 43.

47. YCDOW 6, 362–364.

48. By law his punishment would be 30 lashes. See Hening, *The Statutes at Large*, 2:481.

49. YCDOW 6, 362–364.

50. Amussen, "Punishment, Discipline, and Power," 2–3.

51. YCDOW 6, 360.

52. YCDOW 9, 270–272.

thirteen

THEATER OF TERROR

Domestic Violence in Thomas Thistlewood's Jamaica, 1750–1786

Trevor Burnard

The true hero, the real subject . . . is might. The might that is wielded by men rules over them and before it man's flesh cringes. The human soul never ceases to be transformed by its encounter with force—is swept on, blinded by that which it believes itself able to handle, bowed beneath the power of that which it suffers.[1]

One and a half months after arriving in Jamaica, John Thistlewood, a young Englishman residing with his uncle, Thomas, an overseer on a Westmoreland sugar plantation, had a nasty shock. On April 15, 1764, John "Hard a great Noise" and went to investigate "what the matter was." He found "sum Negroes" who "had been Robbin ours of fish." They fled and John chased; but when he caught up with them, one refused to respect the authority of a new white man and "drew a long Clasp Nife and swore that he would stab me." John "was a little fri[gh]tted and thought myself in a great deal of danger," as he was alone and faced nearly thirty hostile slaves. John saved himself by declaring that "if any of them ofered to stir I would take out my Pistols and blow his Braines out." The bluff worked well enough that "the Fellow that had the Nife in his hand Run immediately into the Bush." Having established that he was master of the situation, John proceeded to demonstrate it in the usual white Jamaican fashion, taking six slaves and giving each "a good whipin."[2]

John Thistlewood's test mirrored a more desperate struggle of twelve years earlier, when his uncle was new to the island. Thomas Thistlewood had encountered Congo Sam, a runaway slave, in a cane field. Sam tried to hack Thistlewood with a machete while a number of slaves watched. Thistlewood wrestled with Sam for over twenty minutes. He managed to subdue the runaway but no bystander helped him; in fact, two female slaves pointedly ignored the confrontation after Congo Sam spoke to them "in his language." Thistlewood barely escaped with his life from what turned out to be Sam's premeditated attempt, supported by "many of the negroes," to murder him. Thistlewood responded with savage brutality. He gave the two women a hundred lashes each and took Sam to the local magistrates in irons, hoping he would be severely punished or mutilated.[3]

Dominant white men in eighteenth-century Jamaica routinely terrorized their bondspeople. They comprised a beleaguered if powerful minority among an oppressed and hostile African majority and were renowned for their violence. As Charles Leslie noted in 1740, "No Country exceeds them in a barbarous Treatment of Slaves, or in the cruel Methods they put them to death." Leslie justified such "Severities" by arguing "how impossible it were to live admidst such Numbers of Slaves, without observing their Conduct with the greatest Niceness, and punishing their Faults with the utmost Severity."[4] Bryan Edwards, a late eighteenth-century historian, commented that fear was the key to white dominance in such a slave system. "Fear," he asserted, "was the leading principle upon which the government was supported." White masters compelled fear through violence, "that absolute coerci[on]" that "supersedes all questions of right."[5]

Violence and fear entwined most forcefully in the personal relations of the household, where the dynamics of power were played out in one of the most brutal slave regimes in history. This essay examines the uses of fear within domestic arenas of a slave society. Extensive physical and sexual violence were both public in the private theater of large Jamaican households and were an essential support of slavery and patriarchy. White-on-black violence, moreover, was replicated in gendered white violence and black-on-black violence as a means of regulating household members and resolving disputes.

The sources for this investigation are the lengthy journals of Thomas Thistlewood, an Englishman who moved to western Jamaica in 1750 and remained there until his death in 1786. He worked as an overseer on a sugar estate before establishing his own plantation in 1767. At his death, Thistlewood was a man of consequence, a justice of the peace and a respected member of the community. His life, however, would be little noted if he had not left an extraordinary diary—a day-to-day account of his activities in Jamaica, amounting to perhaps 500,000 words. It paints a vivid picture of the life of a white of middling status who lived among blacks on the frontier and demonstrates the operation of violence on an eighteenth-century Anglo-American slave plantation in unusual detail.

The diary, nevertheless, is problematic. It must be mediated by its purpose and, most importantly, by Thistlewood's strategies of inclusion and exclusion. Although he never explained why he kept a journal, the way in which entries were recorded reveals something about his motives. He wrote flat, serviceable prose and updated it with machinelike consistency nearly every day until his final illness. It was part of Thistlewood's systematic record-keeping that also included a daily weather journal, commonplace books, and occasional tabulations of his large library.[6] Thistlewood was an inveterate list-maker and collector of facts; his diary was part of his habit of collecting. He wanted to improve his mind, if not his conduct, by recording and ordering his life and intellectual activities. His diary was thus part account book, part *aide-mémoire* and part recapitulation of a life as lived.

The diary's great strength and liability is its extreme lack of self-consciousness—it is a presentation but not an examination of self. Thistlewood may have written it to exert control over himself and his environment but he did not associate this attempted self-control with any moral self-accounting. He made little attempt to justify his behavior and seldom engaged in reflection. This absence of self-scrutiny is most evident in his records of his many sexual encounters. Thistlewood noted where and with whom he had sex in an easily translated form of pig Latin. His matter-of-fact listings did not include explanations of how sex came about or what his partners thought about the couplings. His diary, in short, is one unmediated observation after another. He wrote for himself and was unconcerned with moral improvement or others' perceptions of his actions. Thistlewood lists evidence, facts, and events and almost never describes his emotions. His rare reflective moments, moreover, never revolve around violence or interactions with slaves, all of which he evidently considered natural and unworthy of extended commentary.

Thistlewood did not have an inherently brutal or sociopathic personality, as we will examine later. But his diary details an enormous amount of violence visited on his slaves. That a nonviolent man could be so vicious is stark testimony to the centrality of violence as a way of maintaining control over slaves in Jamaica. Thistlewood would have found nineteenth-century West Indian slaveholders' attempts to downplay slavery's violence puzzling and foolhardy.[7] He knew he was surrounded by huge numbers of slaves who would kill him given the opportunity; he dominated them, in great part, through physical violence.

Thistlewood punished slaves regularly and forcefully. He usually flogged or incarcerated them, but could be creatively sadistic. On one occasion, he forced one slave to defecate in another's mouth, then wired his mouth shut.[8] In Thistlewood's theater of violence, slaves were punished for transgressions

THEATER OF TERROR

solely at his discretion; he ensured that they were unable to escape the constant threat of torture and pain.

Thistlewood accepted that violence was part of the natural order. He never questioned, even on arrival, that whites needed to punish blacks with the utmost brutality. Ten days after arriving in Westmoreland, he noted without comment that his first mentor, William Dorrill, a wealthy planter and leading citizen of the parish, had slave runaways "whipt severely, and rubb'd with pepper, salt, and lime juice." At his first post, Vineyard Pen, Thistlewood established command by whipping the mulatto driver, Dick: "[F]for his many Crimes and Negligences [Dick] was bound to an Orange Tree in ye Garden and Whipt to some Purpose (given near 300 lashes)." Dick received this mind-numbingly severe sentence less for his crimes and negligences than for his challege to Thistlewood's authority. When Thistlewood challenged his slaves, no provocation was required. His public whipping of Dick demonstrated that he was not a man to be trifled with and that he was prepared to control his slaves by force; he dared them to test his authority and suffer the consequences.[9] He was a tough adversary: the slaves at Egypt, whom he managed for over 15 years, called him "abbaumi appea" or "no for play."[10]

The Jamaican frontier required toughness. Westmoreland Parish was rough and ready in Thomas Thistlewood's time, when much of it was barely settled. Its inland portions harbored groups of maroons—rebel slaves, most of them African, who waged an unrelenting war against white control in the early eighteenth century. A treaty between maroons and colonists brought an uneasy peace in 1738, but whites remained wary. Westmoreland, moreover, was prime sugar territory, and the number of enslaved Africans within its boundaries increased quickly. The parish remained almost entirely black during Thistlewood's residence; whites accounted for 6 percent of its population in 1730 and less than 8 percent in 1788. Its slaves were disproportionately male and African, and from many ethnic groups, which limited family and kinship ties. The same gender imbalance prevailed among whites, the great majority of whom were English immigrants.[11]

White men ostensibly controlled the parish through institutional mechanisms of power. The law was in their hands and they did not hesitate to use it to cow recalcitrant slaves or to assert their own rights. But law was not the principal means of slave regulation in Westmoreland—a remarkably underinstitutionalized frontier society even by the standards of plantation America.[12] White men used the law only *after* they asserted domination through physical force. Mastery on a frontier where Europeans were surrounded by hostile and brutalized Africans was, through necessity, supported by unvarnished brutality.

Studies of New World slavery do not ignore its savagery, and masters throughout British America were capable of horrific brutality toward bondspeople.[13] North American masters, however, lived in communities that continually grew more genteel. While slavery remained at heart an institution predicated on violence and inhumanity, the raw savagery evident in the relations of men on the frontier lessened—or was hidden more successfully—over time. By the early nineteenth century, the dominion of white men over slaves, women, and children was checked and its most poisonous effects mitigated: women and slaves won limited advances in individual rights; the state assumed some responsibility for supervising household relations; and, most importantly, the growing importance of stewardship—paternalism—as a governing value for household heads softened patriarchs' overt brutality toward dependents.[14] In North America, patriarchalism gradually metamorphosed into paternalism. Patriarchal masters stressed obedience to authority and resorted to violence when that authority was questioned, but seldom deluded themselves that slaves were content. Paternal masters treated slaves better materially but expected them, in turn, to be grateful for this benevolence. Under paternalism, masters' violence was less openly countenanced and more often condemned as counterproductive and retrogressive.[15] But this shift from patriarchy to paternalism had not occurred in Thistlewood's Jamaica. Patriarchal assumptions remained dominant among eighteenth-century Jamaican slave owners. Patriarchy in Jamaica was "the manifestation and institutionalization" of raw male dominance; masters paid scant regard to mutual obligations or reciprocal rights between household heads and dependents.[16] In fact, the delusions of antebellum Southern paternalists could prove dangerous on Jamaica's frontier.

Although white Jamaicans shared the common British-American impulse for material and cultural improvement, life was generally crude. Most white men lived recklessly, drank heavily, spent extravagantly, and exploded in violent rages. Thomas Thistlewood did not fit that pattern. He was abstemious, a master of his emotions, an avid reader with conventional Enlightenment opinions, and a dedicated amateur scientist; he achieved a level of gentility and cultural attainment not often associated with eighteenth-century Jamaica. Many of his acquaintances, however, were vulgar, coarse, and cruel enough to prove the rule.

In 1752, for example, Thistlewood's friend, the elderly creole planter Tom Williams, came to visit. Thistlewood noted that at home, Williams wore "nothing but a shirt, and fans himself with the forelap before his daughter." When a female domestic cleaned his hall unnecessarily "he shit in it and told her there was something for her to clean," and once "killed a Negro girl of his own that had got looseness, stopping her A—— with a cornstick." White Jamaican men were capable of incredible savagery. In 1765, Thistlewood recorded a conversation he had had with another acquaintance, Harry Weech. Weech had told him that "he cut off the Lips, upper lip almost Close to her Nose, off his Mulatto Sweetheart, in Jealousy, because he said a Negroe should never kiss those lips he had. She having brought a child rather too dark. He kept besides her, her sister and a white woman at the same time."[17] That the

THEATER OF TERROR

perpetrator of such an act could relate it casually to friends speaks volumes about the character of Jamaican slavery.

Thistlewood was not a violent man by eighteenth-century Jamaican standards. He accepted the right of patriarchs to exercise authority as they saw fit, and, on occasion, he punished slaves viciously, brooking no intervention. But he employed violence only when mastering slaves. He was never involved in violence in Britain and exhibited few violent tendencies in his most intimate relationship, his thirty-four-year sexual involvement with the African slave Phibbah.[18] Everything in his diary suggests that his violence was strictly controlled. Thistlewood inflicted violence only on slaves, only in regulated form, and only on people whom he thought deserved punishment. This behavior is not surprising in a man of regular habits determined to exercise great self-control. His use of violence against slaves was a deliberate, rational plan, designed to further his goals of slave management.

He modelled his management strategy on the instructions of the enormously wealthy planter Richard Beckford to his attorneys, which Thistlewood copied out in full and recommended to fellow planters. Beckford advised his overseers, first, to make a clear distinction between white servants, who were "part of his Family," and slaves, whose condition was unalterable. Overseers were to look after slaves' health and allow them to provide for themselves through generous allocations of provision grounds. They were to hear slave complaints "and give them redress when they are oppressed." Their race and status were not "a reason for not treating them as Rational Beings." When they were wronged, they could be vengeful, which often produced "more fatal consequences than desertion." Beckford concluded that "the end of Punishment is ye Example, and that when ye Punishment is unjustly inflicted, it Ceases to have ye Effect intended and inspires a general Rancour and hatred of ye Person who inflicts it."[19] Just punishment, of course, could be ruthless.

Thistlewood tried to adhere to this strategy. He indicated the reasons behind each punishment in his diary, as if to remind himself why he had done what he had. He preferred regulated punishments and disliked losing control over his emotions. When Thistlewood retaliated against a slave who came at him with a stick, he regretted that he had been "forced to knock him down."[20] He believed punishment should be considered, regular, rational, and dispassionate. He disdained fellow whites who punished slaves "like madmen" under the influence of liquor, lust, or fear. As Thistlewood saw it, whites needed to demonstrate firm control—he noted how an overseer evoked community displeasure through overlenient treatment of his slaves[21]—but also needed to exercise self-mastery.

Not many Jamaican whites followed Thistlewood's advice. In practice, white men had complete dominion over slaves and almost complete power over women and children. In 1761, for example, Thistlewood related that a notoriously cruel overseer, Jack Wright, "beat the hothouse girl and that next day she died," but "the Jury brought it in a Natural death" and Wright continued his depredations. Wright killed another woman in 1777; in May 1778, Thistlewood wrote that he heard "Jack Wright has killed a mulatto woman, and is fated for it: this murder the 4th murder, if not more, that he has committed." Only when Wright had proved himself a psychopath did authorities act against him. Even freedom was not sufficient for legal redress: in 1761 one of Thistlewood's friends, John Cunningham, "Shott a Free Negro, Free Dick of Corowina" with complete immunity.[22] White male dominance was close to absolute and was based on white men's ability to dominate blacks physically. As J. B. Moreton commented, "the most insignificant Connaught savage bumpkin, or silly Highland gawky" learned on arrival "to flog without mercy" to "shew [their] authority." They became slave owners "and cowskin heroes"; "proud, insolent, and haughty."[23]

White men, including Thistlewood, also assumed that one privilege of living in a slave society was to be able to molest black women as they pleased. Thistlewood constantly assaulted his female slaves.[24] While some of his sexual connections were consensual—a few women, notably Phibbah, could refuse his advances—others were undoubtedly coercive. Coercion is difficult to establish because Thistlewood—our only source—never suggests that he used threats or force to induce women to have sex, but he almost certainly did. Wandering in the cane fields, for example, he "Found Masie, an Ebo Negroe, Cutting Canes: abt 11 am Cum Illa [had sex] in Calabash Cane piece."[25] It was doubtless clear to Masie what was expected of her and what might happen if she did not comply.

For the most part, Thistlewood thought of such encounters as straightforward transactions, rather than as ways to degrade slaves. He gave many of his sexual partners money after copulation. But sometimes he forced women to have sex with him to prove his dominance over slaves.[26] Early in their relationship, for example, Phibbah discovered an escapade Thistlewood had with the slave Eve almost as soon as the coupling took place. She scolded him and he responded by having sex with another woman, Beck, "in the hothouse" while "Many Negroes" watched. Thistlewood showed Phibbah that his authority on the plantation included the right to have sex when and with whom he wanted.[27] The public nature of Thistlewood's sexual opportunism also sent a message to male slaves. Whatever rights they might possess in regard to slave women were unimportant compared to Thistlewood's—he was indeed cock of the walk.[28] The sexual power of white men in Jamaica was as public as their violence. By exercising prerogatives of coerced sexual access to all slave women, white Jamaican men demonstrated that their patriarchy was unbridled power, not an ideology of metaphoric fatherhood.

Other men's sexual activities make Thistlewood's appear tame. Many white men in Jamaica associated sex with drinking and violence. John Cope, Thistlewood's wealthy employer, was drunk and "in his Tantrums" when he "Forced Egypt Susannah in the Cookroom" and acted "like a Madman most part of the evening." Thistlewood was occasionally obliged to protect women slaves from drunken white men who wandered onto the estate. Resisting white sexual advances was impossible for most black women; when Egypt Susannah and Mazerine refused to sleep with Cope and his friend, they were whipped for their recalcitrance.[29] On another occasion, when Cope "Come home in Liquor," he "Wanted Silvia very much and Was like a Madman almost." Unlike planters in the antebellum American South who had sex with slaves clandestinely and despite moral disapproval, Jamaican planters, like Cope, did so openly and without retribution.[30] Five months previously, Cope had helped instigate a gang rape on Eve. Six white men got "heartily drunk" and four "hawl'd Eve Separately into the Water Room and were Concern'd with her," one man twice. Thistlewood's diary entry was laconic but he obviously found it unjustifiable. When Eve ran away soon after the rape, he did not punish her, presumably interpreting her flight as a legitimate response to excessive abuse.[31]

Because in Jamaica patriarchy equalled male sexual privilege, white men were also able to abuse white women and other dependents with relative impunity. Although Cope's wife, Molly, was the architect of his fortune, he made no attempt to hide his philandering from her, and when she complained, he beat her, smashed her belongings, and turned her out of the house. He also "kicks Mrs C. out of bed and openly takes girls of 8 or 9 years old."[32] On another occasion, he "collared and struck [his adult son] Jack," who was not "reconciled with his father" for over three months.[33] Cope remained a leading citizen of Westmoreland despite his behavior, although Thistlewood was never one of his admirers.

Thistlewood, moreover, did not believe that the violence necessary to restrain slaves should be applied against family members or fellow whites. In this respect, he was quite unlike Cope. White men found it difficult not to be tyrants in all their relationships but Thistlewood was able to avoid domestic tyranny by carefully limiting his violence mostly to slaves. He needed to be greatly provoked before using violence against people who were not enslaved, but it did happen. His son, for example, mulatto John, caused him many heartaches. John lied, stole, and consorted with a runaway female slave. When he was fifteen, Thistlewood apprenticed him to a carpenter, but John's work was unsatisfactory. His employer told Thistlewood that John had "never been at Work since the Races" and that he went "away without leave." He misused other tradesmens' tools, got drunk, and was habitually late and disobedient. Thistlewood's exasperation grew. Finally, after a particularly flagrant transgression, he placed John in the bilboes—stocks—overnight, whipped him, and sent him back to his master with his hands tied behind his back.[34] Although Thistlewood disciplined John harshly, he did so only after many serious transgressions.

Nor was Thistlewood violent toward fellow whites despite considerable provocation. In 1757, his white subordinate Thomas Fewkes became "very abusive" and "Swore he would Set Fire to the Plantation, great House and that he would see my heart's blood in the Morning." Thistlewood did nothing. The next morning, however, Fewkes continued his verbal onslaught and Thistlewood, fearing for his safety, put him "in the Bilboes his insolence was so great." He was, however, careful not to use either considerable force or arbitrary authority over a white man. He went to some effort to obtain a warrant against Fewkes so that he could "discharge" him legitimately. When, in 1762, four drunken soldiers seized one of his slaves and threatened to use their guns if he tried to recover her, Thistlewood called a white witness, warned the soldiers to "take Care What they did lest they Should have Occasion to repent," and complained the next day to their commanding officer.[35] Thistlewood's use of violence, therefore, was reasoned and measured by others' race and status. He did not punish whites; he did not readily discipline his son; he whipped slaves without hesitation. Keeping slaves uneasy was an important means whereby he could control them.

But he restrained the excesses of other white men against his slaves to preserve his own mastery. He would have agreed with Edmund Burke that the unrestrained exercise of terror could diminish respect for authority; such excess led to laws "losing their terror in the minds of the wicked and their reverence in the minds of the virtuous."[36] When a white servant raped a slave woman while drunk, Thistlewood reprimanded him, noting that "the Field Negroes Wanted him away which I perceived."[37] His reprimand was based partly on contempt for the man's lack of self-control and partly on his concern that white authority would be weakened if attacks on slaves were obviously unjustified. Thus, when John Groves began to flog slaves "without much occasion," Thistlewood called him "a Madman" and reprimanded him. A white man's authority was absolute but had to be tempered by justice if slave management were to succeed.[38]

Thistlewood's slaves lived in a fluid, frightening world—beaten, brutalized, and worn down by a harsh and debilitating work regime. Pain and uncertainty accentuated their cultural dislocation and physical discomfort, exacerbated by extraordinarily high mortality rates that resulted in a constant instability in slave communities.[39] The black population of Jamaica suffered a net natural decrease until well into the nineteenth century; planters continually imported new slaves, many of whom died. Those who survived were frequently moved to other plantations or were transported off the island.[40] If their owners died or were heavily indebted, they were sold. As both death and indebtedness were common in Jamaica, many slaves were forcibly removed from their homes. Thistlewood is not the best guide to this phenomenon, as he was long-lived, remarkably settled, and solvent, but dislocations occurred frequently even in his

THEATER OF TERROR

household. In thirty years, he bought 28 slaves, 16 of whom he still possessed when he died. Seven predeceased him, three were sold, and two transported.

In Jamaican slave quarters, therefore, instability predominated. Thistlewood's slaves were involved in a dizzying array of household arrangements, as partners moved in and out of relationships. As a result, family structures were impermanent and immensely varied.[41] Masters' attacks on the integrity of slave family relationships and their continual assaults on slave women further accentuated tensions.[42]

Most male slaves, in particular, found the contours of family life in Jamaica especially difficult. Sex ratios were so skewed toward males that many men never obtained partners. Competition for women was keen and violence resulted frequently, particularly when men found others cuckolding them. Lincoln, for example, an Ebo slave purchased by Thistlewood in 1756, was a man of many attachments; he kept two women and was involved with several others throughout his time in Jamaica.[43] In 1778, Lincoln visited a slave couple, Monday and Maria, at 3 A.M., ostensibly to give Maria some sugar cane. But when he "began to inquire for his countryman" (Maria), Monday refused to let him speak with her. Lincoln persisted. He went "into her room to stay with her." Monday, however, "laid hold of him first" and beat him.[44]

In Jamaica, African women had more control over domestic arrangements than they had had in Africa, a reality that often troubled their men. In many West African cultures, women were expected to live in families and have children who would perpetuate the family. They were "valued for child-producing properties, for their economic contribution to the household, and for the affinal relationship they represent to husband and his kin."[45] Enslaved women, however, recognizing their scarcity value and/or the inability of enslaved men to become the controlling patriarch, insisted on playing the field and refused to countenance male philandering. Maria, for example, whom Lincoln desired, was a sexually independent woman. After several years with Solon, she had an affair with a slave from a nearby estate in 1773. When it foundered, she lived with two men from other estates in quick succession before setting up housekeeping with Monday. By 1787 she lived on her own.[46] Nor was Maria unusual. In 1774 Thistlewood noted "Understand Jimmy wants to throw away Abba, he having long kept Phoebe Slyly, Phoebe has also thrown away Neptune (or wants much to do it) upon Jimmy's account."[47] Aurelia—Thistlewood's principal sexual partner on Kendal estate—did not confine her attentions to her master: Thistlewood was told that "six different men lay with Aurelia last night" by her own volition. Her deviations from models of traditional African female behavior, however, did not lessen her status on the plantation.[48]

Africanists have argued that most West African relationships are marked by an absence of active conflict between partners.[49] Domestic discord between slaves in Thistlewood's household was pronounced, possibly because African

Trevor Burnard

family practices could not be replicated perfectly in slavery. In one tragic episode which arose from a complex exchange of partners, "Moll beat Lydde out of jealousy," then ran to the river and drowned herself. In 1782, Lincoln "Catch'd Shamboy in bed with his wife Sukey" which led to "a great out Cry at the Negro House."

Thistlewood often intervened in these disputes, less to restore harmony between slave couples than to enforce discipline and maintain work routines. In 1773, he "Flogged Maria for Cuckolding Solon at the Retrieve and Stirring up Quarrels." When Jimmy and Phoebe made a secret match, Thistlewood flogged them both for "criminal conversation." He reprimanded one slave "for wanting to take Moll Billy's wife" then whipped Billy and Moll "for fighting" over the incident.[50] When three leading slaves complained to him that Cuffee was "exceeding impudent, quarrelsome, and threatens dick and dawneys lives or to kill himself etc is continually fighting etc," Thistlewood acted immediately, flogging Cuffee "in ye yard before them."[51] His calculated intervention into slaves' domestic affairs and personal lives illustrates his use of violence as a management tool. His forceful adjudication of slave disputes bolstered his authority in a world where custom was attenuated, the law was no avail, and a master's power was close to absolute.

Because Thistlewood calculated his violence even as he used it, because he daily demonstrated his power and his toughness, and because he made his punishments part of a rational scheme rather than random acts of uncontrolled rage, violence worked for him. His slaves resented him and were prepared if the occasion was right to attack him, but they generally acceded to his control.[52]

Thistlewood's measured use of terror and his indifference to slaves' pain suggest an inability to identify with his slaves. He was not a racist as Jamaican historian Edward Long and Thomas Jefferson were racists. He made virtually no reference in his diary or commonplace books to blacks as biologically different or inferior in capacity and ability to whites. He recognized slaves as human, attributing their deficiencies to human frailty rather than imbecility. Yet he never questioned the right of white dominance. Although he read Enlightenment texts, he never internalized the Enlightenment insight that a recognition of humanity might lead to equality. He worked from ancient assumptions that humanity included a hierarchy of degrees between the "noble" and the "base." Within that framework, he recognized slaves' humanity and justified white power based on violence.[53] He was indifferent to the pain he inflicted and recognized violence against slaves only as a weapon in his never-ceasing battle against the threat of rebellion.[54] His physical power greatly facilitated plantation management, but was ultimately deeply ironic. His deliberate savagery destabilized already fragile slave communities. Coupled with the disintegration of African familial ties, Thistlewood's violence itself made his slaves' world inherently volatile and inclined slaves to respond violently. But

247

since he was the only person whose power allowed him to employ violence, he was able to create a self-perpetuating justification for his actions.

Thistlewood also used violence to mediate slaves' disputes when relationships in slave households caused too much friction, especially in cases of property disputes. Jamaican slaves often owned livestock, grew and sold vegetables, or bought and sold property for cash. But no laws and few customs protected slaves' rights to their property. In their efforts to gain economic autonomy through property ownership, slaves trampled on the rights of other slaves seeking autonomy, often enough to cause major disruptions.[55] Thistlewood's ability to punish offenders, therefore, was important for slaves who wished to protect themselves and their property.

Theft of slaves' property was an obvious source of tension. The difficulty of dealing with a persistent thief can be seen in the case of Sally, a Congo slave who refused to accept either Thistlewood's authority or that of senior slaves. She was a habitual thief, who stole "everything left in the cookroom." Thistlewood flogged her constantly, but Phibbah, who was in charge of the cookroom, was more vicious. Exasperated by Sally's thefts, she left her "with her hands tied behind her naked for the mosquitoes to bite her." Sally got her revenge a week later by stealing "a new handkerchief driver Johnie gave her to bring to Phibbah." She continued her depredations until an exasperated Thistlewood sold her off the island in 1784.[56] Her fellow slaves shunned Sally but could do little about her antisocial behavior and were forced to wait until Thistlewood took action against her.

Violence was not problematic for Thistlewood because he saw that unrelenting control was necessary in a Hobbesian slave regime and because he dissociated himself from the violence he committed and the pain he caused. But his violence is problematic for scholars because it does not fit our understanding of the intellectual discourse of violence during the second half of the eighteenth century. Order and civilization became increasingly linked in bourgeois Western thought in the late eighteenth and early nineteenth centuries. The modern civilized personality lay in the slow elaboration of rules about conduct that emphasized emotional self-restraint.[57] As this new intellectual order developed, people who patterned their behavior on rules of conduct that emphasized self-restraint gradually came to eschew the use of personal violence. Instead, they envisioned punishment in new ways. It became less personal and more bureaucratic, less directed by strong-willed individuals and more likely to be exercised by a powerful state.

Harsh, arbitrary corporal punishment exercised by hot-blooded and emotionally unrestrained masters on the bodies of suffering slaves did not fit this new conception of discipline.[58] The deepening value attached to sympathy in late eighteenth-century culture, moreover, encouraged an emotional response to personal suffering.[59] Slaves received increasing sympathy, especially as humanitarian abolitionists highlighted slavery's cruelties and illuminated their deviations from bourgeois conceptions of civility and respectability. Slavery became emblematic of antimodernity, and slaves, exemplary victims of barbarity.[60]

Thistlewood fitted imperfectly into this developing intellectual framework. On one hand, he was consciously modern and "improving." His distaste for freely expressed passion, his obsessive need for order and lists, his search for self-improvement through self-control, and his moderation in eating and drinking all fit into an eighteenth-century "civilizing process." On the other hand, he was no "man of feeling." He subscribed to older notions about the role of violence in society and about the extent to which a modern man should adopt them. If he were aware of David Hume's and Adam Smith's arguments that sympathy and compassion were intrinsic to man's nature and that imaginative projection was the means through which compassion was expressed, he did not act on these insights.[61] He was a patriarch, not a paternalist—a believer in "the great chain of being" who did not need to develop an elaborate theory of scientific racism to justify treating Africans as inferiors. He possessed none of the beliefs necessary to develop a humanitarian sensibility; he did not believe it was "right" to alleviate human suffering, nor did he feel causally involved in creating it.[62] At no point in his long residence in Jamaica nor in his voluminous writings did Thistlewood consider the morality of slavery. Slavery was natural and Africans were natural slaves, less because of their race than because they fell outside the social contract that secured individual rights. Africans were outsiders; he need not consider their rights, especially in a world where white control was always tenuous.[63] Enlightenment writers were ambivalent about treating non-Europeans as slaves without rights, but ambivalence was a luxury that whites on the frontier of western Jamaica could not afford.[64]

Thistlewood died in 1786, before most abolitionist attacks began. The next generation of Jamaican slaveholders, however, was forced to think much more systematically about the violence that engulfed their society and governed relations between masters and slaves. As bourgeois Europeans came to believe in sympathetic responses to suffering, slaveholders were forced to defend their indifference to slaves' pain.

In 1831 to 1832, Jamaican slaves arose in a spectacularly destructive revolt, put down with customary brutality. The power of the whip and the discipline of individual, personalized terror had proved insufficient in a world dominated by humanitarian discourse. Abolitionists, moreover, had final proof of the immorality of slavery. While violence worked in the short term, and worked very well for Thistlewood, it eventually spelled the end of Jamaican slavery.

THEATER OF TERROR

Notes

1. Simone Weil, "The *Iliad*, Poem of Might" in George A. Panichas, *The Simone Weil Reader* (New York, 1977), 153.
2. Diary of John Thistlewood, Monson 31/38, Lincolnshire Archives, Lincoln, England. I thank Lord Monson for permission to cite from the Thistlewood diaries.
3. Diary of Thomas Thistlewood, 12/27/1752, Monson 31/3. All future references to Thistlewood's diary will be by date only.
4. Charles Leslie, *A New and Exact Account of Jamaica* (Edinburgh, n.d., probably 1740), 41.
5. Bryan Edwards, *The History, Civil and Commercial of the British Colonies in the West Indies* (Dublin, 1793), 1:13.
6. The Thistlewood section of the Monson deposit includes 90 books, most of them exercise books, covered with brown paper and neatly labeled.
7. See *Marly; or, a Planter's Life in Jamaica* (Glasgow, 1828). The anonymous author of this novel attempts to deny the reality of whipping while admitting it was necessary to discipline slaves.
8. 5/26/1756; 6/28/1756; 8/27/1756; 10/5/1756.
9. 5/15/1750; 7/16/1750.
10. 2/5/1768.
11. Michael Craton, *Testing the Chains: Resistance to Slavery in the British West Indies* (Ithaca and London, 1982), 61–96. In 1730, 443 whites dwelt in the parish; by 1788 this number had increased to 1495. Westmoreland was prime sugar territory, and the number of slaves increased rapidly from over 7000 in 1730 to 17,486 in 1788. Census of 1730, C.O. 137/19 (pt.2)/48 and Census of 1788, C.O. 137/87, Public Record Office, Kew, London.
12. Philip Morgan, *Slave Counterpoint: Black Culture in Eighteenth-Century Chesapeake and Lowcountry* (Chapel Hill, NC, 1998), 275.
13. Morgan, *Slave Counterpoint*, 266–267.
14. Peter W. Bardaglio, *Reconstructing the Household: Families, Sex, and the Law in the Nineteenth-Century South* (Chapel Hill, NC, and London, 1995), 34.
15. Philip D. Morgan, "Three Planters and Their Slaves: Perspectives on Slavery in Virginia, South Carolina, and Jamaica, 1750–1790," in Winthrop D. Jordan and Sheila L. Skemp, eds., *Race and Family in the Colonial South* (Jackson, MS, and London, 1987), 39.
16. Gerda Lerner, *The Creation of Patriarchy* (New York, 1986), 238–239.
17. 3/19/1752; 12/31/1765.
18. Thistlewood punished Phibbah physically twice. On February 22, 1752, before he was her partner, he gave her 70 lashes for harboring the former overseer of Egypt. He also gave her "some correction" early in their relationship, on December 6, 1755, which he later attributed to the bad influence of a white bookkeeper.
19. Mr Richard Beckford's Instructions to Messrs John Cope, Richard Lewing and Robert Mason, 4/10/1754, Monson 31/86.
20. 12/4/1752.
21. 2/22/1782.
22. 3/1/1761; 3/7/1777; 5/5/1778. Violence against slaves was also permitted to free colored men, especially when a white man could vouch for them. In 1764, Humphrey,

one of Thistlewood's slaves, "a Stout hopefull young Fellow" argued with four men (a white, two mulattos, and a quadroon) in a canoe. The quadroon, James Chisholme, shot and killed Humphrey, afterward confessing to a magistrate that he did so "Wilfully and purposely (out of mere Wantonness)" without any "Manner of Provocation." Thistlewood was incensed at the loss of a slave who "Understood his business" and prosecuted Chisholme at the assizes, but to no avail. Chisholme was "tryed and Acquitted" when the white man in the canoe, Richard Dracott, "swore positively" that mulatto Joseph Hunter (who had left the parish) had shot Humphrey. Dracott's perjured testimony won his companion's acquittal as no white could contradict it. 10/19/1764; 10/25/1764; 9/28/1765.

23. J. B. Moreton, *Manners and Customs of the West Indian Islands* (London, 1790), 81. Most whips were made of cowhide, hence the reference to cowskin.

24. The question of whether sex between a master and a slave could ever be consensual is very contentious. Ann DuCille, "'Othered' Matters: Reconceptualizing Dominance and Difference in the History of Sexuality in America," *Journal of the History of Sexuality* 1 (1990): 116–121. For Thistlewood's sex life, Trevor Burnard, "The Sexual Life of a Jamaican Slave Overseer," in Merril Smith, ed., *Sex and Sexuality in Early America* (New York, 1998).

25. 12/7/1753.

26. 2/1/1753; 9/16/1753.

27. 7/28/1755; 8/22/1765; 8/26/1765.

28. Thistlewood was not indifferent to male slaves' sexual rights. He never had sex in a slave hut, evidently recognizing that slaves had some place that was inviolate.

29. 2/20/1753; 5/5/1756; 10/9/1756; 11/16–17/1759; 10/21/1761; 2/4–6/1765.

30. Catherine Clinton, *The Plantation Mistress: Women's World in the Old South* (New York, 1982); Barbara Bush, *Slave Women in Caribbean Society, 1650–1838* (London, 1990), 33–45.

31. 3/12–14/1755; 8/13/1755.

32. 3/17/1755; 4/19/1755; 10/7/1755; 5/5/1756; 8/11/1782.

33. 8/11/1782; 12/4/1782.

34. 6/28/1777; 7/2/1777; 10/28/1777; 1/6/1778; 5/8/1778; 7/3/1778; 12/28/1778.

35. 4/17–20/1757; 1/17/1762.

36. Edmund Burke, "Letter and Reflections on the Executions of the Rioters," 1780, in *Works and Correspondence* (London, 1853), 5:580–581.

37. 11/16–17/1759. See also 10/21/1761.

38. John Groves left the estate "because he might not flogg the Negroes as he pleased." 1/6–8/1761.

39. Commentors on Jamaican slavery are divided about slavery's effects. Some insist on the vitality of slave culture and emphasize the ways in which slaves constructed institutions without much white interference. See Sidney W. Mintz and Richard Price, *An Anthropological Approach to the Afro-American Past: A Caribbean Perspective* (Philadelphia, 1976); Mervyn Alleyne, *Roots of Jamaican Culture* (London, 1988); Michael Mullin, *Africa in America: Slave Acculturation and Resistance in the American South and the British Caribbean, 1736–1831* (Urbana, IL, 1992). Other historians, especially in older scholarship, stress disorganization and chaos as principal characteristics of Jamaican slavery. Orlando Patterson, *The Sociology of Slavery: An Analysis of the Origins, Devlopment, and Structure of Negro Slave Society in Jamaica* (London, 1967).

251

40. Michael Craton, "Jamaican Slave Mortality: Fresh Light from Worthy Park, Longville and the Tharp Estates," *Journal of Caribbean History* 3 (1971): 1–27.

41. Barry Higman, "Household Structure and Fertility on Jamaican Slave Plantations: A Nineteenth Century Example," *Population Studies* 27 (1973): 527–550; and Higman, "The Slave Family and Household in the British West Indies, 1800–1834," *Journal of Interdisciplinary History* 6 (1975): 261–287, sees more stability than I, possibly because he studies Jamaica in a later, more settled period.

42. Thistlewood tried to honor familial rights. He reprimanded his nephew for sleeping with driver Johnnie's wife, Little Mimber. The fact that he did so, however, demonstrates how easily whites intruded into slaves' domestic arrangements, 2/4–6/1765.

43. Douglas Hall, *In Miserable Slavery: Thomas Thistlewood in Jamaica, 1750–86* (London, 1989), 180–183, 315.

44. 11/13/1778.

45. Mullin, *Africa in America*, 171.

46. Hall, *In Miserable Slavery*, 195–196, 316.

47. 12/11/1774.

48. 10/8/1757; 10/22/1757. Changed gender expectations may have contributed to male demoralization, Patterson, *Sociology of Slavery*, 178–181; Bertram Wyatt Brown, "The Mask of Obedience: Male Slave Psychology in the Old South," *American Historical Review* 93 (1988): 1246–1247.

49. Madeleine Manoukian, *Akan and Ga-Adangme Peoples* (London, 1950), 26–31; M. D. McLeod, *The Asante* (London, 1981), 30–31.

50. 12/8/1756; 11/14/1773; 12/14/1774; 9/10/1780; 11/2/1782.

51. 1/5/1784.

52. Thistlewood knew his slaves were ready to rebel along with Tacky's revolt: "When the report was made of the Old Hope Negroes being rose, perceived a strange alteration in ours. They are certainly ready if they durst, and am pretty certain they were in the plot," 5/28/1760.

53. Gordon K. Lewis, *Main Currents in Caribbean Thought: The Historical Evolution of Caribbean Society in its Ideological Aspects, 1492–1900* (Baltimore, MD, 1983), 109–115; David Brion Davis, *The Problem of Slavery in the Age of Revolution, 1770–1823* (Ithaca, NY, 1975), 184–198.

54. Thistlewood was not incapable of emotional identification, as on the deaths of whites of similar status. He could not sleep when his nephew drowned and was very upset when Dr. Robinson, a botanist whom he greatly respected, died, 5/12/1768.

55. Slave theft could be resistance, see Alex Lichtenstein, " 'That Disposition to Theft, With Which They Have Been Branded': Moral Economy, Slave Management, and the Law," *Journal of Social History* 21 (1988): 415; Marvin L. Michael Kay and Lorin Lee Cary, " 'They are Indeed the Constant Plague of Their Tyrants': Slave Defence of a Moral Economy in Colonial North Carolina, 1748–1772," in Gad Heuman, ed., *Out of the House of Bondage: Runaways, Resistance and Marronage in Africa and the New World* (London, 1986), 38. Lichtenstein and Kay and Cary, however, overemphasize the use of theft to secure social solidarity and underestimate the extent to which it violated slave ideas of right and wrong.

56. Hall, *In Miserable Slavery*, 191–195, 198–201.

Trevor Burnard

57. Norbert Elias, *The Civilizing Process* (Oxford, 1978, 1982). Elias argued that this self-regulating and empathetic personality came into being as a result of the growth of state power, but others, notably Thomas Haskell, think this fundamental change in personality resulted from the ethical outworkings of market capitalism. Thomas Haskell, "Capitalism and the Origins of the Humanitarian Sensibility," *American Historical Review* 90 (1985): 339–361, 547–566. As V.A.C. Gattrell summarises Elias, "from these protracted processes, people and groups learnt to inhibit their aggressions, and rules became part of the taken-for-granted." V.A.C. Gatrell, *The Hanging Tree: Execution and the English People 1770–1860* (Oxford, 1994), 17.

58. Michel Foucault, *Discipline and Punish: The Birth of the Prison*, trans. Alan Sheridan (London, 1977).

59. Gatrell, *The Hanging Tree*, viii. Among a vast literature, see G.J. Barker-Benfield, *The Culture of Sensibility: Sex and Society in Eighteenth Century Britain* (Oxford, 1992); John Dwyer, *Virtuous Discourse: Sensibility and Community in Late Eighteenth Century Scotland* (Edinburgh, 1987); John Mullan, *Sentiment and Sociability: The Language of Feeling in the Eighteenth Century* (Oxford, 1988); Norman Fiering, "Irresistible Compassion: An Aspect of Eighteenth Century Sympathy and Humanitarianism," *Journal of the History of Ideas* 37 (1976): 199–212; Lawrence E. Klein, *Shaftesbury and the Culture of Politeness: Moral Discourse and Cultural Politics in Early Eighteenth Century England* (New York, 1994).

60. Joyce E. Chaplin, "Slavery and the Principle of Humanity: A Modern Idea in the Early Lower South," *Journal of Social History* 24 (1990): 299–315.

61. David Hume, *Treatise of Human Nature* (London, 1739–1740); Adam Smith, *The Theory of Moral Sentiments*, D. D. Raphael and A. L. Macfie, eds., (Oxford, 1976).

62. Thomas Haskell, "Capitalism and the Origins of the Humanitarian Sensibility," in Thomas Bender, ed., *The Antislavery Debate: Capitalism and Abolitionism as a Problem in Historical Interpretation* (Berkeley, CA, 1992), 107–160.

63. David Eltis, "Europeans and the Rise and Fall of African Slavery in the Americas: An Interpretation," *American Historical Review* 98 (1993): 1415–1423.

64. David Brion Davis, *The Problem of Slavery in Western Culture* (Ithaca, NY, 1966), 319–479; Davis, *Slavery and Human Progress* (New York, 1984), 154–158.

fourteen

"I HAVE GOT THE GUN AND WILL DO AS I PLEASE WITH HER"

African-Americans and Violence in Maryland, 1782–1830

T. Stephen Whitman

D omestic violence commonly describes acts that occur in the home or its vicinity among people linked by ties of family or intimacy. It can thus be placed on the "private" side of public/private dichotomies. But violence between masters and slaves often blurred the boundaries of those categories, with the sphere of domestic violence occupying more space than might be expected. This essay looks at violence between African-Americans and whites in early national Maryland and argues that African-Americans could most successfully engage in violence against whites when those actions could be explained by white men as occurring outside the world of public space and public speech they regarded as their exclusive preserve.

Slaveholders in early national America expanded and modified a preexisting patriarchal culture to include slaves as subordinate members of their own families, over whom they ruled paternally, as real or figurative fathers. As fathers, they dispensed rewards to loyal and submissive family members and inflicted punishment, often violent, on those who disobeyed or defied their authority. Emerging paternalist doctrines stressed, however, that authority be exercised benevolently. In this context, black aggression against whites could sometimes be interpreted by whites as domestic violence occurring within the family and could be forgiven rather than being punished by the state.[1]

In post-Revolutionary Maryland, as elsewhere in the South, slaveholders developed a paternalist stance as part of a struggle to reassert control over African-

Americans following the upheavals of the Revolutionary war. Unlike their counterparts in the Deep South, they also dealt with the impact of the manumission of slaves as Northern states gradually abandoned the institution. Recent reexaminations of the first emancipation in the Mid-Atlantic have brought fresh insight into the role played by race in the democratization of politics, the maturation of a market economy, and the reshaping of gender relations.[2]

This essay extends those discussions to the cultural understandings of black violence in Maryland. Between 1780 and 1830, Maryland clung to slavery but also became home to the nation's largest aggregation of free people of color. Over the same time span, Marylanders reshaped their penal laws in company with many other Atlantic coast states. All shifted from reliance on corporal punishment and banishment to a penitentiary system.

Despite these momentous changes, an older practice of mitigating judicial terror with mercy remained a mainstay of Maryland criminal jurisprudence. This practice was manifested as pardons issued in response to petitions for clemency by respectable citizens of an accused or convicted person's community.[3] Pardon petitions and their reception by Maryland's governors and judges illustrate evolving cultural values regarding violence by, against, and among African-Americans.

For example, in 1794 two slaves petitioned the Governor and Council of Maryland seeking pardon for having struck their master, Haden Edwards. Remarkably, their plea was heard with sympathy. The governor quashed their prosecution with a writ of *nolle prosequi*, thereby averting the cropping of their ears, the grisly sentence mandated for slaves who assaulted whites. To achieve this result, Bazil and Philip, aided by powerful patrons, recounted the entire history of their lives, studded with incidents presented to mitigate their crime and revalidate their identities as humble and obedient servants.

The pardoning process that served Bazil and Philip so well was, in theory, open to all Marylanders. Anyone could petition the state's governor and council to have a person pardoned or spared prosecution of virtually any crime. Pardons could quash grand jury indictments, absolve convictions, or commute sentences. In practice, while women, persons of color, and nonresidents of Maryland occasionally filed or signed petitions, most signers were white men from the county in which the crime had been tried. Most petitions, moreover, reached the governor only after they were referred to the judges who had presided over the case.[4]

Judges advised the governor on granting pardons. They explained points of law, frequently commenting on whether a jury's verdict represented a miscarriage of justice or rested on misread evidence. They also spoke to whether carrying out sentences, especially capital sentences, would set appropriate examples for the community and increase respect for the law. Finally, they offered their views on the nature of the defendant's character and reputation. Their assessments carried weight: few pardons were obtained over judicial objection.

"I HAVE GOT THE GUN AND WILL DO AS I PLEASE WITH HER"

Jurors might also become involved, often to circumvent overly rigorous sentencing requirements: when a sixteen-year-old boy was convicted of counterfeiting for having passed a single bad coin, judge and jurors all called for a pardon rather than imposing a mandatory four-year sentence.[5] More commonly, jurors who were forced to convict a defendant in strict adherence to Maryland's harsh laws respecting proof of guilt could then petition to annul their own verdicts based on shaky evidence.[6]

While requests for pardons to avoid miscarriages of justice were numerous, far more petitions accepted the defendant's guilt but argued that justice would best be served by allowing the convict to resume life at large in his or her community. Usually composed by the spouse, friends, or attorney of the defendant and circulated for signatures in the county where the crime occurred, most petitions offered a brief three-part biography of the convict. This sketch aimed to demonstrate that, first, his or her crime represented an isolated, idiosyncratic action that would not recur. Second, some mitigating interpretation could be offered for the crime. Thus, a thief might be presented as having been previously honest and industrious; his crime might be attributed to bad company, drink, or other external evils under whose sway the now repentant criminal would never again fall. Finally, champions of violent offenders would claim that the pardon-seeker had been and would become again an amiable, equable person who had been propelled to assault or homicide by irresistible but unique provocations. The plausibility of these stories and their perceived ability to predict future good conduct turned on the number and prominence of the petition's signers, who were after all "most likely to be injured should [a wrongdoer] err again."[7] Petitioners attested to the character of the pardon-seeker, and the governor and council, aided by judges, assessed the character of both groups in dispensing mercy.

An analysis of pardon recipients reveals, unsurprisingly, that a defendant's race, class, and gender were important predictors of success. White men were far more likely to win pardons or commuted prison terms than African-Americans or women. Beneficiaries of writs of *nolle prosequi* were almost exclusively white males of substance, men who could successfully assert a completely untarnished reputation that would be stained even by a trial ending in an acquittal.[8] Between 1782 and 1830, blacks benefitted from less than one-tenth of the pardons or quashing of prosecutions for felonies, although they comprised half of those convicted of such crimes.[9] Among prisoners, one-third of white men obtained a commuted sentence, compared to one-ninth of black men, one-eleventh of white women, and a minuscule one-thirtieth of black women (see Table 14–1).[10]

Given this pattern, that two slaves could strike a master and escape punishment suggests that the case of Bazil and Philip was amazing indeed. Their petition stated that the young men had grown up near Frederick Town, Maryland, where they lived with their mother and other relatives. They were sold in 1792,

T. Stephen Whitman

Table 14–1. *Maryland Penitentiary Inmates, 1811–1830,*[1] *Proportions Obtaining Pardon*

	# Sentenced	# Pardoned	% Pardoned
White Males	852	264	31
White Females	179	16	9
Free Black Males	596	66	11
Free Black Females	362	11	3

[1] These data include all inmates who entered the penitentiary from 1811 through 1830 who served their full sentence or were pardoned from some portion of it and exclude prisoners who died in the penitentiary or escaped from it. Data compiled from the Prisoner Records, Maryland Penitentiary, 1811–1830, Maryland State Archives, Annapolis.

along with the land they worked, to a Dr. Kerlegand. Two years later, Kerlegand sold them "against their will and entreaty" to Haden Edwards, whose expressed intention was to take them with him into Kentucky. But Bazil and Philip learned that Edwards's true plan was to transport them "to New Orleans . . . to sell them to the Spaniards." When Edwards called on Kerlegand to take possession of the men, they "remonstrated" with him, but Edwards was unyielding and even insisted on tying up the slaves to prevent their flight. At this critical moment, faced with "perpetual separation" from home and loved ones, Bazil, in a "fit of desperation and madness" struck Edwards, and he and Philip escaped.

The fugitives were soon captured and held in the county jail. When Edwards came to Frederick to identify the runaways, he evidently offered to drop the charges against them if they would consent to be sold to a Maryland master. Bazil and Philip agreed, and duly became the slaves of General Otho Williams. Edwards, however, either reneged or was unable to make good on his promise to stay prosecution: "the warrant being issued before Mr. Edwards sold them, he was later [summoned] to appear against them." Professing that they were "truly sorry" for their deed, and seeking not to "justify" their actions, but rather to "offer these circumstances" as a "mitigation" for their offense, Bazil and Philip solemnly concluded their prayer with a "promise to endeavor by an honest discharge of their duty to continue that good character which they heretofore maintained." Williams and Dr. Philip Thomas, a Frederick notable, backed the slaves' version of events and vouched for their "generally peaceable deportment" in letters supporting the petition.[11]

Bazil, Philip, and their adherents missed no opportunity to portray the men as worthy of mercy. They strove to assure readers of their childlike and submissive natures and to steer them away from an image of black rebels challenging white authority. Thus Edwards's duplicity had first aroused the men's fears because of their devotion to family and home. Their terror at leaving Maryland could also be read in a patriotic vein; fear of a Spanish master in far-off New Orleans had provoked Bazil to his rash act. They did not resist their status as chattel, for they had been sold without incident, both before and after the Kerlegand-Edwards transaction. In that fateful sale, the slaves did not dispute their master's authority to dispose of them; rather, they "entreated" a man not yet their master not to remove them to Kentucky and "remonstrated" with him when he arrived to claim them. By placing their fate in the hands of Kerlegard and thus subtly distancing Edwards from the status of true master, with the power and authority that role entailed, the petitioners may have hoped to exculpate their action.

They were not misguided in this strategy. Black-on-white violence was most often forgiven when the victim was an overseer or an outsider, particularly one whose actions were dissonant with a master's policies regarding slave or plantation management. The proper control of slaves was seen as a domestic affair. By stressing Edwards's secret plan to sell them to New Orleans, Bazil and Philip likened him to an overseer deluding or defrauding a "good master," Dr. Kerlegand. They also questioned Edwards's right to discipline the slaves by tying them up, and tinged Bazil's resistance with legitimacy.[12]

Again, the slaves' petition framed the story delicately to minimize Bazil's and Philip's overt resistance. Even Bazil's forbidden punch could be explained. The petition allowed a reader to infer that Edwards had acted badly; he was within his legal right to tie up slaves, but a good and fatherly master would have commanded the situation without such tactics. Bazil's unforgivable blow could not be denied; for it to be forgiven, it must have been motivated by "desperation," not anger or pride, and "madness," not cool calculation. After hitting Edwards once, Bazil and Philip fled, symbolic of their fear and guilt, emotions appropriate to servile natures. They did not persist in beating Edwards nor enjoy revenge. And, most importantly, they said nothing before or afterwards that could suggest a prideful spirit or a sense of rightful resistance. They only "entreated" and "remonstrated" over their removal from Maryland.

Shifting from this precisely etched portrait of a single uncharacteristic misdeed, Bazil and Philip turned to the future. They asked not to avoid punishment—they wrote from jail, where they had been confined for some time—but for a reduction of their sentence to avoid having their ears cropped, a painful and humiliating punishment. They claimed that additional punishment would violate judicial proportionality, a concept with which magistrates and governors were much seized. At this juncture, the petition wove into its story the crucial fact that Haden Edwards, "now in Kentucky," was no longer a member of the community into which Bazil and Philip sought readmission; he had sold them and moved on. Edwards's personal need for retributive justice could be discounted. Foregoing mutilation would not mark a public triumph over Edwards, a factor that lessened the likelihood that such leniency would encourage other blacks to be "impudent" toward whites. Here, the petitioners may have anticipated a counterpetition. Though such counterpetitions opposing clemency were rare, they were most likely to be filed in cases involving black violence or threatening language against whites.[13] Finally, Bazil and Philip reinforced their image as reliably industrious and submissive slaves with their promise to "continue that good character which they heretofore maintained."[14]

Bazil and Philip alone could not put forward this carefully drawn plea. They, like other pardon seekers, had to have witnesses to their lives as sober and honest slaves, contented with their station and mindful of their role. Here, too, their petition hit just the right note. Two prominent local figures stood behind them, slaveholders whose judgments of the petitioners the governor and his council trusted.

Last, but not least, the petition sought relief from a punishment most early national Americans viewed with increasing distaste. By the 1780s Marylanders had begun to protest against colonial statutes that imposed whipping, branding, or mutilation on criminals; by the 1790s most of these punishments had been eliminated for whites.[15] This revulsion extended to the bloody ear cropping imposed upon slaves who raised a hand to their masters, and most vehemently to the requirement that slave murderers or insurrectionists be drawn and quartered. One county sheriff flatly refused to cut off the hand of a slave convicted of murder or to draw and quarter his body following his hanging; a master in Kent County obtained remission of cropping for a slave in a petition that stated that the law was, "like the laws of Draco, written in Blood," and had been enforced only once in the history of the county.[16] Bazil and Philip tapped into this rising opposition to sanguinary punishments in their petition.

Appeals for clemency for Bazil and Philip also followed a pattern for pardons in early national Maryland. Violent offenders were more likely to have convictions absolved or sentences reduced than thieves, perhaps because they could more credibly plead that the act arose in a single misjudgment based on extenuating circumstances rather than in a pattern of behavior. The two most common pleas were, "I didn't mean to do it" and "he really had it coming"; many petitions invoked both excuses. Whites gained pardons more often than blacks, but black pardon rates were significantly higher for violent crimes than for theft (see Table 14–2). Clearly, white Marylanders of the early nineteenth century did not regard all black violence as subversive of racial order. African-Americans also won pardons for rape convictions against white women and for miscegenation. These were extraordinary events, but they underline the importance of patrons in the pardoning process—men who possessed the virtuous reputation they purported to see in the pardon seeker.

Moses Roberts, for example, a free black charged with "intermarrying" with Mary Webb, a white woman, was saved from prosecution through the interces-

"I HAVE GOT THE GUN AND WILL DO AS I PLEASE WITH HER"

Table 14–2. *Pardon Rates for Selected Crime Categories,*
Black and White Men, 1811–1830

	Blacks		Whites	
	% Pardoned	(# Cases)	% Pardoned	(# Cases)
Theft[1]	9	(511)	22	(620)
Vagrancy	0	(8)	6	(33)
Violence[2]	40	(25)	71	(65)
"White Collar"[3]	26	(19)	48	(42)
Horse Stealing	8	(12)	57	(42)
Negro Stealing[4]	9	(11)	76	(17)

[1] "Theft" includes convictions for larceny, stealing, burglary, and undefined felonies.
[2] "Violence" includes assault, robbery, manslaughter, murder, rape, and attempted rape.
[3] "White Collar" crimes include receiving stolen goods, forgery, and perjury.
[4] "Negro Stealing" includes kidnapping free persons of color, enticing slaves, and enticing or assisting runaways.

Data compiled from the Prison Records, Maryland Penitentiary, 1811–1830, Maryland State Archives, Annapolis.

sion of the Dorchester County J.P.s. They concurred with Roberts's contention that "there have been Marriages in the said County similar to his own, and that no prosecutions have taken place in consequence thereof." Persuaded by the judges' statement, the governor issued a *nolle prosequi*.[17]

At least one scholar has suggested that white ferocity toward blacks accused of rape was greater in the post-emancipation South than earlier. That some blacks received pardons in the face of such accusations in early national Maryland supports this view.[18] But, as with cases of black violence against white men, blacks fared best when they could vindicate themselves in white eyes through white constructions of their appearances and actions, rather than their own words.

Two cases may prove instructive. In 1789, Slave Jacob was convicted of raping Henrietta Woodward. His master, Joseph Pigman, petitioned for his pardon. The petition began with the customary depiction of Jacob's "General good Conduct and Behaviour." In particular, he had "a Wife to whom he was Attached in a Singular Manner." Like a good husband, Jacob had been on his way home to his wife at the close of the workday, shortly after Woodward's rape occurred. He was met by a local planter, Mr. Collins, who "Discovered Nothing . . . which induced him to Suppose he had been guilty of Misconduct." Jacob spent the night with his wife and returned to work the next morning, without trying to hide or run away. Pigman advanced this behavior

T. Stephen Whitman

as proof of Jacob's innocence, for he was "so much afraid of punishment that when he . . . had offended his Master he would abscond for a time." In short, Jacob embodied right character for a slave: he was an obedient worker who feared his master's authority, a faithful husband, and, above all, a guileless man who could not have deceived his wife, master, or a white neighboring planter. None of this was indicated by Jacob, but by Pigman, who portrayed Jacob as incapable of conceiving a rape and then feigning innocence.[19]

The victim, Woodward, fell afoul of several gender conventions in her effort to bring an attacker to judgment. Pigman described the spinster Woodward as "far advanced in years." As an older woman, she could exert no sexual attraction. She had therefore probably not been forced into intercourse. Further, he implied that, as a woman alone, she could not truly be raped, as no father or husband's rights were being violated. Most tellingly, Woodward failed to present a clear and convincing case against Jacob; she initially wavered in identifying him as her assailant, despite having known him for years. In short, the governor and council could ignore Woodward's accusations and Jacob's conviction without threatening the social fabric. Woodward did not best embody the principle of female purity—a woman in her prime chastely attached to a husband or father. Jacob, on the other hand, possessed all the virtues of a slave and no disturbing tendencies toward independence or assertiveness that might warrant punishment. Jacob was pardoned.

A second case, with different circumstances, can further illuminate reactions to interracial rape. In 1787, the Maryland governor and council reviewed the case of Negro Adam, who sought pardon for attempted rape. As with Jacob, the evidence was uncertain. Adam's accuser said she had been assaulted at dusk, by a naked Negro man armed with a knife, who fled after failing to overpower her. She identified Adam, whom she had never seen before, by the "Thinness of his Visage . . . and the thickness of his lips." The presiding judges' letter to the governor found Adam's features "regular," and his lips "but little thicker than common." On the other hand, a knife Adam owned had been found at the scene. Finally, although they were not strictly admissible as evidence, three other slaves gave Adam an alibi.[20] But no white observer came forward to vindicate Adam as a faithful, harmless, and obedient slave. The shaky evidence against him was countered only by black testimony of his innocence. Forced to choose between white and black statements, the governor upheld the conviction, though he commuted the death sentence to sale and banishment to the West Indies.[21] Adam, unlike Jacob or Bazil, could not dispel the perception that he had intruded violently into public space, even if he had transgressed against a single woman, herself unentitled to control that public space and speech.

In some instances, therefore, black violence could be forgiven, if and only if circumstances could be interpreted and framed to reinforce white dominance

"I HAVE GOT THE GUN AND WILL DO AS I PLEASE WITH HER"

and black submission. By occasionally granting mercy in a complex case as a narrowly delineated exception to this rule, white men reaffirmed their monopoly on the legitimate use of violence. They successfully demonstrated the justness of their paternal authority and reinforced it through these acts of benevolence.

The converse of this process could be observed when whites sought pardons for violent acts against slaves or free blacks; here, mercy seekers unfailingly harped on the assertive behavior of blacks whose challenges to white authority called forth a justifiably violent response. Such pardon seekers made archetypal claims that a fatal shooting or beating of a slave or free person of color had been actuated by a desire not to kill, but only to "compel a proper submission" from a "daring" or "impudent" black resister. "Impudence" and "insolence" carried a meaning most slaveholders felt easily comprehensible, if the frequency with which they appeared in runaway advertisements is any indicator.[22] When seeking pardon for a felony, petitioners conveyed in unmistakable fashion the attitude and behavior that had led to a slave's deserved punishment and that unexpectedly, if not unreasonably, had resulted in his death. A slave's failure to submit was often underlined in dramatic verbal exchanges, and white recountings of black speech were brought into play to excuse violence.

When Maryland planter Robert Stevens sought a *nolle prosequi* for having killed a slave, he described an elderly neighbor with "ungovernable" negroes and his offer to "assist in correcting them at any time." One of the slaves overheard these remarks, and "came toward the petitioner in a hostile manner and asked if he would correct him." Stevens gave him "one blow" which killed him. Confronted with the ominous image of a slave who advanced on a white man and mocked him, neighbors flocked to sign Stevens's successful petition.[23] Similarly, when overseer Griffen Williams shot and killed Negro Nathan, he called Nathan "refractory and insolent" and told of a threat to "take Williams' life if he should ever attempt to correct him." More than 150 of Williams's supporters argued that "Public Policy and General Security" dictated that his prosecution be quashed. Even to bring Williams to trial "would be considered as a Triumph by a certain description of Population . . . which might induce to dangerous Consequences . . . of the most fruitful Desolation and exquisite Distress." Williams successfully obtained a *nolle prosequi*.[24]

Thus if a clash between black and white men could be represented as black encroachment on white males' public space, blacks, enslaved or free, received no community support, particularly if no white man testified publicly in the blacks' defense. In one case in 1811, John Montgomery stoned Henry Fite, a free black, to death but avoided the hangman's noose. Montgomery described Fite as having dressed above his station in a "ludicrous Stile," and as having "assailed" a passerby with verbal "insolence" while standing in the street before Montgomery's livery stable. Annoyed, Montgomery asked Fite to move on, but he had replied "in a most insulting manner that he would not stir until it

T. Stephen Whitman

suited him." Montgomery then killed Fite with a "brickbat," but obtained a *nolle prosequi* with a petition endorsed by merchants and bankers.[25]

Mob violence as well as individual action could be forgiven if it were seen to restore proper patriarchal relations between white and black men. In 1798, an altercation boiled up between some Irishmen who dined with and may have boarded with a free black family. When Archibald Davelin tried to seduce Henry Brown's wife, the Browns drove most of the Irish party out. The Irishmen came back with a gang, "declaring they would burn every bugger" in the house. The house was duly fired with the inhabitants inside. After watching the fire spread, the attackers "huzza'd for old Ireland and ran off." Brown and his wife escaped, but three children and one Irishman still sleeping in the house were burnt to death.[26] Davelin's petitioners acknowledged that he provoked the fight and organized the arson and murders. They nonetheless urged the governor not to execute him because his death was "not necessary to the public Safety," of which free blacks apparently did not partake. The county chief justice concurred in this appeal, saying that Davelin "appeared to be penitent . . . and said he was drunk at the time, and did not know what he was about." Davelin's death sentence was commuted to a prison term followed by banishment. For whites who attacked blacks, even the barest gestures of remorse and repentance sufficed to win pardon.

These cases demonstrate the power and danger surrounding black speech and movement and the ways in which white pardon-seekers could assemble a moment's impressions into a parable of black aggression that attacked the very basis of society and merited swift and violent redress. Slaves who trespassed on the white preserve of violence could survive only with a letter-perfect story like that of Bazil and Philip, supported by whites. In contrast, when a black man was accused of the rape of a single white woman, where neither party had the privilege to define public space or speech, his chances of gaining a pardon or avoiding death were greater than for resisting or even resenting white male attacks.

Black-on-black violence fell almost entirely beneath the purview of white men, as the case of Mingo and James Saunders illustrates. On December 5, 1784, Mingo, the slave of John Lewis, and several other young Baltimore blacks called on the slave George, who subsequently related the group's doings to the sheriff. A free black, James Saunders, was to hold a dance that night, but Mingo and his friends were not invited. Mingo declared that "he and others had Dances and invited Saunders but that now Saunders had made a Dance and not invited them." They were, as a result, "determined to break up the dance." Mingo went from house to house in Baltimore's Fells Point and Old Town assembling a gang of rowdies. "Negro Jim" begged off, saying "his wife wouldn't let him go," but lent the gang a drum, a fiddle, and a fife. Mingo also got a gun, along with powder and shot. This troubled some of the men. One

"I HAVE GOT THE GUN AND WILL DO AS I PLEASE WITH HER"

participant, Myers, demanded to know what the gun was loaded with, and another, Ben, suggested that if the "Gun was Loaded with anything more than Powder," Mingo "had better not carry her." Mingo scornfully brushed these inquiries aside, telling the men, "if you have a mind to go let us go, if not go about your business and I will go about mine." When a third man, Juba, remonstrated with him, Mingo stated ominously, "I have got the gun and will do as I please with her."

Perhaps hoping to curb Mingo's impetuosity, the men, now eight or nine in number, formed an impromptu militia company that elected Juba captain to accompany Mingo in his mission. Juba "rang[ed] them in order, and flourishing a Stick, order[ed] them to rank two deep . . . threatening to break their Heads if they did not Obey." The company marched on, stopping at the corner of the "new Alley" to bolster their courage with the bottle of rum Juba had brought along. They "gave three cheers and threw up their hats," and then selected Peter to go to Saunders's door, "where the Company were dancing to ask for Grogg." When Peter was refused, Mingo called out, "Won't you, damn you, I'll soon see if I will not have Grogg." A struggle ensued, with Mingo's party trying to shove their way through the door, while "those on the Inside pushed to keep it to." Brickbats flew in every direction. During a lull, Mingo fired the gun into the door, killing Saunders as he opened it, and exulted, "You all thought I was going to shoot Up, but I had the Gun and I shot where I pleased to Shoot." Those inside the house burst out and momentarily routed the attackers, but Mingo rallied men like Bob and Paris, who "wanted to go home," and reminded them that "if you go away without getting your revenge they will have it to say that they drove you." After another round of fighting, both parties broke up and disappeared down Baltimore's back alleys.[27] So concluded George's deposition, delivered "in irons" as the sheriff questioned him.

Trying to wring meaning from this richly detailed story raises numerous questions. To what extent did George shape his story to protect himself or others in Mingo's gang from prosecution for murder or manslaughter? How much of the story did George volunteer, and how much did his white questioners wrest from him? Did they reconfigure what George offered to suit their own ends? While these questions are largely unanswerable, it is possible to infer some of the brawl's meanings by looking at the punishments meted out.

Mingo, as a slave who had committed murder, was sentenced to be hung and drawn and quartered, though a pardon remitted all but the hanging. None of the other men, however, were prosecuted or punished, beyond being whipped for disorderly behavior.[28] A group of slaves had marched through the streets of Baltimore in military fashion, attacked a house of free people and killed one, yet no one was tried for insurrection and only Mingo was hanged.

This lenient outcome was surely influenced by the fact that Mingo's victim was black, but George's deposition also played a part. He described only

T. Stephen Whitman

Mingo as threatening. He recalled violence on the part of everyone in the gang, but only Mingo used the gun and, critically, only Mingo used violent speech. Indeed, George's story showed almost every other man as reasonable. Ben, Myers, and Juba had cautioned Mingo about the gun; Peter had given Saunders a chance to repair his insult by providing grog; Bob and Paris expressed misgivings and wanted to go home. By contrast, Mingo's oft-repeated boast, "I have got the gun and will do as I please with her," singled him out as the truly dangerous slave who knew his will and acted on it.

White reluctance to validate the truth of black speech in the courtroom may also explain the single conviction. As the author of the pardon petition uncomfortably noted, "all the witnesses in the case were Negroes." Could the truth be discovered or the social order be upheld by black words alone? Reflecting a double-bind, just as black witnesses could not save the accused rapist, Adam, from imprisonment, black testimony could not make the assault on Saunders's house into a serious enough matter for conviction. A gun-toting slave who celebrated a murderous revenge was hung; little of consequence had been at stake in a case of black-on-black violence that no white had described, and the public space had not been disturbed.[29]

The picture that emerges from these patterns is one in which whites ascribed meaning to events by listening closely to white words while watching black actions. Black violence against whites could be excused if white witnesses or supporters chose to explain it in ways that did not threaten patriarchal relationships. White violence against blacks carried no social threat when performed by masters or their surrogates; other white perpetrators could still expect to be absolved of wrongdoing if they expressed remorse and repentance and invoked the specter of open black resistance to whites. Black words, in their own right, counted for very little, and blacks, free or enslaved, had no choice but to enact and reenact their repentance.

Notes

1. Sylvia Frey, *Water From the Rock: Black Resistance in a Revolutionary Age* (Princeton, NJ, 1991), links the development of paternalism to the loss of slaveholders' control occasioned by the Revolutionary war, 243–282. For a panoramic treatment of the same themes, Eugene Genovese, *Roll, Jordan, Roll: The World the Slaves Made* (New York, 1974), esp. 3–112. For patriarchy's influence on law in the South, Peter Bardaglio, *Reconstructing the Household: Families, Sex, & the Law in the Nineteenth-Century South* (Chapel Hill, NC, 1995), 3–36; Michael Grossberg, *Governing the Hearth: Law and the Family in Nineteenth-Century America* (Chapel Hill, NC, 1985), 3–31. On public space and power, Stephanie McCurry, *Masters of Small Worlds: Yeoman Households, Gender Relations, and the Political Culture of the Antebellum South Carolina Low Country* (New

"I HAVE GOT THE GUN AND WILL DO AS I PLEASE WITH HER"

York and Oxford, 1995); also Bertram Wyatt-Brown, *Southern Honor: Ethics and Behavior in the Old South* (New York and Oxford, 1982); Dickson D. Bruce, Jr., *Violence and Culture in the Antebellum South* (Austin, TX, 1979).

2. Shane White, *Somewhat More Independent: The End of Slavery in New York City 1770–1810* (Athens, GA, 1991); Gary Nash, *Forging Freedom: The Formation of Philadelphia's Black Community, 1720–1840* (Cambridge, MA, 1988); Nash and Jean Soderlund, *Freedom by Degrees: Emancipation in Pennsylvania and Its Aftermath* (New York, 1991); Graham Hodges, *Slavery and Freedom in the Rural North: African-Americans in Monmouth County, New Jersey, 1665–1865* (Madison, WI, 1997); Shane White, " 'It Was a Proud Day': African Americans, Festivals, and Parades in the North, 1741–1834," *Journal of American History* 81 (1994): 13–50; Paul A. Gilje and Howard B. Rock, " 'Sweep O! Sweep O!': African-American Chimney Sweeps and Citizenship in the New Nation," *William and Mary Quarterly* 51 (1994): 507–538; T. Stephen Whitman, *The Price of Freedom: Slavery and Manumission in Baltimore and Early National Maryland* (Lexington, KY, 1997); Christopher Phillips, *Freedom's Port: The African American Community of Baltimore, 1790–1860* (Urbana and Chicago, 1997); William H. Williams, *Slavery and Freedom in Delaware: 1639–1865* (Wilmington, DE, 1996), 141–184; Patience Essah, *A House Divided: Slavery and Emancipation in Delaware, 1638–1865* (Charlottesville, VA, 1996), 36–74.

3. The Maryland state constitution of 1776 and succeeding laws, notably that of 1795, chap. 82, vested the power to pardon convicted felons and to quash felony indictments through the issuance of a writ of *nolle prosequi* in the Governor and Council of Maryland. After the abolition of the council in 1837, the Governor exercised his pardoning power with the assistance of the Secretary of State of Maryland.

4. *Laws of Maryland*, 1795, chap. 82. The governor's clerk referred the cases back to the presiding judges; his letters appear throughout the pardon papers. Governor and Council, Pardon Papers, 1782–1830 (hereafter Pardons), Maryland Hall of Records (hereafter MHR).

5. Pardons, Box 18, Folder 17 [18:17]. The governor agreed that the sentence was too harsh, and issued a *nolle prosequi* quashing the case, an option kept open by the judges' having suspended sentencing the convict, delaying the trial's formal conclusion.

6. Maryland law positively required juries to convict all defendants charged with larceny on the testimony of a single disinterested witness as well as black defendants charged with virtually all felonies, including capital offenses. *Laws of Maryland*, 1715, chap. 26, and 1751, chap. 14.

7. Pardons, 17:7 (1806).

8. White men received 438 of 510 (86 percent) *nolle prosequi* writs issued by governors in felony cases between 1782 and 1830. Compiled from Pardons.

9. State figures for felony convictions are not available for this period, but the racial makeup of persons imprisoned in the state penitentiary from 1811 to 1830 is. During its first 20 years, 1136 of 2263 prisoners were identified as persons of color (50 percent). Over the same time, the governor and council showed mercy to over 700 whites, but fewer than 70 blacks. Data from Maryland Penitentiary, Prisoner Records, 1811–1830 (hereafter Prisoner Records), and Pardons, MHR.

10. These data exclude those who died in jail or escaped. Of 852 white men, 264 were pardoned before serving their full sentence (31 percent). Of 596 black men, 66

were pardoned (11 percent), as were 16 of 179 white women (9 percent), and 11 of 362 black women (3 percent), Prisoner Records.

11. Pardons, 6:100. Williams or Thomas probably assisted Bazil and Philip in composing their petition or provided them with a lawyer. The petition came from and was signed by the two slaves.

12. Of 1300 pardon petitions filed between 1782 and 1830, seven involved cases of slaves obtaining pardon or a writ of *nolle prosequi* for charges of assault or attempted murder against a white. In none of these cases did a slave attack his master; in six, the master supported the petition, Pardons.

13. See, for example, Pardons, 11:14, Petition of the Citizens of Dorchester County Respecting Negro Doff, 1805. Doff was convicted of using insurrectionary language, and was not pardoned.

14. Pardons, 6:100.

15. *Laws of Maryland*, 1790, chap. 52, and 1793, chap. 57. Corporal punishments were replaced with labor performed in chains on the roads or in dredging Baltimore's harbor, popularly referred to as the "wheelbarrow law."

16. These harsh laws had been passed early in the eighteenth century, as Marylanders began to import more slaves. *Laws of Maryland*, 1715, chap. 23 and 1729, chap. 4. For the reluctant sheriff, Pardons, 7:60. Also Pardons, 7:7.

17. Pardons, 7:66 (1797).

18. Martha Hodes, "The Sexualization of Reconstruction Politics: White Women and Black Men in the South after the Civil War," *Journal of the History of Sexuality* 3 (1993): 402–417.

19. Pardon, 4:65.

20. Maryland, like most slave states, forbade the consideration of black testimony that challenged that of white witnesses. But the rule was bent, judging from the petitions, to allow statements that indirectly undermined white testimony.

21. Pardons, 3:96. Given the nature of slavery on sugar plantations, the governor's action probably gave Adam little solace.

22. Latham A. Windley, *Runaway Slaves: A Documentary History from the 1730s to 1790* (Westport, CT, 1983); T. Stephen Whitman, *The Price of Freedom*, 61–92.

23. Pardons, 12:73 (1807).

24. Pardons, 15:76 (1812).

25. Pardons, 15:24 (1811).

26. Pardons, 8:30 (1798).

27. Pardons, 3:12 (1785). Luther Martin, Baltimore attorney and politician, and George's owner submitted the petition.

28. Mingo's petition refers to the other men "having already been whipped," and no other petitions were filed in this case. I infer that none of the other slaves were convicted of the capital offenses of murder or manslaughter. Subsequent bills of sale and pardon petitions prove that Paris, Peter, Ben, Myers, and George were at large in Baltimore in the late 1780s; I believe this was also true for Jack, Juba, and Bob.

29. Pardons, 3:12 (1785). The lone white witness was not at the brawl and testified only to seeing black men flee down the street afterwards.

"I HAVE GOT THE GUN AND WILL DO AS I PLEASE WITH HER"

fifteen

WITHIN THE SLAVE CABIN

Violence in Mississippi Slave Families

Christopher Morris

" "W hile I had the good luck to have a kind master," George Weatherby recalled in the late 1930s, prodded by a writer with the Federal Writers' Project (FWP), "I had the bad luck to have a cruel pa. He was mean to us children and especially to ma. He made it powerfully hard on us all, Ma, she had to work in the fields from early to late, and then with pa cruel to her, made it terrible for her to get along." George's brother, Steve, concurred. "My father was cruel to my mother. She had a mighty hard time with him, and us children little and having to be a slave too was too much for her to stand." When George was seven years old, his family moved to a different plantation and a new master. "He weren't kind like our first master. Ma just couldn't stand that with pa rough too, so as soon as it could be arranged she took us children and went back to Marse Owens." The father stayed behind.[1]

Abuse, sometimes incredibly violent and destructive, occurred within slave families just as it occurred within free families. Within the context of slavery, however, the impact of domestic violence on the people it touched was unique. No matter how bad it was, it was never a slave's worst problem; that was slavery itself. Partners and parents could be vicious, but a troubled family life only made the primary ordeal for slaves—the relationship with the master—harder to endure. Like many of the FWP narrators, Weatherby recalls that his master was kind, although his remark about how his mother had to work in the fields "from early to late" is revealing, as is Steve's comment, that a mean husband in addition to "having to be a slave too was too much for her to stand." For the Weatherbys' mother, the combination of cruel master and abusive husband—of ill-use in both slavery and family—was unbearable.

Historians have long debated the legacy of slavery for African-American families. Over fifty years ago, E. Franklin Frazier argued that bondage had stripped blacks of their African heritage, in particular traditional notions of family, leaving them ill-prepared for freedom. The consequences, including female-headed households, rootless men, high divorce rates, promiscuity, and family "disorganization," mired descendents of slaves in poverty and ignorance. In the 1960s, when policy makers eager to address poverty and violence in black communities and families drew on Frazier's work, they stimulated a backlash among historians, most notably Herbert Gutman, who were concerned that slavery and slaves' descendents would be blamed for problems that lay within the structures of modern society. They argued that the black family, which survived both slavery and poverty as a vital institution within the black community, was hardly pathological. More recently, scholars have revisited the idea that slavery did leave deep scars on the people it touched. Cases of violence within slave families reflect on both these positions. Intimate violence between some enslaved people, however, does not negate the viability and durability of the ideals of family life most slaves held.[2]

The topic of domestic violence in many historical contexts risks being anachronistic. Some family violence—corporal punishment of children, for example—was clearly considered legitimate during the eighteenth and nineteenth centuries. It is difficult for modern Americans, moreover, to appreciate how trivial much violence must have been in a society saturated with it. In the slave South, people wore signs of brutality—brands, lacerated backs, cropped and bitten ears—as naturally as if they had been born with them. Whipping was, in Winthrop Jordan's words, "a fixture of life as real as rain, and like rain it would happen again because it had happened before." Despite the pain, early Americans did not view violence with the same sensibilities we do. And they rarely wrote about it.[3]

Both slaves and slave owners sought stable slave families, albeit for very different reasons. As masters saw it, slaves did not live in autonomous families, but within a larger plantation household. Relations within slave families always involved the master, at least indirectly, and this connection affected the internal dynamics of slave families.[4] The potential sources of conflict between intimates are many, and violence is only one possible response. But slave owners could soothe or exacerbate such problems and were always present in slaves' internal family affairs. From the slaves' perspective, domestic violence invited a master to intervene and turned their own weapon of resistance against them. From the master's perspective, violence among slaves marked a breakdown in

WITHIN THE SLAVE CABIN

plantation order that required intervention. Slave family violence, therefore, destabilized the relationship between masters and slaves, and both sought to minimize conflict within families.

Much has been written during the last three decades about strong and supportive slave marriages and kinship, and the ways in which they helped shield slaves from oppression. Despite the difficulties of marriage across plantation boundaries ("abroad marriages"); long working hours that kept parents away from children and too exhausted to interact when they were with them; and the forced separation of spouses and parents and children, most dramatically at the auction house, against all odds, many enslaved men and women formed lasting relationships, and most children lived with one or both parents. The family persisted as a strong ideal among slaves. Some scholars have argued that because they were so inimical to the institution of slavery, slave families must be seen as a form of resistance.[5]

But slave family life was also wholly entangled with master/slave relations, adding a degree of complexity not present in free families. Slave owners had a stake in maintaining stable marriages, which discouraged runaways and encouraged plantation discipline. Healthy children added to owners' assets. Many owners, moreover, idealized their legal responsibility for their slaves through the lens of paternalism. Some, like George Fitzhugh, a proslavery theorist, defended slavery in part because he believed it reduced domestic violence by checking the patriarchal despotism inherent in free families. Working-class women and children, he argued, were more likely to be abused than their enslaved counterparts, who were protected from tyrannical husbands and fathers by paternalistic masters.[6] In April 1865, planter William J. Minor testified in the same vein about domestic violence under slavery. "On all well regulated plantations, previous to this matter [Emancipation] excessive drinking was prohibited, also gambling, beating of wives, [and] excessive punishment of children." Minor claimed that freedmen "are now beating their wives to excess." He noted that he had "had three or four instances of wife-beating on my own plantation in the last two or three months, where men have tied their wives up to the house & whipped them. One man, an elder of a church, tied up his wife & beat her with an ox whip." Under slavery, Minor explained confidently (if unrealistically), beaten wives could always seek protection from their masters; without this paternal figure, nothing could be done.[7]

On occasion, the master himself and the conditions of slavery could be the source of domestic strife. The Weatherby case is revealing. Unkind masters and frequent sales created a precarious family life, made more so by a cruel father. But the ideal of a protective family remained strong. When George recalled, for example, that his mother arranged for the return to Owens's plantation, he recalled a patriarchal ideal. She could have only appealed to her masters, who possessed sole legal authority to separate the Weatherbys from their father.[8]

The law supported masters' intervention in slaves' families in cases of domestic violence. It recognized neither slave marriages nor the responsibility of enslaved parents for their children; legal authority over slaves and their families belonged entirely to slave owners. With the exception of murder, moreover, and, after 1860, rape, slaves were not legally accountable for violent attacks on each other. Slave owners settled disputes among slaves as they saw fit. Some established plantation courts that mimicked those of the legal system, with the master as judge, to mediate troubled relations between husbands and wives. Others handled slave domestic violence individually and irregularly. Without the support of law, the slave family was structurally and institutionally weak and dependent on individual masters.[9]

Unlike most free families in the antebellum era, enslaved families were not patriarchal. Enslaved men lacked legal authority and economic influence over wives and children. On one hand, this encouraged egalitarian relationships between men and women which some scholars have perhaps romanticized. On the other, it left men and women few means to protect their families from the legal patriarch—the master. Despite a strong family ideal, slaves' power to shape family life was severely limited by their relationship with a master, as was their ability to work out domestic problems.[10]

Violence in slave families is elusive, because it existed largely outside the law and its records. What we know of it (short of murder) surfaces in the documents of the few masters and slaves who wrote or spoke of it, but plantation records, magazine articles about slave management, personal memoirs, newspapers, and the FWP slave narratives all contain clues to the internal dynamics of slave families. The FWP papers for Mississippi alone yield twenty obvious cases of family violence. While frequency of violence is impossible to determine from this handful of surviving accounts, the cases tell us a great deal about slaves' experiences.

Federal Writers' Project interviewers often drew stories of family violence out of ex-slaves when they asked about whippings. "Marse Matthew whupped me and so did my mammy," responded Jim Martin. Emily Dixon of Simpson County claimed "Ole missus was kinder to me than ma was. She used to make her quit whipping me for ma beat me too hard." Former slaves often softened violent masters' images for white interviewers by claiming that their parents, whom they loved, could be violent too. With this caution in mind, the FWP tales and other cases of intimate violence are revealing.[11]

The perpetrators of slave family violence were as likely to be women as men. Alex Montgomery recalled that on one occasion his mother whipped him for breaking some jasmine flowers off a bush in his master's front yard and bringing them home to her. As Montgomery noted, "the overseer never did whup" him, although "my mammy worked on my back" frequently. The punishment, however, might have spared him a more severe whipping by the master. Lucindy

Shaw said of both her parents, "they used to beat me like I was a dog; the white folks'd beat me and the colored folks'd beat the same as the white folks." When Anna Baker's mother ran away from the sexual advances of an overseer, Anna was left to the care of her aunt Emmaline, who whipped her and on one occasion clubbed her on the head with an iron implement. Ebenezer Brown reported that he received his worst whippings from his grandmother.[12]

Violent women were often described with affection or even pride. Chaney Mack remembered that his mother "whupped my daddy just the same as de rest of us." Mack claimed his mother was part Cherokee and took tremendous pride in her ability to stand up to any man, black or white. "They call her 'Big Sarah,' and nobody fooled with her. She walk straight and hold her head high. . . . She'd grab a man by the collar, throw him down and set on him." Charlie Davenport's mother was also part Indian. "Her pa was a full blooded Choctaw and, young as she was, I is been told that nobody doest meddle her." Women who suffered abuse and acted to stop it became heroic figures. Annie Coley told a story about an overseer who struck a woman, causing her to miscarry. The other female slaves jumped him and took him to a brush pile where they planned to burn him alive. They loosed him only at the urging of their men.[13]

Some violent men received grudging respect as well. One woman described the husband who beat her as "too mean to die." Another man whipped his daughter "for burning up all the coffee she was parching." He was a driver and familiar with whipping; when he whipped his daughter the other slaves on the plantation thought he "whipped justly." Working as a driver could put a slave at odds with his community, but in this case, he earned respect for treating his daughter as he would any other slave.

In general, though, surviving recollections of violent husbands and fathers are unrelentingly negative. A violent mother could represent opposition to male authority—patriarchy—and thus to slavery. A violent father or husband, however, recalled the master. George Weatherby explicitly compared his "cruel" father to his "kind" master. Manus Robinson told of how "My pa used to whip me with the plow lines to make me work," as a master or overseer would have done.[14]

The absence of legal and economic bases for patriarchy did not prevent some slave men from asserting authority over wives and children through violence. Indeed, some husbands insisted on proprietary privilege over their wives. In a case in Mississippi, for example, the slave Harrison faced a murder charge for killing another slave. He claimed the deceased had taunted him, saying he "was inside of the House with his [Harrison's] wife and that he might help himself if he could." In a similar case in Louisiana, Lewis killed Henry "Because I found him in my cabin with my wife." Masters and overseers also threatened some slaves' claims to possession of their wives. In one case a slave killed his overseer for habitually coming to his cabin at night and raping his wife while he, the helpless husband, lay in the same bed. A furious slave in Issequena County struck his overseer four times with an axe as the overseer whipped the slave's wife. Males slaves' frustration with their inability to control or protect their wives often led to violence, domestic and otherwise.[15]

In the South, especially Mississippi, being a man meant (among other things) the right to authority over family, by violent means if necessary. Courts granted free husbands the right to "moderate chastisement" of wives and children, a right some interpreted as a symbol of freedom. William Johnson of Natchez was born into slavery. Manumitted at age eleven, he eventually purchased slaves himself. He not only whipped his slaves, but on one occasion gave his own mother, whose disorderly public behavior embarrassed him, "a few Cuts" with a whip. He immediately regretted what he had done. His mother dared him to hit her again, "which I would not do for anything in the world. I shoved her back from me three times." But the woman had very publicly challenged his ability to control the family he headed. From Johnson's perspective, she challenged his mastery not only over her but over his slaves.[16]

Masters' legal control and intervention prevented male slaves from using violence to demonstrate their power. Henry Jones lived near Natchez in the early nineteenth century. When his master told him he had been sold and would be moved to another part of the state, he decided to run away, and asked his wife Diana to run with him. When she refused, he exploded with rage, not at the master who had disrupted his life, but at his wife. He kicked Diana in the stomach, knocked her about the head and stabbed her to death. Jones and his wife illustrate the tenuousness of slave family structures; they could be destroyed in a moment by a master, whom slaves dared not challenge. Although the master threatened to dissolve Jones's family, from his perspective, Diana was also at fault. Husbands like Henry expected loyalty in marriage but could not enforce it except with violence.[17] Wives like Diana doubtless thought of their families, but also had to think of themselves—Jones may have abused her before this incident.

The absence of patriarchal control on the part of slave men, therefore, refutes the simple conclusion of some scholars that patriarchal families are the only settings for domestic violence. Patterns of violence within slave families doubtless differed from those in free families, especially in the proportion of female perpetrators. It was also easier for enslaved women to escape violent husbands or fight back because they could seek assistance from their master, the patriarch outside the family. Enslaved women, unlike free black women, posed no social threat to whites. Married or not, they were legally bound to their owner—they would never become vagrant or unprotected. A "divorced" slave woman could not become a public charge. Most masters saw little point in forcing slave couples to remain together, especially if a woman of childbearing age could find another partner quickly, and granted divorces easily.[18]

The mere presence of a master, however, could tacitly permit domestic violence to escalate. When a woman at Burleigh plantation in Mississippi "after many attempts, succeeded one day in stabbing her husband to death," a jury acquitted her on the grounds that she had acted in self-defense. Such a decision might have left a free woman a charity case or a vagrant, a matter no juror would ignore in reaching a verdict. But a slave's master would care for her if she posed no insurrectionary threat. The slave community may or may not have shunned her for her deed, although, as we have seen, strong slave women were much admired and a little feared.[19]

Masters usually worked to keep the peace in the quarters. Articles appeared periodically on this issue in plantation advice journals. "I never permit a husband to abuse, strike or whip his wife," wrote a Georgia planter in the *Southern Agriculturalist*, "and tell them it is disgraceful for a man to raise his hand in violence against a feeble woman, and that woman, too, the wife of his bosom, the mother of his children and the companion of his leisure, his midnight hours." In a similar vein, a contributor to the *Southern Cultivator* advised that "Men should be taught that it is disgraceful to abuse or impose on the weaker sex, and if a man should so far forget and disgrace himself as to strike a woman, the women should be made to give him the hickory and then ride him on a rail. The wife, however, should never be required to strike her husband, for fear of its unhappy influence over their future respect for and kindness to each other."[20]

While treatises on slave management describe an ideal for correcting family violence, in practice discipline was often left to overseers, whose responses frequently fell short of the ideal. An overseer hung Nathan Best "up in a peach tree and whupped me. Cause I stuck a knife in a gal's arm—she got mad at me and slapped me in the mouth, and I had that ole knife and stuck it in her arm." A Louisiana planter fired his overseer for beating a slave to death. In his defense, the overseer claimed he beat the slave for beating his wife. Netty Rant Thompson recalled that the overseer whipped slaves for, among other things, "fighting amongst themselves."[21]

Slaves did not always appreciate the efforts of masters to teach them to work out their differences or to protect them when they could not. Jefferson Davis, for example, presided over a slave court on his Mississippi plantation. On one occasion, Davis found a serious bruise on Julia Ann, but she refused to tell him how she had gotten it. "Negroes only conceal injuries when received in some manner which they fear to relate," he claimed, "and unless her husband struck her she is so quiet that I cannot imagine how she should have received a blow." Julia Ann may indeed have protected her husband with her silence; she obviously did not welcome Davis's intrusion.[22] Masters also interfered in child raising. Polly Turner recalled her master "wouldn't let the mammies whip their own children either; if he come across a woman whupping her child he say, 'Get away woman; that's my business,' and he'd give one or two little whacks." [23]

Domestic violence was bad for slave owners' business. At market, slaves with reputations for violence brought lower prices and made for difficult sales. [24] Infants and children who died of parents' negligence (at least in the master's opinion) were lost to both labor and sales. Upon returning to his plantation after a brief absence, slave owner Newit Vick, Jr., learned that Hetty and Adam had been fighting, "and Hetty being in Family way was severely injured having a [hemorrhage?] and losing her child. I feared she would not leave [live] for some time, but Dr. Stansbury pronounces her out of danger now." Vick's words indicate paternalistic concern but also the business instincts of a man interested in seeing his women deliver healthy infants. [25]

As masters and mothers had different reasons for wanting to raise healthy children, it is hardly surprising that masters' efforts to control slave children's upbringing led them into conflict with mothers. Planter Walter Wade, for example, sought to encourage a sense of responsibility for children among enslaved women, even though he remained convinced that most were incapable of being good mothers. Wade's diary records slave births and deaths at his plantation, Rosswood, from 1838 to 1858. During those years, 103 children were born, at least 28 of whom died before their second birthday. Across the South, as many as 35 percent of enslaved infants may have died during their first year of life. But Wade was a physician, and if infant mortality on his plantation was lower than average—though higher than that of the free population—their deaths interested and concerned him. He recorded his diagnoses for over half of the cases. [26]

Regardless of the cause of death, Wade nearly always held mothers responsible, even though he often placed babies with nurses. Thus, for example, he noted that one child died from "starvation," due to "want of a good mother," while another died at 22 months from "want of good nursing and general good treatment." He also noted that several mothers "overlaid" or accidently smothered their babies in bed. Wade acknowledged that such deaths were accidental, but attributed them to mothers' negligence. [27] In 1851, he even constructed a "nurse house" to give him greater control over infants than their irresponsible mothers.

For Wade, deaths from tetanus due to "inattention to the naval" were most frustrating. As he wrote, "Judy's child died this evening from tremus nascentium—or lockjaw—from bad management of the navel—one week old; to the Hour!!!—Feel very much hurt—at the frequency of such cases on this place: notwithstanding the cautions and directions I have given the nurses." Some mothers were more likely than others to lose children this way. "Judy's child . . . dead," he wrote in July, 1850, "from irritation of navel!!!" This was "the 3rd child she has lost in succession from same cause." Judy's babies may have been especially prone to infection. Or Judy may have purposefully ignored her children precisely because her master explicitly ordered her to wash their navals thoroughly; the children may well have been casualties of the struggle between master and slave. At least one infant on the Wade plantation was a clear victim of that struggle, "A mulatto . . . murdered!!" The master ventured no guess in his journal as to the culprit.[28]

Wade never realized why so many babies died; he could not admit the possibility that women who struggled to care for their children found that a nearly unbearable burden in addition to the burden of slavery. Women who "starved" their children or left them vulnerable to infection may have done so willingly to deny them to their master. They may themselves have been overworked, underfed, and living in filth.

To a master, a child's death could be evidence of maternal incompetence, a business expense, or even a sign of failure to meet paternalistic responsibilities, but it was probably cause for no emotion greater than regret. To a mother, however, the loss of a child could be a catastrophic tragedy. Tabby Abbey "had one baby in my life, a long time ago," she recalled, "but I went to sleep one day when I was Nursing him and rolled over on him and smothered him to death. I like to went crazy for a long time after that." Slave Betty of Georgia lost a child the same way, but we learn of her case from the very different perspective of slave traders. They claimed Betty suffered "from imbecility of mind," and that she "had not sense to raise her child and they [her owners] took it from her and raised it in the house for she had overlaid her first one." Betty's condition caused a breach of warranty suit between her new and former masters.[29]

Domestic violence within slave families, as in all families, existed in the eye of the beholder, who might be perpetrator or victim, slave or free, black or white, male or female, master or slave, household member or outsider. The boundary separating legitimate "correction" and abuse was never absolute. Each instance of family violence became an occasion for establishing its meaning. To this end, some cases were more illuminating than others, with none more so than that of Marie Glass. Glass was not a slave but a free woman of color who owned bound laborers, and her history reveals a great deal about family and violence within the slave South.

This mid-eighteenth century case unfolded during a period when Mississippi's society was more fluid than it would be a half century later. By the mid-nineteenth century, Marie Glass's case would have been handled decisively, even preemptively, by a mature, confident white patriarchy. But the tangled mix of race, gender, and class it contained laid bare the contest for control over the domestic sphere, slave and free, that continued long after Glass's death.[30]

In 1780 the British colonial court at Baton Rouge charged Marie Glass "free Mollattress" with "suspicion of having Cruelly Ill treated and Murdered one white Girl named Emelia Davis an apprentice and servant." Glass had been born in "the North of Carolina" of free parents and had come to Natchez, where she married John Glass before settling near Baton Rouge. Davis, a girl of fifteen, had been indentured to loyalist William Walker, who fled during the Revolution, leaving his servant in Glass's hands. Over the next year and a half she tortured Davis to death and hid the body. But the girl's disappearance raised suspicions among neighbors, and an investigation ensued.[31]

The investigation uncovered extensive violence within Glass's household. A white woman who had worked for her claimed she had suffered "the most cruel treatment and was several times lashed with a cowhide." She displayed "the marks she still carries" to the court. Another servant, a black man, also bore the scars of his violent mistress, while still another, a freeborn black boy, horrified investigators inured to late eighteenth-century standards of violence. "This young child . . . is scarred from head to foot, front and back . . . bearing nine scars on his head and having had his arm broken."

Marie Glass was an imposing and ferocious figure. A peddler who tangled with her over the precise weight of some coffee and sugar came away with a bloody nose. She was, he confessed, "quicker and more skilful with a stick than I am." A passing fur trader accused Glass of beating his Indian guide. The trader prevented his guide "from taking his revenge," however, because he feared it "would have gone badly with him." Glass's husband John explained that he was so cowed by his wife that he was not able to intervene. The court believed him.

The death of Emelia Davis finally brought Glass, a "more than Savage Woman," down. But authorities moved painstakingly slowly. Initially they were bewildered that anyone could be capable of "such cruelties as the human mind can not conceive," as one court officer noted. But as inconceivable accusations became inescapable facts, the court remained hesitant, fearful of abridging the right of household heads to employ violence when disciplining or punishing servants.[32]

Neighbors witnessed Molly Glass's (Marie's nickname) treatment of her apprentice Emelia. One, Sarah West, heard strange noises coming from the Glass cabin, crept up to it, and spied through a crack in the wall. She saw "Molly Glass with a fork heated in the fire apply the same to the Tongue of Emelia, with which she scar[r]ed or burnt it." Her sister Catherine watched Glass "suspend Emelia and light a fire near her, not to burn her but to smoke her and smother her by a thick smoke." Neither woman did anything to stop the violence. In a society based on bound labor, masters' prerogatives were vital; they had to be permitted to discipline their servants. Although fascinated by Molly Glass's theater of torture, the community looked away because it was "improper for a man to behold so indecent a spectacle." They dared not interfere.

Legal authorities intervened upon Emelia's death, as the bounds of legitimate punishment had been breached. In building its case against Glass, however, court representatives had to demonstrate that the servant had not died ac-

277

cidentally at the hands of a well-intentioned master administering proper corporal punishment. Neighbors now came forward to testify to the outrageous violence they had witnessed. Sarah West said that she had seen Marie beat Emelia with "the handle or Butt end of the whip . . . larger than a mans thumb." Glass had broken "the rule of thumb," a traditional common law measure distinguishing acceptable discipline from unlawful abuse. Her extreme cruelty—branding Emelia's tongue, suffocating her with smoke—strengthened the case against Glass.[33]

Glass defended herself by claiming the patriarchal privilege to discipline household members when they behaved improperly. She lashed one servant with a cowhide because she "was fond of men and was lazy." The young black boy was guilty of "lying and was greedy to the extreme." "Is it not so, my child, that I corrected you only when you deserved it?" Glass challenged him in court. "Yes, Mistress," he answered. Emelia Davis was "an outrageous liar," had stolen watermelons, and had given chickens and milk to runaway slaves. The last explanation was calculated to convince a community of slaveholders that Emelia indeed deserved punishment. She was, moreover, "a child," whom Marie "corrected . . . for her good." It "was as a mother that she inflicted such corrections."[34]

Race and status became important issues as the trial progressed. Glass was a free mulatto, Davis a bound white. Sarah West believed that Molly Glass dressed Emelia in a petticoat "unfitt for a negroe slave," and that "of all peoples, Negroes or other, she hath never seen a poor wretch so miserably hacked and cut as this poor white girl was." Several blacks gave evidence against Glass as well. The prosecution described them as "sensible" and "intelligent," to demonstrate a broad consensus that Glass had stepped beyond her place in society. Three Choctaw Indians swore that they had asked Marie "what right she had to whip a White Girl?" "A white woman," they insisted, "was not whipped." Glass answered them "that Emelia was her Slave and that she had a right to do with her as She pleased and added when She is dead it will be well." The Choctaw men told the court "that they were Red men, but that seeing this young girl so badly whipped made their hearts ache." The court was assured that even "savages," as the record calls them, were horrified by Glass, and by the race role reversal she embodied.[35] One witness summed up the issues clearly when she described Davis as black with bruises. Glass, a mulatto woman master, had literally turned a white servant black.

If race roles were reversed in this case, so too were gender roles. Marie was a very strong woman. Until she murdered Emelia, Glass, like the slave women discussed above, attracted notoriety and even admiration because she challenged patriarchal power directly. The peddler who was bloodied by Marie immediately went to his boat for his gun, presumably to put her in her place. Two women who had watched the fight stopped him. They stated in court that the peddler struck the first blow, and that Glass had defended herself against an abusive man. These women returned to court later, however, to present evidence that would condemn Molly Glass. Her reputation for confrontation may in part explain the community's initial hesitation to stop her.

No one was more awed than Glass's husband John. Legally, he was the head of the household, but he did not act it. John told the court "that he proposed all he could to his wife and advised her several times to send [Davis] away rather than keep a bad subject." When asked "why he had not beaten his wife" to restrain her, he answered "that he did not like quarrels and that he was not the master." While his wife placed a red-hot fork on Davis's tongue, John Glass lay in bed and listened to the girl's screams. When a neighbor questioned Marie about the way she treated Emelia, he noted that John "never opend his Lips." Instead, "[h]e hung down His Head" and sat "with His Gun between His legs, sitting on a chair and seemed more than ordinary pensive and thoughtful." When Emelia died, John "fell into such imbecility that he was not able to bury" her, although he moved the body at his wife's command. His long silence after her murder "proceeded from a Dread of Molly Glass' resentment." Glass proclaimed his innocence. But if John Glass was innocent, it was because he was innocent of being a man. Marie, not he, was master.[36]

The court referred to John Glass as Marie's "pretended" husband, although they had documents to prove their marriage. Over the course of the trial, however, it became increasingly clear that John Glass *was* a pretended husband, legal documents or no. At first, the court assumed he was master of his household and of his wife. But contrary to expectations, John could not control his wife. In his report to the governor of Spanish Louisiana, Captain Favrot, commander of Baton Rouge, noted that John "was no more than the slave of this mulatress who had a despotic power over him." The governor agreed, and referred to Molly as John's "concubine." If John Glass was neither a master nor a man, he could not be a husband nor Marie a wife. They were not, therefore, a family properly entitled to privacy, but a household of outlaws demanding intervention and control.[37]

The British court at Baton Rouge found Marie Glass guilty of murder and sentenced her to death; the Spanish court in New Orleans confirmed the sentence. Marie was to have her hand severed, to be hanged by the neck until she was dead, to have her head severed and, with her hand, placed on a pole and displayed for all to see. On July 26, 1781, she died on the gallows in the New Orleans public square.

The court also sentenced John to be hanged. It had little choice—as Marie's husband, he was legally responsible for her behavior. The court appealed to the governor for clemency, however, on the grounds that John Glass was not capable of meeting this legal expectation. The Governor reduced John's sentence to five years in the Castillo at Veracruz.[38]

279

Witnesses speculated about the root of Marie Glass's violence. Sarah and Catherine West told the court that when they asked Glass why she abused Emelia Davis, Glass stated ambiguously that she did so because "she would not forgive her [own?] father." This puzzling statement together with Glass's behavior suggests patriarchal governance was the real target of her violence. For nearly two years, at least, she inverted the social order and played the role of a white male slave owner and father convincingly and cast her husband in the role of mistress; few dared challenge her. She claimed to discipline her servants for their own good, and for the good of the community of masters. In their efforts to build a case against Glass, authorities accused her of harboring runaways. Yet like a proper slaveholder, Glass claimed to have controlled her servants strictly to protect them from runaways, some of whom had attacked and scarred Emelia.

Intentionally or otherwise, Marie Glass upended a world that condoned violence from men and whites but accepted only meekness from women and blacks. By condemning her and seeking clemency for her husband, the court helped reestablish white patriarchal authority in a place and time when such authority was uncertain. By the nineteenth century, nonpatriarchal, black, enslaved families would exist entirely within patriarchal, white, free households. Powerful black women would still be found *within* slave families where, unlike Marie Glass, they posed no threat to the white patriarchy, but only to black male sensibilities. And men such as John Glass, because they were free, white, and male, would be held to their patriarchal responsibilities.[39]

The end of slavery altered relations within black families in ways that emphasized their peculiar structure during slavery. With freedom, men became legal patriarchs; some used their new authority over wives and children unhesitatingly. While a slave, Henry Lewis McGaffey watched his master whip his mother until "the blood run down her bare back," but could do nothing about it. When McGaffey married after emancipation, he claimed he had to "whup" his wife, Mary, "every time the moon changed." She no longer had a master to whom to appeal. The couple had ten children, but Mary "turned out so bad, I left her." After slavery Barney Alford married Josephine Williams, "and she made me a good wife. She stayed with me forty one years and had seven children. Oh, yes, I had to whup her some times, but then we always would get along better after that."

In freedom, men also took responsibility for family in ways they never could in slavery. Annie Coley's brother took her and her three children into his home when she fled her abusive husband. Some parents told FWP interviewers they passed along to children and grandchildren harsh lessons given them by masters. Lizzie Brown once lied to her master and was whipped for it. The master, she recalled, "said, 'Liz, I'm not whipping you for not locking the henhouse door, but for not telling the truth.' And that was what learned me to tell the truth. And I does that same thing by my grandchildren now."[40]

Christopher Morris

With freedom, former slaves acquired the right to accept responsibility for their families. Family structures became more economically and legally patriarchal, a form often associated with domestic violence. The pressures, disappointments and sense of powerlessness associated with poverty and racism as well as family violence continued and in some ways worsened after Emancipation. But the power to refrain from using violence, to settle disputes peacefully within families and without outside interference, was now in their hands. James Cornelius stated proudly that in 51 years of marriage he hit his wife only once.[41]

In freedom, former slaves' families became their own. Outside agents, such as the Freedman's Bureau, continued to exert pressure, but the slave owners were gone. Masters had been powerful presences in slave families, a third party in marriages, and legal meddlers between parents and children. Masters' interest in slave families was keen and blended profit motives with paternalistic responsibilities. The masters' presence shaped the structure of slave families, which had both advantages and disadvantages. On the one hand, enslaved men who wanted authority were unable to gain it. On the other, women who sought autonomy or a divorce from an abusive husband could obtain them. While family life could provide essential emotional, psychological, or even material comfort crucial to surviving slavery, many slaves were unable to achieve it, a fact of slavery illustrated during episodes of domestic violence. That is why slave family violence and the overshadowing presence of the master was doubly tragic.

Notes

1. George P. Rawick, ed., *The American Slave: A Composite Autobiography, Supplement, Series 1* (Westport, CT, 1977), 10: 2232–2233, 2246. In quoting from the FWP narratives, I have corrected spellings used by writers who presumed the illiteracy of their subjects. For example, writers often recorded "was" as "wuz," as if in speaking the subject mispelled. I have not changed syntax nor constructions.

2. E. Franklin Frazier, *The Negro Family in the United States* (Chicago, 1939); Lee Rainwater and William L. Yancey, eds., *The Moynihan Report and the Politics of Controversy* (Cambridge, MA, 1967); Herbert G. Gutman, *The Black Family in Slavery and Freedom, 1750–1925* (New York, 1976); Bertram Wyatt-Brown, "The Mask of Obedience: Male Slave Psychology in the Old South," *American Historical Review* 93 (1988): 1228–1252; William Dusinberre, *Them Dark Days: Slavery in the American Rice Swamps* (New York, 1996); Fox Butterfield, *All God's Children: The Bosket Family and the American Tradition of Violence* (New York, 1995). Jacqueline Jones has argued that blacks' "attempts to sustain their family life amounted to a political act of protest against the callousness of owners, mistresses, and overseers," *Labor of Love, Labor of Sorrow: Black Women, Work and the Family from Slavery to the Present* (New York, 1985), 12; Ariela

Julie Gross, "Pandora's Box: Slavery, Character, and Southern Culture in the Courtroom, 1800–1860," Ph.D. diss., Stanford University, 1996, 187.

3. Quotation from Winthrop D. Jordan, *Tumult and Silence at Second Creek: An Enquiry into a Civil War Slave Conspiracy* (Baton Rouge, LA, 1993), 90. Mississippi courts were very tolerant of domestic violence in free families. See Elizabeth H. Pleck, "Wife Beating in Nineteenth-Century America," *Victimology* 4 (1979): 60–74.

4. Ann Patton Malone, *Sweet Chariot: Slave Family and Household Structure in Nineteenth-Century Louisiana* (Chapel Hill, NC, 1992), 16; Gutman, *The Black Family*; Larry E. Hudson, Jr., *To Have and to Hold: Slave Work and Families in Antebellum South Carolina* (Athens, GA, 1997). Violence within families has been mentioned in only a few studies. Deborah Gray White, *Ar'n't I a Woman? Female Slaves in the Plantation South* (New York, 1985), 156; Brenda Stevenson, "Distress and Discord in Virginia Slave Families, 1830–1860," in Carol Bleser, ed., *In Joy and Sorrow: Women, Family, and Marriage in the Victorian South, 1830–1900* (New York, 1991), 113–117; Wilma King, *Stolen Childhood: Slave Youth in Nineteenth-Century America* (Bloomington and Indianapolis, IN, 1995), 97; Elizabeth Fox-Genovese, *Within the Plantation Household: Black and White Women of the Old South* (Chapel Hill, NC, 1988), 327.

5. For examples of this voluminous literature, see Gutman, *The Black Family*; Malone, *Sweet Chariot*; Hudson, *To Have and to Hold*; Cheryll Ann Cody, "Naming, Kinship, and Estate Dispersal: Notes on Slave Family Life on a South Carolina Plantation, 1786–1833," *William and Mary Quarterly* 39 (1982): 192–211; Charles Wetherell, "Slave Kinship: A Case Study of the South Carolina Good Hope Plantation, 1835–1856," *Journal of Family History* 6 (1981): 294–308; Orville Vernon Burton, *In My Father's House Are Many Mansions: Family and Community in Edgefield, South Carolina* (Chapel Hill, NC, 1985), 148–190.

6. George Fitzhugh, *Sociology for the South: The Failure of Free Society* (Richmond, VA, 1854), 105.

7. Ira Berlin et al., eds., *Freedom: A Documentary History of Emancipation 1861–1867* series 1, vol. 3: *The Wartime Genesis of Free Labor: The Lower South* (Cambridge, MA, 1990), 601–602.

8. For sociological inquiries into the causes of domestic violence, see Murray A. Straus and Gerald T. Hotaling, eds., *The Social Causes of Husband-Wife Violence* (Minneapolis, MN, 1980); Richard J. Gelles and Murray A. Straus, *Intimate Violence in Families* (New York, 1988), 17–36; and Richard J. Gelles, "Family Violence," in Robert L. Hampton et al., eds., *Family Violence: Prevention and Treatment* (Newbury Park, CA, 1993), 1–24.

9. *The Revised Code of the Statute Laws of the State of Mississippi* (Jackson, MS, 1857), 248; Mark V. Tushnet, *The American Law of Slavery 1810–1860: Considerations of Humanity and Interest* (Princeton, NJ, 1981), 72–90; Fox-Genovese, *Within the Plantation Household*, 326.

10. White, *Ar'n't I a Woman?*, 158–159; Jacqueline Jones, " 'My Mother Was Much of a Woman': Black Women, Work, and the Family Under Slavery," *Feminist Studies* 8 (1982): 235–270.

11. Rawick, *American Slave* 9:1441; 7:621.

12. Rawick, *American Slave* 9:1524–1525; 10:1926; 6:93–94. On corporal punishment as a way to teach children to be wary of masters, see Thomas L. Webber, *Deep Like the Rivers: Education in the Slave Quarter Community, 1831–1865* (New York, 1978), 165–166.

282

13. Rawick, *American Slave* 9:1419–20, 1424; 7:559; 7:441.

14. Rawick, *American Slave* 7:444, 579; 10:2232; 9:1858. Gabe Butler thought his father's abuse made his mother insane. "My pappy was named Aaron Butler . . . when he would fight my mammy he hit her ober de head and was what run her crazy," Rawick, *American Slave*, 6:325.

15. *State v. Harrison*, a slave, Criminal Court Record (February 1862), Old Court House Museum, Vicksburg, Mississippi; *Arnault v. Deschapelles*, 4 La. 41 (1849); *State v. Henry, a slave*, Warren County Circuit Court Papers, Criminal Cases 105 (May 1852a), and "Habeus Corpus Petition for Frank," folder 31 (1845), Old Court House Museum, Vicksburg, Mississippi. See also *State v. Peter, a slave*, #10 (1857), drawer 340, box 5, Historic Natchez Foundation, Natchez, Mississippi. As Fox-Genovese has noted "a high level of violence resulted from slave men's inability to exercise the domination over women that most societies have awarded to men," *Within the Plantation Household*, 327.

16. William Ransom Hogan and Edwin Adams Davis, eds., *William Johnson's Natchez: The Antebellum Diary of a Free Negro* (Baton Rouge, LA, 1993), 183. On the connection between gender, freedom, and slavery, see Stephanie McCurry, *Masters of Small Worlds: Yeoman Households, Gender Relations, and the Political Culture of the Antebellum South Carolina Low Country* (New York, 1995); and Bertram Wyatt-Brown, *Southern Honor: Ethics and Behavior in the Old South* (New York, 1982).

17. May Wilson McBee, comp., *Natchez Court Records 1767–1805: Abstracts of Early Records* (Baltimore, MD, 1979), 101, 104, 222–224.

18. On domestic violence and patriarchy, see R. Emerson Dobash and Russell P. Dobash, *Violence Against Wives: A Case Against Patriarchy* (New York, 1979); Kersti A. Yllo and Murray A. Straus, "Patriarchy and Violence Against Wives: The Impact of Structural and Normative Factors," in Murray A. Straus and Richard J. Gelles, eds., *Physical Violence in American Families: Risk Factors and Adaptations to Violence in 8,145 Families* (New Brunswick, NJ, 1990), 403–424; Murray A. Straus, "Ordinary Violence, Child Abuse, and Wife Beating: What Do They Have in Common?" in the same volume, 383–399. Deborah Gray White argues that slave marriages were "unusually egalitarian," and "equality within the slave family was founded on complementary roles, roles that were different yet so critical to slave survival that they were of equal necessity." White, *Ar'n't I a Woman?*, 158. Jacqueline Jones points out, however, that equality did not extend into reproduction. Patriarchal masters burdened women only with raising the future workforce. Jones, *Labor of Love*, 11–43.

19. Susan Dabney Smedes, with introduction and notes by Fletcher M. Green, ed., *Memorials of a Southern Planter* (New York, 1965), 89. According to Webber, slaves ostracized abusers. When fights erupted they tried to keep them from the sight of whites, *Deep Like the Rivers*, 64.

20. James O. Breedon, ed., *Advice Among Masters: The Ideal in Slave Management in the Old South* (Westport, CT, 1980), 51, 55.

21. Rawick, *American Slave* 6:130; Helen T. Catterall, ed., *Judicial Cases Concerning American Slavery and the Negro* (Washington, D.C., 1926), 2:651–652; Rawick, *American Slave* 8:1186.

22. Jefferson Davis to William Burr Howell, April 24, 1859, Howell (William Burr) Papers, folder 4, Mississippi Department of Archives and History, Jackson, Mississippi.

23. Rawick, *American Slave*, 7:341.

WITHIN THE SLAVE CABIN

24. Gross, "Pandora's Box," 35–46.

25. Eugene D. Genovese, *The World the Slaveholders Made: Two Essays in Interpretation* (New York, 1971), 195–211; Newit Vick, Jr., to his sister, August 16, 1843, Newit Vick Papers, Natchez Trace Collection, The Center for American History, The University of Texas at Austin, Austin, Texas.

26. Wade recorded infant deaths irregularly, making it difficult to determine the number of deaths in the first year after birth, a standard measure of infant mortality. Wade (Walter) Plantation Diary, typescript, 1:101–03, 125; 2:1–2, 36–38, Mississippi Department of Archives and History, Jackson, Mississippi. Richard Steckel estimated that 35 percent of enslaved infants died before their first birthday in "A Dreadful Childhood: The Excess Mortality of American Slaves," *Social Science History* 10 (1986): 427. William Dusinberre argues that this figure is too high, and puts infant mortality (death before first birthday) for slaves at 27.5 percent in *Them Dark Days*, 537. A reliable estimate puts infant mortality in the U.S. in 1859–1860 at 16 to 20 percent. See Michael R. Haines and Roger C. Avery, "The American Life Table of 1830–1860: An Evaluation," *Journal of Interdisciplinary History* 11 (1980): 88.

27. Wade Plantation Diary, typescript, 2:1–2, 36–38; 1:101–103, 125, 131.

28. Wade Plantation Diary, typescript, 1:156, 1011; 2:214. Wade mentions deaths from lockjaw as 3.8 percent of births; Steckel estimates the average rate for all slaves at 7.5 percent, Steckel, "A Dreadful Childhood," 456. Dusinberre questioned this estimate. Dusinberre, *Them Dark Days*, 241, 537.

29. Rawick, *American Slave* 6:3; Gross, "Pandora's Box," 186 n368. An unknown number of infants probably died of sudden infant death syndrome. See Michael P. Johnson, "Smothered Slave Infants: Were Slave Mothers at Fault?" *Journal of Southern History* 47 (1981): 493–520.

30. The following discussion is drawn from Henry P. Dart, comp., "Trial of Mary Glass for Murder, 1780," *Louisiana Historical Quarterly* 6 (1923): 591–654 [hereafter Mary Glass], an English translation from original Spanish and French documents.

31. Dart, "Mary Glass," 600, 619.

32. Dart, "Mary Glass," 596, 597, 607, 608, 609, 645, 646.

33. Dart, "Mary Glass," 614–615, 626. William Blackstone observed that common law gave husbands the right to give wives "moderate correction," but that this correction had fallen into disfavor with all but the "lower rank," William Blackstone, *Commentaries on the Laws of England*, Facsimile of First Edition of 1765–1769 (Chicago, 1979): 1:432, 433. As late as 1782, one English justice asserted that it was lawful for husbands to beat their wives provided the stick were no thicker than the husband's thumb, Lawrence Stone, *The Family, Sex and Marriage in England 1500–1800* (New York, 1977), 326. In 1850, John Stuart Mill and Harriet Taylor complained that working class men believed "the law permits them to beat their wives," A. James Hammerton, *Cruelty and Companionship: Conflict in Nineteenth Century Married Life* (New York, 1992), 53.

34. Dart, "Mary Glass," 609, 610, 624, 630.

35. Dart, "Mary Glass," 613, 615, 618, 622, 639–640, 645.

36. Dart, "Mary Glass," 617, 630, 631, 632, 638.

37. Dart, "Mary Glass," 646, 649. Witnesses reported having seen John take Marie "to task for her tongue which with her love for liquor would cause her ruin." They claimed to have seen John scold his wife, telling "her to be silent and not to talk in that

way, that she always had a bad tongue." His admonitions had little effect. Dart, "Mary Glass," 611.

38. Dart, "Mary Glass," 642, 643, 644–645, 648. There was a final ironic twist to the story. When the executioners arrived at her jail cell, Marie told them she was pregnant. The sentence could not be enacted until the child was born. This "manly" woman sentenced to death for killing a child postponed her execution by claiming that she was about to become a mother. Time soon told otherwise, Dart, "Mary Glass," 650–654.

39. Dart, "Mary Glass," 624.

40. Rawick, *American Slave* 9:1396, 1400; 6:45; 7:444; 6:257. Freedom also allowed a few former slaves to escape family responsibilities. One woman, not wishing to be hindered by an eight-month-old baby when free, tossed him into a well before leaving the plantation. The child survived. In the disarray of Reconstruction, authorities could or would not press charges against the mother. Rawick, *American Slave*, 9:1449.

41. On "enhanced masculine authority" after emancipation, see Lesley A. Schwalm, *A Hard Fight for We: Women's Transition from Slavery to Freedom in South Carolina* (Urbana, IL, 1997), 260–268. At the turn of the twentieth century, the South was unconcerned with wife-beating. While the rest of the U.S. debated the problem and three states punished abusers with whipping, southern whites were so consumed by holding the color line with lynchings that they paid little attention to family problems, in particular the way in which black men treated black women. To question white men's treatment of white women questioned their whiteness and their masculinity, neither of which authorities wished to do. Elizabeth Pleck, *Domestic Tyranny*, 116; Straus, "Ordinary Violence," 403–424; Rawick, *American Slave* 7:506.

WITHIN THE SLAVE CABIN

CONTRIBUTORS

JENIFER BANKS is a professor in the English Department at Michigan State University. Most recently she has delivered papers on Caroline Kirkland and Catharine Sedgwick. She is co-editor of *The Collected Letters of Washington Irving,* Volumes 1–4 (Twayne, 1978–1982) and is currently working on a critical edition of the selected letters of Catharine Sedgwick.

EDWARD E. BAPTIST is the Charlton B. Tebeau assistant professor of history at the University of Miami. He is the author of several articles on antebellum southern culture.

TREVOR BURNARD is Senior Lecturer at the University of Canterbury, New Zealand where he teaches American and New World history. He has published many articles on early Chesapeake and Caribbean history and is finishing books on free society in early Jamaica and on the life of a Jamaican slave overseer.

STEPHANIE COLE is assistant professor of history at the University of Texas at Arlington. She is currently completing her manuscript entitled "Servants and Slaves: Domestic Service in the North/South Border Cities, 1800–1850."

CHRISTINE DANIELS has published a number of articles on labor and the family in colonial America. She is the co-author, with T. Stephen Whitman, of a book on apprenticeship in Maryland, 1640–1860 (University of Kentucky Press, 2000).

ED HATTON earned his doctorate in American history from Temple University in 1997 with a dissertation on spousal and intimate murder in the antebellum middle class. He has published book reviews and articles in the *Journal of American History,* the *Journal of Social History,* the *Journal of the Early Republic,* the *Journal of Popular Culture, H-Net,* and the *Irish Times.* He is currently the head of instructional design at an educational software company located in Dublin, Ireland.

MICHAEL V. KENNEDY has written several articles on early American industries and on eighteenth-century family economic strategies. He also co-edited, with William G. Shade, *The World Turned Upside Down* (Lehigh University Press, 1999).

JACK D. MARIETTA is the author of *The Reformation of American Quakerism, 1748–1783* (University of Pennsylvania Press, 1984), which dealt with the history of Quakers in Pennsylvania. He has moved from the analysis of Quaker religious delinquency to public crime in the Quaker province. He has been a member of the history department at the University of Arizona since 1968.

JACQUELYN C. MILLER received her doctorate from Rutgers University in 1995 and now teaches at Seattle University in Seattle, Washington. Her recent publications include "The Body Politic and the Body Natural: Benjamin Rush's Fear of Anarchia and His Treatment for Yellow Fever." in *"A Centre of Wonders": The Body in Early America,* edited by Michele Tarter and Janet Lindman (Cornell University Press, 1999) and "An 'Uncommon Tranquility of Mind': Emotional Self-Control and the Construction of a Middle-Class Identity in Eighteenth-Century Philadelphia" in *Journal of Social History,* 1996.

CHRISTOPHER MORRIS is associate professor of history at the University of Texas at Arlington. He is the author of *Becoming Southern: The Evolution of a Way of Life, Warren County and Vicksburg, Mississippi, 1770-1860,* as well as several articles on slavery and the Old South. He is currently working on a social-environmental history of the Lower Mississippi Valley, from 1500 to present.

JAMES D. RICE is assistant professor of history at Central Washington University. His research and publications focus on Native Americans and frontier societies in early America, and on the social history of crime and punishment.

JEFFREY H. RICHARDS is associate professor of English and chair of the department at Old Dominion University. In addition to articles on eighteenth- and nineteenth-century American drama and fiction, he is the author of *Theater Enough: American Culture and the Metaphor of the World Stage, 1607–1789* (Duke University Press, 1991) and *Mercy Otis Warren* (Twayne, 1995) and the editor of an anthology of plays, *Early American Drama* (Penguin, 1997).

RANDOLPH A. ROTH teaches history at the Ohio State University. His publications include *Democratic Dilemma: Religion, Reform, and the Social Order in the Connecticut River Valley of Vermont, 1791–1850* (Cambridge University Press, 1987) and "Is History A Process: Nonlinearity, Revitalization Theory and the Central Metaphor of Social Sciences History" in *Social Science History*, 1992.

G. S. ROWE is professor of history at the University of Northern Colorado. Professor Rowe is the author of *Thomas McKean: The Shaping of an American Republicanism* (Colorado Associated University Press, 1978), *Embattled Bench: The Pennsylvania Supreme Court and the Forging of a Democratic Society, 1684–1809* (University of Delaware Press, 1994), and numerous articles on Pennsylvania's early legal community. Currently he is completing a book on crime and its resolution in pre-19th century Pennsylvania in collaboration with Jack D. Marietta.

MERRIL D. SMITH received her doctorate in history from Temple University. She is the author of *Breaking the Bonds: Marital Discord in Pennsylvania, 1730–1830* (New York University Press, 1991) and the editor of *Sex and Sexuality in Early America* (New York University Press Press, 1998). She is currently teaching at Widener University and working on a further study of Elizabeth Wilson, motherhood, sex, and crime in the Mid-Atlantic.

TERRI L. SNYDER is a member of the Department of American Studies at California State University, Fullerton. She is currently completing a manuscript on gender, law, and society in early colonial Virginia.

T. STEPHEN WHITMAN teaches history at Mount St. Mary's College in Maryland. His published work includes *The Price of Freedom: Slavery and Emancipation in Baltimore and Early National Maryland.*

INDEX

Fischer, Mary Anne, 193-195; Foster, Titus, 82; Gallagher, Hugh, 159–160; Gill, Jane, 26; Gordon, Jean, 31; Griffin, Mary, 159; Griffin, Richard, 159; Halleday, Margaret, 158; Hart, Shadrick, 153; Hauser, John, 43n; Heger, Catherine, 32; Heger, Phillip, 32; Hemphill, Thomas, 31; Hicks, William, 161; Higgert, Ann, 32; Higgert, Henry, 32; Hill, James, 227; Hill, William, 195; Hoisington, Arminda, 70; Holgate, Mrs., 71; Holloway, James, 225–226; Hooper, James, 195; Jennings, John, 161; Jennings, Patrick, 161; Kain, Margaret, 178; Keister, Jacob, 178; Kennedy, Robert, 34; Leader, Henry, 82, 88; Leader, Lucinda, 88; Lewis, John, 31; Loggins, Sheldon, 77; Love, Elizabeth, 32; Lusk, Naomi, 70; Macartey, John, 229–232; McArther, Alexander, 32; McArthur, Sarah, 32; McNeil, Catherine, 32; McNeil, Elizabeth, 70; McNeil, Hector, 32; McNeil, Josiah, 70; McVey, John, 31; Miller, Appelona, 34; Miller, John, 34; Montgomery, John, 262; Morris, John, 148; Mull, Jacob, 195; Murray, Alexander, 195; Myriak, John, 31; Norris, Mary, 32; O'Brien, Michael, 156; O'Hara, Peter, 156; Owle, Ann, 227; Owle, Richard, 227; Patterson, Mrs., 71; Perkins, Daniel, 161; Pinkett, Thomas, 231; Plater, George, 188; Popp, Gertrude, 33; Powell, James, 82; Powell, Mary, 70; Pyle, Henry J., 117; Ramage, Josiah, 32; Randol, George, 34; Rauch, Margaret, 42n; Regan, Anne, 31; Rodgers (Rogers), George, 194–195; Rogers, Kelly, 32; Rosen, Woley, 31; Ryan, Peter, 148; Sampson, Elizabeth, 231; Savory, Henry, 227; Savory, Mary, 226–227; Schaeffer, "Fat John," 36; Selby, John, 199; Shurlin, Jane, 223; Slate, Robert, 227; Slate, Mrs., 227–228; Smart, Benjamin, 73; Smart, Nancy, 73; Smith, Jean, 31; Spearman, Anne, 189–190, 193–195; Starr, John, 148; Sweeney, James, 82; Tebbetts, Hannah, 82; Tebbetts, Jonathan, 82; Tilden, Elizabeth, 70; Young, Ann, 32; Young, John, 32; Wade, William, 226; Wallingford, David, 71; Wallingford, Sarah, 71; Warner, July, 158; Welch, Mary, 80; Welch, Nathaniel, 80; West, Catherine, 277; West, Sarah, 277; Whipple, Abigail, 70; Whipple, Oliver, 70; Williams, John, 226; Williams, Mrs., 226; Wilson, Frances (Fanny), 193–195; Wilson, Mrs., 76; Wilson, Theodore, 82; Woodward, Henrietta, 260–261; Woodyard, Elizabeth, 31; Wyriak,

Nicholas, 32; Yarnell, Philip, 31; Young, Brewster, 83, 86–88; Young, Emerritta, 83, 86–88; see also African-Americans, free, proper names; masters, proper names; servants, proper names; slaves, proper names
Austen, Jane, *Pride and Prejudice, Sense and Sensibility*, 203
Authority, female, 219–225, 229–232, 272–280; as disorderly, 12–13, 224–226, 276–280; and race, 12–13, 232, 276–280

"Baby dropping," 33, 178, 285n
Bacon, Nathaniel, 219, 234n
Bacon's Rebellion, 219, 222
Bakhtin, Mikhail, 107n
Ballads, 94, 224; about murder, 94–95; and objective style, 103–105; by title: "Banks of the Ohio," 94; "Little Ellen Smith" ("Poor Ellen Smith"), 94, 103, 109n; "Miller's Apprentice" ("Oxford Tragedy"), 98; "Omie Wise," 94–105, 106n, 107n, 109n; "Tom Dula" ("Tom Dooley"), 94, 102; and narrator-switching, 15, 103–104; diffusion of, 97–98; performance of, 102–104
Baltimore, Maryland, 6–7, 148–163, 185–197, 262–265
Bangor, Maine, 81
Baptists, 174
Beattie, John, 28
Biddle, Charles, 52, 177, 180, 182n
Birdsell, James, 121–122
Blackstone, William, 192, 163n, 200n, 284n, *Commentaries on the Laws of England*, 163n, 192
Blumin, Stuart, 59n
Boardinghouses, 117–118, 124
Bordentown, New Jersey, 111, 118–119, 123–124, 127
Bradley v. State, (1824), 9, 18n, 163n–164n
Breast feeding, 180–181, 274–276
Brown, Charles Brockden, 203–204; *Edgar Huntley, Wieland*, 203
Brown, William Hill, *The Power of Sympathy*, 202
Brown, David Paul, 116
Buchan, William, 49, 60n, 178, 180; *Advice to Mothers*, 180
Burke, Edmund, 245
Bushnell, Horace, *Views of Christian Nature*, 127

Carey, Mathew, 57
Charivaris, 95, 97, 104, 106n, 274
Chester, Pennsylvania, 173–174
Cheyne, George, 49

Index

Lynching, 95, 104, 109n, 285n

Magistrates, see Justices of the Peace
Manners, and violence, 116, 204–214
Manumission, 150, 255; see also emancipation
Markets, and domestic abuse, 99, 108n, 136
Maroons, 240
Marriage, 46, 125–126, 174
Masculinity, and creativity, 131n; and self-control, 55–56, 111, 113–116, 127–130; and violence, 7, 15, 88, 99–101, 104–105, 111, 113–116, 121–122, 124, 127–130, 149–; ideal of, 15, 85–88, 102, 124
Massey, Ann, 52
Massey, Samuel, 52
Masters, proper names: Babe, Richard, 36; Batten, Anne, 223; Batten, Ashaell, 223, 225; Beckford, Richard, 242; Browning, Humphrey, 229–232; Cloud, William, 36; Cope, John, 243–244; Cope, Molly, 244; Cunningham, John, 243; Davenport, John, 36; Davis, Jefferson, 274; Dorrill, William, 240; Edgar, Charles, 37; Edwards, Haden, 255, 257–258; Fishbaugh, Dominick, 44n; Gather, Elizabeth, 36; Gibson, Use, 229; Glass, John, 277, 279–280; Glass, Marie (Mary, Molly), 12–13, 276–280, 284–285n; Hyde, Mrs., 223, 225; Hyde, Robert, 225; Jagler, Charles, 36; Johnson, William, 273; Kerlegand, Dr., 257–258; Lawrence, John, 36; Lewis, John, 263; McAuliffe, Timothy, 36; Minor, William J., 270; Morley, Thomas, 234n; Nicholas, John, 36; Pigman, Joseph, 260–261; Prichard, Robert, 223; Pride, Chatmall, 36; Reigert, Christopher, 36; Reynold, Henry, 36; Russell, John, 228; Scott, Samuel, 36; Stevens, Robert, 262; Thomas, Philip, 257; Tilghman, William, 188; Vaulx, Elisheba, 219–220, 222, 227, 229–232, 233n; Vaulx, James, 233n; Vick, Newit Jr., 275; Wade, Walter, 275–276, 284n; Walker, William, 277; Weech, Harry, 241; Williams, Otho, 257; Williams, Tom, 241; Williamson, Mrs., 225
Masters, and homosocial violence, 223, 236n
Matron juries, 42n, 229
Medical advice manuals, 7, 49–51, 56–57, 59n–60n, 111, 113–115, 178–180, 205–206
Mens rea doctrine, 121
Middlebury, Vermont, 76
Mill, John Stuart, 284n
Milton, Vermont, 71
Ministers, 128–129
Mittelburger, Gottlieb, 22
"Modern" family, 23, 248

Montacute, 138; see also Pinckney, Michigan
Montesquieu, 22
Moore, Charles, 48
Moore, Margaret King, 180
Moore, Milcah, 48
"Moral sense," 121
Moreton, J.B., 243
Morris, Abigail, 48, 54–55
Morris, Hannah, 54
Morris, John, 47, 54
Morris, Margaret, 47, 52, 54–56
Morris, Milcah, 56
Morris, Richard, 54–56
Morris, Robert Hunter, 22
Morris, William, 47
Mortality rates, 5, 221, 233n
Morton, Mary, 57–58
Motherhood, 157, 173–181, 184n; class-based expectations, 175–181, 190; republican, 8, 46, 175–177, 179–181, 190–192, 207
Murder, acts of, 71–73, 81–82, 95–97, 111–113, 124, 126, 156–157, 173, 263; vs. manslaughter, 73, 81, 166n
Murder rates, see homicide rates

Nassy, David, 57
Natchez, Mississippi, 273
Neighbors, and household violence, 4, 13–14, 17n, 20n, 30–31, 70–72, 75–78, 80–89, 95–97, 100–101, 137–138, 153–154, 186–198, 199n–200n, 226–228
New Jersey, Supreme Court of, 116
New Orleans, Louisiana, 257–258
New York City, New York, 58, 118–120, 123, 185
Newark, New Jersey, 57–58
Newspapers, and "postings" of abusers, 79–81
Newton, Isaac, 47
Nolle prosequi, writs of, 255–256, 260, 262–263, 266n–267n
Novels, 116, 202–203
Overseers, 237–238, 258, 262

Passion, suppression of, 114
Paternalism, and responsibility, 5, 9–12, 97, 151, 163, 276; and slavery, 149–151, 241, 240–243, 254, 258, 265n–266n, 270; see also patriarchy
Patriarchy, and civil governance, 9, 16, 30, 97, 113, 137–138, 149–151, 176–177, 191–192, 220, 232, 240–245, 280; and common law, 16, 145n; 150–153, 192, 200n, 278, 284n; and female masters, 6, 11–13, 16, 206, 219–225; and legitimate correction, 9, 137, 148–149, 152–153, 220, 276, 280; and manhood, 95–96, 113, 244, 273, 279; and negotiation,

Index

23586764R00359